KEY MATHS 8

© David Baker, Paul Hogan, Barbara Job, Renie Verity 1996, 2001

The right of David Baker, Paul Hogan, Barbara Job, Renie Verity to be identified as authors of this work has been asserted in accordance with the Copyright, Designs and Patents Act 1988.

All rights reserved. No part of this publication may be reproduced or transmitted in any form or by any means, electronic or mechanical, including photocopy, recording, or any information storage and retrieval system, without permission in writing from the publisher or under licence from the Copyright Licensing Agency Limited. Further details of such licences (for reprographic reproduction) may be obtained from the Copyright Licensing Agency Limited, of Saffron House, 6-10 Kirby Street, London, EC1N 8TS.

First published in 1996
Second edition published in 2001 by
Nelson Thornes Limited
Delta Place
27 Bath Road
CHELTENHAM GL53 7TH

08 09 / 10 9

A catalogue record for this book is available from the British Library.

ISBN 978 0 7487 5984 2

Original design concept by Studio Dorel
Cover design by John Christopher, Design Works
Cover photographs: Roger Howard/Ace Photo Agency (front); Chris Fairclough Colour Library (spine); Baron Wolman/Tony Stone Images (back)
Artwork by Maltings Partnership, Eric Apsey, David Oliver
Cartoons by Clinton Banbury
Typeset by Tech Set Ltd
Printed and bound in China by Midas Printing International Ltd

Acknowledgements

The publishers thank the following for permission to reproduce copyright material:
Aerofilms, p. 152; Ancient Art & Architecture Collection (Ronald Sheridan), p. 239 (bottom); ED142018 The Thinker, Bronze by Rodin (front view) Musee Rodin, Paris/Bridgeman Art Library, London, p. 205; British Broadcasting Corporation, p. 52; British Mensa Ltd, p. 327; Central Statistical Office, p. 281; Channel Four Television, p. 52; Collections, p. 252 (Michael Allen), p. 292 (bottom left – Brian Shuel); The Hulton Deutsch Collection, p. 51; Independent Television, p. 52; Milepost 9½, p. 147; National Savings, p. 164; The National Blood Service, p. 291; Reproduced from the Ordance Survey mapping with permission of The Controller of Her Majesty's Stationery Office © Crown copyright (07000U), pp. 228, 241, 242, 244, 246; Produced by courtesy of Lord Bath and Longleat Estate, p. 81; Sky Television, p. 52; Sporting Pictures (UK) Ltd, p. 249; Tony Stone Images, p. 11 (John Lamb, p. 94 (John Lawrence), p. 236 (Dale Durfee), p. 292 (bottom right – Kevin Kelley); York City Archives, p. 250.
All other photographs by Martyn F. Chillmaid.

The publishers have made every effort to contact copyright holders but apologise if any have been overlooked.

David Baker
The Anthony Gell School, Wirksworth

Paul Hogan
Fulwood High School, Preston

Barbara Job
Christleton County High School, Chester

Renie Verity
Pensby High School for Girls, Heswall

Contents

1 Graphs

CORE

1 Conversion graphs

2 Graphs and rules

3 Time

4 Using time

QUESTIONS

EXTENSION

SUMMARY

TEST YOURSELF

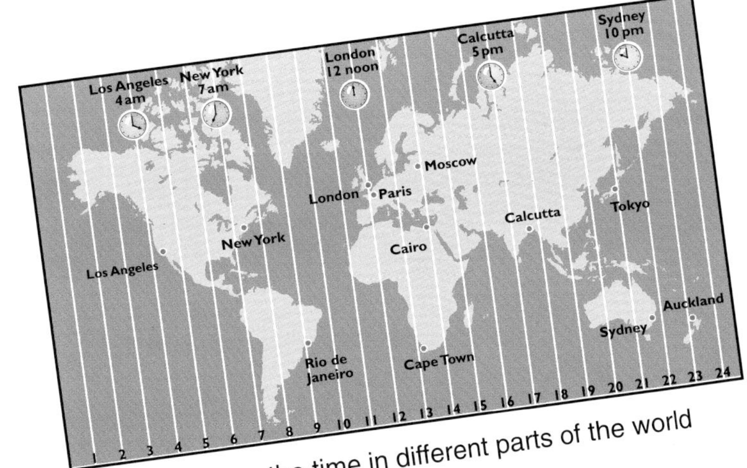

The map shows the time in different parts of the world when it is 12 noon in UK winter time.

Do you have any relations in New Zealand? Be careful if you telephone them. It is nearly 12 midnight in New Zealand when it is 12 noon in the UK!

Look in a world atlas to find out:

- how continents such as Africa arrange time zones to fit countries' borders
- what happens when a traveller crosses the International Date Line.

1 Conversion graphs

Class 8J are in Paris on an exchange visit. They are buying presents for their friends.
They want to convert the prices from francs to pounds.
They have a conversion graph.

Exercise 1:1

This is the graph that 8J are using:

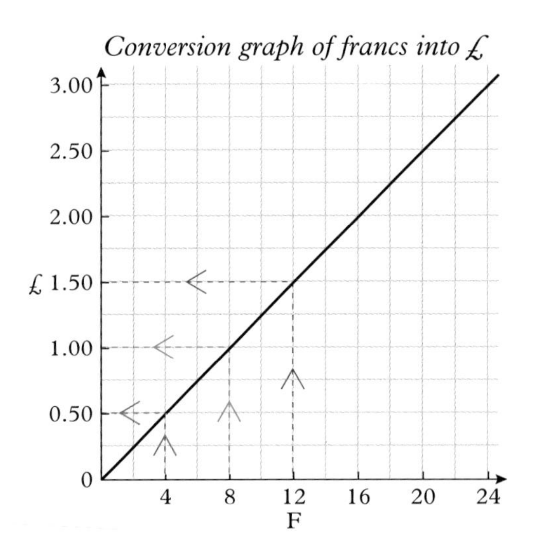

1 Anne is buying a model of the Eiffel Tower. It costs 12F.
Find 12F on the bottom scale of the graph.
Follow the red line to the graph.
Read off the price in £ from the side scale.

2 Ned is buying a picture of Paris. It costs 8F.
Follow the green line to see how much this is in £.

3 Danielle is buying two pens. They cost 4F each.
  a Follow the blue line to find out how much one pen costs in £.
  b How much do the two pens cost in £?

4 Terry wants to buy three boxes of chocolates. A box costs 16F.
  a How much does one box cost in £?
  b How much do three boxes cost in £?
  c Terry has 50F.
  Has he enough money to buy the chocolates *and* a pen?

Conversion graph

We use a **conversion graph** to change from one unit to another.
Conversion graphs are always straight lines.

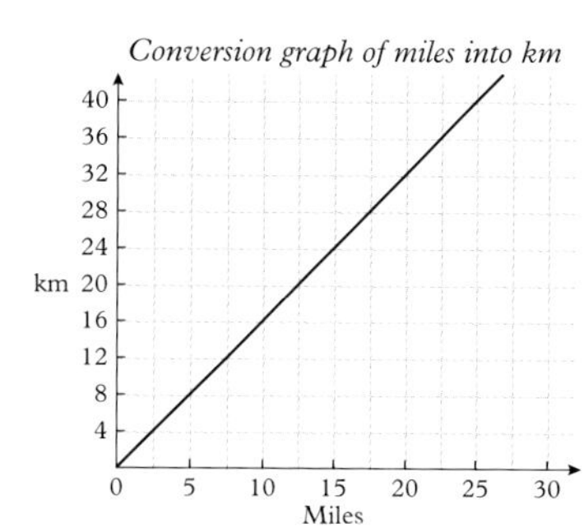

Exercise 1:2

1 Here is a conversion graph for US dollars ($) into £.

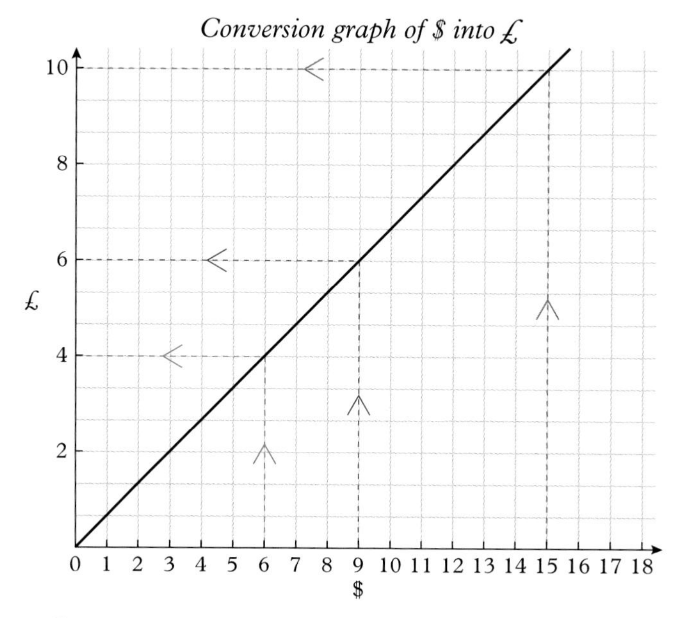

  a Convert $9 into £ (red line).
  b Convert $15 into £ (blue line).
  c Convert $6 into £ (green line).

2 This graph converts miles into kilometres.

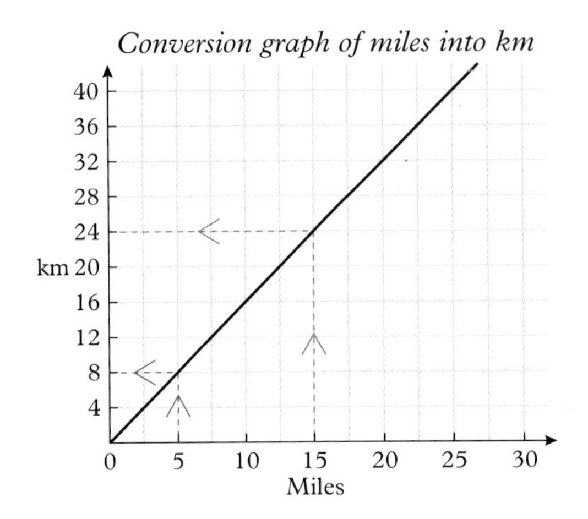

a Convert 5 miles to km (red line).
b Convert 15 miles to km (blue line).
c Convert 20 miles to km.

3 This graph converts kilograms into pounds (lbs).

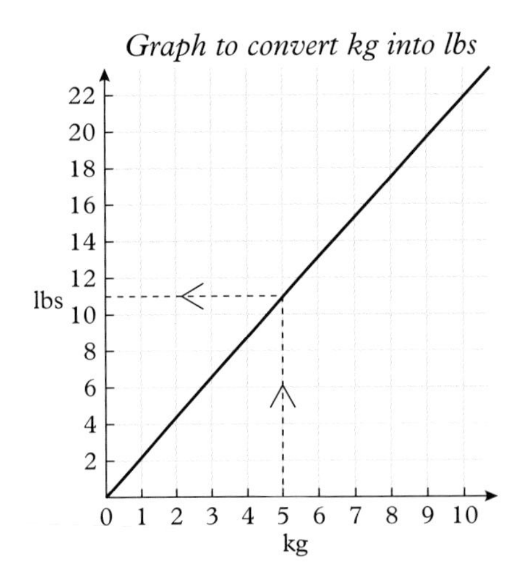

a Convert 5 kg into pounds.
b Convert 10 kg into pounds.
c A bag of sugar weighs 1 kg.
About how many pounds is this?
d A large bag of potatoes weighs 8 kg.
About how many pounds is this?

2 Graphs and rules

Exercise 1:3

1 David is taking part in the school sponsored walk.
He is being sponsored £2 per mile by his family. The further he walks the more money he will collect.
He works out the amount in a table.

Number of miles	1	2	3	4	5
Amount £	2	4			

a Copy the table.
b Fill in the last three columns of the table.

Here is a graph of David's table:

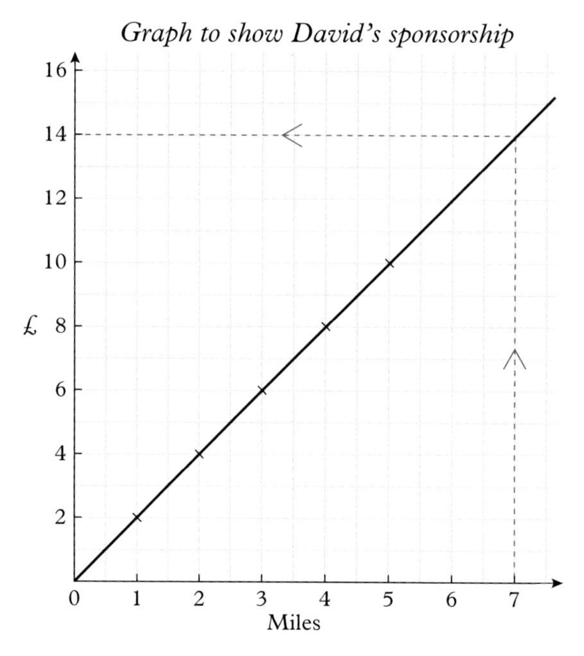

c Follow the red line.
How much will David get if he walks 7 miles?

2 Nicky is also doing the sponsored walk.
He is being sponsored £3 per mile.

a Copy the table for Nicky.
Fill in the last three columns.

Number of miles	1	2	3	4	5
Amount £	3	6			

Here is the graph of the table.

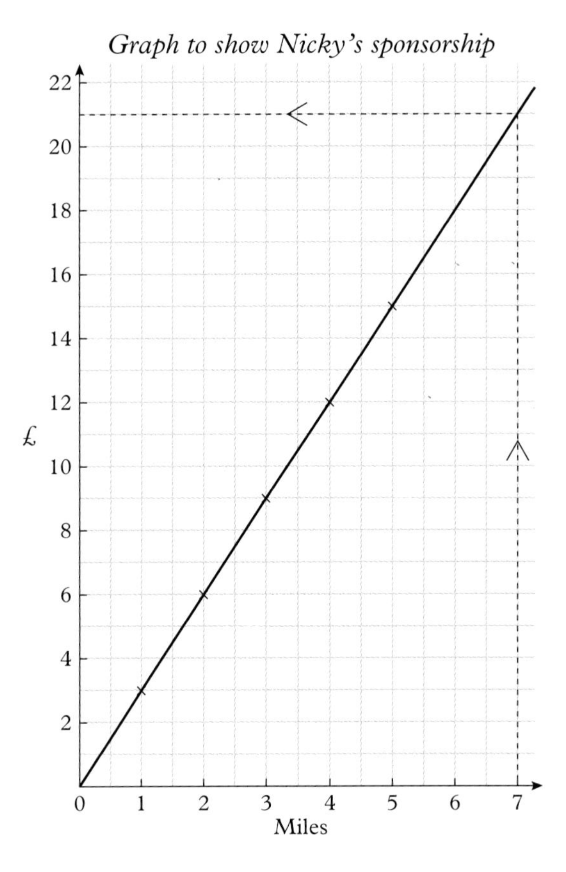

b How much will Nicky get if he walks 7 miles?

● **c** How much will he get if he walks $4\frac{1}{2}$ miles?

3 Yasmin is being sponsored £1.50 per mile.

a Fill in the rest of the table on your worksheet.

Number of miles	1	2	3	4	5
Amount £	1.50	3.00			

b Plot the points from the table on the graph on your worksheet. (The first two are done for you.)

c Join the points with a ruler to make a straight line. Continue the line to the edge of the graph.

d Use your graph to work out how much Yasmin will get if she walks
(1) 8 miles (2) 9 miles

◀◀REPLAY▶

Formula A rule written out in algebra is known as a **formula**.

Example Nicky is being sponsored £3 per mile.
The *t*otal he collects equals £**3** × number of *m*iles.
In short form this is: $t = 3 \times m$

Exercise 1:4

Write down the short form of these rules.
Use the red letters and numbers.

1 The *t*otal amount raised in a sponsored walk at £**2** for each *m*ile.

2 The *t*otal amount raised in a sponsored swim at £**6** for each *l*ength.

3 The *w*ages earned by someone earning £**4** per *h*our.

4 The *h*eight of a plant which grows at **3** cm per *m*onth.

5 The *d*istance covered by a car travelling at **30** miles per *h*our.

6 The *a*mount of money Joanna saves if she saves £**6** per *m*onth.

Sometimes it is useful to draw a graph of a rule.

Example

Tim has a part-time job as a waiter.
He earns £3 for every hour that he works.
He works out a table to show how much he can earn.

Number of hours	1	2	3	4	5
Wages £	3	6	9	12	15

His rule is: ***w***ages equals £3 × number of ***h***ours worked.
In algebra this is: $w = 3 \times h$

Tim draws a graph of his table:

Graph to show Tim's wages

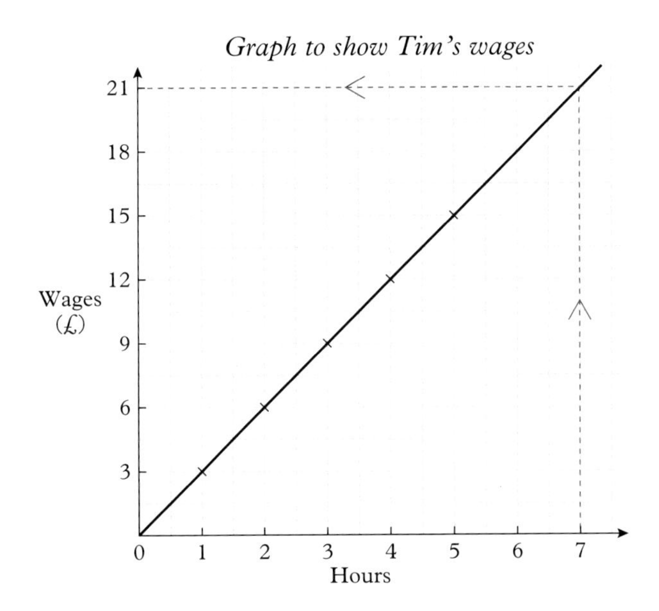

He can now see how much he would earn for 7 hours' work.
Follow the red line.

Exercise 1:5

1 Anisha works in the same cafe as Tim.
She is older and earns £4 per hour.

Her rule is: *w*ages equals £4 × number of *h*ours worked

a Write Anisha's rule in algebra: $w = \ldots \times \ldots$

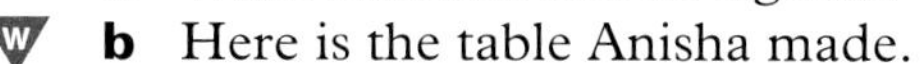

b Here is the table Anisha made.

Number of hours	1	2	3	4	5
Wages £	4	8			

Fill in the rest of the table on your worksheet.

c Plot the points on the graph on your worksheet.
(The first two are done for you.)
Join the points with a ruler to make a straight line.
Continue the line to the edge of the graph.

d Use your graph to work out how much Anisha will earn if she works:
(1) 4 hours
(2) 6 hours
(3) 8 hours
• (4) $5\frac{1}{2}$ hours

2 Nathan's new video recorder has a counter on it.
He plays a video and works out a rule for the counter.

Nathan's rule is
*c*ounter equals 50 × number of *m*inutes.

a Write Nathan's rule in algebra: $c = \ldots \times \ldots$

b Here is Nathan's table.

Number of minutes	10	20	30	40	50
Counter	500	1000			

Fill in the rest of the table on your worksheet.

c Plot the rest of the points on the graph on your worksheet.
Join the points with a ruler to make a straight line.
Continue the line to the edge of the graph.

d Use your graph to find out what the counter will show after:
(1) 30 minutes
(2) 50 minutes
(3) 70 minutes
(4) 45 minutes
(5) 75 minutes

3 Joel and Lianne are jogging together. Lianne soon gets ahead of Joel.
Lianne jogs at 4 metres per second (m/s).
Joel jogs at 3 metres per second.
They each work out a rule for the distance they jog.

Lianne's rule is: ***d***istance equals 4 × number of ***s***econds

a Write Lianne's rule in algebra: $d = \ldots \times \ldots$

b Copy this table for Lianne's rule.
Fill in the gaps.

Number of seconds	10	20	30	40	50
Distance (m)	40	80			

c Draw a graph to show Lianne's rule.
Use this scale.

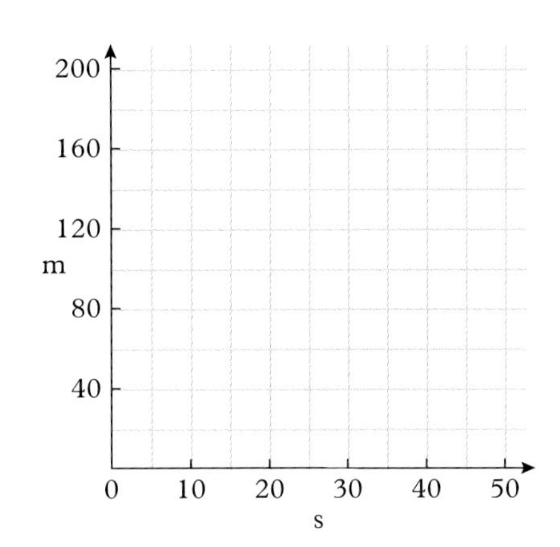

d Write down Joel's rule in words: distance equals …

e Write Joel's rule in algebra: $d = \ldots \times \ldots$

f Make a table using Joel's rule.

g Draw the graph for Joel's rule on the same diagram as Lianne's.

h Describe the differences between the two graphs.

3 Time

This is the most famous clock in the world.
Most people think the clock is called Big Ben.
In fact Big Ben is the name of a bell.
It is the bell with the loud, deep note that we count to get the hour.

Times after midnight and in the morning are am.
Times in the afternoon and evening are pm.

Exercise 1:6

1 Write down the times shown on these clocks.
Use am and pm.

a
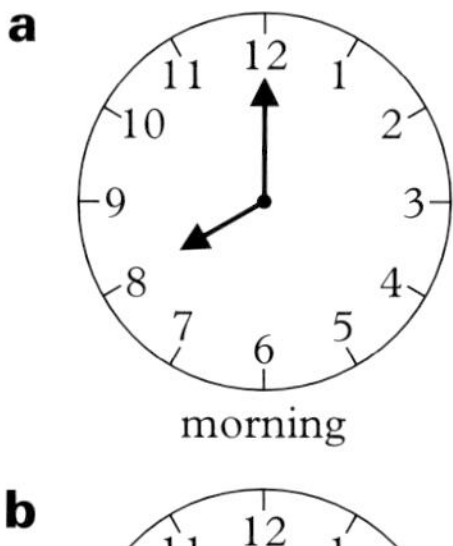
morning

b
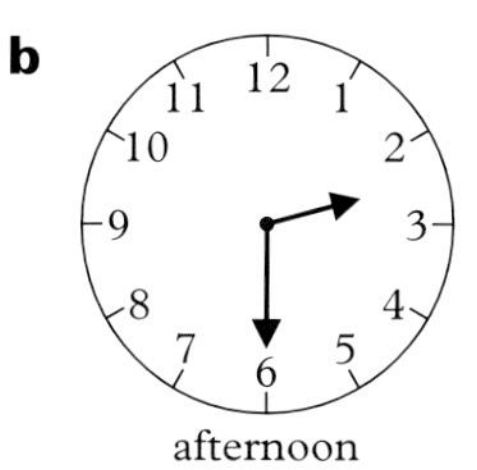
afternoon

c
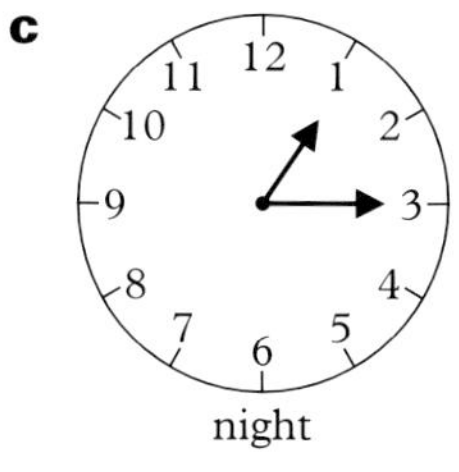
night

d
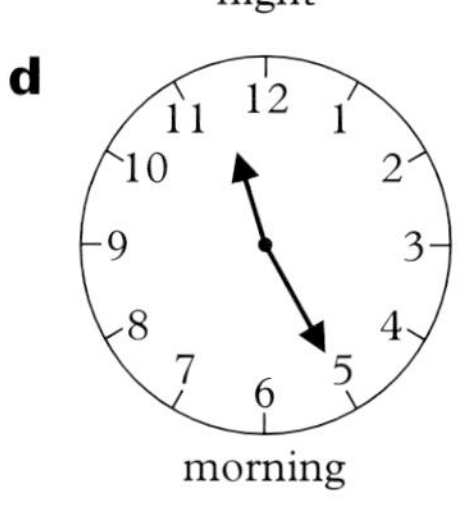
morning

e
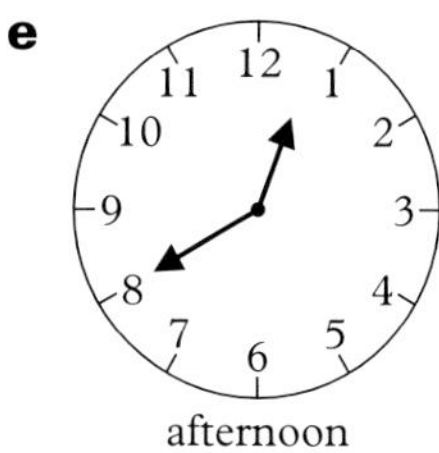
afternoon

f
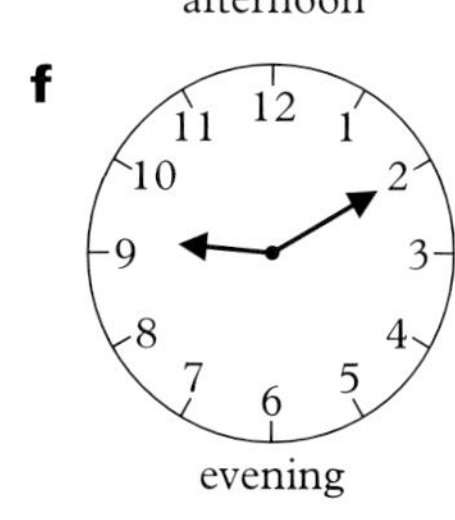
evening

Examples

Draw each time on a clock face.

a 8.10 am **b** 3.30 pm **c** 10.50 pm

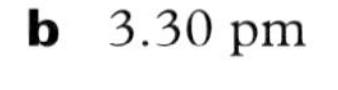

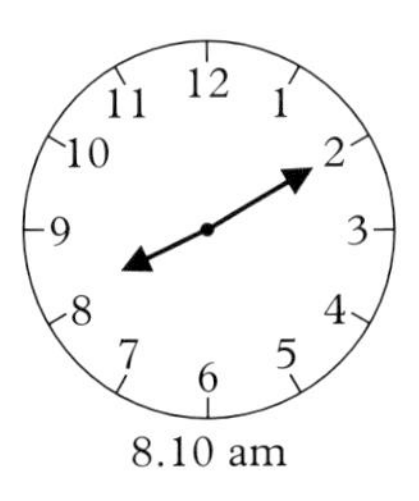

8.10 am

The hour hand has moved a bit past the 8.

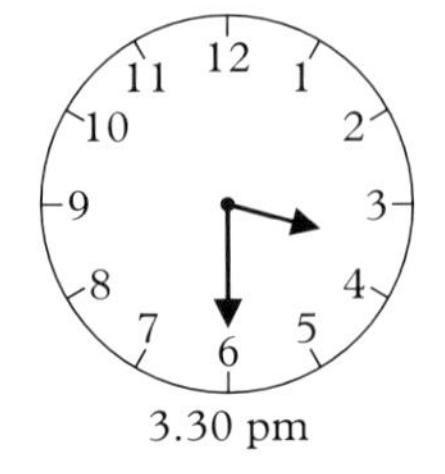

3.30 pm

The hour hand has moved halfway to the 4.

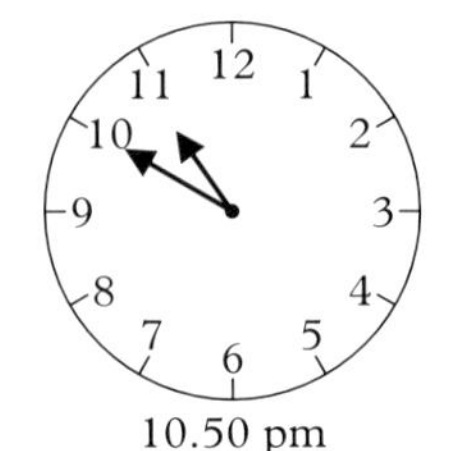

10.50 pm

The hour hand is nearly at the 11.

2 You need a worksheet with clock faces for this question.

3 Write these as am or pm times.
- **a** Ten past six in the morning.
- **b** Quarter past eight in the evening.
- **c** Twenty past ten in the morning.
- **d** Twenty-five past seven in the evening.
- **e** Half past eleven in the morning.

4 Write these as am or pm times.
- **a** Ten to five in the afternoon.
- **b** Quarter to four in the morning.
- **c** Twenty to one in the afternoon.
- **d** Twenty-five to nine in the morning.
- **e** Five to eleven in the evening.

Timetables for buses and trains use the 24-hour clock.

Examples

We always have four figures.
7.55 am is the same as **07** 55
3 pm is the same as 15 **00**

Midnight is 00 00
Midday is 12 00

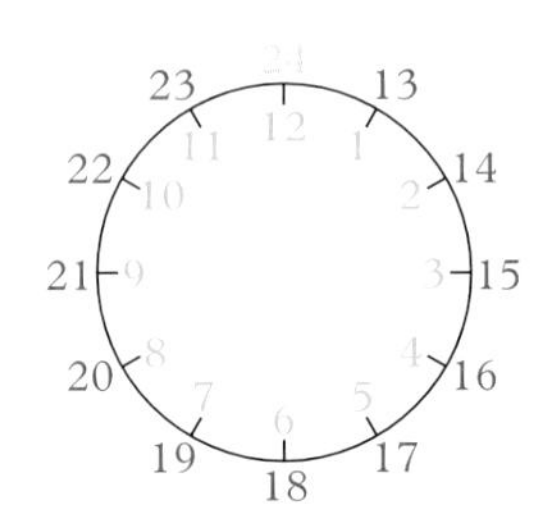

Exercise 1:7

Copy these tables.
Fill them in.

1

	am/pm	24-hr clock time
a	3 am	03 00
b	6 am	
c	2 am	
d	10 am	
e	1 pm	
f	5 pm	
g	9 pm	
h	3 pm	

2

	am/pm	24-hr clock time
a	1 am	01 00
b		05 00
c		09 00
d		11 00
e		14 00
f		18 00
g		20 00
h		23 00

3 Write these 24-hour clock times.
a 8.30 am **b** 1.15 pm **c** 7.05 pm **d** 11.45 am

4 Write these as am or pm times.
a 06 30 **b** 11 20 **c** 13 50 **d** 22 40

Amarjit wants to record EastEnders at 7.30 pm.
Her video uses the 24-hour clock.

Amarjit knows that 7.30 pm is 19 30.

Exercise 1:8

These things happened during Parvinda's day.
Copy this table.
Fill it in.

	am/pm	what happened	24-hr clock time
1	7.15 am	woke up	07 15
2	7.20 am	got up	...
3	...	had breakfast	07 30
4	...	left for school	08 20
5	8.45 am	arrived at school	...
6	...	break	11 00
7	11.20 am	break ended	...
8	12.30 pm	lunch	...
9	...	afternoon school	13 30
10	3.40 pm	school ended	...
11	...	arrived home	15 55
12	5.45 pm	had tea	...
13	...	started homework	18 25
14	8.00 pm	watched TV	...
15	...	went to bed	21 30

This timetable gives the times of some trains from London to Norwich.
The times are given using the 24-hour clock.

Mondays to Fridays	✕	✕	✕						
London Liverpool Street	**1330**	**1430**	**1530**	**1555**	**1630**	**1700**	**1725**	**1730**	**1800**
Colchester	**1418**	**1518**	**1618**	**1645**	**1718**	—	**1824**	—	—
Harwich International Port	—	—	—	—	—	—	**1855**	—	—
Ipswich	**1436**	**1536**	**1636**	**1711**	**1736**	**1801**	—	**1841**	**1905**
Stowmarket	**1447**	**1547**	**1647**	—	**1747**	—	—	**1852**	**1916**
Diss	**1459**	**1559**	**1659**	—	**1800**	—	—	**1905**	**1929**
Norwich	**1523**	**1623**	**1723**	—	**1824**	**1836**	—	**1929**	**1953**

Restaurant ✕

Exercise 1:9

1 Three trains have restaurants.

a Write down the times that these three trains leave London.

b Convert these times to am or pm times.

2 Only one train stops at Harwich International Port.
 a What time does the train arrive at Harwich?
 b Convert this time to am or pm time.

3 **a** What time does the 17 30 from London arrive at Norwich?
 b Convert this time to am or pm time.

• **4** Mary arrives at London Liverpool Street at 4.15 pm.
 a What time does the next train leave for Norwich?
 b What time does this train arrive in Norwich?
 c Convert these times to am or pm times.

The calendar

Example

It is Jason's birthday on 24th August.
He wants to know which day of the week it will be.

Jason's birthday is on a Wednesday.

August

S	M	T	W	T	F	S
...	1	2	3	4	5	6
7	8	9	10	11	12	13
14	15	16	17	18	19	20
21	22	23	(24)	25	26	27
28	29	30	31	...	...	...

Exercise 1:10

Use Jason's calendar to answer these questions.

1 Write down the days of the week for these dates.
 a 8th August **b** 13th August **c** 30th August **d** 14th August

2 **a** July comes before August.
 Write down the day of the week for 31st July.
 b September comes after August.
 Write down the day of the week for 1st September.

3 **a** Copy this number pattern.
 1, 8, 15, ..., ...
 Find the next two terms.
 b The number pattern gives the dates of the Mondays in August.
 Write down the number pattern for the Wednesdays.

Not all months have the same number of days.
Here is an easy way to remember the number of days in a month.

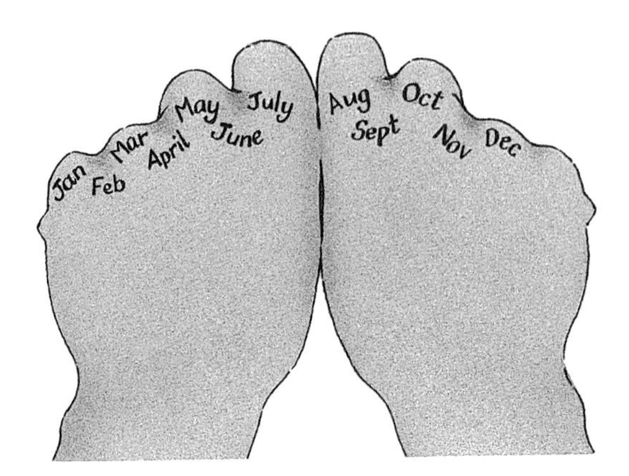

The months on the 'bumps' all have 31 days.
April, June, September and November have 30 days.
February has 28 days unless it is a leap year. In a leap year February has 29 days.
Leap years are …, 1996, 2000, 2004, 2008, 2012, …

4 Write down the number of days in:
a January **b** June **c** August **d** November

5 There are 365 days in most years.
How many days are there in a leap year?

6 **a** Write down the number of days in February in these years:
(1) 1999 (2) 2000 (3) 2009 (4) 2012
b 2000, 2004, 2008, 2012, … is a number pattern.
(1) Write down the rule for the pattern.
(2) Write down the next year in the pattern.

4 Using time

The time is 7.55 am.
Stan's bus journey to school takes 47 minutes.
He wants to know if he will be at school by 8.45 am.

Exercise 1:11

1 1 week = 7 days
Write down the number of days in:
a two weeks **b** four weeks **c** 10 weeks

2 1 hour = 60 minutes
Write down the number of minutes in:
a two hours **b** five hours **c** 24 hours

Example

A video lasts 137 minutes.
Convert this to hours and minutes.

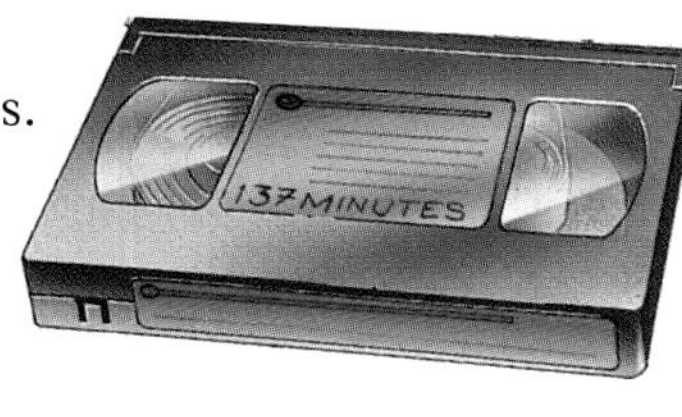

There are 60 minutes in one hour.
Keep taking away 60 to find the whole hours.

137 − 60 = 77
77 − 60 = 17

We have taken 60 away twice. This gives two hours.
There are 17 minutes left over.

Answer: 2 h 17 min

3 Convert these video times to hours and minutes.
a 112 minutes **c** 96 minutes
b 134 minutes **d** 128 minutes

● **4** Liam is recording a film on his video.
He has a 180-minute tape.
a How long does his tape last in hours?
b The film lasts 150 minutes.
Convert this to hours and minutes.
c Liam has recorded the film.
How much free time is left on his tape?

Example

Claire is catching a bus to school.
The bus arrives at 8.14 am.
The bus journey takes 25 minutes.
When does Claire arrive at school?

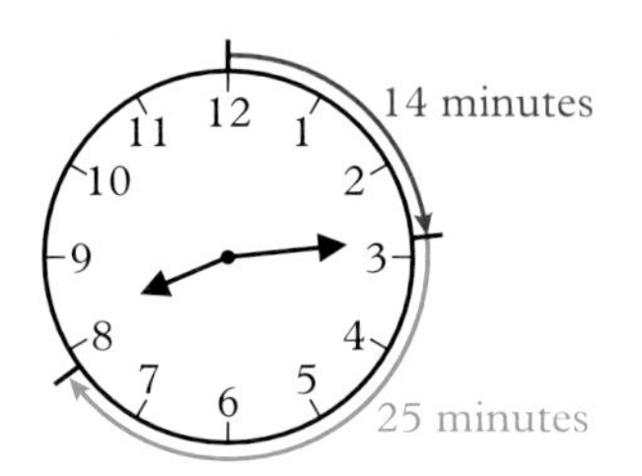

14 + 25 = 39

Claire arrives at 8.39 am.

Exercise 1:12

1 Work out the times when these buses arrive.
a Bus leaves at 7.05 am and takes 10 minutes.
b Bus leaves at 3.30 pm and takes 20 minutes.
c Bus leaves at 7.25 am and takes 30 minutes.
d Bus leaves at 12.30 pm and takes 25 minutes.
e Bus leaves at 9.04 am and takes 32 minutes.
f Bus leaves at 4.16 pm and takes 8 minutes.

Example

The time is 7.55 am.
Stan's bus journey to school takes 47 minutes.
He wants to know if he will be at school by 8.45 am.

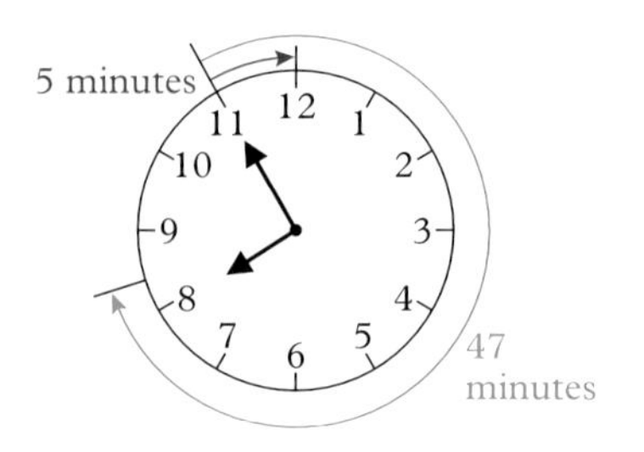

At 7.55 am it is 5 minutes to the next hour.
47 − 5 = 42
The bus arrives at 8.42 am.

2 Work out the times when these buses arrive.

a Bus leaves at 7.55 am and takes 25 minutes.
Copy this and fill it in.

At 7.55 am it is … minutes to the next hour.
25 − 5 = …
The bus arrives at 8. … am

Do these in the same way.

b Bus leaves at 3.40 pm and takes 50 minutes.

c Bus leaves at 7.45 am and takes 30 minutes.

● **d** Bus leaves at 11.37 am and takes 25 minutes.

Example How long is it from 9.10 am to 9.37 am?

37 − 10 = 27
Answer: 27 min

Exercise 1:13

1 How long is it between these times?

a 8.15 am to 8.20 am

b 10.30 am to 10.45 am

c 3.25 pm to 3.35 pm

d 6.12 pm to 6.36 pm

Example How long is it from 8.35 am to 9.12 am?

From 8.35 to 9.00 is 25 minutes.
From 9.00 to 9.12 is 12 minutes.
25 + 12 = 37

Answer: 37 min

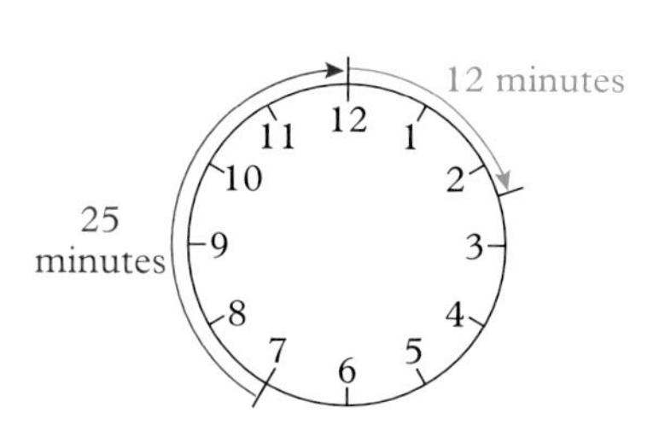

---

2 How long is it between these times?

a 7.25 am to 8.17 am

b 09 34 to 10 28

c 6.48 pm to 7.15 pm

d 16 35 to 17 33

Example How long is it from 8.35 pm to 11.12 pm?

8.35 to 9.00 is 25 min

11.00 to 11.12 is 12 min

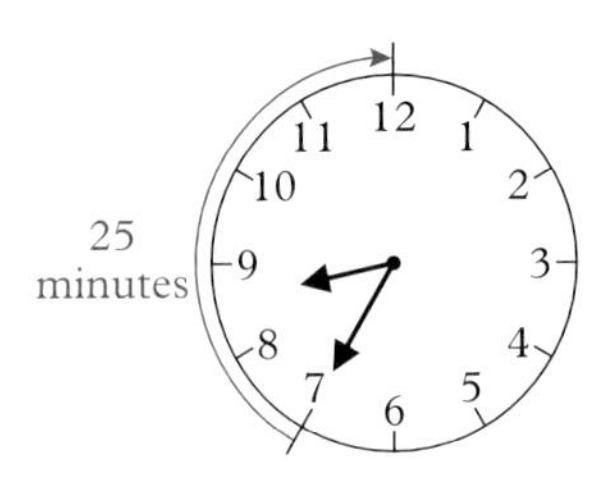

25 min + 12 min = 37 min

9.00 to 11.00 is 2 h

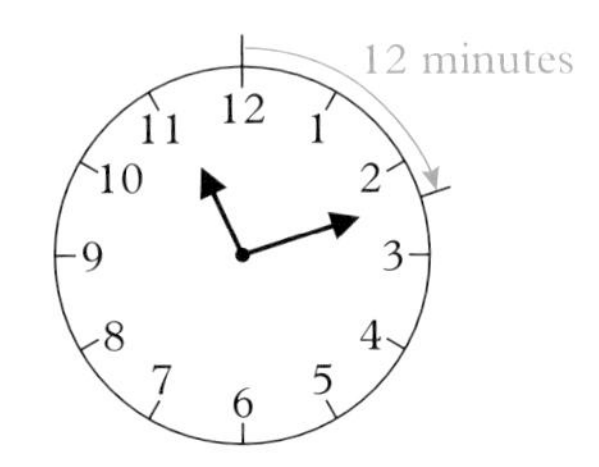

Answer: 2 h 37 min

---

3 How long is it between these times?

a 8.40 am to 10.15 am

b 3.30 pm to 6.05 pm

c 6.45 pm to 9.10 pm

d 9.25 am to 1.15 pm

e 4.42 pm to 6.17 pm

f 7.34 pm to 9.07 pm

• **4** Sian's school day starts at 8.50 am and finishes at 3.35 pm.

a How long is Sian at school?

b Morning break is 15 minutes and lunch is 1 hour.
How long is Sian with her class?

Exercise 1:14

1 An express train travels at 200 km an hour.
How far does it travel in:

a one hour

b two hours?

2 The rule for the *d*istance travelled by the express train is:
200 × the number of *h*ours. $d = 200 \times h$
Copy this table.
Use the rule to fill it in.

Number of hours	0	1	2	3
Distance in km	0	200		

3 Copy the axes on to squared paper.
Plot a graph for the express train.

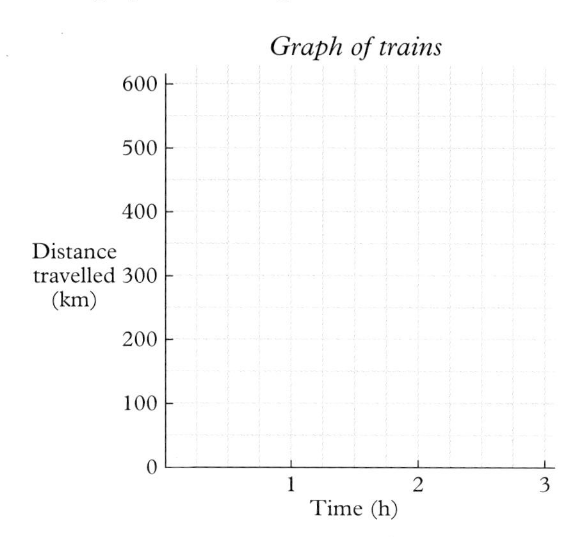

4 A goods train travels at 150 km an hour.
How far does it travel in:

a one hour **b** two hours?

5 The rule for the ***d***istance travelled by the goods train is:
150 $\times$ number of ***h***ours. $\boldsymbol{d = 150 \times h}$

Copy this table.
Use the rule to fill it in.

Number of hours	0	1	2	3
Distance in km	0	150		

6 Plot a graph for the goods train.
Use the same diagram as before.

● **7** **a** Which train is faster?
b How can you tell which train is faster from the graph?

1 This graph converts inches into centimetres.

a How many centimetres are there in 4 inches?

b A ruler is 6 inches long.
About how many centimetres is this?

c A book measures 4 inches by 8 inches.
What is the size of the book in centimetres?

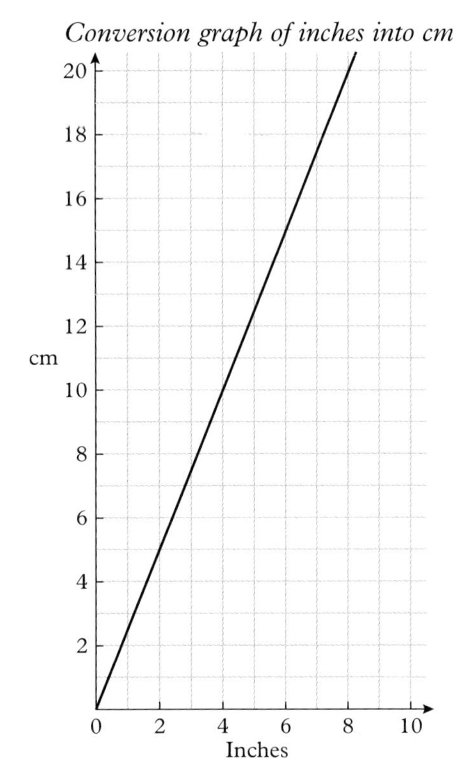

2 Keeping a cat costs about £4 per week.

a This table shows the costs.
Copy it and fill it in.

Number of weeks	1	2	3	4	5
Cost £	4	8			

b Plot a graph of the cost.
Use this scale.

c Continue the line to the edge of the graph.
How much does it cost to keep a cat for 6 weeks?

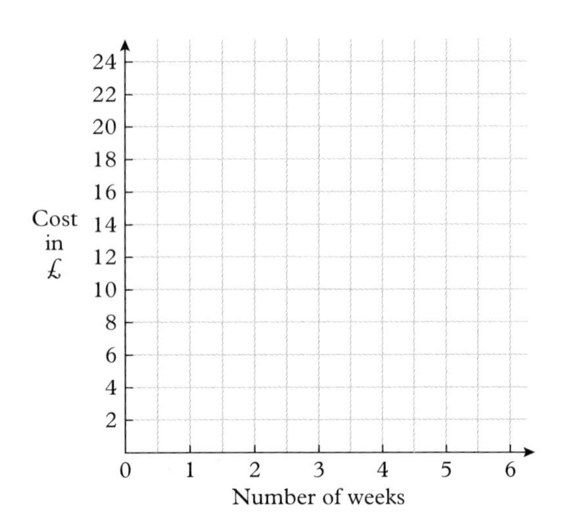

3 **a** Write these as 24-hour clock times.
(1) 3.20 am (2) 7.55 pm (3) 5.05 pm (4) 6.15 am (5) 11.30 pm

b Write these as am or pm times.
(1) 05 25 (2) 15 20 (3) 12 30 (4) 14 45 (5) 01 00

4 Write down the number of days in:

a July
b October
c April
d February in the year 2003

5 Work out the times when these buses arrive.

a Bus leaves at 8.25 am and takes 15 minutes.
b Bus leaves at 4.40 pm and takes 25 minutes.
c Bus leaves at 3.55 pm and takes 20 minutes.
d Bus leaves at 12.20 pm and takes 45 minutes.

6 Eileen leaves for school. She walks for 7 minutes to her bus stop. She waits 2 minutes for a bus. The bus ride takes 10 minutes.

a How long does Eileen take to get to school?
b She leaves at 8.05 am.
When does she arrive?

7 The timetable shows some trains from Liverpool to London.

Liverpool Lime Street	0600	—	0710	0745	—	0845	0945
Runcorn	0617	—	0727	0802	—	0902	1002
Hartford	—	0648	—	—	0856	—	1013
Crewe	0639	0702	0753	—	0914	0925	1025
Stafford	0700	—	—	0837	0935	0944	1047
Tamworth	0720	—	—	—	—	—	—
Nuneaton	0735	—	—	—	—	1008	—
Rugby	—	0802	—	—	—	1023	1125
Milton Keynes Central	—	—	—	0933	1031	1049	—
Watford Junction	—	—	0930	—	—	—	1214
London Euston	0853	0912	0953	1020	1117	1136	1237

a (1) What time is the earliest train from Liverpool to London?
(2) What time does the train get to London?

b Which trains from Liverpool to London stop the most times?

c One train from Liverpool does not stop at Crewe.
What time does this train leave Liverpool?

d (1) At what time does the 07 45 from Liverpool arrive in London?
(2) How long does this train take to get to London?

1 This table shows the exchange rate for Spanish pesetas and £.

£	1	2	3	4
Spanish pesetas	200	400	600	800

a Draw a conversion graph. Use these scales.

b Continue your graph to the edge of the scale.

c Use your graph to work out the cost of these items in £:

(1) A toy donkey costing 1000 pesetas

(2) A picture of Madrid costing 700 pesetas

(3) A straw hat costing 900 pesetas

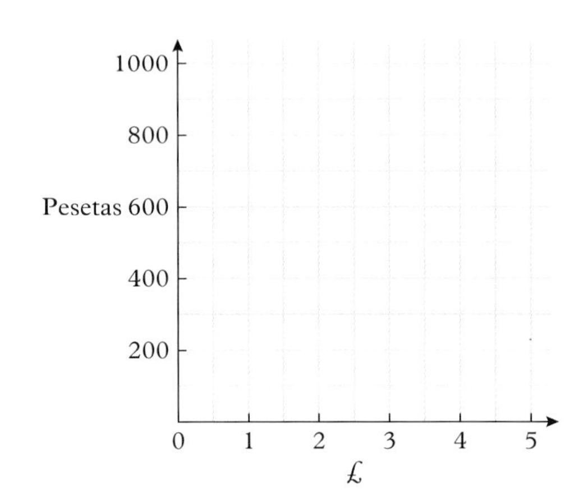

2 Maureen wants to record *Mission of the Shark*.

a Maureen programmes her video using the 24-hour clock. Write down the start time and the finish time of the film in this way.

b Maureen has a blank 240-minute tape. How much time will be left on her tape? Give your answer in hours and minutes.

7.20 **Pets Win Prizes (T) (S)** Including racing millipedes and llamas. *686320*

8.00 **The National Lottery Live (S)** *118097*

8.15 **Casualty** Facts of Life **(T) (S) (R)** Ash (Patrick Robinson) is in the limelight this week, suspended in mid-shift after an article in the local paper. *134287*

9.05 **News; Sport; (T)** weather *364320*

9.25 **Bob Monkhouse On The Spot (S)** *225897*

9.55 **Film** **Mission Of The Shark** (Robert Iscove, 1991, TVM) **(T)** Stacy Keach leads this fact-based survival drama as the commander of a US warship torpedoed in shark-infested waters in 1945. *935436*

11.30 **Film** **The File Of The Golden Goose** (Sam Wanamaker, 1969) Yul Brynner is an American agent sent to London to infiltrate a counterfeiting gang in this strictly formulaic crime drama. **(T)** *577981*

1.15 **Weather;** close *950036*

3 Jaswinder is revising for GCSE. He wants to do three hours' revision each night.
Jaswinder starts at 4.25 pm. He breaks for tea which takes 45 minutes.
At 7.40 pm he stops to watch television.

a How long has Jaswinder worked?

b The television programme ends at 8.35 pm. Jaswinder starts his revision again.
When will he finish his three hours?

- **Conversion graph**

  We use a **conversion graph** to change from one unit to another.
  Conversion graphs are always straight lines.

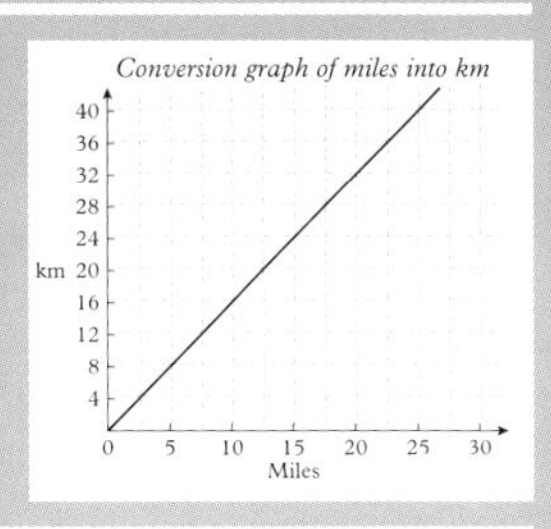

- **Graphs and formulas**

  Nicky is being sponsored £3 per mile
  The *t*otal he collects equals £3 × number of *m*iles.
  In algebra this is $t = 3 \times m$

  To draw a graph of a formula first fill in a table:

Number of miles	1	2	3	4	5
Amount £	3	6	9	12	15

  Then draw the graph.

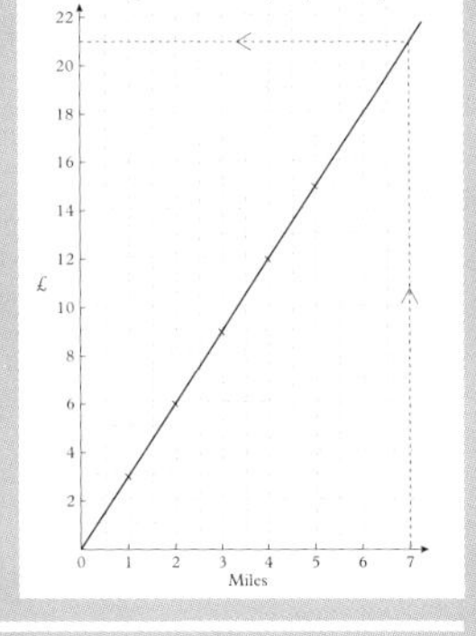

- Times after midnight and in the morning are am.
  Times in the afternoon and evening are pm.

  Timetables for buses and trains use the 24-hour clock.

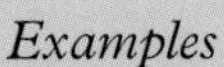

  Examples
  We always have four figures.
  7.55 am is the same as **07** 55
  3 pm is the same as 15 **00**

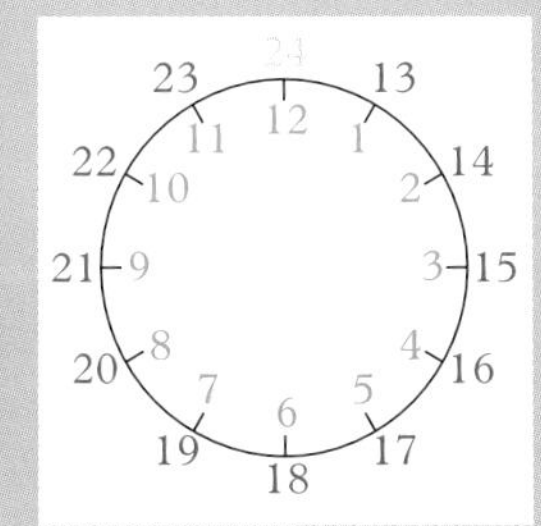

- *Example*
  The time is 7.55 am.
  Stan's bus journey to school takes 47 minutes.
  He wants to know if he will be at school by 8.45 am.

  At 7.55 am it is **5 minutes** to the next hour.
  $47 - 5 = 42$
  The bus arrives at 8.42 am.

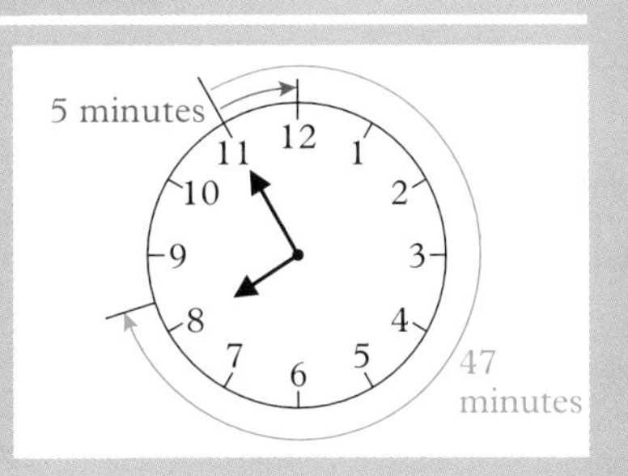

- *Example*
  How long is it from 8.35 am to 9.12 am?

  From 8.35 to 9.00 is 25 minutes.
  From 9.00 to 9.12 is 12 minutes.
  $25 + 12 = 37$

  Answer: 37 min

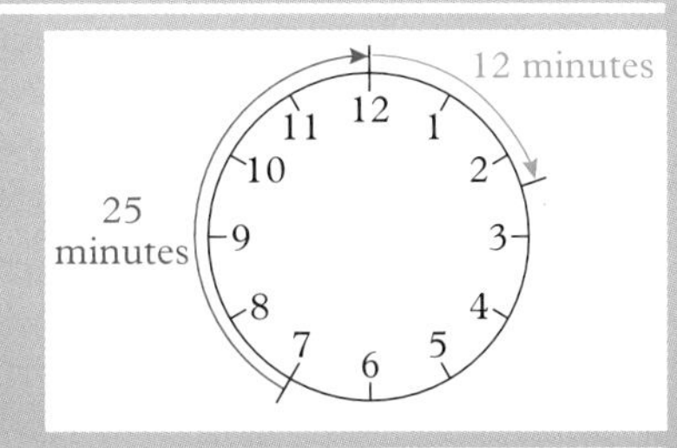

1 TEST YOURSELF

1 This is a conversion graph for German marks (DM) into £.

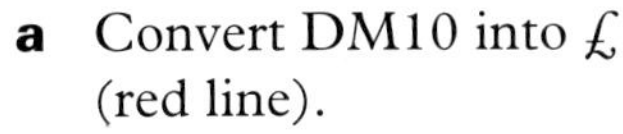

a Convert DM10 into £ (red line).
b Convert DM12 into £ (blue line).
c Convert DM6 into £.

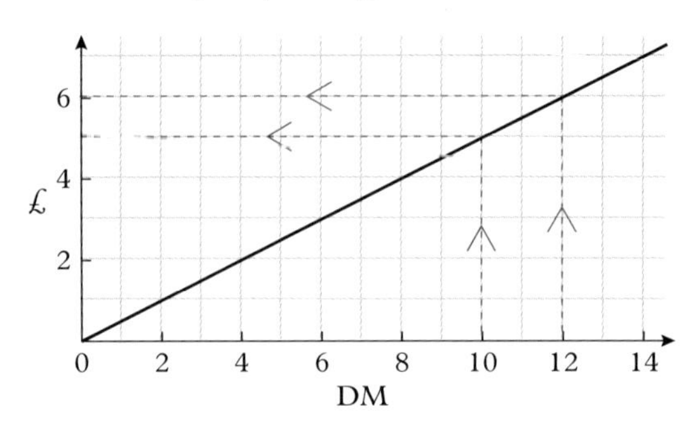

2 Alison earns £5 per hour as a waitress.

a This table shows her wages.
Copy the table and fill it in.

Number of hours	1	2	3	4	5
Wages £	5	10			

b Draw a graph of Alison's wages.
Use these scales.

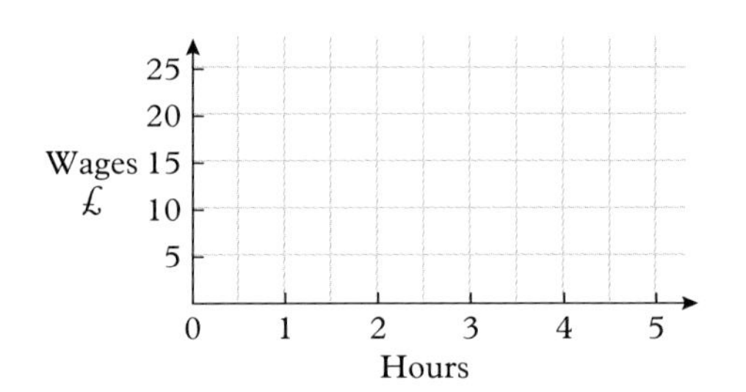

3 **a** Convert these to am or pm times.
(1) 06 30 (2) 11 40 (3) 15 02 (4) 22 57

b Convert these to 24-hour clock times.
(1) 7.15 am (2) 12.30 pm (3) 5.27 pm (4) 9.25 pm

4 How many days are there in:
a May **b** November **c** February 2010 **d** year 2007

5 Work out the times when these buses arrive.
a Bus leaves at 11.25 am and takes 15 minutes.
b Bus leaves at 3.40 pm and takes 45 minutes.

6 How long do these journeys take?
a Bus leaves at 4.50 pm and arrives at 5.08 pm.
b Train leaves at 08 56 and arrives at 11 23.

2 Estimating your mental power

CORE

1 **Squares and roots**
2 **Mental maths**
3 **Estimation**

QUESTIONS
EXTENSION
SUMMARY
TEST YOURSELF

The number 10^{100} is called a googol.

This is a 1 and one hundred zeros.

$\mathbf{10^{100}}$ = 10 000 000 000 000 000 000 000 000 000 000 000 000 000 000 000 000 000 000 000 000 000 000 000 000 000 000 000 000 000 000 000 000 000 000 000 000 000

It takes Kerry $\frac{1}{4}$ second to write a zero and $\frac{1}{5}$ second to write the 1.

How long does it take her to write a googol?

1 Squares and roots

This number pattern is special.

The dots always form a square.

◀◀ **REPLAY** ▶

$1 \times 1 = 1$ $2 \times 2 = 4$ $3 \times 3 = 9$

For 1×1 we write 1^2 (one squared).
For 2×2 we write 2^2 (two squared).
For 3×3 we write 3^2 (three squared).

Square numbers

The **square numbers** are 1, 4, 9, ...
We get them from 1^2, 2^2, 3^2, ...

Exercise 2:1

1 Copy this table of square numbers.
Fill it in.

1^2	2^2	3^2	4^2	5^2	
1	4	9			36

2 For 3×3 we write 3^2
Write these in the same way.

a 4×4
b 6×6
c 7×7
d 9×9
e 11×11
f 14×14

3 $5^2 = 5 \times 5$
Write these in the same way.

a 4^2 **b** 3^2 **c** 6^2 **d** 8^2 **e** 10^2 **f** 16^2

4 Use your calculator to work out:

a 6×6 **b** 8×8 **c** 9×9 **d** 12×12 **e** 14×14 **f** 15×15

5 Use your calculator to work out:

a 7^2 **b** 5^2 **c** 11^2 **d** 10^2 **e** 13^2 **f** 16^2

We can use the **x^2** key on a calculator to work out square numbers.

Example Work out 6^2

Key in:  **x^2** 

Answer: 36

Exercise 2:2

1 Use **x^2** to work out:

a 3^2 **b** 5^2 **c** 7^2 **d** 9^2 **e** 10^2 **f** 13^2

2 Use **x^2** to work out:

a 21^2 **b** 26^2 **c** 31^2 **d** 43^2 **e** 29^2 **f** 45^2

3 Use **x^2** to work out:

a 20^2 **b** 30^2 **c** 40^2

Without using your calculator, write down the answers to:

● **d** 50^2 ● **e** 60^2 ● **f** 70^2

4 Use **x^2** to work out:

a 4.3^2 **b** 3.5^2 **c** 2.6^2 **d** 7.5^2 **e** 1.9^2 **f** 5.8^2

● **5** Use **x^2** to work out:

a 31.2^2 **b** 58.1^2 **c** 68.4^2 **d** 24.5^2 **e** 100^2 **f** 130^2

Example

Find the area of this square.

Area = length × width
= 4 × 4
= 16 cm^2

4 cm (side) × 4 cm (base)

4 × 4 is 4^2. You can use **x^2**

Key in: **4** **x^2** **=**

Answer: 16 cm^2

---

6 Use **x^2** to find the areas of these squares:

a 7 cm × 7 cm

b 12 cm × 12 cm

c 17 cm × 17 cm

d 2.3 cm × 2.3 cm

7 This bowling green is a square.
The length of a side is 25 m.
Find the area of the bowling green.

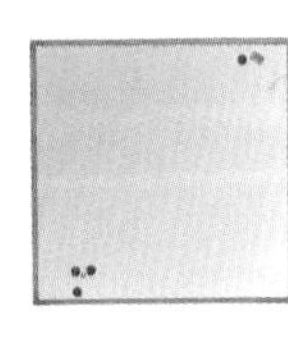

8 Mrs Brown has a square carpet
The length of a side is 3.6 m.
Find the area of the carpet.

9 Find the area of this square chessboard.
The length of a side is 48 cm.

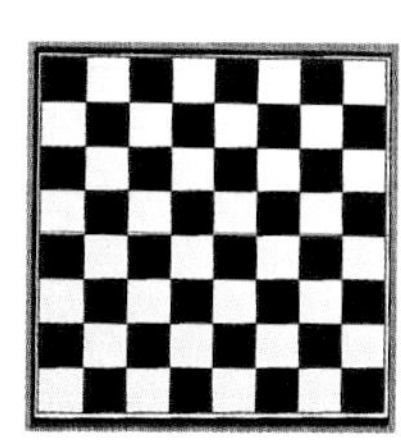

Example

The area of this square is 25 cm^2.
What is the length of a side?

area = 25 cm^2

We know that
$5 \times 5 = 25$
So the length of a side is 5 cm.

Exercise 2:3

1 Find the length of a side of these squares.

a

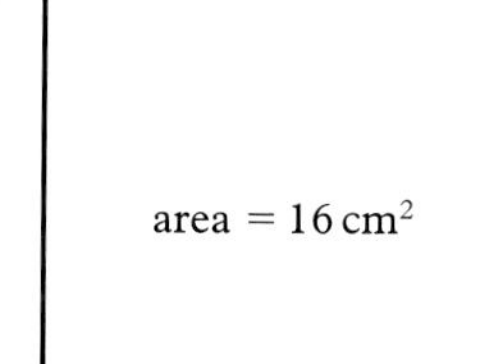

b

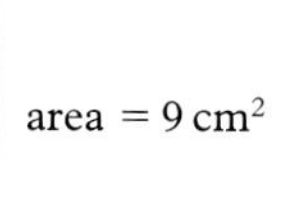

c

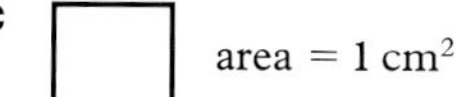

Square root

On a calculator there is a $\sqrt{}$ key.
This is called a **square root** key.
This key will find the length of a side of a square for you.

Example

The area of this square is 16 cm^2.
The length of a side is $\sqrt{16}$

Key in: $\sqrt{}$ 1 6 =

Answer: 4 cm

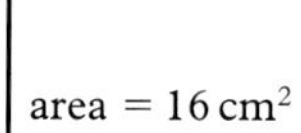

---

2 Use [√] to find the length of a side of a square with area:

a 36 cm^2 **b** 49 cm^2 **c** 121 cm^2 **d** 81 cm^2

3 Work out:

a $\sqrt{25}$	**d** $\sqrt{169}$	**g** $\sqrt{361}$	**j** $\sqrt{676}$
b $\sqrt{64}$	**e** $\sqrt{196}$	**h** $\sqrt{225}$	**k** $\sqrt{900}$
c $\sqrt{144}$	**f** $\sqrt{324}$	**i** $\sqrt{256}$	**l** $\sqrt{3136}$

The area of this square is 7 cm^2.
The length of a side is $\sqrt{7}$

[√] [7] [=] on the calculator gives

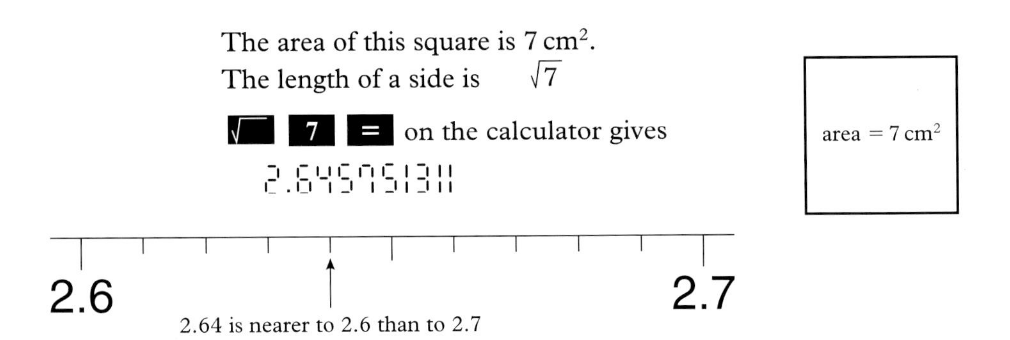

The length of the side is 2.6 cm correct to one decimal place (1 dp).

Exercise 2:4

1 Copy this table.
Fill it in.

	Area of square	[√] from calculator	Length of side (to 1 dp)
a	11	3.31662479	
b	20		4.5
c	34		
d	19		
e	43		

2 Find the length of a side of these squares.
Add four more rows to your table from question **1**.
Write your answers in the new rows.

a area $= 14\ \text{cm}^2$

c area $= 92\ \text{cm}^2$

b area $= 50\ \text{cm}^2$

● **d** area $= 15.4\ \text{cm}^2$

3 Work these out.
Give your answers correct to 1 decimal place.

a $\sqrt{29}$	**d** $\sqrt{189}$	**g** $\sqrt{378}$	**j** $\sqrt{674}$
b $\sqrt{60}$	**e** $\sqrt{200}$	**h** $\sqrt{205}$	**k** $\sqrt{809}$
c $\sqrt{42}$	**f** $\sqrt{567}$	**i** $\sqrt{287}$	**l** $\sqrt{5231}$

4 This floor tile is a square.
The area is $800\ \text{cm}^2$.
Find the length of a side.

5 This record sleeve is a square.
The area is $920\ \text{cm}^2$.
Find the length of a side.

2 Mental maths

Ruth, Andrew and Allison have £2 to spend on ice cream. They need to know which ice creams they can buy.

Sometimes we have to work things out in our heads.

Exercise 2:5 Adding

1 Work these out in your head.
Write down the answers.

a	**b**	**c**	● **d**
6 + 5	4 + 7	13 + 4	17 + 8
8 + 4	8 + 8	14 + 2	13 + 9
7 + 6	6 + 9	17 + 3	8 + 15
9 + 5	5 + 8	15 + 4	17 + 9
8 + 3	4 + 9	4 + 14	19 + 5
7 + 7	5 + 7	3 + 15	7 + 16
7 + 9	8 + 9	6 + 13	8 + 14
9 + 3	7 + 8	5 + 12	12 + 9

2 9 + 1 = 10 and 1 + 9 = 10
1 and 9 are a pair of numbers which add up to 10.

Write down all the pairs of numbers that add up to 10.

3 Write down all the pairs of numbers that add up to 20.

4 Copy this addition table on to squared paper.
Fill it in.
Stick your table into your book.

+	5	6	7	8	9	10
5	10	11				
6						
7						
8						
9						
10						

Game Pairs to eleven

This is a game for two players.
You will need a pack of cards. Take out the kings, queens and jacks.
An ace counts as one.

Dean and Rachel play the game.
Dean deals 10 cards like this.

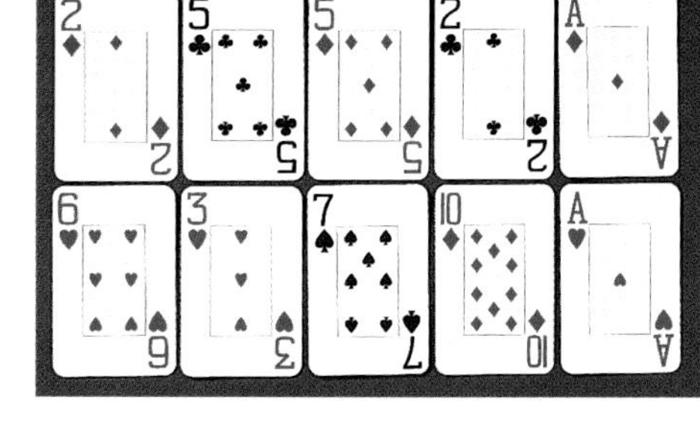

Dean then looks for all the pairs of cards that add up to 11.
He takes them out and keeps them.

Rachel fills in the gaps from the pack.
She looks for pairs that make 11.
She takes them out and keeps them.
Then it is Dean's turn again.

The game ends when all the cards are collected.
The player with the most cards wins.

Sometimes there aren't any pairs that make 11.
Keep the pairs you have already.
Pick up the cards on the table and the pack.
Shuffle them. Deal 10 new cards.

Play this game with a partner.

Exercise 2:6 Subtracting

1 Work these out in your head.
Write down the answers.

a	**b**	**c**	• **d**
$10 - 7$	$20 - 12$	$15 - 12$	$16 - 7$
$10 - 4$	$20 - 15$	$13 - 11$	$13 - 6$
$10 - 3$	$20 - 17$	$17 - 14$	$15 - 7$
$10 - 9$	$20 - 18$	$14 - 13$	$14 - 5$
$10 - 5$	$20 - 13$	$15 - 11$	$17 - 8$
$10 - 2$	$20 - 16$	$16 - 13$	$13 - 4$
$10 - 6$	$20 - 14$	$18 - 12$	$18 - 7$
$10 - 8$	$20 - 11$	$19 - 15$	$15 - 6$

◀◀ REPLAY ▶

Example Write down the rule for this pattern.
Find the next two terms.
22, 20, 18, 16, 14, …, …

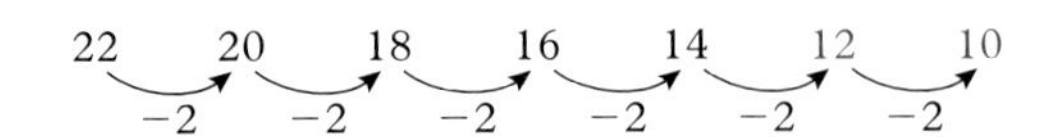

The rule is −2. The next two terms are 12, 10.

2 Copy each number pattern.
Write down its rule.
Use your rule to fill in the missing numbers.

a 19, 16, 13, …, …, …
b 23, 19, 15, …, …, …
c 29, 24, 19, …, …, …
d 26, 22, 18, …, …, …

The addition table that you made in Exercise 2:5 can help you subtract.

Example

a Use your addition table to answer this:
$7 + 9 =$

b Write two take aways using the same numbers.

+	5	6	7	8	9	10
5	10	11	12	13	14	15
6	11	12	13	14	15	16
7	12	13	14	15	16	17
8	13	14	15	16	17	18
9	14	15	16	17	18	19
10	15	16	17	18	19	20

a $7 + 9 = 16$
b $16 - 9 = 7$ $16 - 7 = 9$

3 Use your addition table from Exercise 2:5 to answer these.
Write two take aways using the same numbers.

a $8 + 5 =$ …
… $- 8 = 5$
… $- 5 = 8$

b $9 + 6 =$ …
… $- 9 = 6$
… $- 6 = 9$

c $5 + 9 =$ …
… $- 5 = 9$
… $- 9 = 5$

4 Do these in the same way as question **3**.

a $7 + 6 =$
b $6 + 8 =$
c $7 + 5 =$

Game *Take away dice*

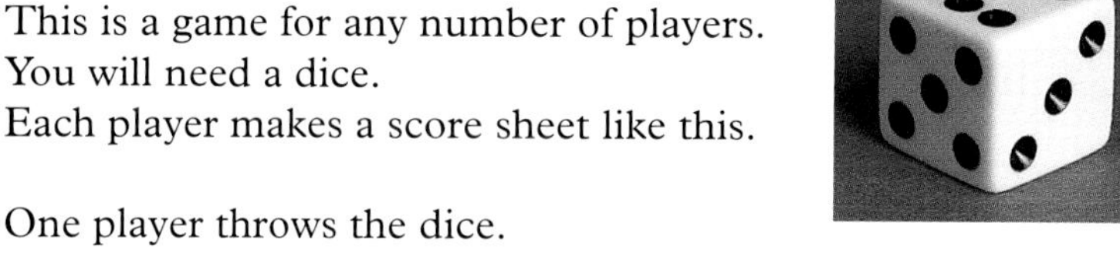

This is a game for any number of players.
You will need a dice.
Each player makes a score sheet like this.

One player throws the dice.
All the players write the number somewhere above the line on their score sheet.
You cannot move a number once you have written it down.
After 8 throws all the boxes will be filled up.

Game 1

6	2	5	4
4	3	4	2

Now do 4 subtraction sums.
Take the bottom number away from the top one.
If the top number is smaller than the bottom one, leave the answer blank.
Cross out any answers that are the same.
Add the rest of the answers together to get your score.

6	2	5	4
4	3	4	2
~~2~~		1	~~2~~

Score: 1

Game 2

5	6	4	6
3	2	1	6
2	4	3	

Score: 2 + 4 + 3 = 9

The player with the highest score wins.

Play this game with some friends.

Exercise 2:7 Multiplying

1 Copy this multiplication table.
Fill it in.

×	1	2	3	4	5	6	7	8	9	10
1	1	2								
2	2	4								
3										
4										
5										
6										
7										
8										
9										
10										

2 Use your multiplication table to help you answer these.

a 6×5
b 7×4
c 8×6
d 7×8
e 9×10
f 6×9
g 6×7
h 9×5
i 10×7
j 8×9
k 7×7
l 5×8

3 **a** How many times is 40 written in your multiplication table?
b Write down all the pairs of numbers that multiply to give 40.

4 **a** How many times is 24 written in your multiplication table?
b Write down all the pairs of numbers that multiply to give 24.

W Game 3 in a line

Ask your teacher for a worksheet.

Exercise 2:8 Dividing

Example $5 \times 4 = 20$
We can write down two divisions using the same numbers.
$20 \div 5 = 4$ $20 \div 4 = 5$

1 Copy these.
Fill in the missing numbers.

a $3 \times 4 = \ldots$
$\ldots \div 3 = 4$
$\ldots \div 4 = 3$

b $8 \times 10 = \ldots$
$\ldots \div 8 = 10$
$\ldots \div 10 = 8$

c $4 \times 7 = \ldots$
$\ldots \div 4 = 7$
$\ldots \div 7 = 4$

2 Do these in the same way as question **1**.
a 4×5 **b** 3×6 **c** 10×7

Example Use your multiplication table to answer this:
$24 \div 6 =$

×	1	2	3	4	5	6	7	8
1	1	2	3	4	5	6	7	8
2	2	4	6	8	10	12	14	15
3	3	6	9	12	15	18	21	24
4	4	8	12	16	20	24	28	32
5	5	10	15	20	25	30	35	40
6	6	12	18	24	30	36	42	48
7	7	14	21	28	35	42	49	56
8	8	16	24	32	40	48	56	64

Answer: $24 \div 6 = 4$

3 Use your multiplication table to help you answer these.

a	$35 \div 7$	**c**	$36 \div 9$	**e**	$56 \div 8$	**g**	$54 \div 6$
b	$48 \div 6$	**d**	$42 \div 7$	**f**	$64 \div 8$	**h**	$72 \div 8$

Game *Dividing line*

This is a game for two players.
It is like noughts and crosses.
You need a dice, some red and
blue counters and a 3×3 square.
The square has the numbers 2–10.
The numbers can be put in any order.

2	3	7
4	5	8
6	9	10

Alice and Carl play this game.
Alice throws the dice. She gets a four.
She wants to cover the centre square.
Alice needs to think of a division
sum for it.

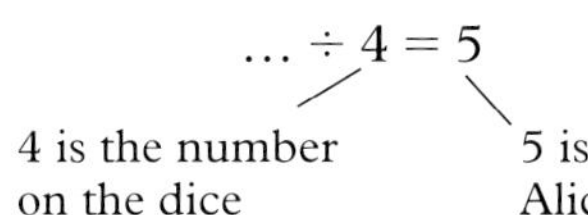

Alice says that $20 \div 4 = 5$.
Carl checks this using his multiplication table.
Alice is right so she covers the 5 with a red counter.

Carl wants to cover the 3.
He throws a six.

$$\ldots \div 6 = 3$$

Carl says that $18 \div 6 = 3$.
Alice checks this.
Carl is right so he puts a blue
counter on the 3.

2		7
4		8
6	9	10

The first person to get three
counters in a line (like noughts
and crosses) wins the game.

Play this game with a partner.

3 Estimation

Susan is choosing the wallpaper for her bedroom.
She knows that she needs 7 rolls.

The flowers pattern costs £6.30 a roll.
The teddy bears pattern costs £7.85 a roll.
Susan's mum has £50 to spend.

Susan estimates the cost of each type of paper.
She says that the flowers cost about £6 a roll,
7 rolls cost about 7 × £6 = £42

She says that the teddy bears cost about £8 a roll,
7 rolls cost about 7 × £8 = £56

Susan knows that she can only have the flowers.

◀◀ REPLAY ▶

Rounding to the nearest whole number

Examples

1 Round the number 5.7 to the nearest whole number.

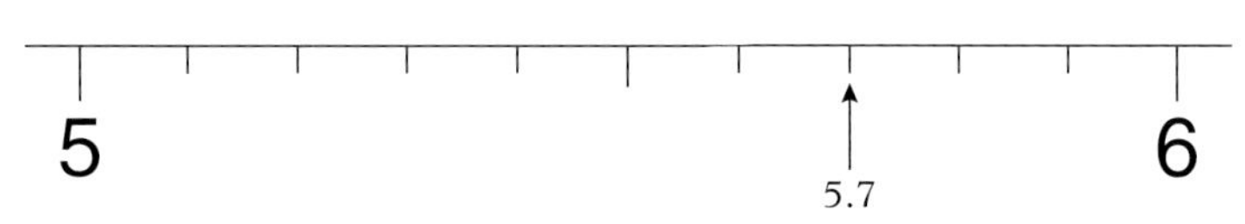

5.7 is nearer to 6 than to 5. It is rounded to 6.

2 Round the number 3.5 to the nearest whole number.

3.5 is halfway between 3 and 4. It is rounded to 4.

Exercise 2:9

1 Round these numbers to the nearest whole number.

a 4.6	**d** 6.5	**g** 9.9	**j** 12.9
b 3.8	**e** 8.1	**h** 13.6	**k** 21.6
c 5.9	**f** 4.3	**i** 10.2	**l** 13.5

Rounding to the nearest 10

Examples

1 Round the number 63 to the nearest 10.

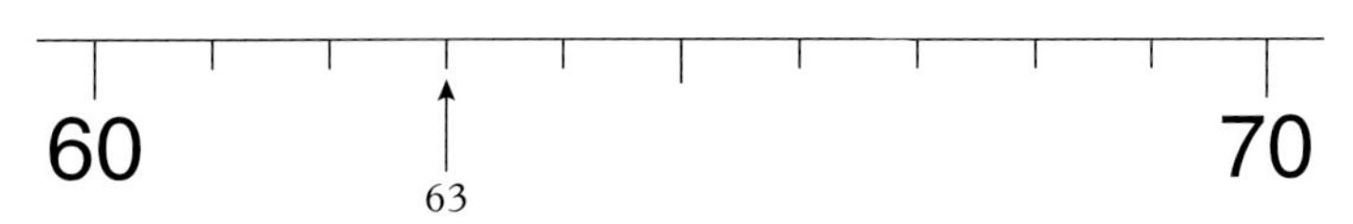

63 is nearer to 60 than to 70.
So 63 is rounded to 60 to the nearest 10.

2 Round the number 85 to the nearest 10.

85 is halfway between 80 and 90.
So 85 is rounded to 90 to the nearest 10.

3 Round the number 138 to the nearest 10.

138 is nearer to 140 than to 130.
So 138 is rounded to 140.

2 Round these numbers to the nearest 10.

a 18	**d** 55	**g** 99	**j** 134
b 46	**e** 91	**h** 48	**k** 247
c 57	**f** 52	**i** 101	**l** 185

Rounding to the nearest 100

Examples

1 Round the number 633 to the nearest 100.

633 is nearer to 600 than to 700.
So 633 is rounded to 600 to the nearest 100.

2 Round the number 650 to the nearest 100.

650 is halfway between 600 and 700.
So 650 is rounded to 700 to the nearest 100.

3 Round these numbers to the nearest 100.

a 127	**c** 757	**e** 411	**g** 699
b 426	**d** 650	**f** 635	**h** 581

- **4** Round these numbers:
  a 27 to the nearest 10
  b 13.5 to the nearest whole number
  c 243 to the nearest 100
  d 3678 to the nearest 100

Estimating

We often work things out on a calculator.
It is a good idea to check that your answer is about right.
It is very easy to hit the wrong key by accident!

Example Work out 4.9×3.2

Calculation: 4 · 9 × 3 · 2 =
Answer: 15.68
Estimate: 4.9 is about 5
3.2 is about 3
4.9×3.2 is about $5 \times 3 = 15$

15 is near to 15.68. So the answer is probably right.

Exercise 2:10

1 Copy these.
Fill in the missing numbers.
a $5.9 \times 7.2 = \ldots$
Estimate: 5.9×7.2 is about $\ldots \times \ldots = \ldots$
b $4.6 \times 3.1 = \ldots$
Estimate: 4.6×3.1 is about $\ldots \times \ldots = \ldots$

2 Work these out.
Write down the answer and estimate for each one as in question **1**.

a 2.7×8.4 **c** 8.6×1.1 **e** 8.5×4.8 **g** 5×2.3
b 5.6×8.1 **d** 4.9×2.1 **f** 3.3×6.5 **h** 8×4.1

Example

Work out 36×82

Calculation: **3** **6** **×** **8** **2** **=**

Answer: 2952

Estimate: 36 is about 40
82 is about 80
36×82 is about $40 \times 80 = 3200$

3200 is near to 2952. So the answer is probably right.

3 Copy these.
Fill in the missing numbers.

a $54 \times 36 = \ldots$
Estimate: 54×36 is about $\ldots \times \ldots = \ldots$

b $26 \times 72 = \ldots$
Estimate: 26×72 is about $\ldots \times \ldots = \ldots$

4 Work these out.
Write down the answer and an estimate for each one.

a 58×23 **c** 23×37 **e** 35×21 **g** 40×23
b 39×21 **d** 11×29 **f** 98×12 **h** 80×45

Example

Work out 352×286

Calculation: **3** **5** **2** **×** **2** **8** **6** **=**

Answer: 100 672

Estimate: 352 is about 400
286 is about 300
352×286 is about $400 \times 300 = 120\,000$

120 000 is near to 100 672. So the answer is probably right.

5 Copy these.
Fill in the missing numbers.

a $124 \times 356 = \ldots$
Estimate: 124×356 is about $\ldots \times \ldots = \ldots$

b $278 \times 312 = \ldots$
Estimate: 278×312 is about $\ldots \times \ldots = \ldots$

6 Work these out.
Write down the answer and an estimate for each one.

a 578×123 **c** 213×667 **e** 349×398 **g** 800×233
b 234×652 **d** 111×909 **f** 564×345 **h** 400×897

● **7** Work these out.
Write down the answer and an estimate for each one.
You need to decide how to round the numbers in the questions.

a 3.3×21 **d** 1.9×435 **g** $8.9 - 2.7$ **j** $234 + 567$
b 4.9×35 **e** 55×246 **h** $21.5 \div 4.3$ **k** $315 - 189$
c 231×34 **f** 5.3×867 **i** $18 \div 4.8$ **l** $535 - 95$

When you answer questions you should always make an estimate to check your answer.

Exercise 2:11

In this exercise:
a work out the answers using a calculator
b write down an estimate to check that each answer is about right.

1 Sunita has saved £48.
Her mum gives her another £28.
How much has she got now?

2 Year 8 have a day out in London.
They go in 3 coaches.
The first coach takes 53 people, the second takes 38 people and the third takes 67 people.
How many people go to London?

3 Four of the classes in Year 8 collect bottles for recycling.
The table shows how many bottles they collect.

8D	8F	8M	8P
246	624	335	479

How many bottles are collected altogether?

● **4** The height of the television and the stand is 118 cm.
The height of the stand is 53 cm.
What is the height of the television?

118 cm

53 cm

● **5** Daniel runs the Year 8 snack bar.
A can of cola costs 38 p.
A packet of crisps costs 23 p.
He buys 180 of each.
How much does he spend?

6 Find the cost of:
a 13 rolls of this wallpaper
b 3 of these borders

● **7** This set of garden furniture costs £137.50.
The table costs £39.50.
a How much do the four chairs cost?
b How much is it for one chair?

8 Veronica is having a party. Her mum buys a jar containing 396 sweets.
18 people come to the party.
How many sweets does each person get?

9 54 pupils from Year 8 have a day out at Alton Towers.
It costs £375.30.
How much does each pupil have to pay?

10 126 pupils from Year 8 go ten-pin bowling.
Only six people can play in one lane.
How many lanes do they need?

1 Use x^2 to work out:

a 16^2 **b** 12^2 **c** 1.7^2 **d** 61.3^2 **e** 140^2

2 Use $\sqrt{}$ to work out:

a $\sqrt{1764}$ **b** $\sqrt{1600}$ **c** $\sqrt{2.89}$ **d** $\sqrt{1.44}$ **e** $\sqrt{96}$

3 **a** Copy this pattern.
Use $\sqrt{}$ to fill in the missing numbers.

$\sqrt{1} = \ldots$
$\sqrt{10} = \ldots$
$\sqrt{100} = \ldots$
$\sqrt{1000} = \ldots$

b Predict $\sqrt{10\,000}$
Use your calculator to check your prediction.

4 **a** Use x^2 to find the area of this square carpet.

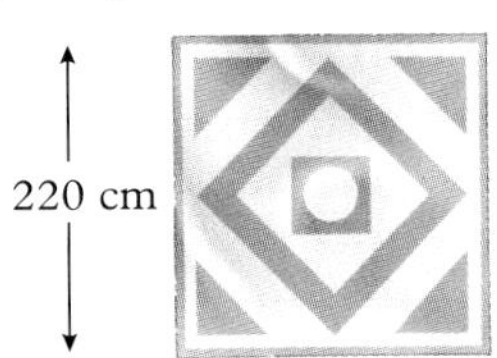

b Use $\sqrt{}$ to find the length of a side of this square paving stone.

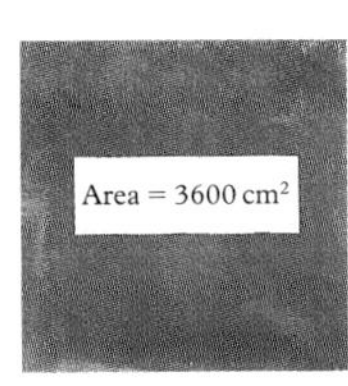

5 Copy these.
Fill in the missing numbers.

a $14 + 8 = \ldots$
$\ldots - 8 = 14$

b $26 - 19 = \ldots$
$\ldots + 19 = 26$

c $3 \times 8 = \ldots$
$\ldots \div 8 = 3$

d $32 \div 4 = \ldots$
$\ldots \times 4 = 32$

6 **a** How many times is 36 written in your multiplication table?
b Write down all the pairs of numbers that multiply to give 36.

7 Work these out in your head or use an addition or multiplication table.
Write down the answers.

a	**b**	**c**	**d**
$4 + 2$	$8 - 4$	5×4	$36 \div 4$
$3 + 5$	$9 - 3$	6×6	$24 \div 6$
$3 + 8$	$20 - 9$	3×9	$49 \div 7$
$9 + 9$	$18 - 13$	7×5	$28 \div 4$
$14 + 5$	$14 - 8$	8×8	$32 \div 8$
$7 + 12$	$13 - 6$	7×9	$25 \div 5$
$22 + 6$	$19 - 14$	10×8	$70 \div 7$
$7 + 23$	$20 - 8$	8×4	$27 \div 3$

8 $11 + 1 = 12$ and $1 + 11 = 12$
1 and 11 are a pair of numbers which add up to 12.
Write down all the pairs of numbers that add up to 12.

9 Make an estimate for each of these.
Find the accurate answer.

a	$34 + 63$	**c**	$317 - 179$	**e**	32×63	**g**	$678 + 205$
b	$89 - 57$	**d**	6.8×31	**f**	$51 \div 1.7$	**h**	$24.3 \div 4.8$

10 **a** Which of these answers is the best estimate for 6.3×51?
(1) 3 (2) 300 (3) 30 (4) 3000
b For each of these say if the estimate is good or bad.
(1) 4.2×7.8 estimate 320 (2) $28 + 53$ estimate 80
c Write a good estimate for any parts of **b** you think are bad.

11 Jane has £50 to spend on clothes for her holiday.
She wants an estimate to see if she can afford everything.
Here is Jane's list.
a Write down an estimate for Jane.
b Work out the exact cost of the clothes.

Game *Number guesses*

This is a game for two or more people.

One person chooses a calculation like
$14 + 8 = 22$ or $6 \times 7 = 42$
The other players have to guess the numbers and if it is add, take away, multiply or divide.
They are allowed 10 guesses.

8W are playing Number guesses.
Sadie has chosen $24 \div 6 = 4$
Sadie starts like this:

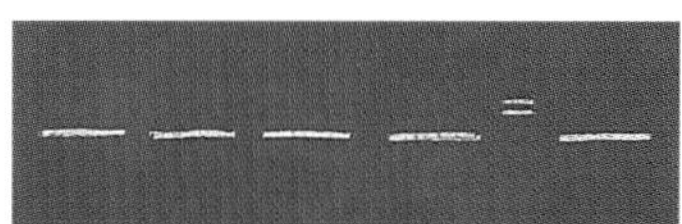

After seven wrong guesses and three correct ones it looks like this:

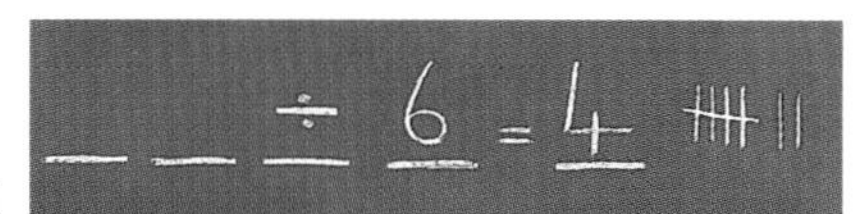

If there are 10 wrong guesses Sadie will win and get another turn.
Leroy guesses the missing numbers.
Now it is his turn.

Play this game with some friends.

1 **a** Use x^2 to work out:
(1) 13^2 (2) 4.2^2 (3) 54^2 (4) 0.2^2 (5) 0.4^2

b Write down the numbers that get smaller when you press x^2
What can you say about these numbers?

c Use $\sqrt{\ }$ to work out:
(1) $\sqrt{0.09}$ (2) $\sqrt{1225}$ (3) $\sqrt{0.0036}$ (4) $\sqrt{10\,404}$ (5) $\sqrt{0.0081}$

d Write down the numbers that get bigger when you press $\sqrt{\ }$
What can you say about these numbers?

2 **a** Use $\sqrt{\ }$ to calculate the length of a side of this square silk scarf.
The area of the scarf is 3721 cm^2.

b The scarf has a narrow hem round its edge.
Use your answer to **a** to find the length of the hem.

3 Round these numbers:

a 5.5 to the nearest whole number
b 790 to the nearest 100
c 4.612 to 1 dp
d 17.45 to the nearest whole number
e 23 to the nearest 10
f 514 to the nearest 100
g 85 to the nearest 10
h 3894 to the nearest 100
i 13.915 to 1 dp
j 12.1 to the nearest whole number

4 **a** Round these amounts:
(1) £328 (to the nearest £100)
(2) £54 (to the nearest £10)
(3) £563 (to the nearest £100)
(4) £1150 (to the nearest £1000)

b Use your answers to **a** to estimate the answers to these.
(1) £328 + £54
(2) £563 − £328
(3) £1150 − £563
(4) £328 + £563 + £1150
(5) £563 ÷ 2
(6) £54 × 3

c Work out the accurate answers to **b**.
Compare the answers with your estimates.

5 **a** James and Sarah are surprised that their bill in Jo's Burger Cafe is so large.
They use estimates to check it.
Write down the estimates they could use.
How many mistakes has Jo made?

b Copy the bill and correct it.

Jo's
BURGER·CAFE

4 Cola's at 68p	£3.12
2 burgers at £1.75	£4.50
2 chips at 65p	£1.30
2 Sweets at £1.95	£3.90
TOTAL	£14.82

- We can use the x^2 key on a calculator to work out square numbers.

Example Work out 6^2

Key in: 6 x^2 =

Answer: 36

You can use x^2 to find the areas of squares.

Example The area of this square is 4×4 or 4^2

4 x^2 =

Answer: $16\,\text{cm}^2$

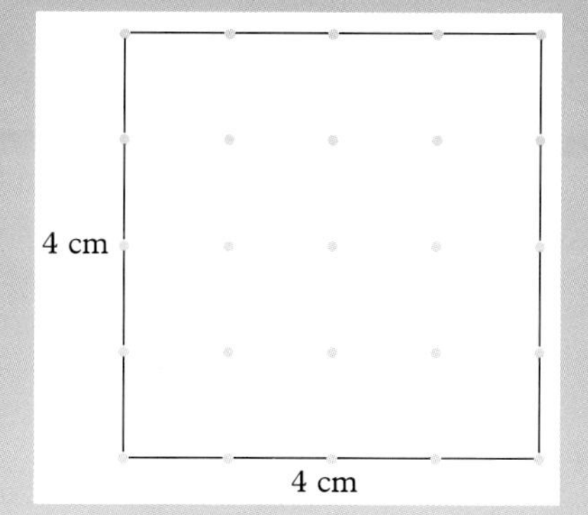

- √ is the **square root** key.
It will work out the sides of squares.

Example The length of a side of this square is $\sqrt{25}$

Key in: √ 2 5 =

Answer: 5 cm

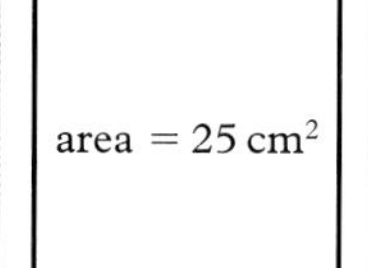

- $\sqrt{7} = 2.645\,751\,3$

$\sqrt{7}$ is 2.6 correct to 1 dp

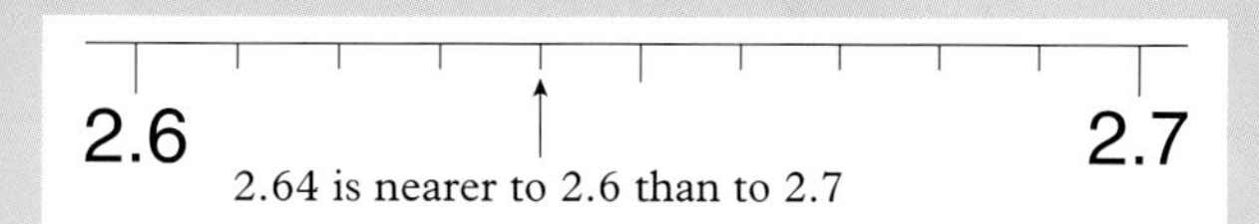

- You can work out some questions in your head or use a multiplication table.

Examples
1 $8 + 14 = 22$
2 $23 - 7 = 16$
3 $7 \times 5 = 35$
4 $48 \div 6 = 8$

- *Examples* 5.7 rounded to the nearest whole number is 6.
63 rounded to the nearest 10 is 60.
633 rounded to the nearest 100 is 600
'Halfway' numbers are always rounded up.
85 rounded to the nearest 10 is 90.

- To make an estimate, round each number.

Examples

1 2.8×34
Estimate: $3 \times 30 = 90$
Answer: 95.2

2 $589 - 128$
Estimate: $600 - 100 = 500$
Answer: 461

3 $38 - 12$
Estimate: $40 - 10 = 30$
Answer: 26

4 $183 \div 25$
Estimate: $200 \div 20 = 10$
Answer: 7.32

The estimate and the answer should always be quite close.

1 Use x^2 to work out:

a 17^2 **b** 3.6^2 **c** 80^2

2 Use $\sqrt{\ }$ to work out:

a $\sqrt{625}$ **b** $\sqrt{1600}$ **c** $\sqrt{0.04}$ **d** $\sqrt{196}$

3 Use $\sqrt{\ }$ to work these out.
Give your answers correct to 1 dp.

a $\sqrt{6}$ **b** $\sqrt{7.9}$ **c** $\sqrt{600}$ **d** $\sqrt{45}$

4 Use x^2 to find the area of this square.

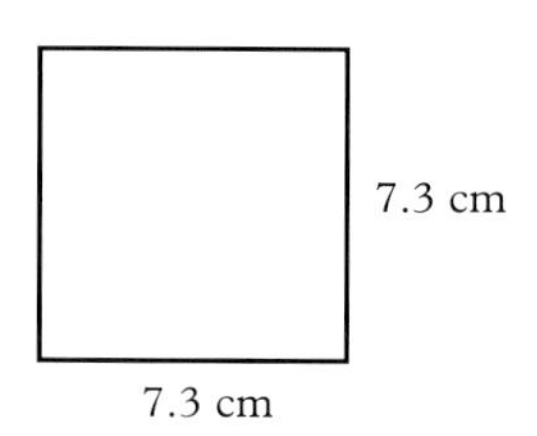

5 The area of this square is 250 cm^2.
Use $\sqrt{\ }$ to find the length of a side.
Give your answer correct to 1 dp.

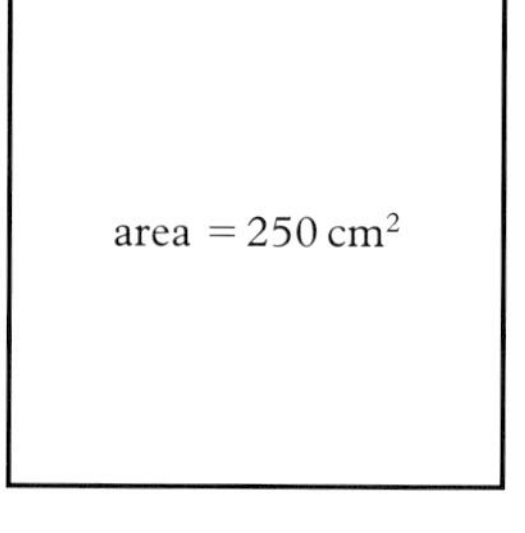

6 Do these in your head or use an addition or a multiplication table.
Write down the answers.

a $17 + 6$ **c** $20 - 8$ **e** 7×5 **g** $18 \div 3$
b $9 + 14$ **d** $18 - 9$ **f** 6×6 **h** $21 \div 7$

7 **a** Round 5.6 to the nearest whole number.
b Round 65 to the nearest 10.
c Round 640 to the nearest 100.
d Round 1731 to the nearest 100.

8 **a** Make estimates for these.
(1) $27 + 89$ (3) 5.6×3.2
(2) $72.5 - 43.2$ (4) $54 \div 1.8$
b Work out the answers.
Compare them with your estimates.

3 Statistics: questions and answers

CORE

1 **Diagrams and charts**

2 **Pie-charts**

3 **Designing a questionnaire**

QUESTIONS

EXTENSION

SUMMARY

TEST YOURSELF

The first opinion poll was done by **George Gallup** in **1935**.

Opinion polls are now often called Gallup polls. Gallup is one of the biggest survey companies in the world.

1 Diagrams and charts

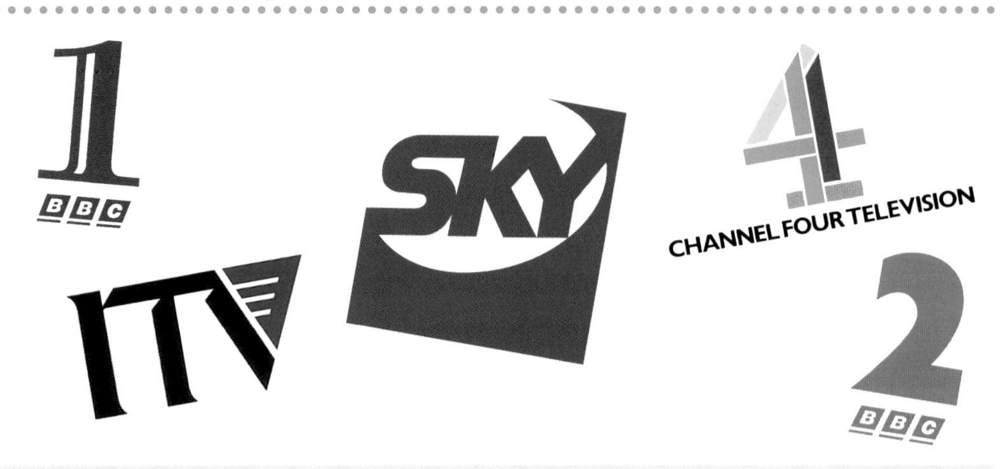

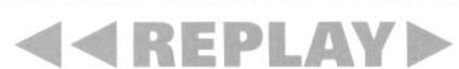

All of Year 8 have taken part in a survey.
The questions were about how much TV they watched.
They were also asked about their favourite type of programme and their favourite channel.

Here are the results of the survey.

Number of hours watched per day

Hours per day	0	1	2	3	4	5	6
Number of pupils	20	45	75	60	10	5	5

Favourite type of TV programme

Type of programme	children's	soaps	sport	comedy	films	drama	news
Number of pupils	15	55	40	25	35	25	25

Favourite channel

Channel	BBC1	BBC2	ITV	C4	Sky	other
Number of pupils	73	22	66	19	24	16

Year 8 display this data.
Here is some of their work.

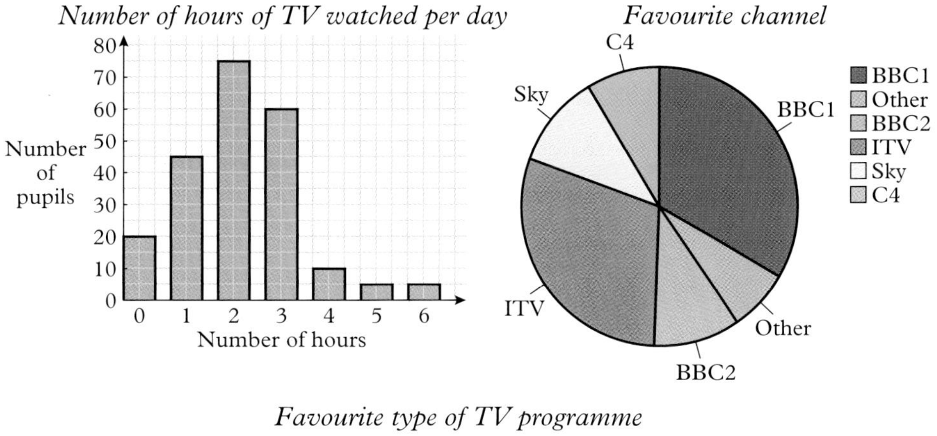

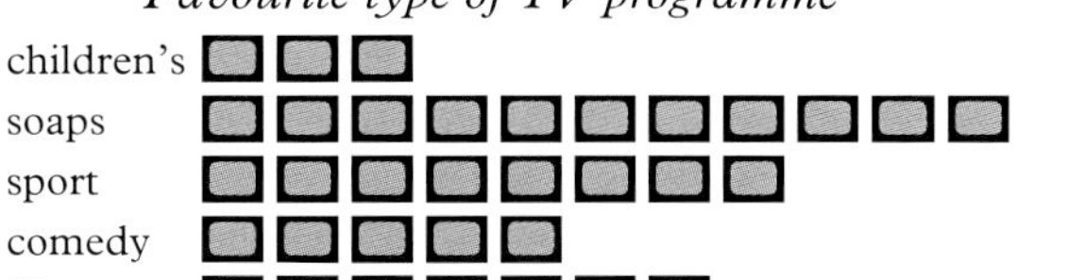

Exercise 3:1

1 Look at the bar-chart.

a Add up the heights of all of the bars.
How many pupils are there in Year 8?

b Which is the highest bar?
What does this tell you?

c How many people watch TV for *more* than 3 hours a day?

• **d** There are 20 people in the 0 hours bar.
Do you think they watch no TV at all?
Explain your answer.

2 Look at the pictogram.

a How many people does ▢ stand for?

b How many people said films were their favourite?

c How many more people liked soaps than liked news?

d What is the least popular type of programme?

• **e** How could you show 3 people on this diagram?

3 Look at the pie-chart.

a What colour is the biggest slice?
What is the most popular channel?

b What is the least popular channel?

• **c** Can you tell how many people liked BBC2 the most?
Explain your answer.

Exercise 3:2

1 **a** Copy the axes on to squared paper.

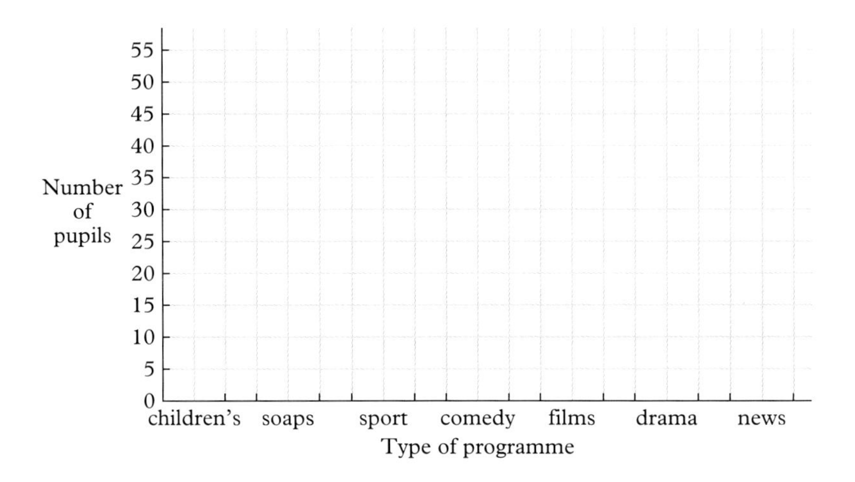

b Draw a bar-chart of the favourite types of programme.
c Put a title on your diagram.

2 Draw a bar-chart to show the favourite channel.
Don't forget a title and labels.

3 **a** Copy the outline of the pictogram.
b Draw a pictogram of the number of hours of TV watched.
Choose your own symbol to represent 5 pupils.
c Make sure that your diagram has a key.

Hours
0
1
2
3
4
5
6

4 Draw a pictogram of the favourite channels.
Choose a different symbol.
Don't forget the key.

Year 8 were also asked how many videos they had hired in the last month.

Here are the answers from 8J and 8K.

8J

0	6	9	5	4	6	0	4	5	11
3	6	5	8	7	4	6	2	2	0
11	3	1	9	7	5	6	2	3	10

8K

2	5	4	9	6	8	2	3	4	0
1	8	5	3	10	5	9	4	2	6
4	5	8	9	6	3	5	10	2	0

Exercise 3:3

1 **a** Copy this tally-table for 8J.
Fill it in.

Number of videos hired by 8J

Number of videos	Tally	Total
0		
1		
2		
3		
4		
5		
6		
7		
8		
9		
10		
11		

b Draw a pictogram of these results.

2 **a** Make another tally-table for 8K.
b Draw a pictogram of these results.

It can be useful to collect data into groups.
It makes diagrams easier to draw.

For the numbers of videos hired sensible groups might be:

0–2 3–5 6–8 9–11

These are called equal groups.
They are all three videos wide.
For example 3–5 has 3, 4 and 5 in it.

Number of videos hired by 8J

Number of videos	
0 1 2	this becomes group 0–2
3 4 5	this becomes group 3 –5

Exercise 3:4

1 **a** Copy this tally-table for 8J.
Fill it in.
You can use your chart from Exercise **3:3** to help you.
You do not have to start all over again!

Number of videos	Tally	Total
0–2		
3–5		
6–8		
9–11		

b Copy the axes on to squared paper.

c Draw a bar-chart of your grouped data.
Remember that bar-charts of grouped data have their bars touching.

d Put a title and labels on your graph.

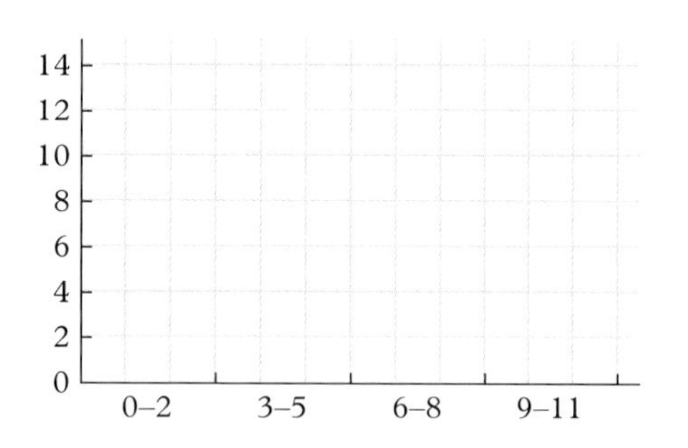

2 **a** Make a grouped tally-table for 8K.
Use the same groups.

b Draw a bar-chart for this data.
Use the same scale as in question **1**.

● **3** Here is the data for the videos hired by 8L.

5	1	9	0	0	6	7	10	5	9
8	3	5	6	8	9	0	0	1	4
5	10	1	7	3	6	7	7	5	4

a Make a grouped tally-table for this data.

b Draw a bar-chart for 8L.

2 Pie-charts

Pie-chart

A **pie-chart** shows how something is divided up.
The angle of the slice represents the number of items.

Example

Class 8N were asked their favourite subject.

Out of the 28 pupils:
14 said Maths
7 said PE
7 said French

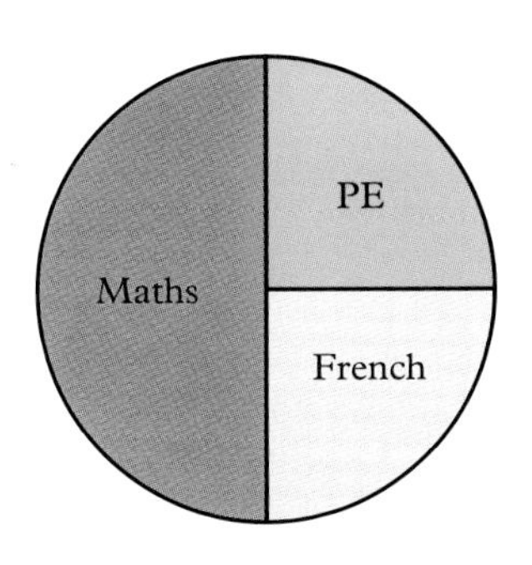

14 pupils is half the class.
Maths gets half of the pie.

7 pupils is a quarter of the class.
PE and French both get one quarter of the pie.

Exercise 3:5

1 Class 8N were also asked where they had lunch.
One half used the canteen. One quarter went out of school and the other quarter brought sandwiches.
Draw a pie-chart to show this information.

2 100 people were asked to name a city in England.
Here are the results: London 50
Birmingham 25
York 25

a Write down what fraction named each city.
b Draw a pie-chart to show this information.

3 80 people were asked to name a city in Scotland.
Here are the results: Edinburgh 20
Aberdeen 20
Glasgow 20
Inverness 10
Dundee 10

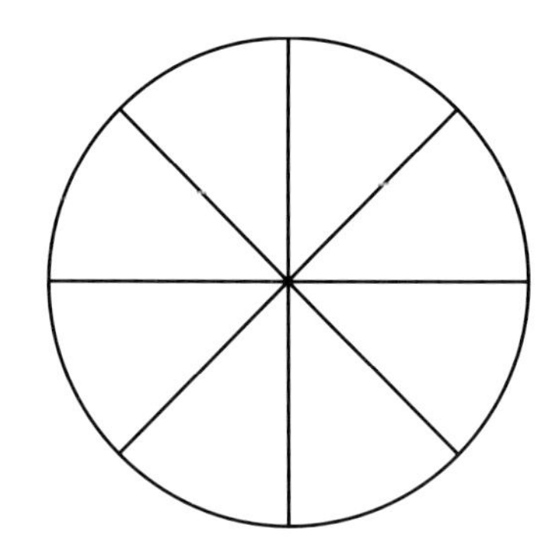

a Draw a circle.
Split it into 8 equal pieces.
You could do this by cutting out the circle and then folding it.

b Use your circle to draw a pie-chart.

4 The same 80 people were asked to name an Irish city.

40 people said Dublin
30 people said Belfast
10 people said Galway

a Split a circle into 8 equal pieces as you did in question **3**.

b Draw a pie-chart to show this information.

Sometimes the data does not work out into simple fractions.
When this happens you have to work out angles.

Remember: there are 360° in a full turn.
This means a pie-chart has 360° in the middle.
This 360° needs dividing up.

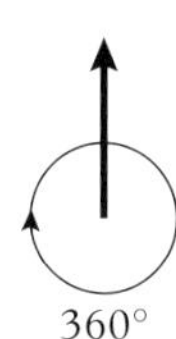

Example
30 people were asked which national newspaper they read.
The results were:

The Guardian	8	*The Sun*	6
Daily Mirror	7	*Daily Express*	6
The Times	3		

Show these results in a pie-chart.

1 Divide up the 360°.

There are 30 people in the survey so 360° ÷ 30 = 12°
This means that each person gets 12° of the circle.

2 Work out the angle for each newspaper. This is easy to do in a table.

Newspaper	Number of people	Working	Angle
The Guardian	8	$8 \times 12° =$	96°
Daily Mirror	7	$7 \times 12° =$	84°
The Times	3	$3 \times 12° =$	36°
The Sun	6	$6 \times 12° =$	72°
Daily Express	6	$6 \times 12° =$	72°

3 Check that the angles add up to 360°.
$96° + 84° + 36° + 72° + 72° = 360°$

4 a Draw a circle. Mark the centre. Draw a line to the top of the circle.

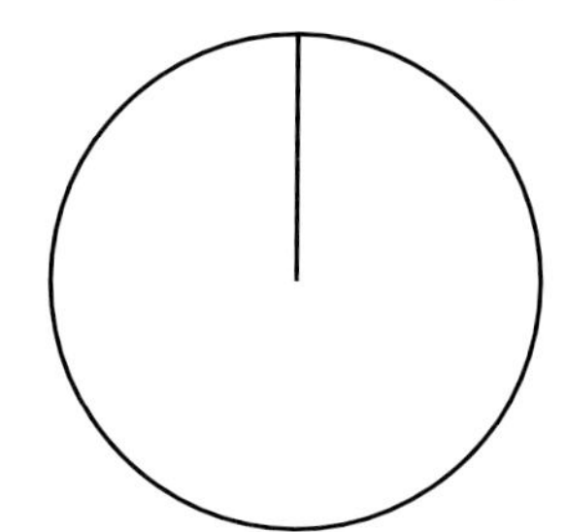

b Draw the first angle (96°).

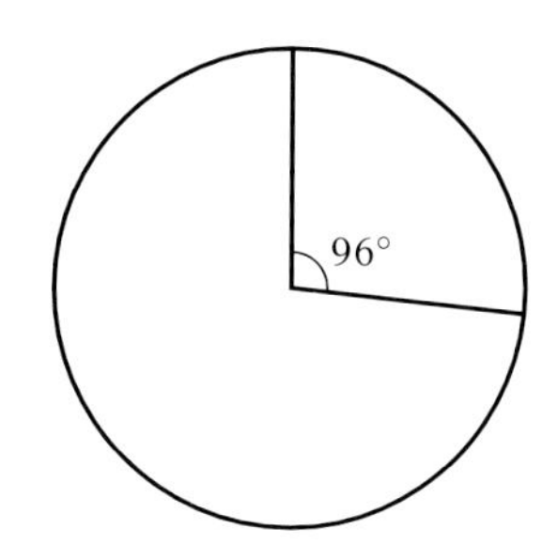

c Measure the next angle (84°) from the line that you have just drawn.

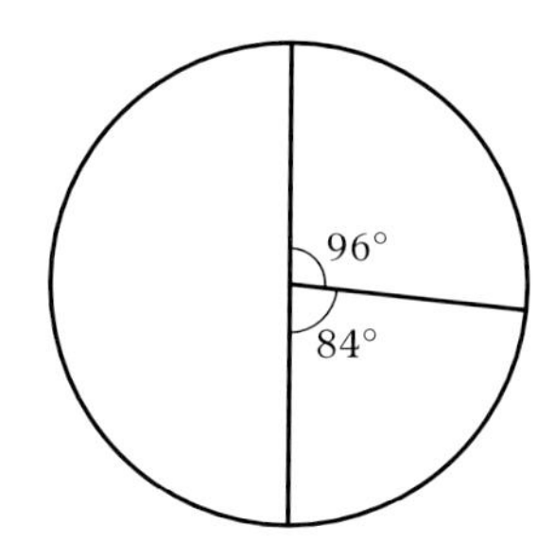

d Carry on until you have drawn all the angles.

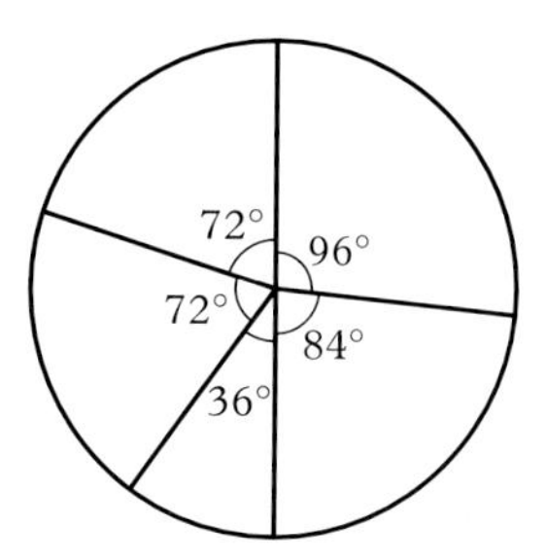

e Colour your pie-chart. Add a key.

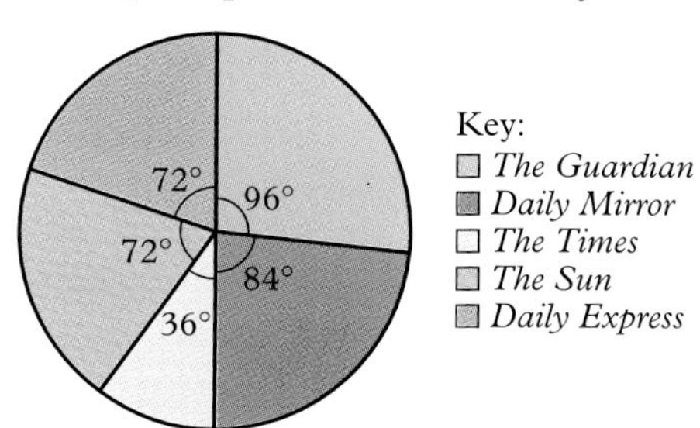

Exercise 3:6

1 Class 8J were asked what they usually have for breakfast.

a Copy this table.

Breakfast	Number of pupils	Working	Angle
cereal	9	$9 \times 12° =$	108°
toast	8	$8 \times 12° =$	96°
cooked	2	$2 \times$	
drink only	6	$6 \times$	
nothing	5	$5 \times$	
Total	30		360°

The angle we need for each pupil is
$360° \div 30$ pupils $= 12°$

b Fill in the rest of the working and angle columns of the table.

c Draw a circle for your pie-chart.

d Draw a line from the centre to the top of the circle.

e Draw the first angle (108°).

f Measure the next angle (96°) from the line that you have just drawn.

g Carry on until you have drawn all the angles.

h Colour your pie-chart. Add a key.

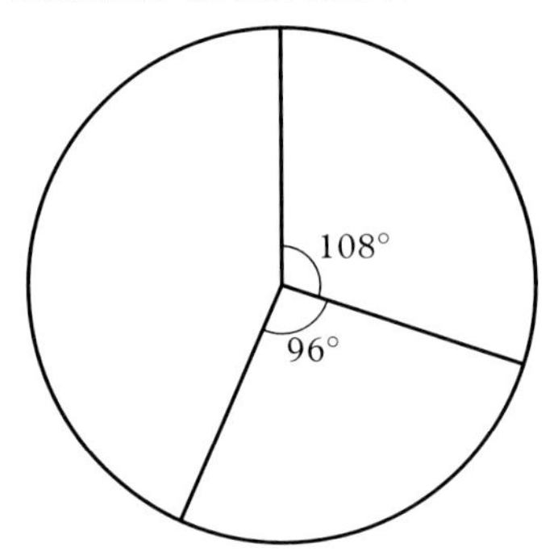

2 Class 8J were also asked how they travelled to school.

a Copy this table.

Method of travel	Number of pupils	Working	Angle
walk	14		
bus	7		
car	6		
bike	3		
private jet	0		
Total	30		360°

b Copy and fill in:
$360° \div 30 = \ldots°$ for each pupil.

c Fill in the working and angle columns of the table.

d Draw a circle for your pie-chart.

e Draw a line from the centre to the top of the circle.

f Draw the first angle (168°).
g Measure the next angle (84°) from the line that you have just drawn.
h Carry on until you have drawn all the angles.
i Colour your pie-chart. Add a key.

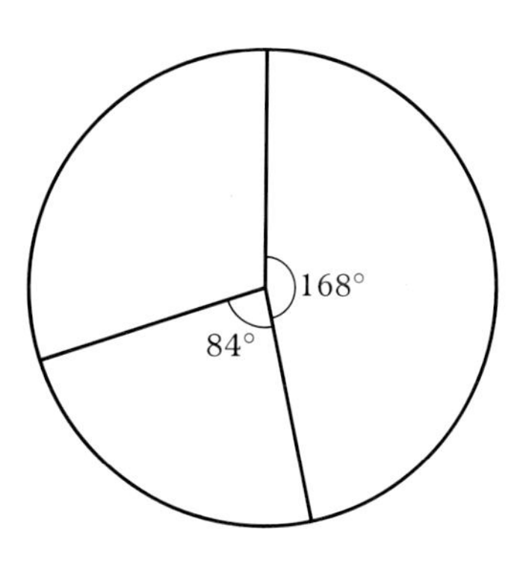

● **3** Class 8P has 24 pupils.
Here are their answers to the travel survey.

Method of travel	Number of pupils	Working	Angle
walk	10		
bus	7		
car	6		
bike	1		
Total	24		360°

a Copy the table.
b Work out the angle for each person.
360° ÷ 24 =
c Fill in the rest of the table.
d Draw a pie-chart to show this information.
Don't forget the key.

3 Designing a questionnaire

To get information, you need to ask questions.

You need to think carefully about the questions that you ask.
You must make sure that you get all the information that you need.
Your questions must be easy to answer.

Questionnaire

A **questionnaire** is a set of questions on a given topic.

There are two types of questionnaire.
Sometimes an interviewer asks the questions and fills in the answers.
Sometimes you are given a form to fill in yourself.

There are some rules that you need to know when you write your own questionnaire.

Rule 1

Questions should not be **biased**. They should not make you think that a particular answer is right.
A question that does is called a **leading question**.

Example

Normal people like to watch football.
Do you watch football?

This question is biased.
The first sentence should not be there.
It makes you think that you aren't normal if you don't watch football.

Exercise 3:7

Here is a list of questions.

a Most people think that you should be able to learn to drive at 16. Do you agree?
b Do you think you should eat less chocolate and more fruit?
c How many weeks of school holiday should children get each year?
d Most clever pupils watch the TV news. Do you watch the news?
e Do you read a daily newspaper?

1 Which of these questions do you think are biased? Write down their letters.

2 Write down what makes each of these questions biased.

● **3** Write better questions to replace the ones that you thought were biased.

Rule 2 Questions should not upset people or embarrass them.

Exercise 3:8

Here is a list of questions.

a How much do you weigh?
b How much money have you got in your bank account?
c How often do you have a shower?
d Do you have any pets at home?
e Most people use a deodorant. Do you?

1 Which of these questions do you think are upsetting or embarrassing? Write down their letters.

2 Write down what is wrong with each of the questions that you chose.

● **3** Write better questions to replace the ones that you didn't like.

Rule 3 Questions can give a choice of possible answers.
This could be:

A Yes, No or Don't know.
B Agree, Disagree or Don't know.
C A set of boxes with answers that you tick.
D A scale where you circle your choice.
This can be useful when you are asking for an opinion.

Exercise 3:9

Here is a list of questions.
Choose the style of answer that you would use for each one.
Write down **A, B, C** or **D**.

A	☐ Yes	☐ No	☐ Don't know
B	☐ Agree	☐ Disagree	☐ Don't know
C	☐ 0–2	☐ 3–5	☐ more than 5

D Strongly agree 1 2 3 4 5 Strongly disagree

1 How many chocolate biscuits do you eat each day?

2 The National Lottery is a good way of raising money for charity.

3 Do diesel cars cause less pollution than petrol cars?

4 Will you vote in the next general election?

5 How many brothers and sisters do you have?

Rule 4 Questions should be clear.
If people do not know what you mean you will not get the information that you need.

Rule 5 Don't ask questions that allow people to give lots of different answers.
This makes it very difficult to draw diagrams to show your results.

Rule 6 Don't ask questions that have nothing to do with your survey.

Rule 7 Questions should be in a sensible order.
Don't jump from one idea to another and back again.

Exercise 3:10

W You need the **Fitness questionnaire worksheet** for this exercise.

1 Fill in the questionnaire.

2 For each question, write down the number of the rule that it has broken.

3 Rewrite the questionnaire using the rules that you have learned.

Exercise 3:11

You are now going to design your own questionnaire.
You can choose any topic that interests you.

You can't 'do' a wide topic like 'sport'. You need to focus on one particular thing.
For example, you could find out how much sport pupils in Year 8 play.

You should plan your work like this:

1 Decide on your topic.
2 Decide who you will ask to fill in the questionnaire.
3 Write the questions for your questionnaire.
4 Try the questionnaire out on a friend.
5 Change the questions if you need to.

Planning

6 Do your survey!

Doing

7 Tally your results.
8 Decide which type of diagrams to use.
9 Draw your diagrams.
10 Work out some averages if you can.
11 Write up your results.

Analysing

1 Class 8J were asked to name their favourite TV soap.
Their answers are shown in this table.

Soap	*EastEnders*	*Coronation St*	*Brookside*	*Neighbours*	*Home and Away*
Number of pupils	6	3	9	8	4

a How many pupils are there in Class 8J?

b Copy the axes on to squared paper.
Draw a bar-chart to show this information.
Don't forget a title and labels.

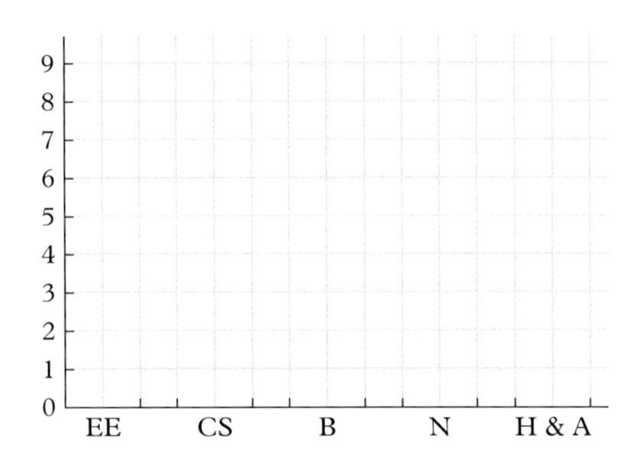

c Draw a pictogram to show the same information.
Don't forget to put a key and a title on your diagram.

2 100 people were asked what sort of butter or margarine they use.

50 people said sunflower margarine
25 people said butter
25 people said low-fat spread

a What fraction of the people said sunflower margarine? ($\frac{1}{4}$ or $\frac{1}{2}$)

b What fraction said butter? ($\frac{1}{4}$ or $\frac{1}{2}$)

c Draw a pie-chart to show this information.

3 Look at the pie-chart. It shows the results of a survey of 80 people.
They were asked how many cars their family had.

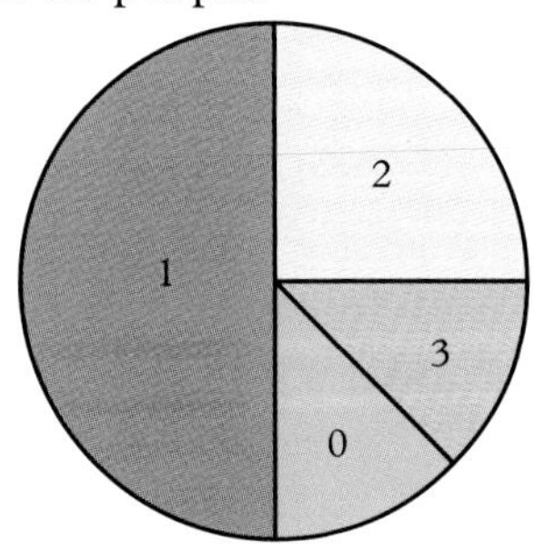

a What is $\frac{1}{2}$ of 80?

b What is $\frac{1}{4}$ of 80?

c What is $\frac{1}{2}$ of 20?

d How many families had 1 car?

e How many families had 2 cars?

f How many families did not have a car?

4 In a survey of 30 trains: 12 were on time, 10 were early and 8 were late.

a Copy and fill in:
$360° \div 30 = \ldots°$ for each train.

b Copy this table. Fill it in.

	Number of trains	Working	Angle
on time	12	$12 \times 12° =$	
early	10	$12 \times 12° =$	
late	8		

c Draw a pie-chart to show this information.

d Colour your chart. Add a key.

5 Class 8J were asked how long it took them to get to school.

The results are given correct to the nearest minute.

Time taken	Number of pupils
1–5	6
6–10	3
11–15	5
16–20	4
21–25	8
26–30	4

a Copy the axes on to squared paper.

b Draw a bar-chart to show this information.
Don't forget a title and labels.

c How many pupils took 15 minutes or less to get to school?

d How many pupils took more than 20 minutes to get to school?

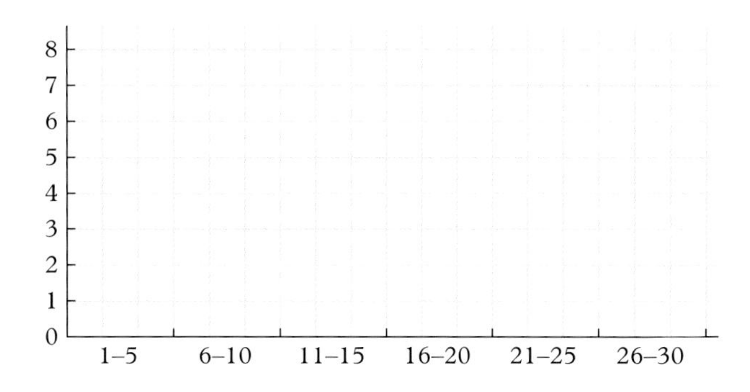

1 A doctor recorded the length of time she spent with each patient.
Here are the times correct to the nearest minute.

10	5	9	20	14	3	8	6	9
4	25	16	11	15	17	8	6	3
9	5	6	8	19	21	6	10	11
5	9	29	3	6	14	18	17	8

a How many patients did she see?
b Copy this table.

Number of minutes	Tally	Total
1–5		
6–10		
11–15		
16–20		
21–25		
26–30		

c Fill in the tally-table.
d Draw a bar-chart to show this information.

2 90 Year 8 pupils were asked whether they preferred Children's BBC or Children's ITV.
38 pupils said Children's ITV.
a Work out the angle for each pupil.
$360° \div 90 = \ldots°$
b Work out the angle for each channel.
c Draw a pie-chart to show this information.

3 Rajiv is planning a survey on smoking.
He has written some questions.
a Which of Rajiv's questions do you think are biased?
b Which questions should have boxes to tick?
c Which questions are not clear enough?

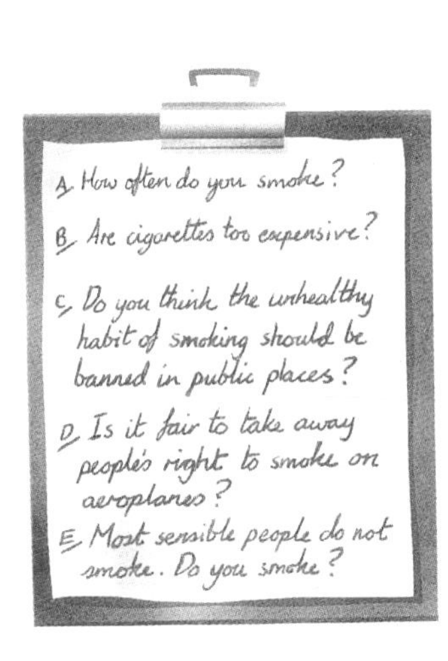

A How often do you smoke?
B Are cigarettes too expensive?
C Do you think the unhealthy habit of smoking should be banned in public places?
D Is it fair to take away people's right to smoke on aeroplanes?
E Most sensible people do not smoke. Do you smoke?

- **Pie-chart**

A **pie-chart** shows how something is divided up.
The angle of the slice represents the number of items.

Example
Class 8N were asked their favourite subject.

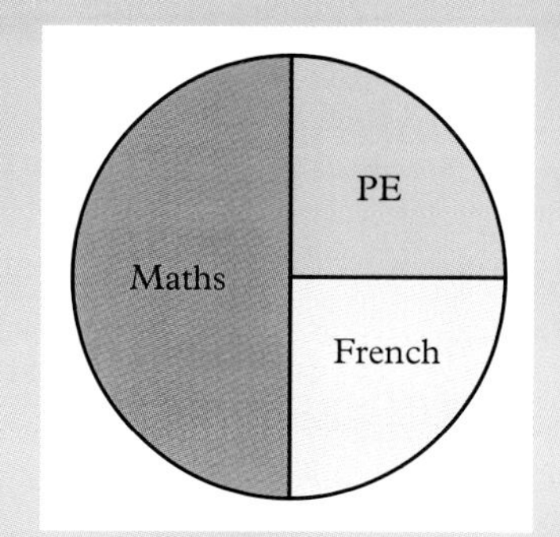

Out of the 28 pupils: 14 said Maths
7 said PE
7 said French

14 pupils is half the class.
Maths gets half of the pie.

7 pupils is a quarter of the class.
PE and French both get one quarter of the pie.

- **Questionnaire**

A **questionnaire** is a set of questions on a given topic.
There are two types of questionnaire.
Sometimes an interviewer asks the questions and fills in the answers.
Sometimes you are given a form to fill in yourself.

Remember:
1 Questions should not be biased.
2 Questions should not upset people or embarrass them.
3 Questions can give a choice of possible answers.
4 Questions should be clear.
5 Don't ask questions that allow lots of different answers.
6 Don't ask questions that have nothing to do with your survey.
7 Questions should be in a sensible order.

1 Phil is doing a survey into the most popular type of music in Year 8.
He has put his results into a table:

Type of music	pop	rock	dance	soul	classical
Number of pupils	80	60	20	30	30

Copy the axes on to squared paper.

a Draw a bar-chart to show this information.
Put a title and labels on your diagram.

b What is the most popular type of music?

c What is the least popular type of music?

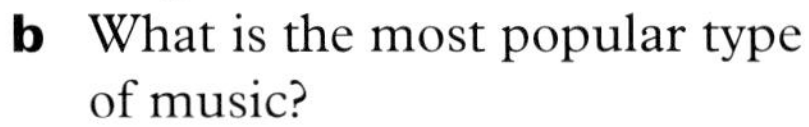

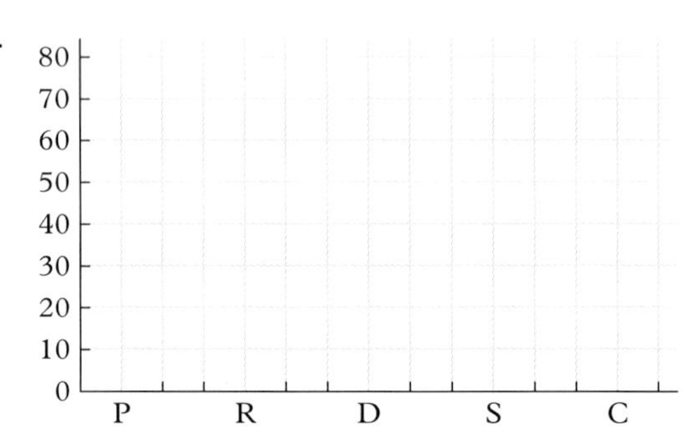

2 Year 8 were also asked which was their favourite radio station.
Half said Radio 1, one quarter said Atlantic 252 and one quarter said Radio 5 Live.

a Draw a circle and mark the centre.

b Draw a pie-chart to show this information.

c Give your diagram a title and a key.

3 Pritti asked 8J to choose their favourite radio station.
Their answers were:

Radio 1	12
Radio 5 Live	10
Atlantic 252	8

a Copy and fill in:
$360° \div 30 = \ldots°$ for each pupil.

b Copy this table. Fill it in.

	Number of pupils	Working	Angle
Radio 1	12	$12 \times$	
Radio 5 Live	10	$10 \times$	
Atlantic 252	8	$8 \times$	
Total			

c Use the table to help you draw a pie-chart of 8J's answers.
Don't forget the key.

4 Algebra

CORE

QUESTIONS
EXTENSION
SUMMARY
TEST YOURSELF

Muhammed ibn Musa al-Khwarizmi c780 – c850

Al-Khwarizmi was a well known mathematician and astronomer who lived in Baghdad in the early 9th century. He wrote a book called *Kitab al-jabr wa al-nuqabalah*, which was about solving equations.

The word algebra comes from the word *al-jabr*.

1 Number patterns

Steve is making patterns with counters.
They are in the shapes of capital letters.

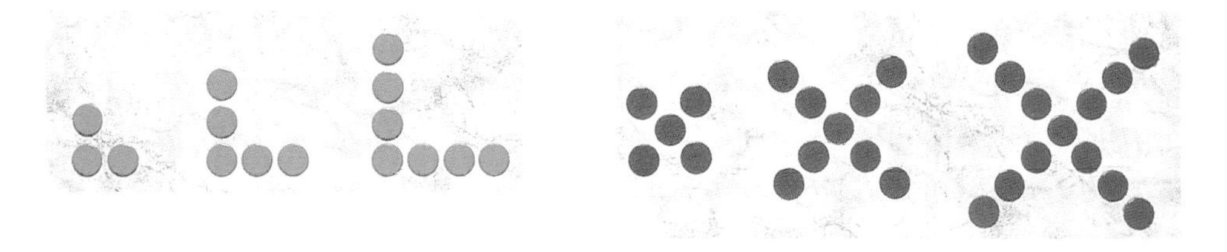

He wants to find the rules for his patterns.

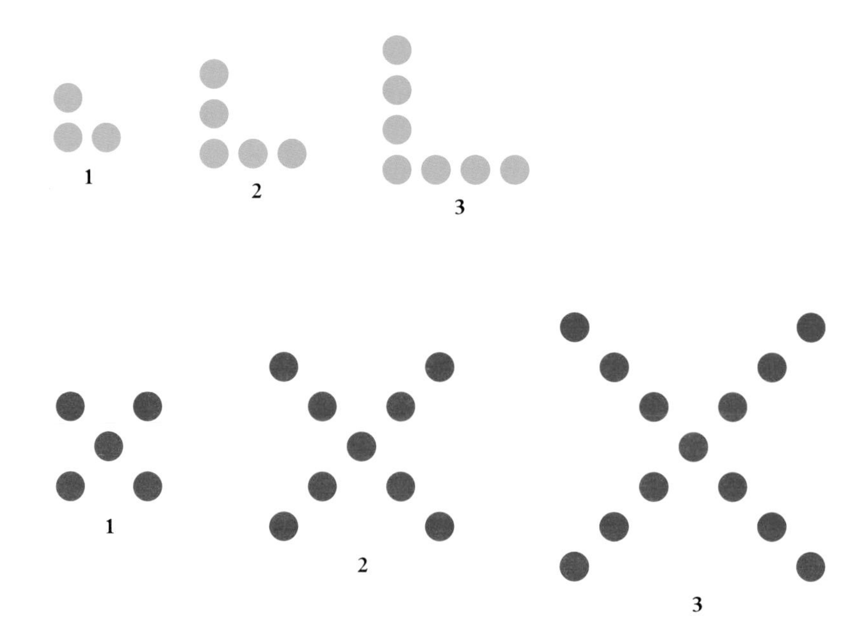

Exercise 4:1 Alphabet patterns

1 **a** Copy L shapes 1, 2 and 3 from the picture.
b Draw L shapes 4 and 5.
c Count the number of circles in each shape.
d Copy this table.
Fill it in.

L shape number	1	2	3	4	5
Number of circles	3	5			

e Look at your table.
How many circles are you adding each time?
f Copy and fill in:
The rule is add … circles each time.

2 **a** Copy X shapes 1, 2 and 3 from the picture.
b Draw X shapes 4 and 5.
c Count the number of circles in each shape.
d Copy this table.
Fill it in.

X shape number	1	2	3	4	5
Number of circles	5	9			

e Look at your table.
How many circles are you adding each time?
f Copy and fill in:
The rule is add . . . circles each time.

3 Can you find some more letters that give patterns?
Draw your letters.
Fill in a table and find the rule.

◀◀ **REPLAY** ▶

Exercise 4:2

1 Write down the rule for each number pattern.
a 1, 3, 5, 7, 9
b 20, 40, 60, 80, 100
c 5, 10, 15, 20, 25
d 900, 800, 700, 600

2 Each pattern has a rule and a starting number.
Copy the table.
Fill in the next four numbers in each pattern.
The first one has been done for you.

Rule	Starting number	Next four numbers
+3	5	8, 11, 14, 17
+10	3	
+2	20	
×2	1	
×10	4	

3 Write down the rule that belongs on each robot's screen.

a 1 → ? → 5
6 → ? → 10
8 → ? → 12

b 2 → ? → 10
4 → ? → 20
5 → ? → 25

Example

Lizzy is making triangles out of matchsticks.

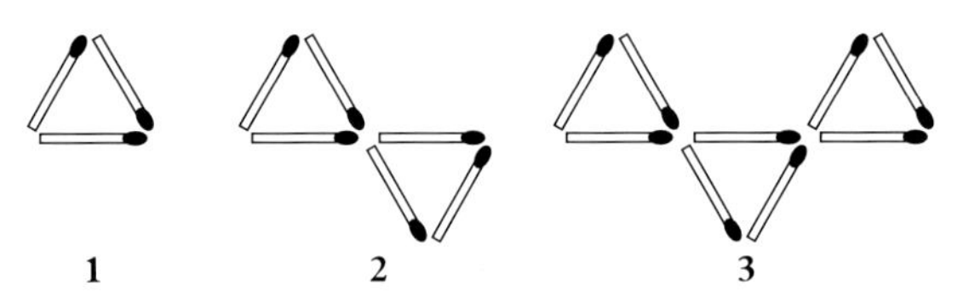

This table shows how many matchsticks she needs.

Number of triangles	1	2	3	4	5
Number of matchsticks	3	6	9	12	15

+3 +3 +3 +3

The rule is shown in red. It is +3.

Lizzy also finds a formula.
If she knows the number of triangles, she can work out the number of matchsticks.

Her formula is:

number of ***m***atchsticks equals 3 × number of ***t***riangles.

In algebra this is $m = 3 \times t$

Exercise 4:3

1 Hitesh is making pentagons out of matchsticks.

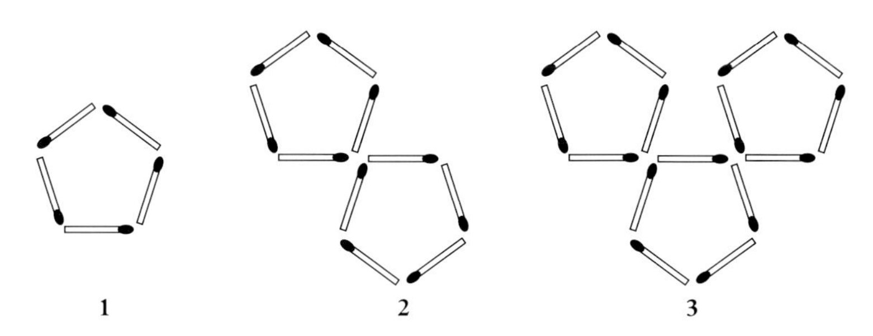

a Copy this table.
Fill it in.

Number of pentagons	1	2	3	4	5
Number of matchsticks			15		

+? +? +? +?

b Fill in the rule on your table.

c Copy and fill in:

The formula is:

number of ***m***atchsticks = … × number of ***p***entagons

d Write this formula in algebra. $m = \ldots \times \ldots$

2 Apples are sold in trays of four.

a Copy this table.
Fill it in.

Number of trays	1	2	3	4	5
Number of apples					

b Copy and fill in:
The formula is:

number of ***a***pples = … × number of ***t***rays

c Write this formula in algebra. $a = \ldots \times \ldots$

• **3** Computer disks are sold in boxes of 10.
  a Make a table to show the number of boxes and the number of disks. Go up to 5 boxes.
  b Copy and fill in:
  The formula is:
  number of ***d***isks = … × ………………………
  c Write this formula in algebra. $d = \ldots \times \ldots$

Example

The formula for the disks is:

number of ***d***isks = **10** × number of ***b***oxes

We can use this formula to work out the number of disks in any number of boxes.

Use your formula to find the number of disks in 20 boxes.

number of ***d***isks = 10 × 20
= 200

---

4 Use the disks formula to find the number of disks in:
a 6 boxes **b** 9 boxes **c** 100 boxes

5 The formula for the trays of apples in question 2 is:
number of ***a***pples = **4** × number of ***t***rays

Use this formula to find the number of apples in:
a 8 trays **b** 11 trays **c** 25 trays

6 Sonya is making octagons out of matchsticks.

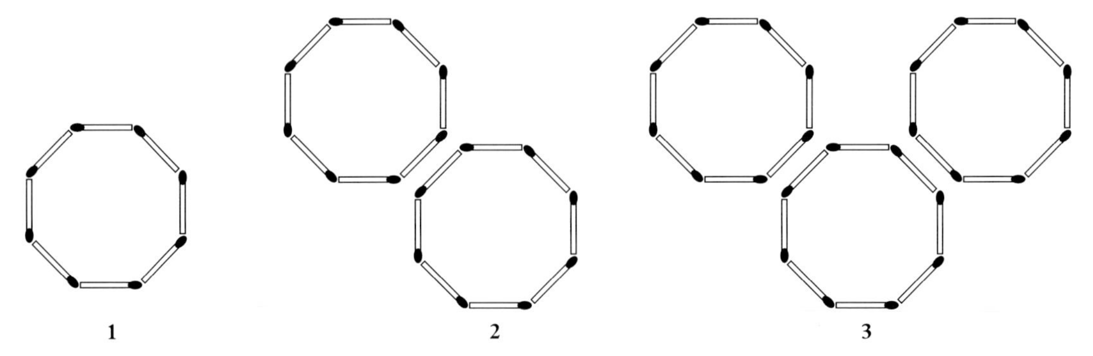

Her formula is:
number of ***m***atchsticks = **8** × number of ***o***ctagons

Use this formula to find the number of matchsticks in:
a 4 octagons **b** 7 octagons **c** 50 octagons

● **7** Lucy is making ***h***exagons out of ***m***atchsticks.

The formula is: $m = 6 \times h$

Use this formula to find the number of matchsticks in:

a 3 hexagons **b** 12 hexagons **c** 100 hexagons

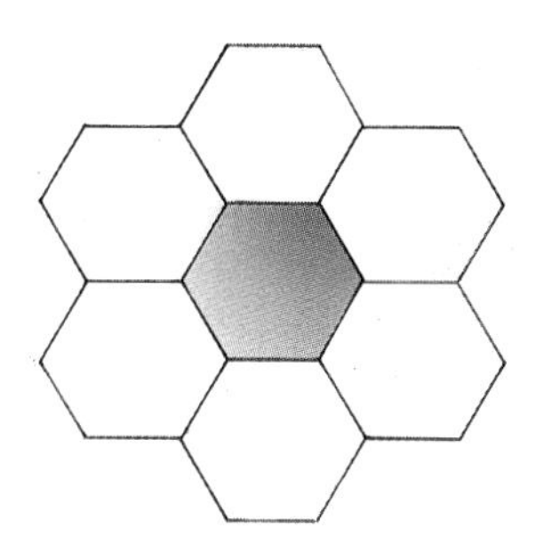

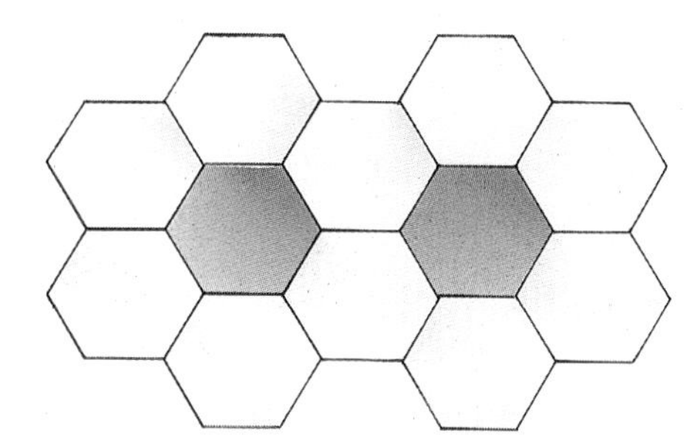

Rod is building a new patio.
He is using red and white slabs.
He wants to work out how many white slabs he needs for each red slab.

The formula is:

number of ***w***hite slabs = **4** × number of ***r***ed slabs + **2**

or $w = 4 \times r + 2$

Example Use this formula to find the number of white slabs that Rod needs for 5 red slabs.

number of ***w***hite slabs = **4** × number of ***r***ed slabs + **2**
= **4** × 5 + **2**
= 20 + 2
= 22

Exercise 4:4

1 Use the slabs formula to find the number of white slabs needed for:

a 7 red slabs **b** 10 red slabs **c** 16 red slabs

2 Angela is tiling her bathroom.
She uses a formula to work out the number of tiles she needs.
The formula is:

number of ***t***iles = **10** x length of ***w***all + **8**

The length of the wall is measured in metres.

Work out the number of tiles she needs if the length of the wall is:

a 3 metres **b** 5 metres **c** 9 metres

3 This formula tells you how long to cook a turkey.

time = **10** × *weight* + **30**

The weight is in kilograms and the time is in minutes.
How long will it take to cook a turkey which weighs:

a 3 kg **b** 6 kg **c** 7 kg

4 David sells computers. The more computers he sells the more he gets paid.
David gets paid £170 each week + £10 for each computer he sells.
The formula for his wages is:

wages = **10** × *computers* + **170**

Work out how much David earns if he sells

a 3 computers
b 9 computers
c 7 computers
● **d** 0 computers

5 Joe is building a fence.
He has bought the fence posts.
He wants to know how many planks he will need.
The formula is:

planks = **3** × *fence posts* − **3**

Joe has 45 fence posts.
How many planks does he need?

2 Reversing rules

Angela has been making patterns with matchsticks.

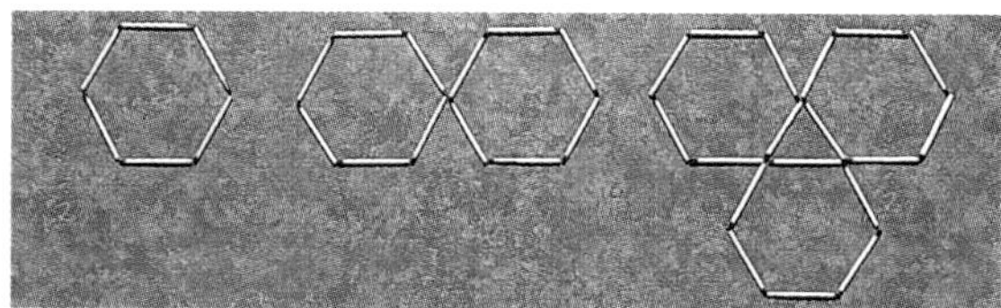

She made some hexagon patterns.
She found a formula.

The formula is: *h*exagons × **6** = *m*atchsticks

Angela sets her friend Kirsty a problem.
Angela says that she used 42 matchsticks to make some hexagons.
She wants to know how many hexagons she made.

Kirsty reverses Angela's rule using robot screens,

hexagons ⟶ [× 6] ⟶ matchsticks

hexagons ⟵ [÷ 6] ⟵ matchsticks

Kirsty's rule is called the **inverse** of Angela's rule.
She uses it to find the answer to the puzzle:

7 ⟵ [÷ 6] ⟵ 42

◀◀ REPLAY ▶

Exercise 4:5

1 Write down the inverse of these.

a add 6
b subtract 7
c multiply by 4
d divide by 5

2 Draw the inverse function machine for each of these.

a → [− 6] →

b → [× 7] →

c → [÷ 4] →

3 The formula for making hexagons with matchsticks is:

hexagons → [× 6] → matchsticks

a Draw the inverse machine for this formula.

b Use your inverse to work out how many hexagons you can make with:

(1) 24 matchsticks
(2) 30 matchsticks
(3) 48 matchsticks

4 Morgan puts some numbers into this function machine.

? → [− 6] → 8
? → [− 6] → 14
? → [− 6] → 27

Work out the numbers that Morgan used.

Rod has ordered 26 white slabs for his patio.
He has forgotten how many red slabs he needs.

Rod needs the inverse of his formula.
The formula is: $w = r \times 4 + 2$

First he writes his formula on robot screens.

r → [× 4] → [+ 2] → 26

The inverse machine is:

6 ← [÷ 4] ←24— [− 2] ← 26

He needs 6 red slabs.

Exercise 4:6

1 How many red slabs does Rod need for:

a 34 white slabs **b** 22 white slabs **c** 42 white slabs

2 Zeta needs a new cycle helmet. The helmet costs £23.

Zeta earns money delivering leaflets.
Her wages are £2 for every packet of leaflets she delivers.
She also gets £5 for lunch and bus fares.

The formula is: *w*ages = **2** × number of ***p***ackets + **5**
or: $w = 2 \times p + 5$

a Write this formula on robot screens.
b Draw the inverse machine.
c How many packets does Zeta need to deliver to buy her cycle helmet?

3 George takes part in a sponsored silence.
His parents give him £5.
His friends sponsor him £2 per hour.

The formula is: *m*oney raised = **2** × number of ***h***ours + **5**

a Write George's formula in algebra.
b Draw the formula on robot screens.
c Draw the inverse machine.
d How long does George need to stay silent to raise:

(1) £11 (2) £23 (3) £53

● **4** Some Year 8 pupils are going to Longleat.

The total cost (in £) is worked out using the formula:

cost = **7** × number of ***p***upils + **80**

Work out the cost for:

a 20 pupils **b** 36 pupils

3 Finding your own rules

Aisha is working on an investigation into squares.

She has to find the formula for the number of matchsticks.

She has made a table.

Number of squares	1	2	3	4	5
Number of matchsticks	4	7	10	13	16

+3 +3 +3 +3

Aisha notices that the pattern goes up in 3s.
She knows that this means that the first part of the formula will be:

number of ***m***atchsticks = 3 × number of ***s***quares

She needs to work out the second part.
So far, her formula gives the green numbers in the table.

Number of squares	1	2	3	4	5
	3 +1	6 +1	9 +1	12 +1	15 +1
Number of matchsticks	4	7	10	13	16

Aisha needs to add 1 to get the right answers.

She writes the full formula:

number of ***m***atchsticks = **3** × number of ***s***quares +1

Aisha uses her formula to work out how many matchsticks she will need to make **6** squares:

number of ***m***atchsticks = 3 × **6** + 1
= 19

She makes 6 squares with matchsticks to check that her answer is right.

Exercise 4:7

1 These patterns are made from square tiles.

1

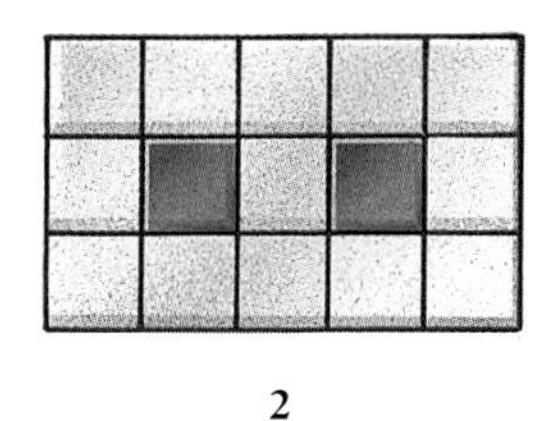

2

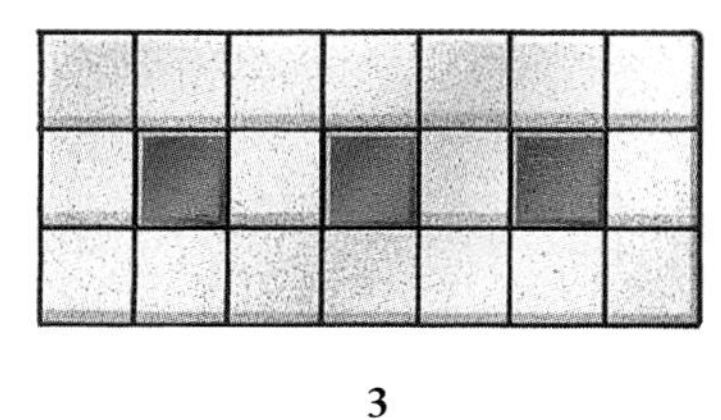

3

a Look at the patterns
Draw the next two.

b Copy this table.
Fill it in.

Number of blue tiles	1	2	3	4	5
Number of yellow tiles	8	13			

+? +? +? +?

c How many yellow tiles do you add each time?

The first part of the formula is:
number of yellow tiles = **5** × number of blue tiles

d Copy this table.
Finish the row of green numbers.
Use the first part of the formula.

Number of blue tiles	1	2	3	4	5
	5 +?	10 +?	+?	+?	+?
Number of yellow tiles	8	13			

e What do you have to add to the green numbers to get the number of yellow tiles?

f Copy and fill in the full formula:
number of yellow tiles = … × number of blue tiles + …

Finding the first part of the formula

Look at your table of results.
See what you have to add each time.
This is the number that you multiply by in your formula.

2 Here are some diagrams of C shapes made out of squares.

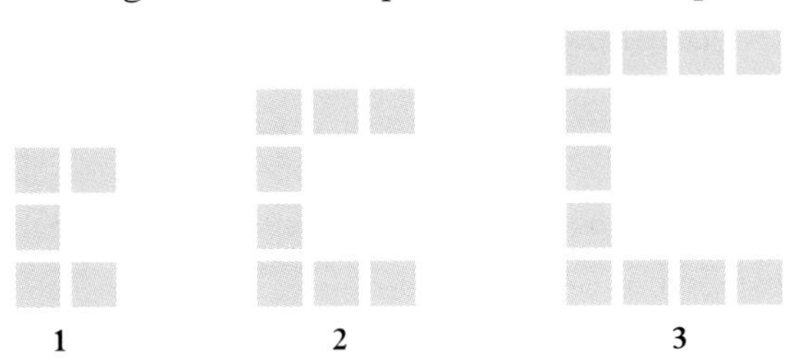

a Copy these diagrams.
Draw the next two.

b Copy this table.
Fill it in.

Diagram number	1	2	3	4	5
Number of squares	5	8			

+? +? +? +?

c How many squares do you add each time?

d Copy and fill in:
The first part of the formula is:

number of squares = … × diagram number

e Copy this table.
Finish the row of green numbers.
Use the first part of your formula.

Diagram number	1	2	3	4	5
	3 +?	6 +?	+?	+?	+?
Number of squares	5			14	

f What do you have to add to the green numbers to get the numbers of squares?

g Copy and fill in the full formula:

number of squares = … × diagram number + …

h Use your formula to work out the number of squares in the 10th diagram.

- **3** **a** Copy these dot diagrams.

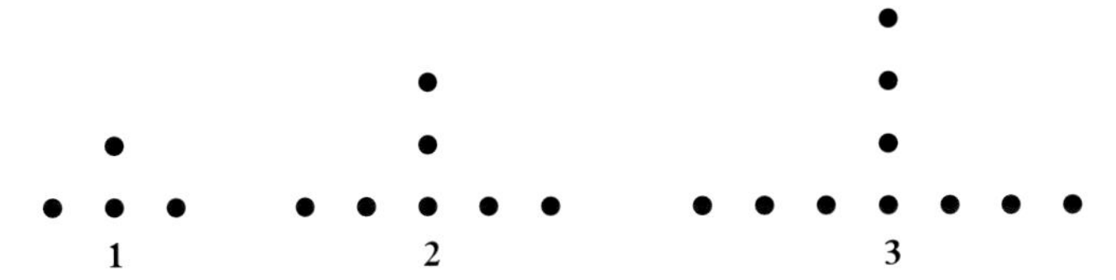

b Draw the next two diagrams.
c Count the the dots in each diagram.
d Make a table of your results.
e How many extra dots do you need each time?
f Write down the first part of the formula.
g Write down the number which needs adding on.
h Write down the full formula.
i Check that your formula works with the next diagram.
j Use your formula to work out the number of dots in the 20th diagram.

Later in this chapter you are going to find some patterns using cubes. You will need to use isometric paper to draw the models.

◀◀REPLAY▶

Exercise 4:8

1 Draw this cube on isometric paper.

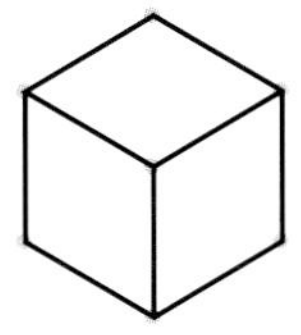

2 Copy these diagrams on to isometric paper.

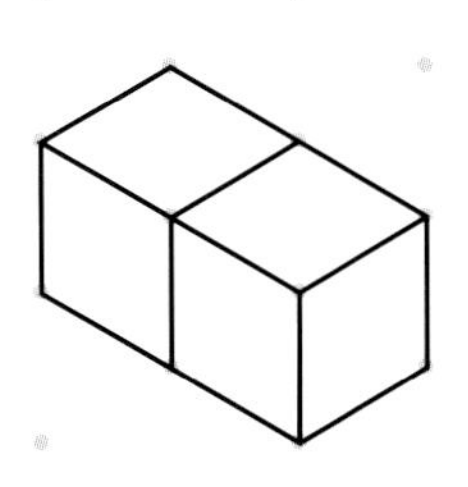

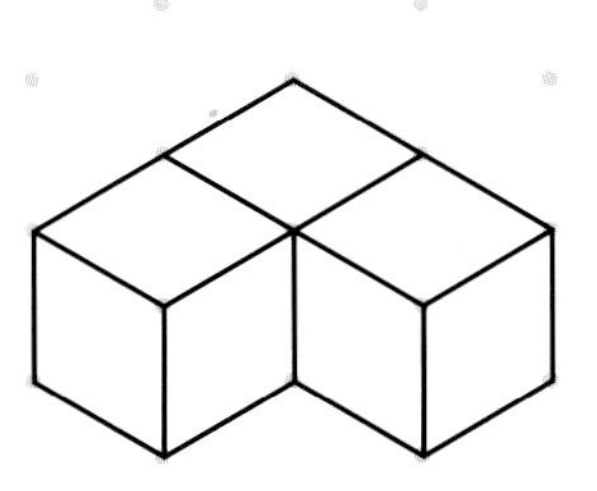

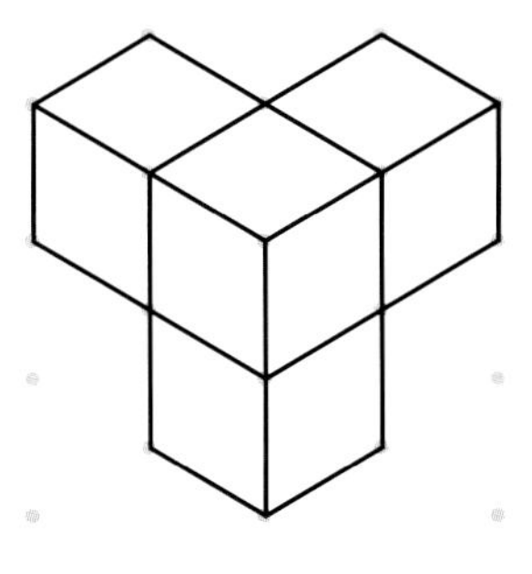

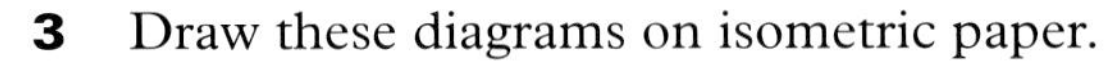

3 Draw these diagrams on isometric paper.

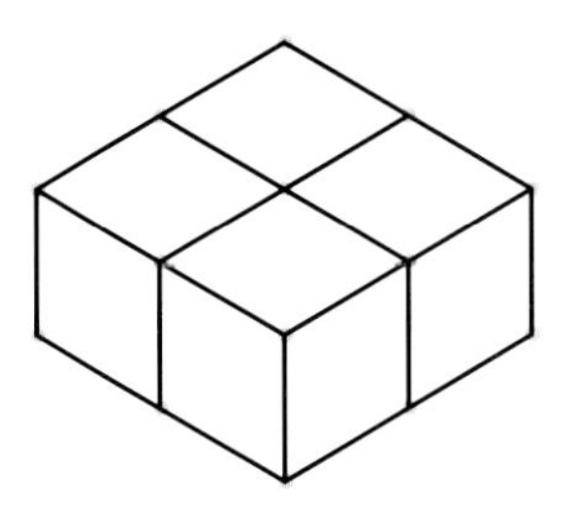

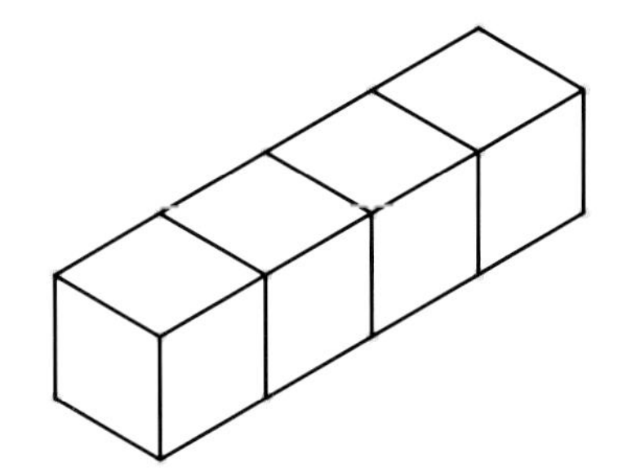

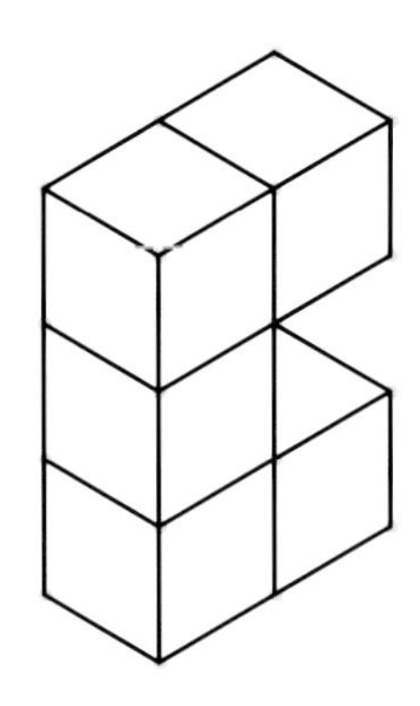

Exercise 4:9

1 **a** Draw these diagrams on isometric paper

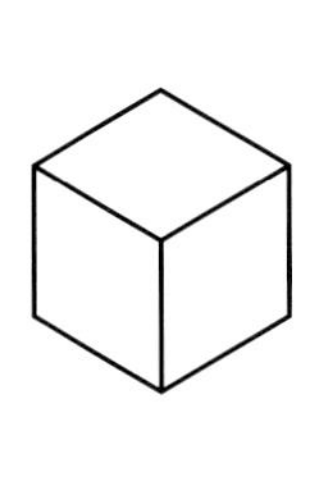

1

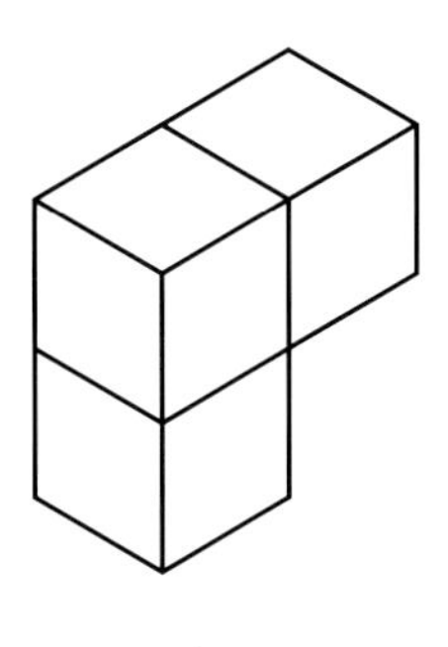

2

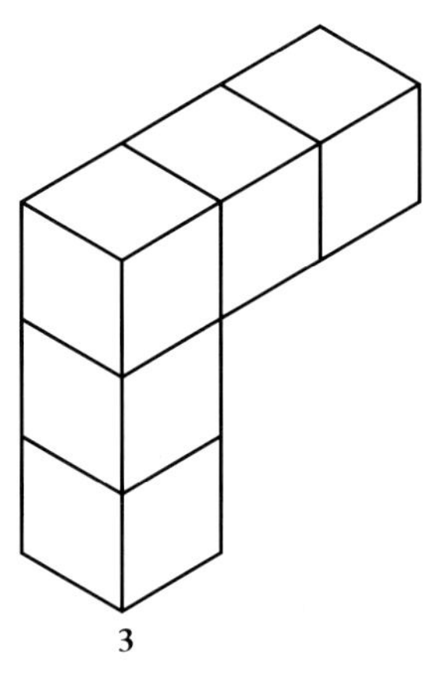

3

b Draw the next two diagrams.
c Count the number of cubes in each diagram.
d Copy this table.
Fill it in.

Diagram number	1	2	3	4	5
Number of cubes					

We want to find a formula for the number of cubes.

e Find the first part of the formula.
f Find the number which needs adding on.
g Write down the full formula.
h Check that your formula works with the next diagram.
i Use your formula to work out the number of cubes in the 30th diagram.

2 **a** Make these models out of cubes.

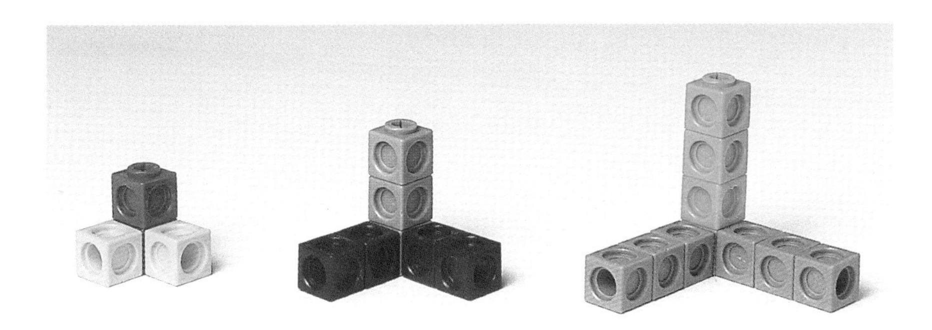

- **b** Draw your models on isometric paper.
- **c** Make a table of the number of cubes in each model.
- **d** Find the formula for the number of cubes.
- **e** Check that your formula works.
- **f** How many cubes would you need to build the 15th model ?

Exercise 4:10 Traffic light squares

Look at these patterns of coloured squares.

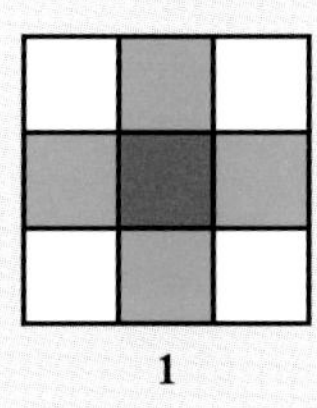

1

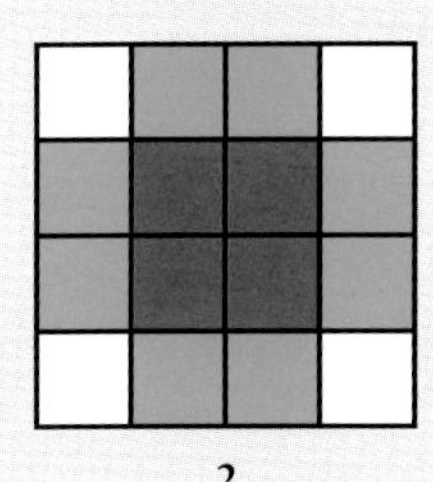

2

How many yellow and green squares would there be in the 50th traffic light square?
How many red squares would there be in the 50th traffic light square?

Design some square patterns of your own.
You could use more colours.
For each pattern, work out how many squares of each colour there would be in the 50th square.

1 Alan is making hexagons out of matchsticks.

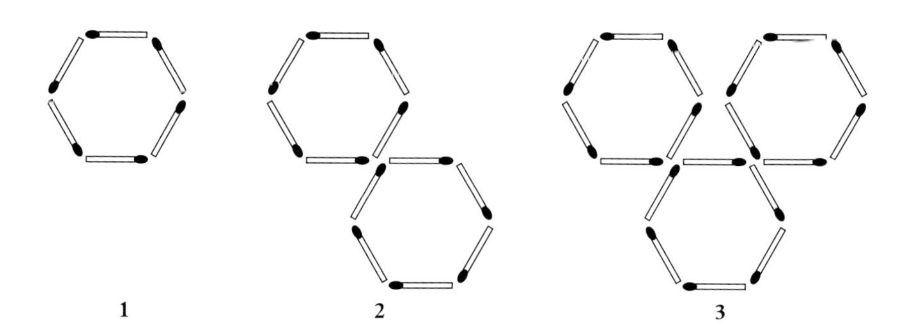

a Draw the next two patterns.

b Copy this table.
Fill it in.

Number of hexagons	1	2	3	4	5
Number of matchsticks	6	12			

+? +? +? +?

c Fill in the rule on your table.

d Copy and fill in:
The formula is:
number of ***m***atchsticks = … × number of ***h***exagons

e Write this formula in algebra
$m = \ldots \times \ldots$

2 Maths books cost £17 for a box of 100.

a Copy this table.
Fill it in.

Number of boxes	1	2	3	4	5
Cost of books £	17	34			

b Copy and fill in:
The formula is:
cost of ***b***ooks = … × ……………………………

c Write your formula in algebra.

d Use your formula to find the cost of 16 boxes of books.

3 These letter I shapes are made from circles.

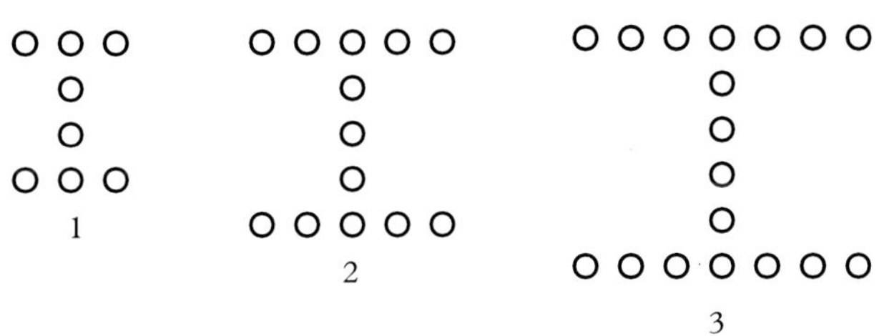

a Copy this table.
Fill it in.
You will need to draw some more diagrams.

Diagram number	1	2	3	4	5
Number of circles	8				

+? +? +? +?

b How many circles do you add each time?

c Copy and fill in:
The first part of the formula is:
number of circles = … × diagram number

d Copy this table.
Finish the row of green numbers.
Use the first part of your formula.

Diagram number	1	2	3	4	5
	5 +?	10 +?	+?	+?	+?
Number of circles	8				

e What do you have to add to the green numbers to get the number of circles?

f Copy and fill in the full formula:
number of circles = … × diagram number + …

g Use your formula to find the number of circles in the 20th diagram.

4 A formula for the number of circles in letter U shapes is:
number of circles = **3** × ***d***iagram number + **4**
or $c = 3 \times d + 4$

a Use the formula to find out how many circles there would be in:
(1) the 10th diagram
(2) the 100th diagram

b Write the formula on robot screens.

c Draw the inverse machine for the formula.

d Use your inverse to work out which diagram uses 124 circles.

1 A cattle farmer wants to work out how many cows he can keep in each of his fields.
Each cow needs enough space to graze.

The formula for working out the area needed is

$$Area = \mathbf{6} \times \text{number of cows} + \mathbf{10}$$

or $A = \mathbf{6} \times c + \mathbf{10}$

a Write this formula on robot screens.
b Draw the inverse machine.
c Write the inverse as a formula.
d This table gives the areas of the farmer's fields in square metres.

Use your inverse to work out how many cows he can keep in each field.

Field	A	B	C	D	E	F
Area of field	40	190	220	165	16	310

2 Look at these number patterns.
For each one copy it and fill in the gaps.
Write down the rule.

a 7 9 11 … …
b 5 8 11 … …
c 6 10 14 … …
d 20 30 40 … …
e 18 36 54 … …
f 18 16 14 … …

3 Copy these number patterns and fill in the gaps.
Write down the rules.

a 8 10 … 14
b 7 … 13 16
c 4 9 … …
d 12 … … 33

- You can look for patterns in tables.

Number of triangles	1	2	3	4	5
Number of matchsticks	3	6	9	12	15

+3 +3 +3 +3

The rule in this pattern is +3

You can work out a **formula**.
The formula tells you how to work out the number of matchsticks if you know the number of triangles.

The formula for this pattern is:

number of *m*atchsticks = 3 × number of *t*riangles

You can write this in algebra $m = 3 \times t$

- You can use a formula to work out more of the **pattern**.

Example
Work out how many matchsticks you would need to make 15 triangles.

number of *m*atchsticks = 3 × number of *t*riangles
= 3 × 15
= 45

- You can work backwards by reversing the formula.
This is called **finding the inverse**.

If the formula is $w = r \times 4 + 2$
First write it on robot screens.

Then reverse it to find the **inverse**.

r ← ÷ 4 ← − 2 ← w

- When looking for the rule first look for a pattern in the numbers.
This gives you the first part of your formula.
Then see what you have to add on.

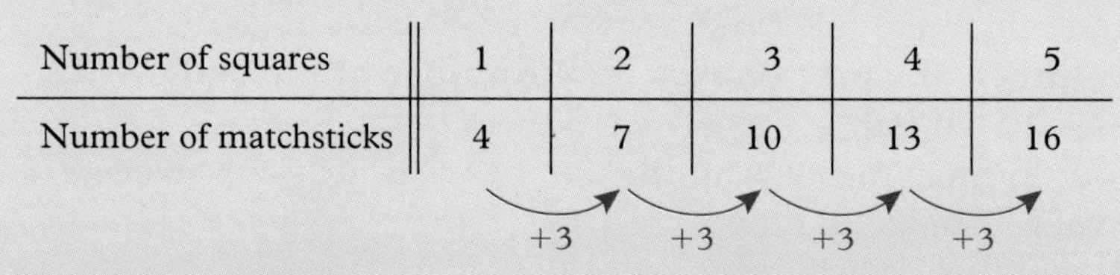

Number of squares	1	2	3	4	5
Number of matchsticks	4	7	10	13	16

+3 +3 +3 +3

In this example the formula is *m*atchsticks = 3 × *s*quares + 1

1 Draw the inverse function machine for each of these.

a → + 3 → **b** → ÷ 7 → **c** → × 5 →

2 Draw the inverse function machine.

3 Jake is laying square paving slabs like this:

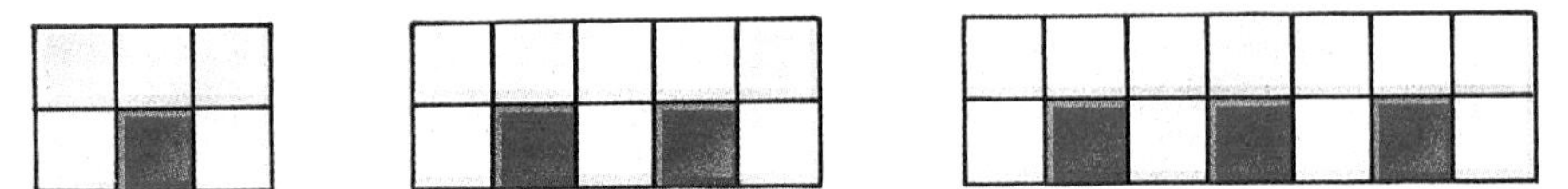

a Copy these patterns
Draw the next two.

b Copy this table.
Fill it in.

Number of red slabs	1	2	3	4	5
Number of white slabs	5	8			

c How many white slabs do you add each time?

d Copy and fill in:
The first part of the formula is:
number of white slabs = … × number of red slabs

e Copy this table.
Finish the row of green numbers.
Use the first part of the formula

Number of red slabs	1	2	3	4	5
	3 +?	6 +?	+?	+?	+?
Number of white slabs	5	8			

f What do you have to add to the green numbers to get the numbers of white slabs?

g Copy and fill in the full formula:
number of white slabs = … × number of red slabs + …

h Jake uses 20 red slabs.
Use your formula to work out the number of white slabs he needs.

i Write your formula on robot screens.

j Draw the inverse machine.

k Jake has 62 white slabs.
How many red slabs does he need?

5 Transformations

CORE

1 **Reflections**

2 **Movement – translations**

3 **Rotation**

4 **Enlargement**

QUESTIONS

EXTENSION

SUMMARY

TEST YOURSELF

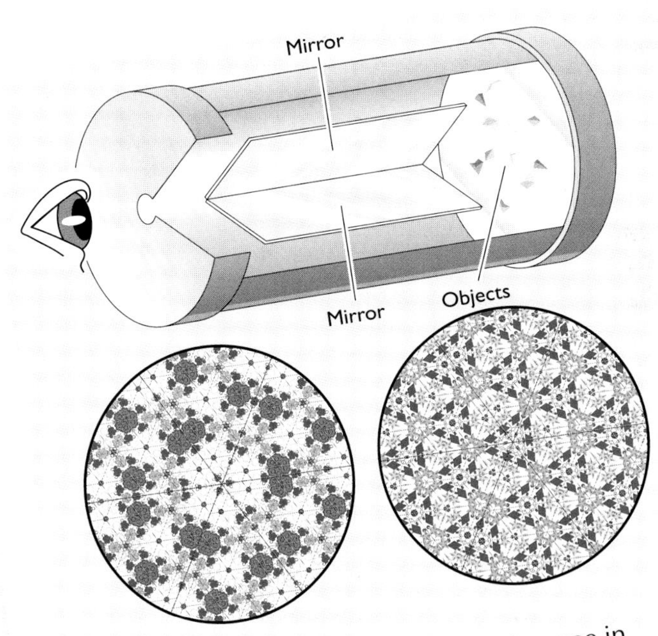

David Brewster invented the kaleidoscope in 1816. It is made with two mirrors in a tube. The angle between the mirrors can be 45° or 60°. When the end of the tube is rotated, coloured pieces of plastic between the two mirrors are reflected to make symmetrical patterns.

Which other angles would work? Why?

1 Reflections

The lake acts like a mirror.
The trees are reflected in it.
The mirror line is a line of symmetry.

◀◀ REPLAY ▶

Exercise 5:1

Copy these diagrams on to squared paper.
Draw their reflections in the mirror lines.

1

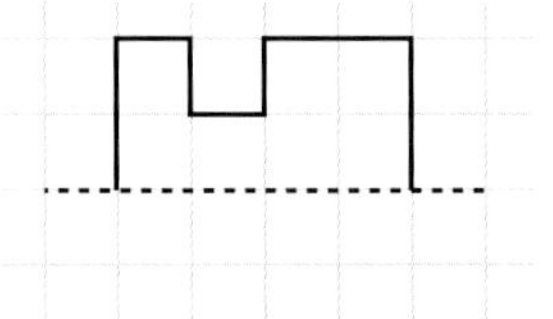

2

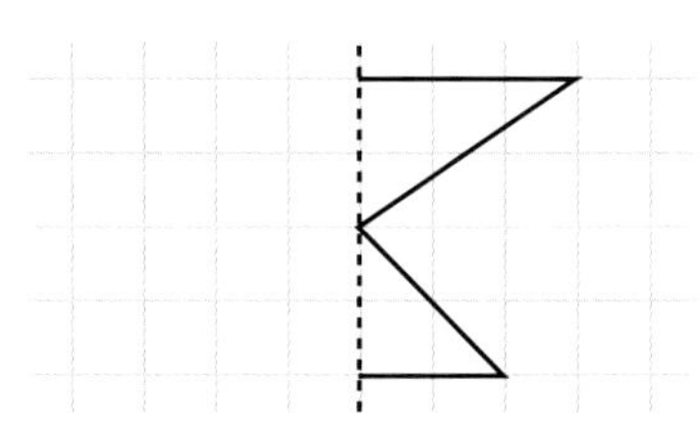

The object does not have to touch the mirror line.
The reflection is the same distance from the mirror line as the object.

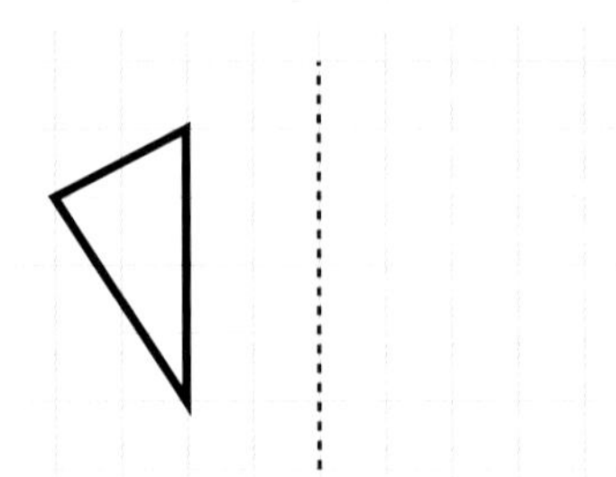

Put an object 2 squares in front of a mirror line.

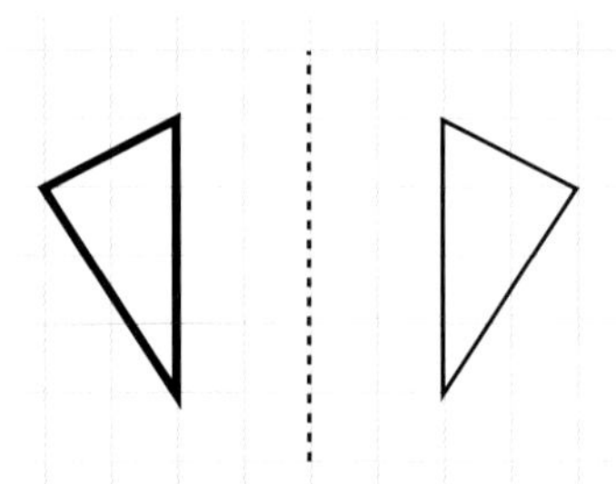

Its reflection is 2 squares behind the mirror line.

Copy these diagrams on to squared paper.
Draw their reflections in the mirror lines.

3

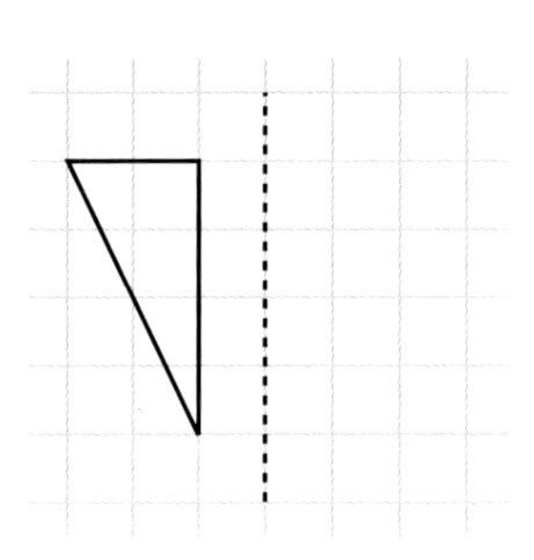

4

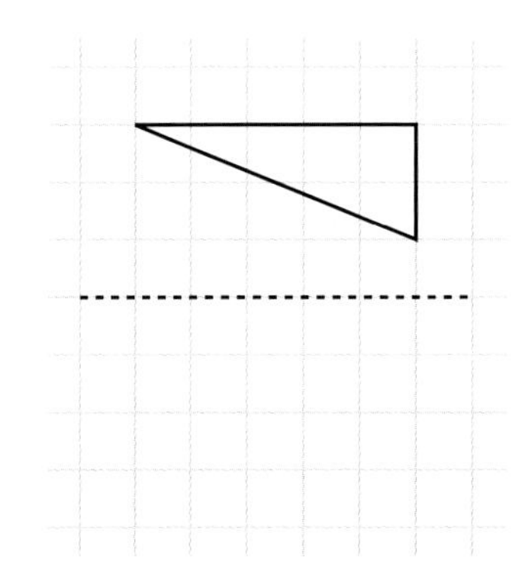

5

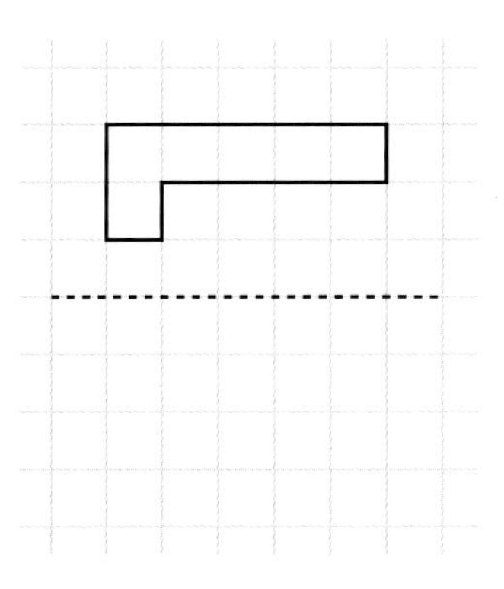

6

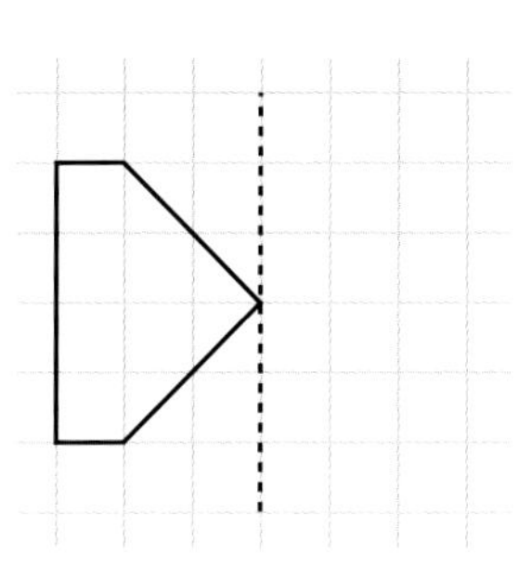

7

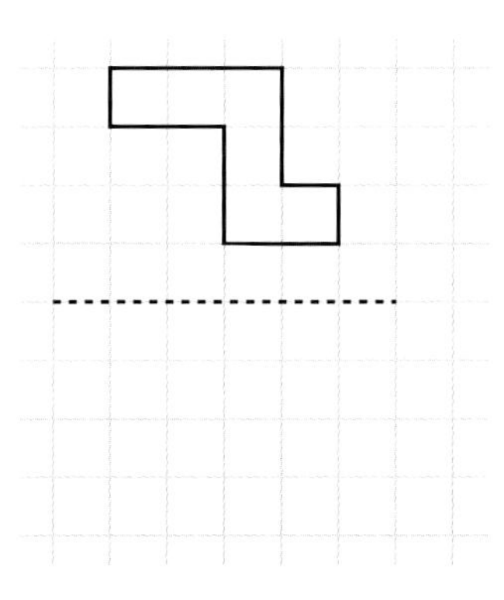

8

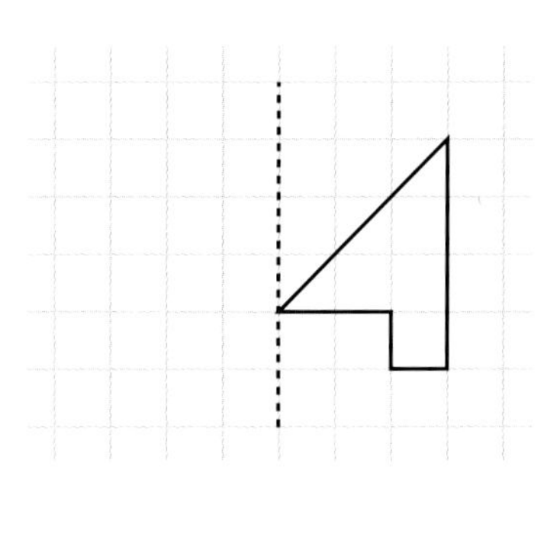

Exercise 5:2

1 Copy these axes on to squared paper.

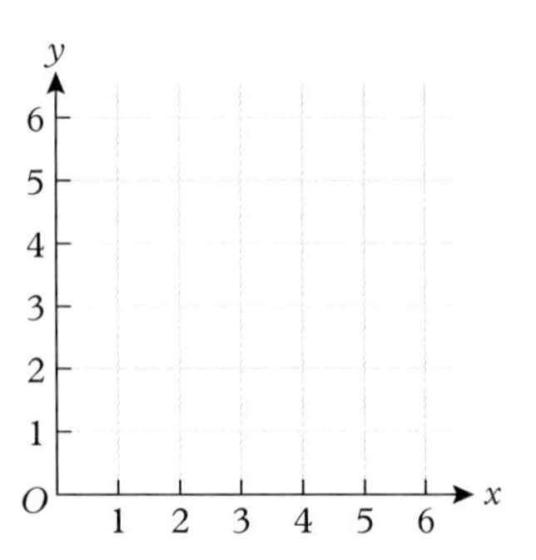

a Plot these points.
(3, 0) (3, 1) (3, 2) (3, 3)
(3, 4) (3, 5) (3, 6)
Join the points with a ruler.
This is your mirror line.

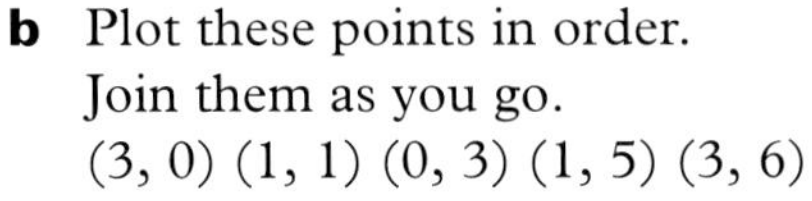

b Plot these points in order.
Join them as you go.
(3, 0) (1, 1) (0, 3) (1, 5) (3, 6)

c Reflect the shape in your mirror line.

d Write down the name of this regular polygon.

2 Draw a new set of axes on squared paper.

a Plot these points.
(0, 3) (1, 3) (2, 3) (3, 3) (4, 3) (5, 3) (6, 3)
Join the points with a ruler.
This is your mirror line.

b Plot these points in order.
Join them as you go.
(0, 4) (2, 6) (6, 6) (4, 4) (0, 4)

c Reflect the shape in your mirror line.

d Write down the name of this quadrilateral.

This shape made from cubes is reflected in a mirror.

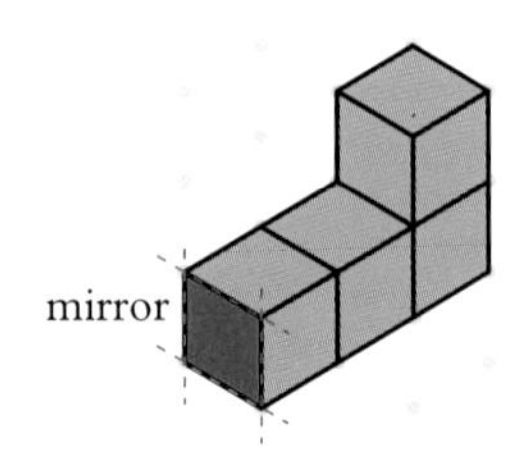

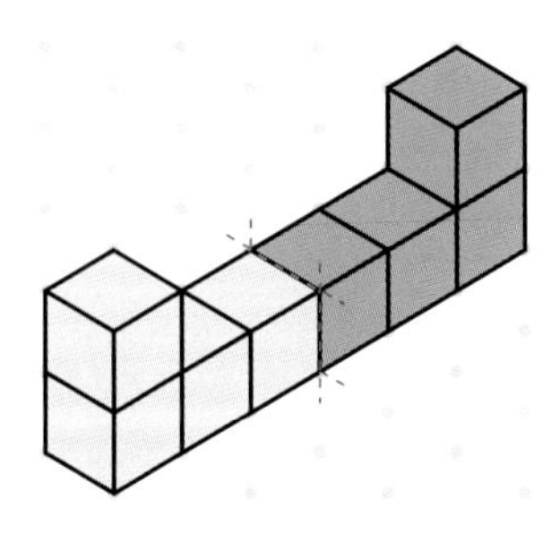

Exercise 5:3

You will need some cubes and some dotty isometric paper for this exercise.

1 Make these shapes from cubes.
Make their reflections.

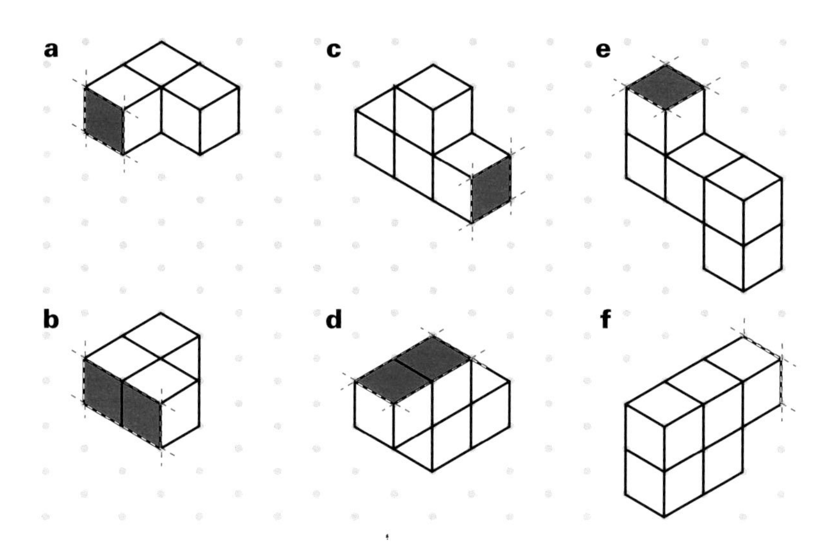

● **2** **a** Make this shape and its reflection.
b Draw your shape on isometric paper.

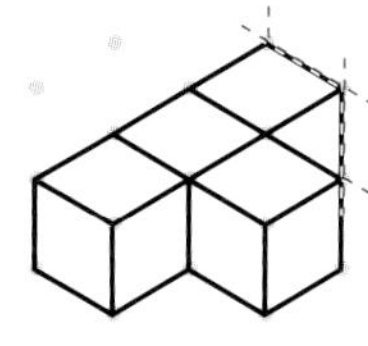

3 Make some shapes and their reflections of your own.

2 Movement – translations

There are different rides at the fair.
You can go straight down the field on the train.
You can go round and round on a roundabout.

Translation	A **translation** is a movement in a straight line.
Rotation	A **rotation** is a movement round in a circle.

Exercise 5:4

1 Write down whether these movements are translations or rotations.
  a opening an ordinary door
  b running 100 metres
  c going up in a lift
  d opening a book
  e swimming a length
  f unscrewing the top of a bottle

2 Give two examples of your own of translations.

3 Give two examples of your own of rotations.

Translations

Example

Translate the L shape 4 squares to the right.

Choose one point.
Move the point 4 squares to the right.
Move the other points in the same way.

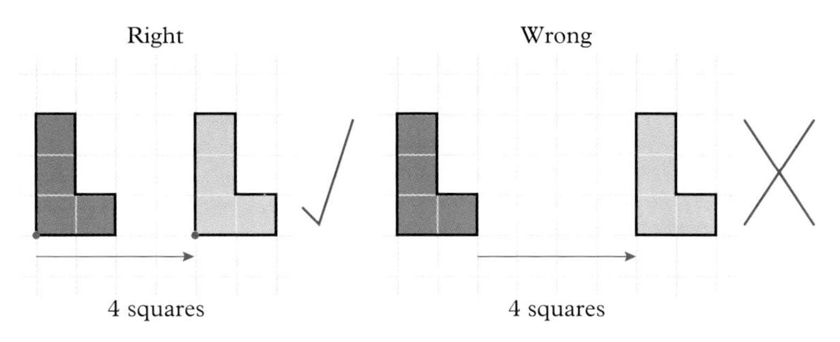

Exercise 5:5

You will need squared paper for this exercise.

1 Copy this L shape on to squared paper.
You will need a new copy for each part of the question.
Label each copy with the question number.

Translate your L:

a 5 squares to the right
b 4 squares down
c 3 squares to the left
d 5 squares up
e 6 squares down
f 5 squares to the left

2 The dark blue L has moved 4 squares to the right and 3 squares up.

a Copy the diagram on to squared paper.
b Draw a new L on the same piece of paper.
Translate it 2 squares to the left and 4 squares down.

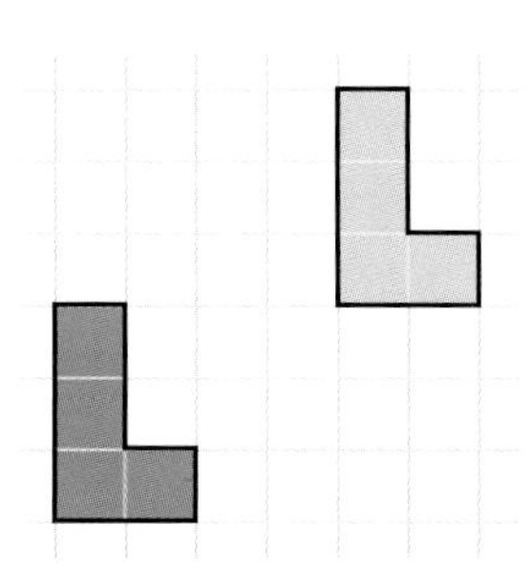

3 Write down the number of squares that the dark blue L has moved.
Write down if it went left, right, up or down.

a

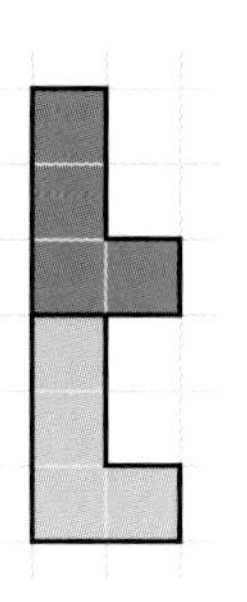

c

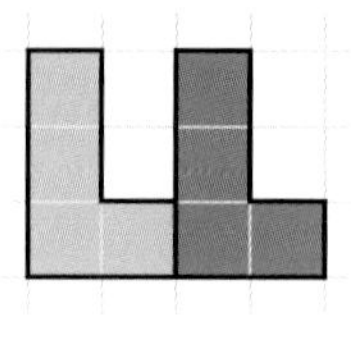

e

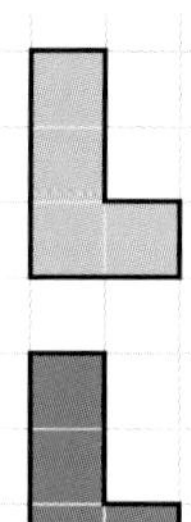

b

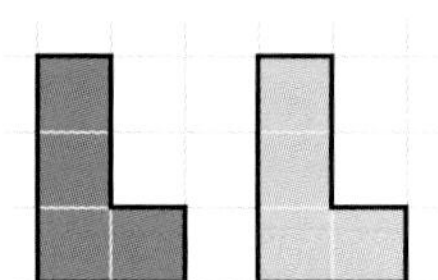

d

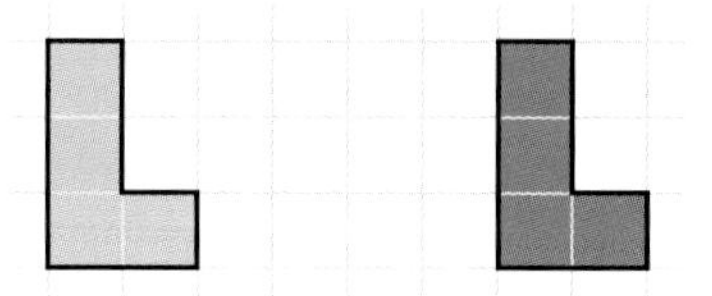

4 **a** Copy these axes on to squared paper.
b Plot these points:
(1, 4) (3, 4) (3, 6)
Join the points to make a triangle.
Put a big T in the triangle.
c Translate T 3 units to the right.
Put a big U in the new triangle.
d Translate U 4 units down.
Put a big V in the new triangle.
e Translate V 3 units to the left.
Put a big W in the new triangle.
f Write down how triangle T moves to get straight to W.

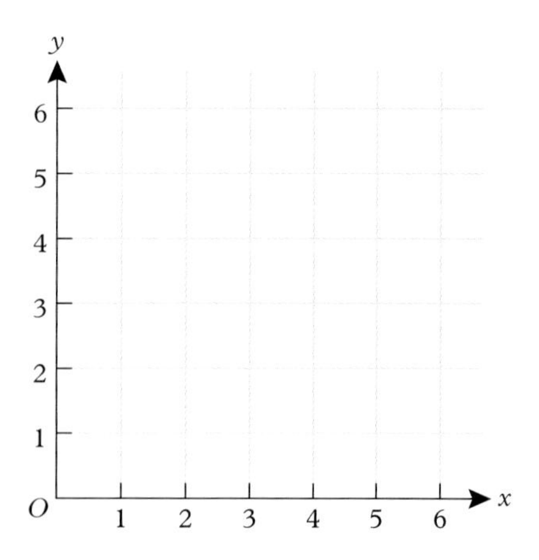

Game Translate a cube

This is a game for two players.
You need a board like this,
a red dice and a blue dice, and
a small cube.
Put the cube on 'start'.

The first player rolls both dice.

The red dice gives the number of squares to move the cube across.
You can move left or right.
The blue dice gives the number of squares to move the cube up or down.
The first player moves the cube.

The second player now rolls both dice and moves the cube.

You score points if you land on a coloured square.

= 1 point   = 3 points

The first person to score 5 points or more wins.

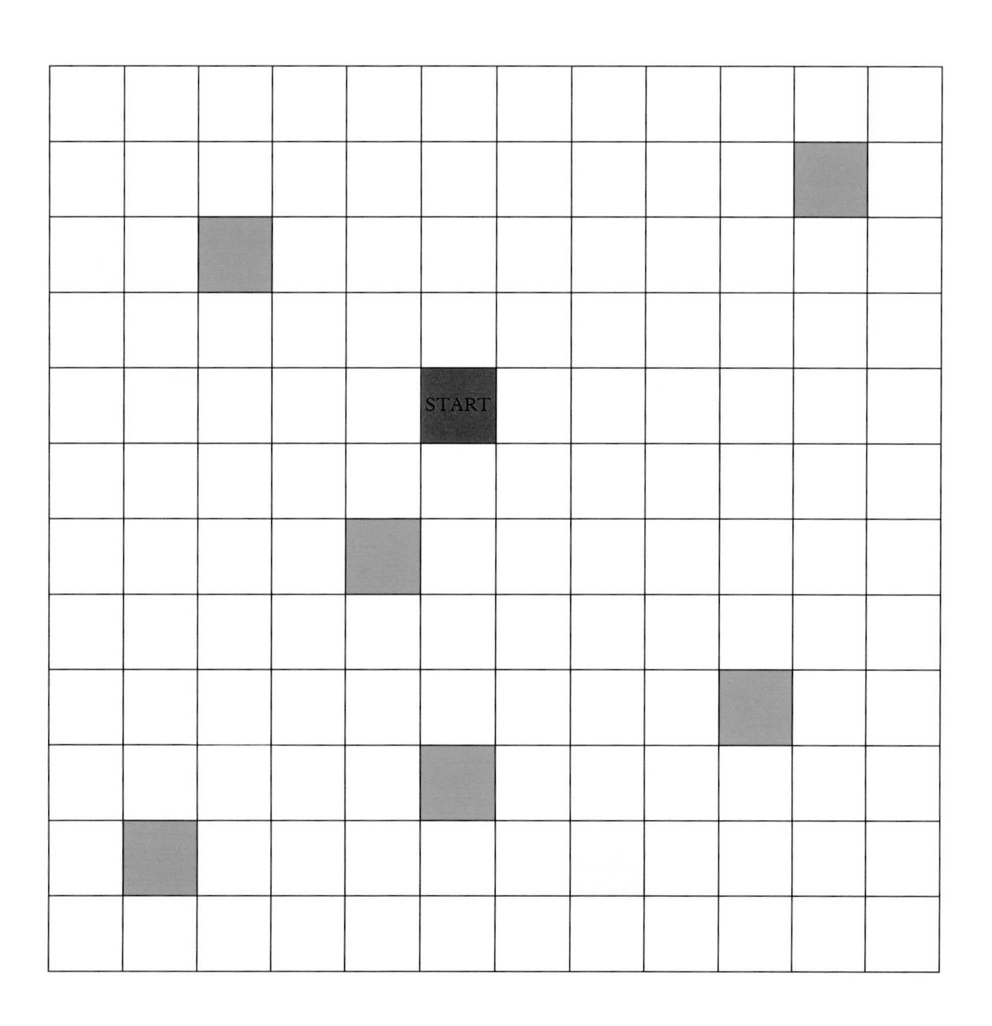

3 Rotation

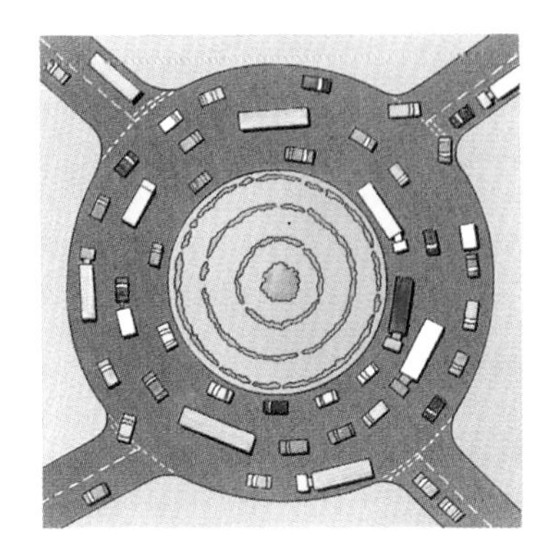

When the traffic is on the roundabout it goes in circles. The centre of the circles is the middle of the roundabout.

◀◀ REPLAY ▶

A rotation or turning can be clockwise or anti-clockwise.
The amount of turning can vary.

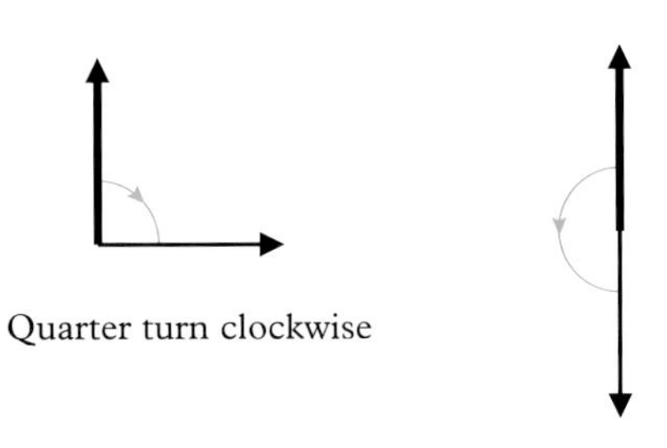

Exercise 5:6

1 Are these rotations clockwise or anti-clockwise?
How much have they turned?

a
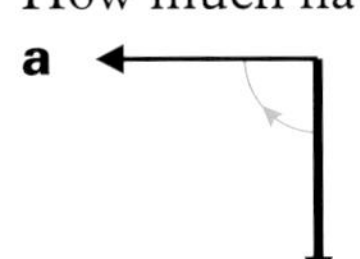

b
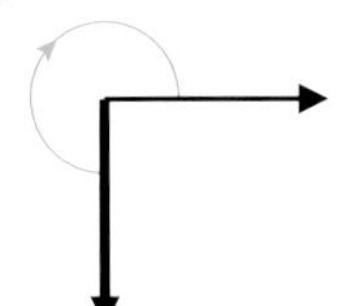

c
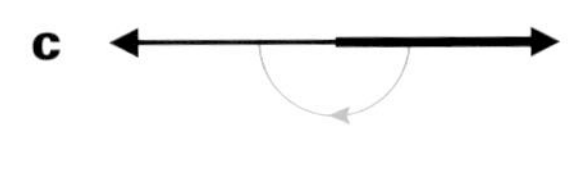

d
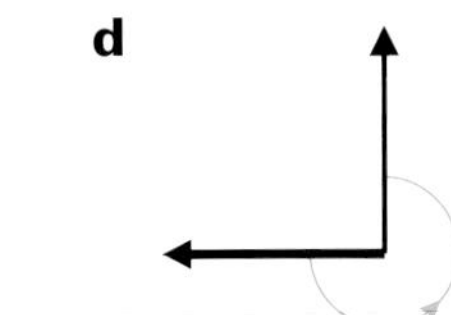

2 Start with this arrow each time.
Draw the arrow after each rotation:

a a quarter turn anti-clockwise
b a half turn clockwise
c a three-quarter turn clockwise

Centre of rotation

When an object rotates it turns about a **centre of rotation**.

The centre of rotation can be in different places.

The arrow has moved a quarter turn clockwise about different centres.

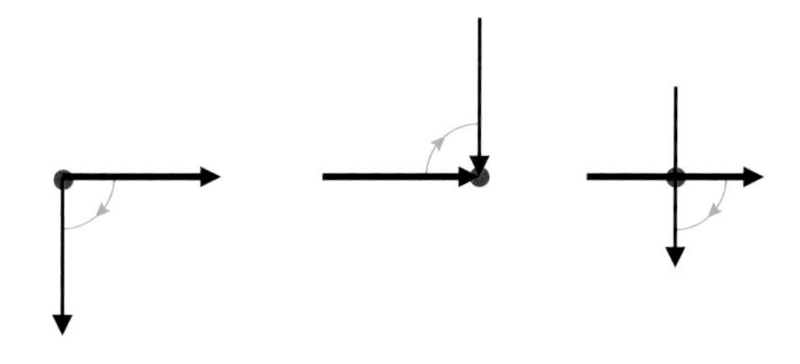

In this exercise centres of rotation are shown in red.

Start by copying an arrow into your book.
Use tracing paper to trace the arrow.
Put your pencil point on the centre. Rotate the tracing paper.
The tracing paper shows you the new position of the arrow.
Draw the new position of the arrow in your book.

Rotate the tracing paper

3 Give the arrow a quarter turn anti-clockwise about the centre.
The centre each time is marked with ●

a **b** **c**

4 Give the arrow a half turn clockwise about the centre.

a

b

c

The centre of rotation does not have to be on the arrow.

The arrow has moved a quarter turn clockwise about different centres. The arc showing the turn has not been drawn.

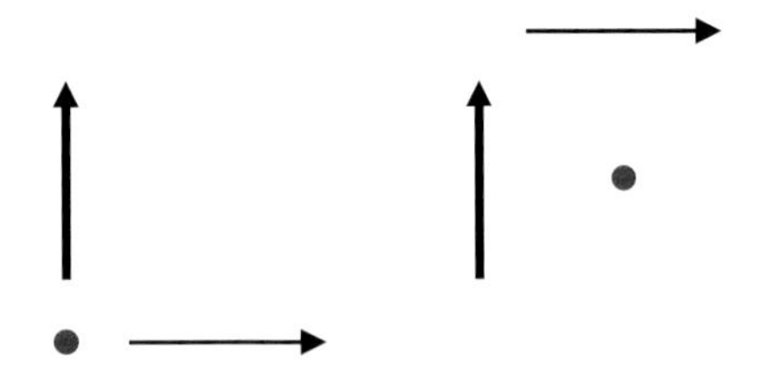

5 Give the arrow a quarter turn anti-clockwise about the centre.
Use tracing paper to help you.
Do not draw the arc showing the turn.

a

b

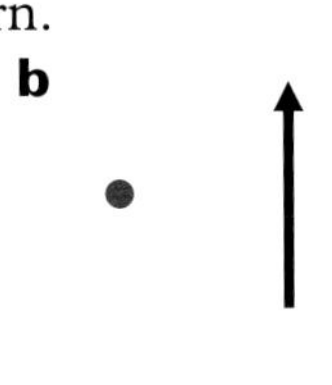

6 Give the arrow a half turn clockwise about the centre.

a

b

Rotational symmetry	A shape has **rotational symmetry** if it fits on top of itself more than once as it makes a complete turn.
Order of rotational symmetry	The **order of rotational symmetry** is the number of times that the shape fits on top of itself. This must be 2 or more.

These shapes have rotational symmetry.

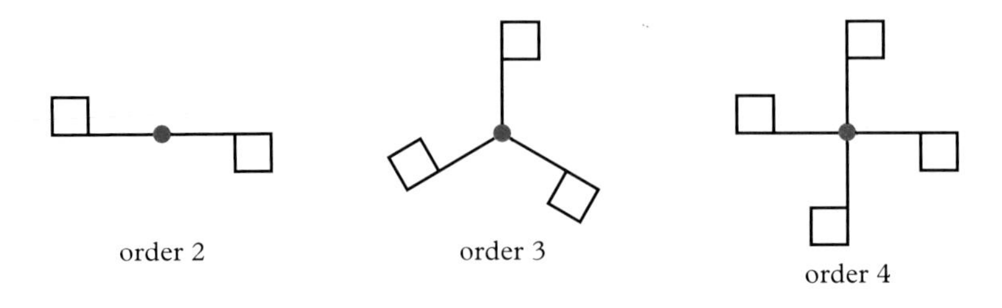

Exercise 5:7

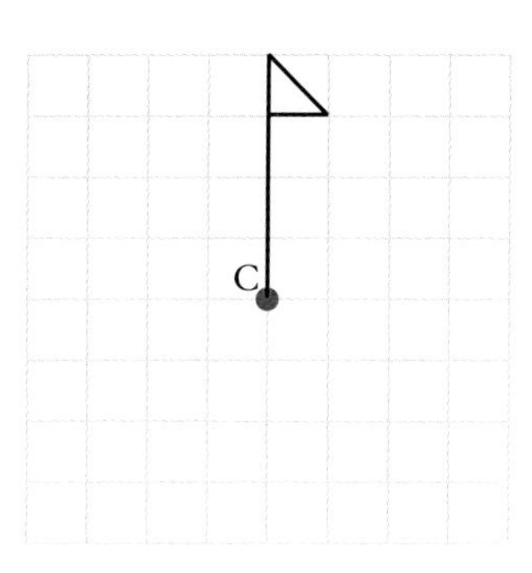

C marks the centre of rotation.

1 **a** Copy the diagram on to squared paper.
b Give the flag a half turn about C. Draw the new position.
c Write down the order of rotational symmetry of your diagram.

• **2** **a** Copy the diagram for question **1** on to squared paper.
b Give the flag a quarter turn clockwise about C. Draw the new position.
c Give the flag another quarter turn clockwise about C. Draw the new position.
d Give the flag another quarter turn clockwise about C. Draw the new position.
e Write down the order of rotational symmetry of your diagram.

3 Design a shape of your own.
Rotate your shape to get new diagrams with rotational symmetry:
a of order 2 **b** of order 4

Patterns with reflections, translations and rotations

You need some large squared paper.
Cut out a 4×4 grid of squares.

Draw a pattern in the top left-hand corner.

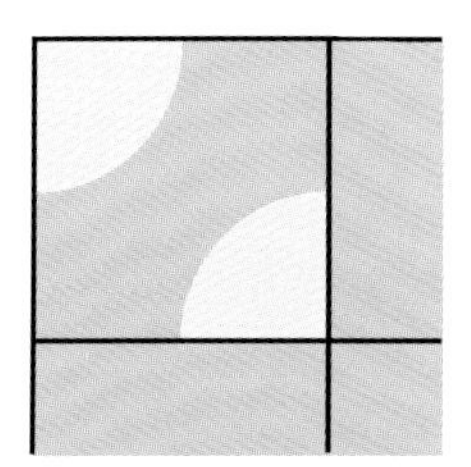

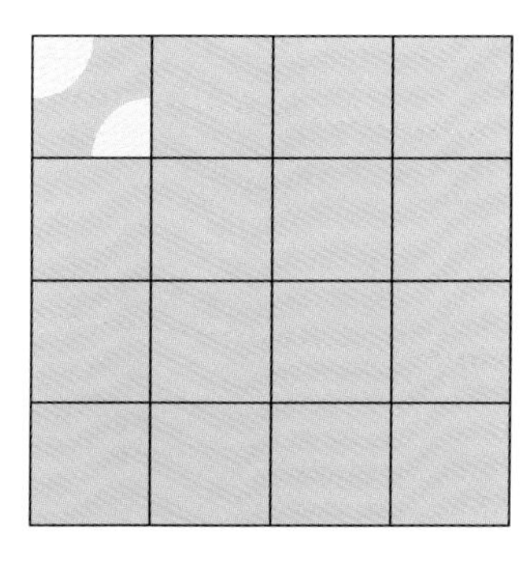

Translate the pattern to each square to get this.

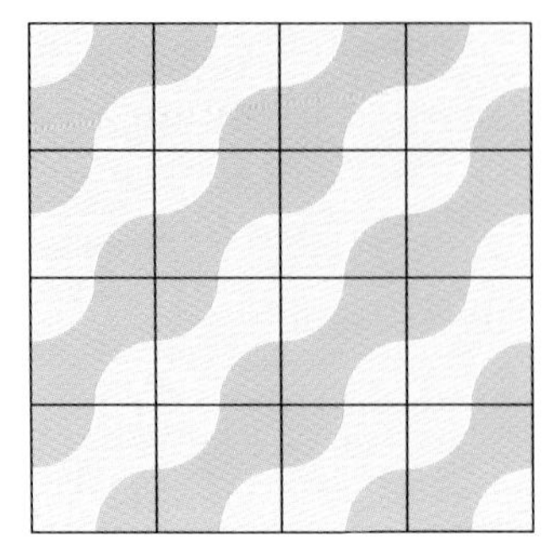

Reflect the pattern in each line of the grid to get this.

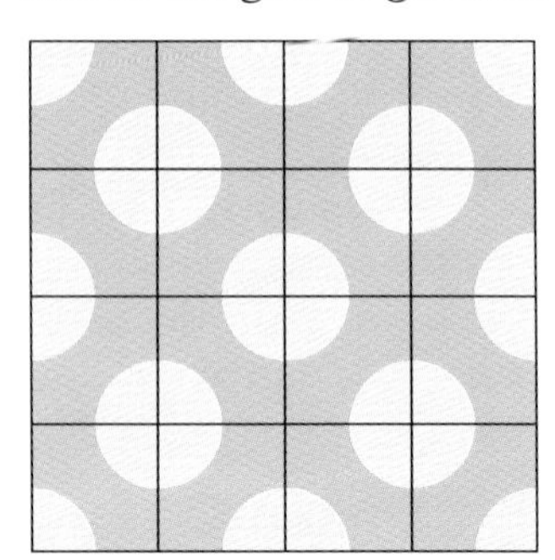

This pattern has been rotated through a quarter turn clockwise each time.

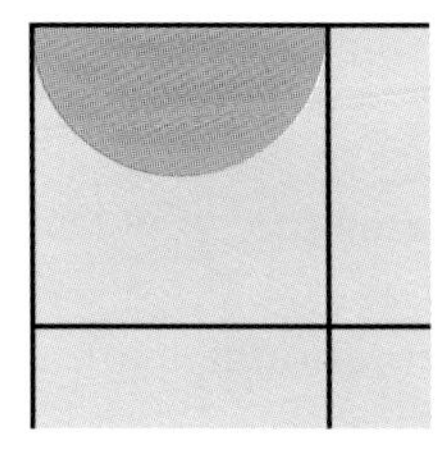

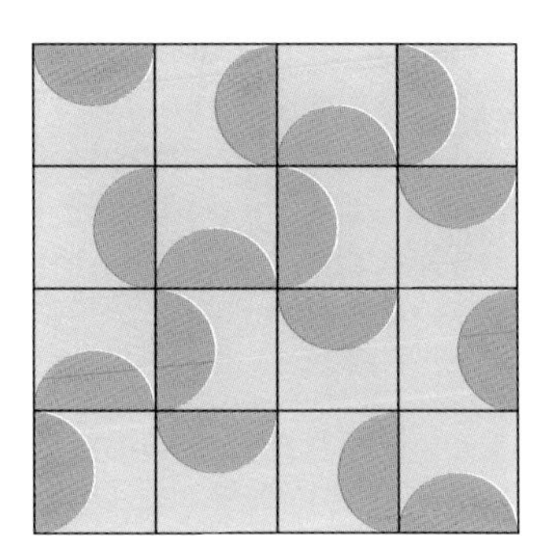

Try some patterns of your own.

4 Enlargement

The photographs of the school play at Stanthorne High are ready.

There is a standard size or an enlargement.
The enlargement is twice as wide and twice as long as the standard size.

Enlargement An **enlargement** changes the size of an object. The change is the same in all directions

Scale factor The **scale factor** tells us how many times bigger the enlargement is.

Example Enlarge the rectangle by a scale factor of 2.

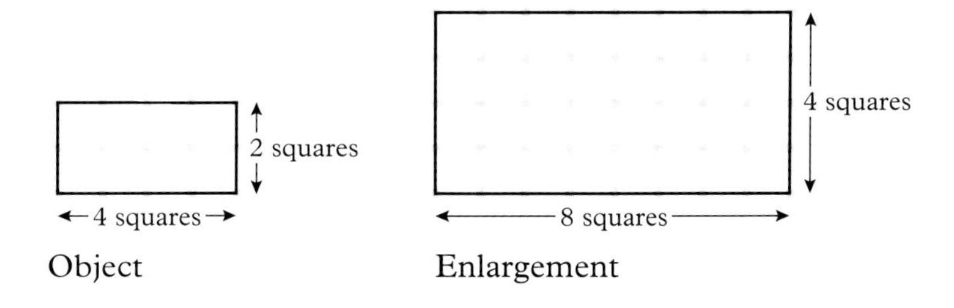

The enlargement is 2 times as long and 2 times as wide as the object.

Exercise 5:8

1 Copy these shapes on to squared paper.
Enlarge each shape by a scale factor of 2.

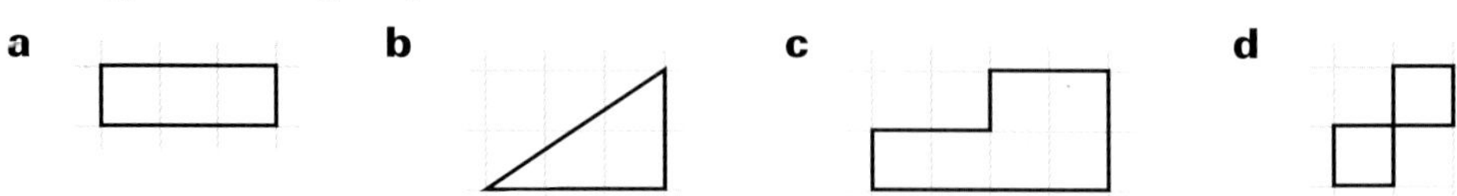

2 Enlarge the shapes in question **1** by a scale factor of 3.

3 Write down the scale factor of each of these enlargements.

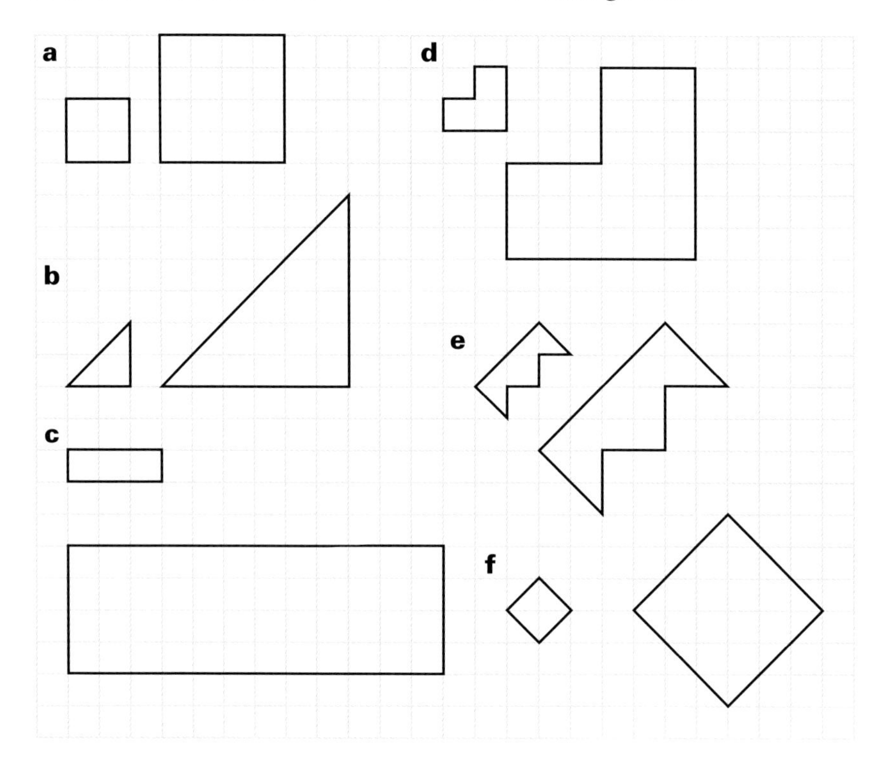

● **4** Measure the sides of these shapes.
Copy them into your book.
Enlarge them by a scale factor of 2.

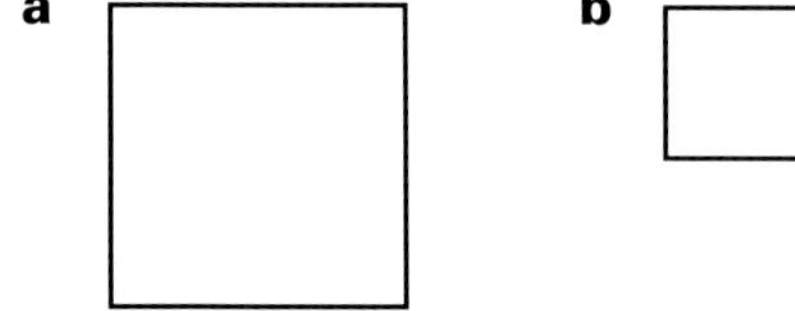

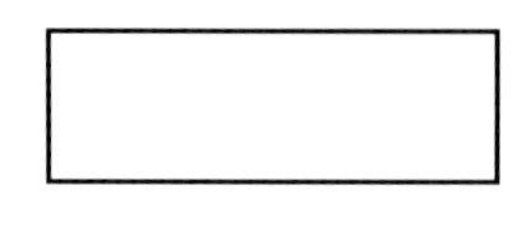

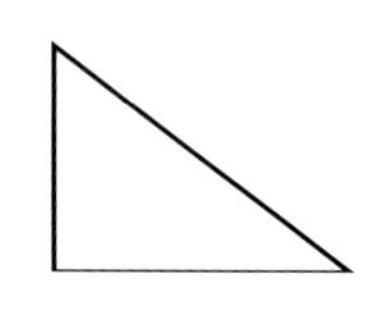

Exercise 5:9

1 Copy these axes on to squared paper.

a Plot these points in order.
Join them as you go.
(2, 2) (2, 4) (1, 6)
(3, 6) (3, 2) (2, 2)

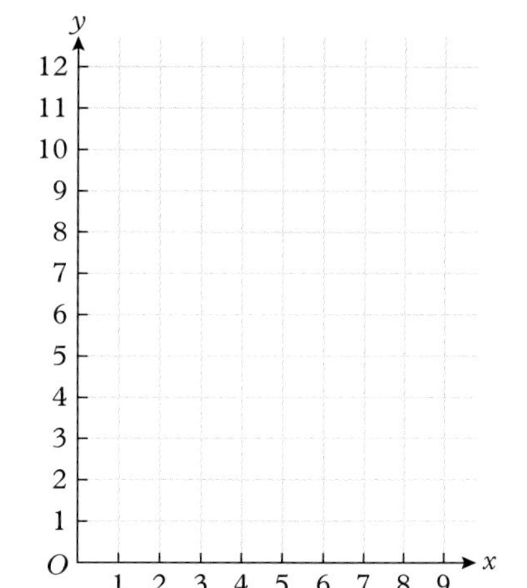

b Copy this table.
Fill it in.
Multiply the co-ordinates on the top line by 2 to get the bottom line.

Co-ordinates of object	(2,2)	(2,4)	(1,6)	(3,6)	(3,2)	(2,2)
Co-ordinates × 2	(4,4)	(4,8)	(…,…)			

c Plot the new co-ordinates in order.
Join them as you go.

d Write down the scale factor of the enlargement.

2 Copy the axes from question **1** on to squared paper.

a Plot these points in order.
Join them as you go.
(1, 1) (1, 4) (2, 4) (3, 2) (3, 1) (1, 1)

b Copy this table.
Fill it in.

Co-ordinates of object	(1,1)	(1,4)	(2,4)	(3,2)	(3,1)	(1,1)
Co-ordinates × 3	(3,3)	(3,12)	(…,…)			

c Plot the new co-ordinates in order.
Join them as you go.

d Write down the scale factor of the enlargement.

1 Copy these diagrams on to squared paper.
Draw their reflections in the mirror lines

a

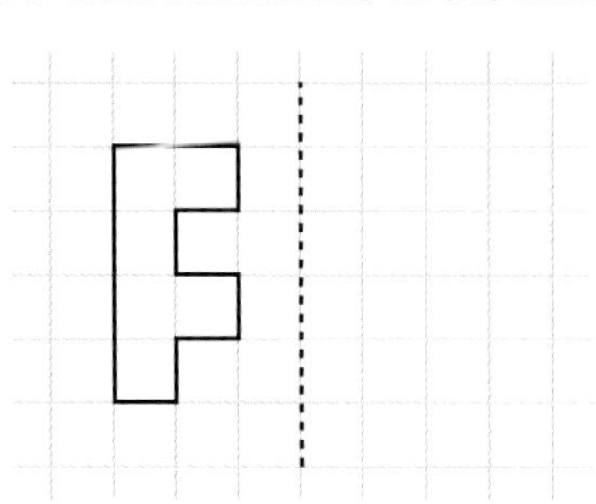

c

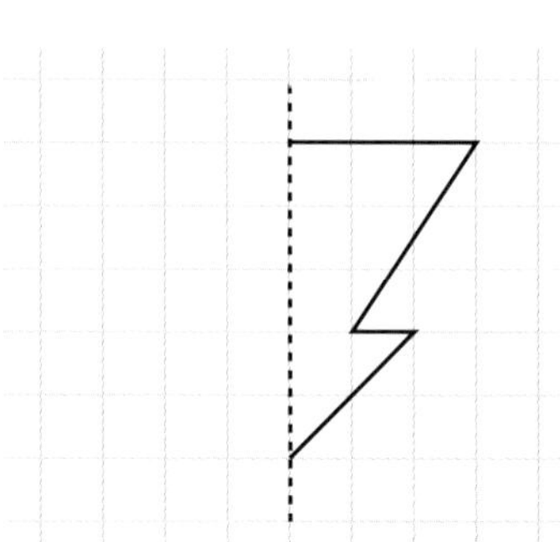

b

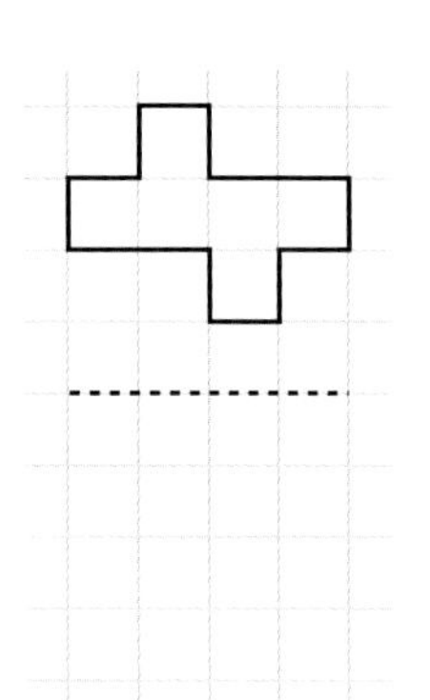

d

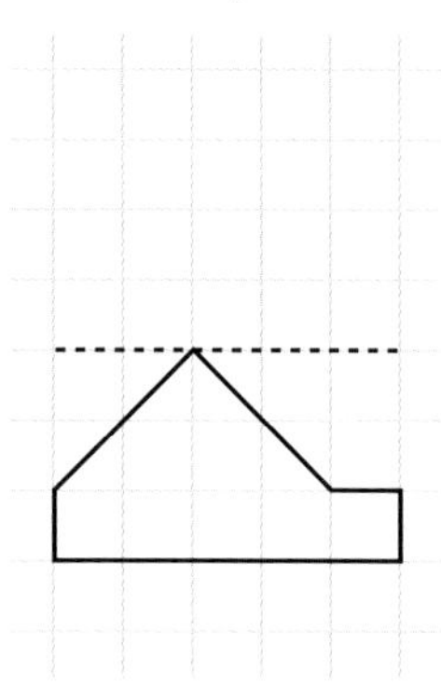

2 Copy this flag on to squared paper.
You will need a new copy for each part of the question.
Label each copy with the question number.

Translate your flag:

a 2 squares to the right
b 3 squares down
c 3 squares to the left
d 4 squares up
e 1 square to the right and 4 squares up
f 2 squares to the left and 5 squares down

3 Write down the number of squares that the dark blue L has moved.
Write down if it went left, right, up or down.

a

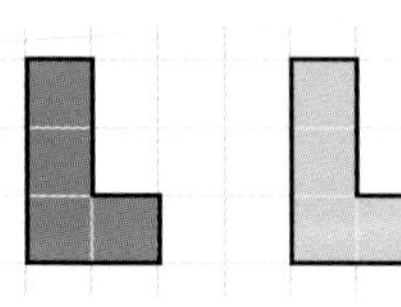

b

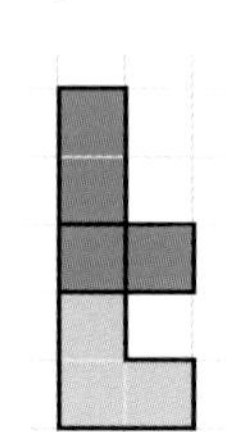

c

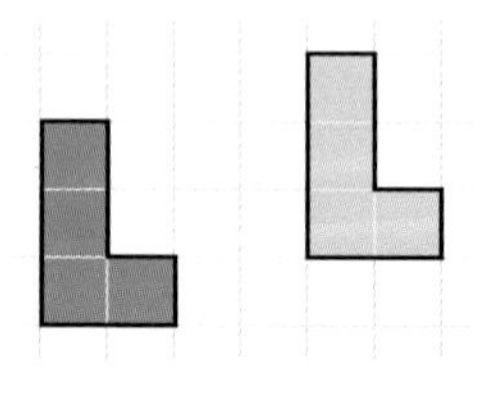

4 **a** Give the arrow a half turn anti-clockwise about each centre.

(1) (2) (3)

b Give the arrow a quarter turn clockwise about each centre.

(1) (2) (3)

5 **a** Copy the diagram on to squared paper.

b Give the arrow quarter turn clockwise about C.
Draw the new position.

c Give the arrow another quarter turn clockwise about C.
Draw the new position.

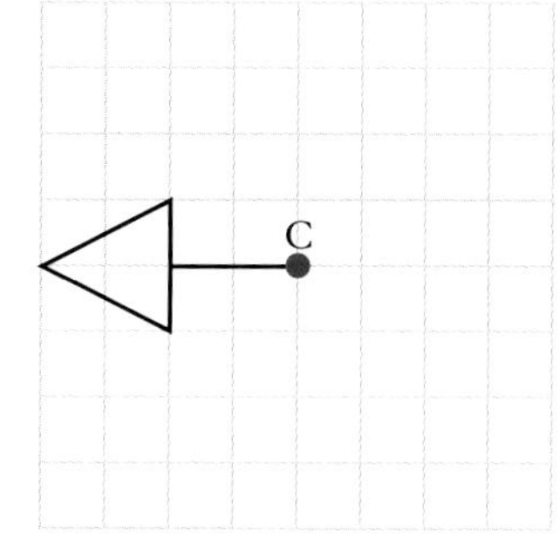

d Give the arrow another quarter turn clockwise about C.
Draw the new position.

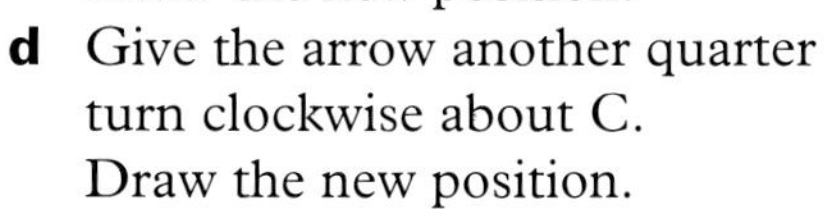

e Write down the order of rotational symmetry of your diagram.

6 **a** Copy these shapes on to squared paper.
Enlarge them by a scale factor of 2.

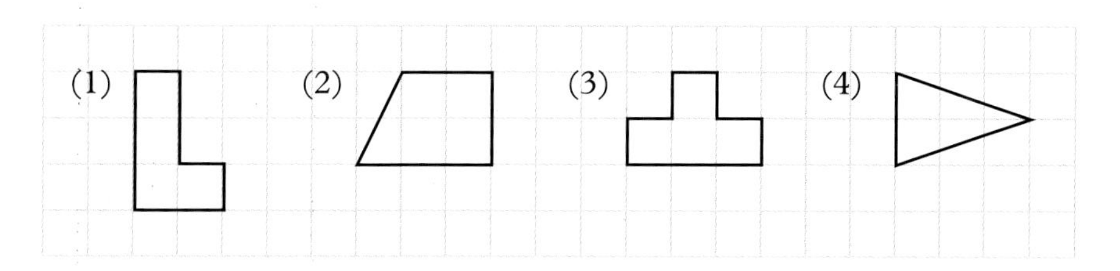

b Repeat part **a** but use a scale factor of 3.

c Write down the scale factor of each of these enlargements.

(1)

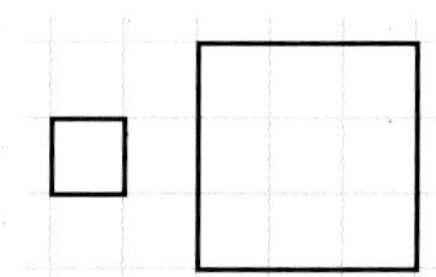

(2)

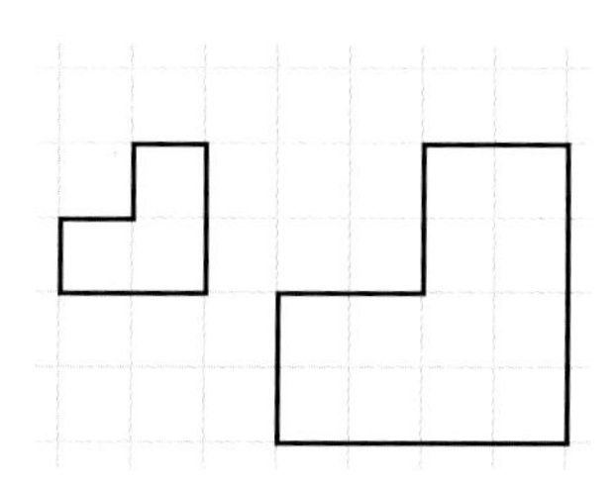

1 Traditional Islamic patterns are made like this.

Make a pattern in a square.

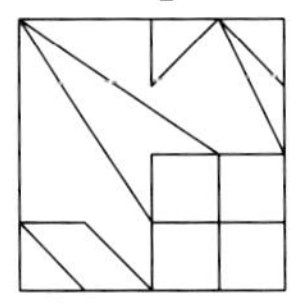

Reflect the pattern across and down.

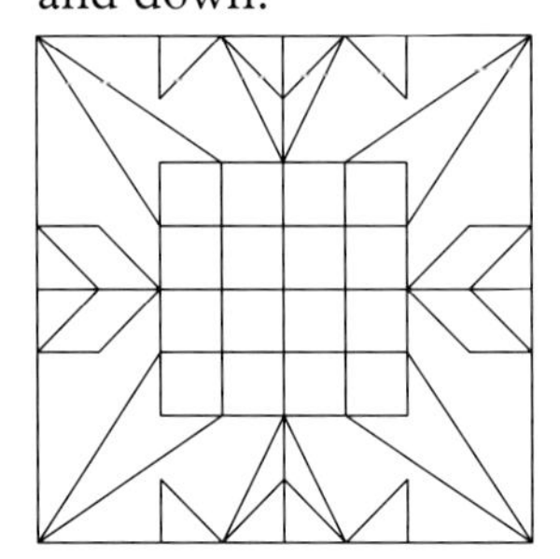

Colour the pattern.

Make your own pattern like this.

2 **a** Make these arrangements of cubes.
Imagine a mirror to the right of each shape.
Make a reflection of each shape in the mirror.
The first one has been done for you.

(1)

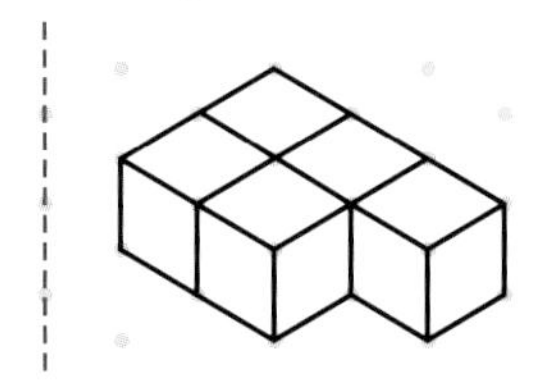

(2)

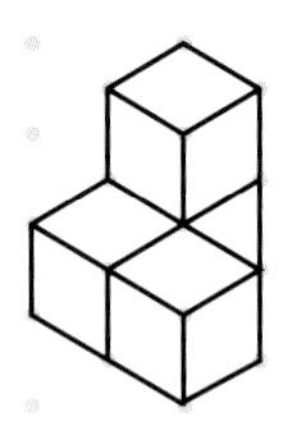

(3)

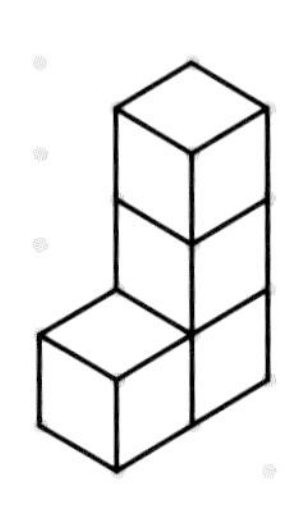

(4)

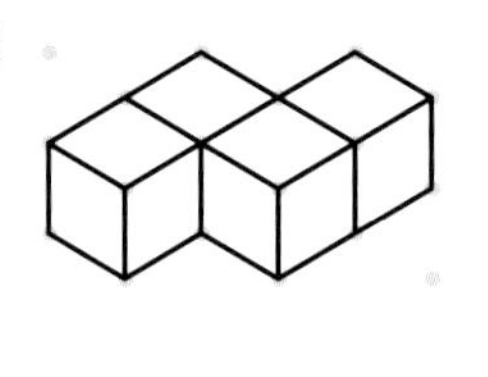

(5)

b Choose one shape and its reflection.
Draw them on isometric paper.

3 Give the arrow a quarter turn clockwise about the centre.

a ● ⟶ **b** ⟶

●

4 Start with a simple shape that tessellates.
You can make a more interesting shape with rotations and translations.

Cut a semicircle from the shape.
Give the semicircle a half turn.

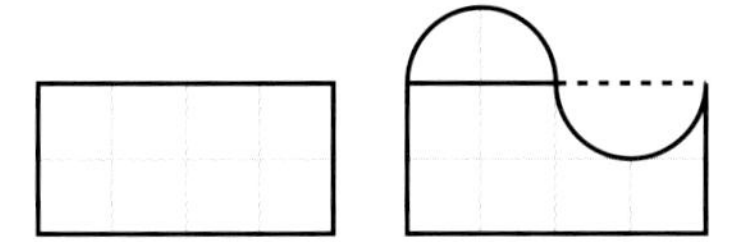

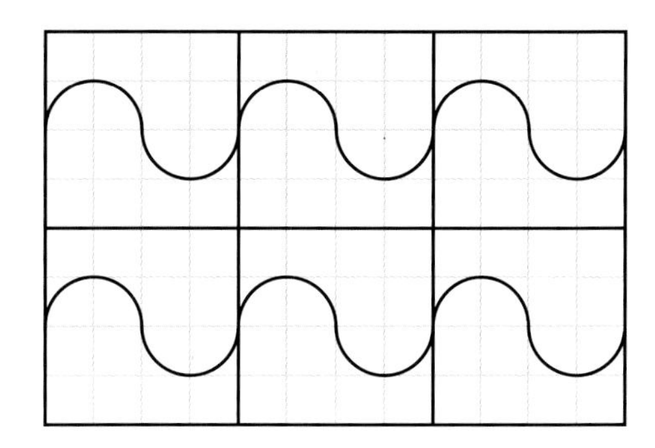

Cut a triangle from the shape.
Translate the triangle to the opposite side.

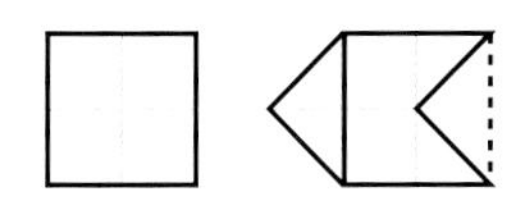

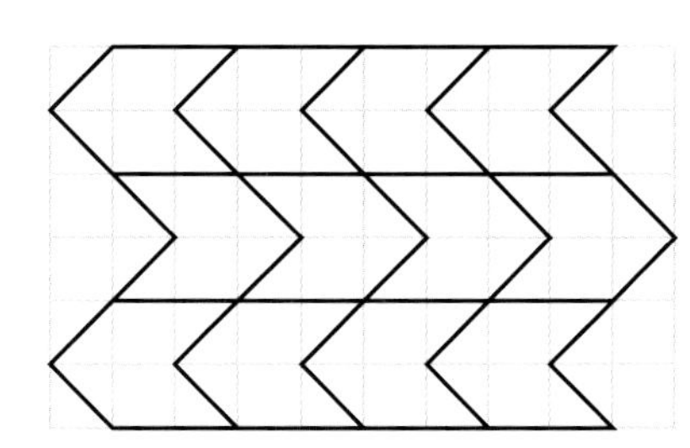

Try some patterns of your own.

5 Copy these axes on to squared paper.

a Plot these points:
(4, 1) (9, 1) (9, 3) (4, 3)
Join the points to make a rectangle.
Translate the rectangle 5 units up.

b Plot these points:
(2, 13) (4, 13) (4, 16)
Join the points to make a triangle.
Translate the triangle 5 units down.

c Plot these points:
(0, 8) (1, 10)
Join the points to make a line.
Translate the line 9 units to the right.

d Plot these points:
(0, 5) (0, 6) (1, 6)
Join the points to make a triangle.
Translate the triangle 4 units to the right.
Translate the triangle another 4 units to the right.

e Plot the point (1, 4)
Translate the point 2 units to the right and 5 units up.

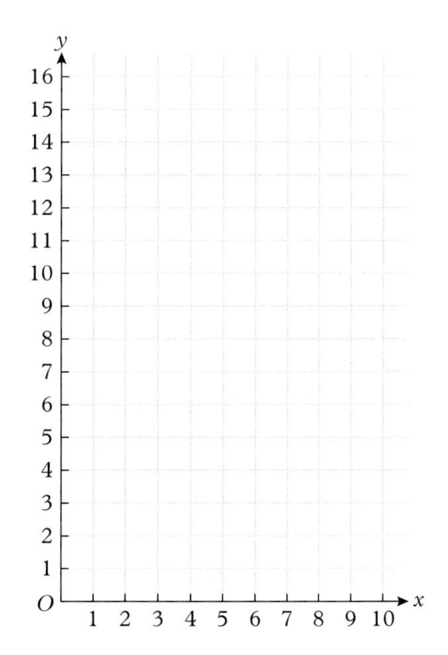

6 Start with a flag like this each time.
Use tracing paper to help you.

a (1) Give the flag a half turn clockwise about C.
(2) Give the flag a half turn anti-clockwise about C.
(3) Write down what you notice.

b (1) Give the flag a quarter turn anti-clockwise about C.
(2) Give the flag a three-quarter turn clockwise about C.
(3) Write down what you notice.

c (1) Give the flag a full turn clockwise.
(2) Give the flag a full turn anti-clockwise.
(3) Write down what you notice.

7 This triangle has been given a half turn about the midpoint of one of its sides.
The triangle and its rotation make a parallelogram.

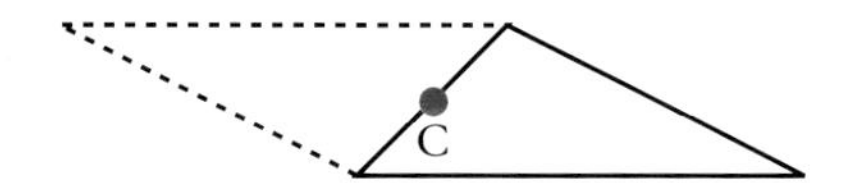

Copy each diagram.
Use tracing paper to give each triangle a half turn about C.
Write down the name of each quadrilateral that you get.
Choose from: square, rectangle, rhombus, parallelogram

a

c

e

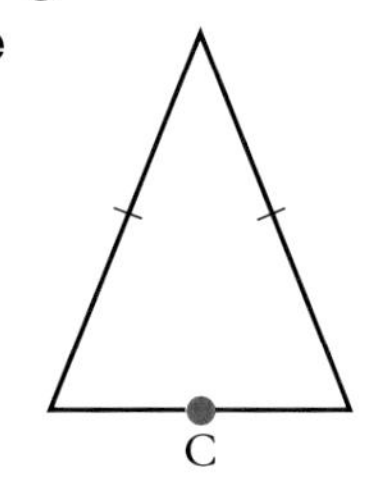

b

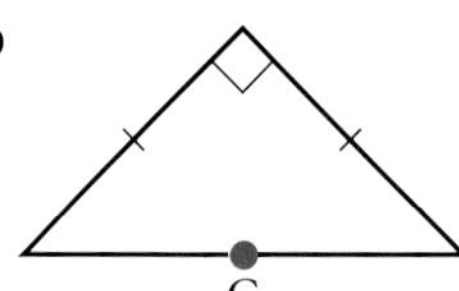

d

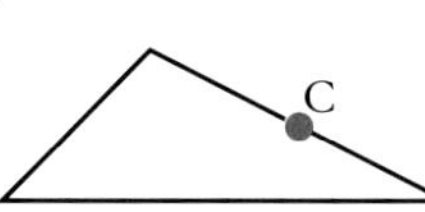

8 Copy these shapes on to squared paper.
Enlarge them by a scale factor of 3.

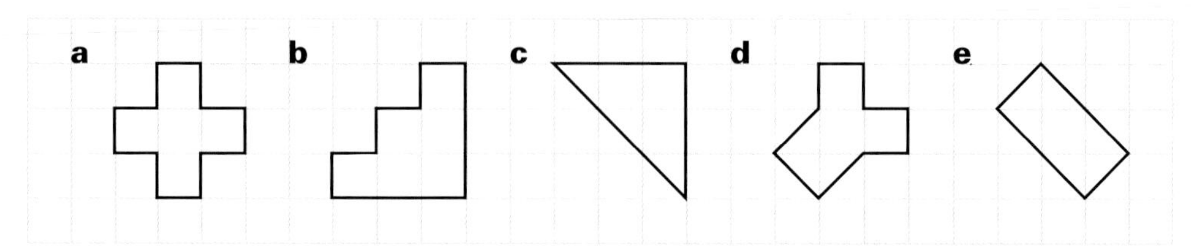

S U M M A R Y 5

- 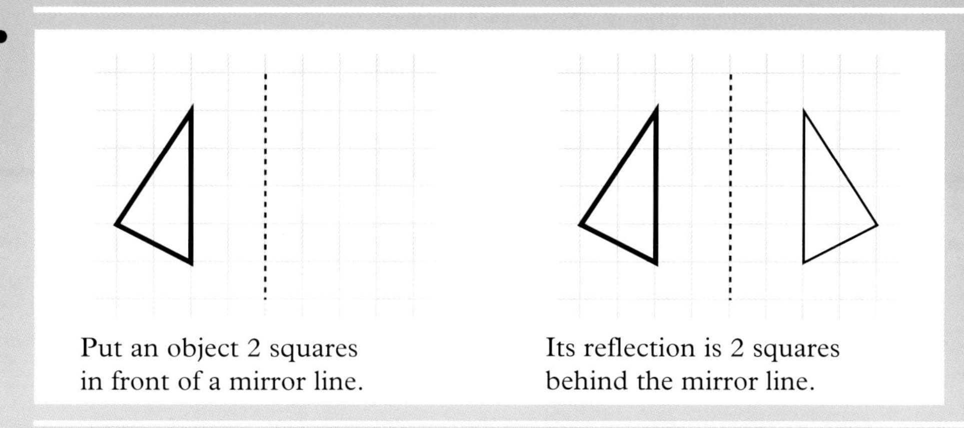

Put an object 2 squares in front of a mirror line.

Its reflection is 2 squares behind the mirror line.

- **Translation** A **translation** is a movement in a straight line.
Rotation A **rotation** is a movement round in a circle.

- *Example* Translate the L shape 4 squares to the right.

Choose one point.
Move the point 4 squares to the right.
Move the other points in the same way.

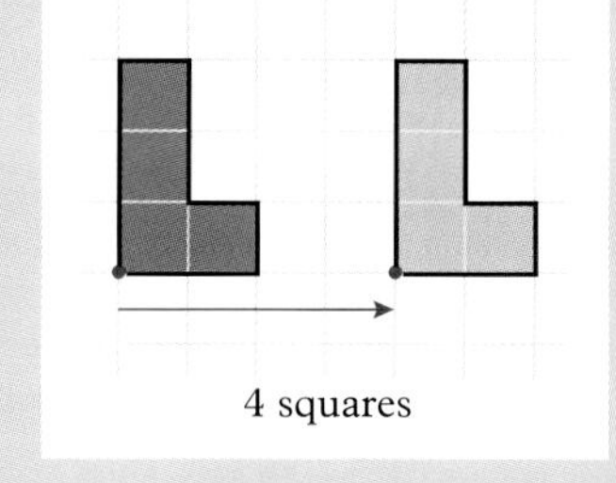

- The centre of rotation can be in different places.

The arrow has been moved a quarter turn clockwise about different centres.

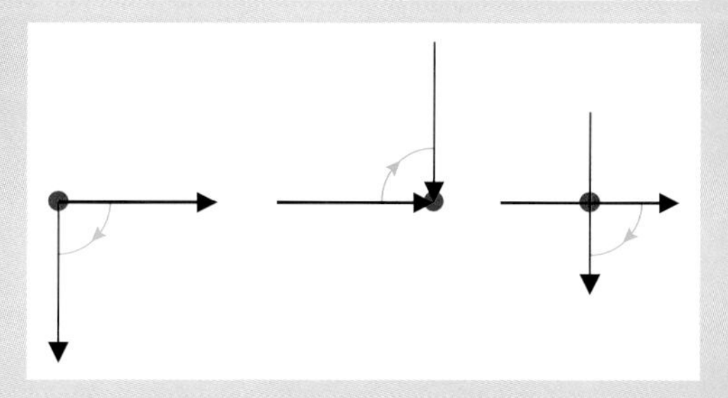

- **Enlargement** An **enlargement** changes the size of an object.
Scale factor The **scale factor** tells us how many times bigger the enlargement is.

Example
Enlarge the rectangle by a scale factor of 2.

The enlargement is 2 times as long and 2 times as wide as the object.

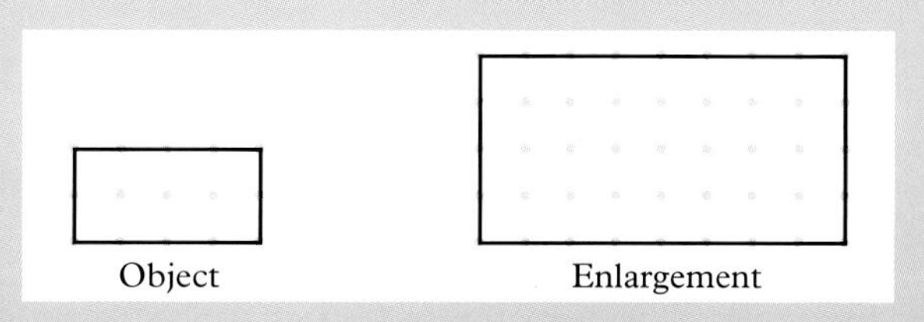

1 Copy these diagrams on to squared paper.
Draw their reflections in the mirror lines.

a

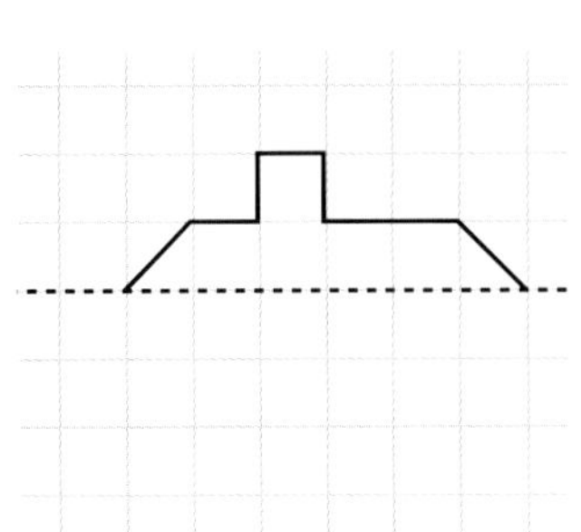

b

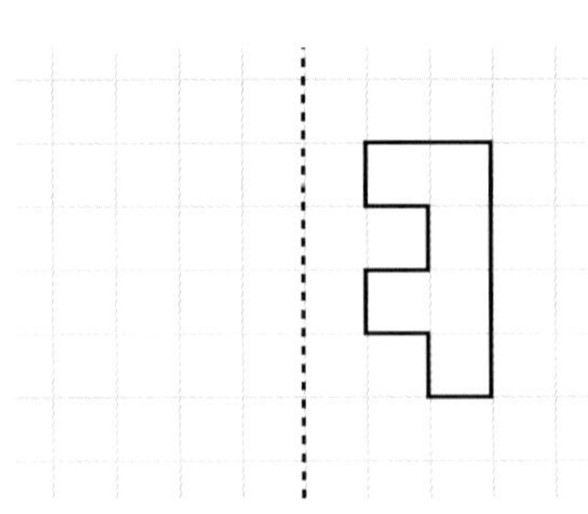

2 Copy this L shape on to squared paper.
Use a new copy for each part of the question.
Label each copy with the question number.

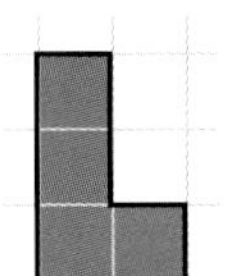

Translate your L:

a 3 squares to the right
b 5 squares down
c 2 squares to the left and
4 squares up

3 **a** Copy the diagram.
Give the flag a
quarter turn anti-clockwise
about C.

b Copy the diagram.
Give the flag a
half turn clockwise
about C.

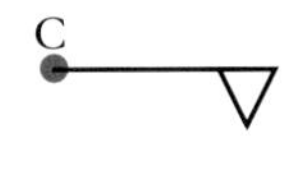

4 Copy the diagram on to squared paper.
Rotate this shape about C a
quarter turn at a time.
Make a new shape with rotational
symmetry of order 4.

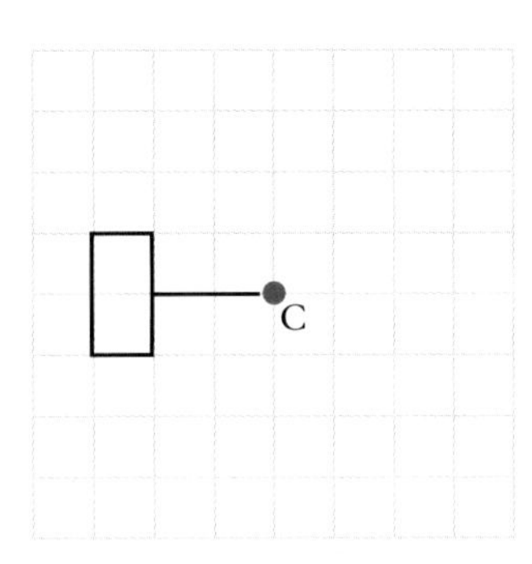

5 Copy this shape on to squared paper.
Enlarge this shape:

a by a scale factor of 2
b by a scale factor of 3

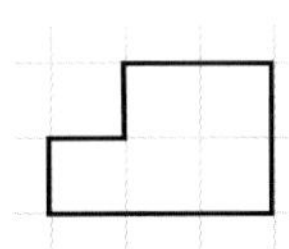

6 Don't be negative!

CORE

1 ◄◄ REPLAY ►

2 Using money

3 The calculator

QUESTIONS

EXTENSION

SUMMARY

TEST YOURSELF

The coldest place in the world is the Pole of Inaccessibility in Antarctica. Its annual mean temperature is −58 °C.

Braemar, in Scotland, is the coldest weather station in the UK. Its annual mean temperature is 6.3 °C. On cold nights, Braemar has had temperatures down to −27 °C.

The lowest temperature possible is absolute zero, 0 K on the Kelvin scale or −273.15 °C. The lowest temperature reached on Earth is 0.000 000 000 28 K. This was at the Low Temperature Laboratory of Helsinki University, Finland, in February 1993.

BRAEMAR

1 ◀◀REPLAY▶

You have already met negative numbers.

Negative numbers **Positive** numbers	Numbers with minus signs in front are called **negative** numbers. Other numbers except nought are **positive**. Positive numbers are sometimes written with a plus sign in front. Nought is not positive or negative.
Examples	Negative numbers −2, −5, −32 Positive numbers 7, +3, 25

Exercise 6:1

1 From this list: 6, −3, 0, −5, +2, −1, +7, 9
- **a** Write down the positive numbers.
- **b** Write down the negative numbers.
- **c** Which number is left?
  Why is it left?

Look at this thermometer scale.

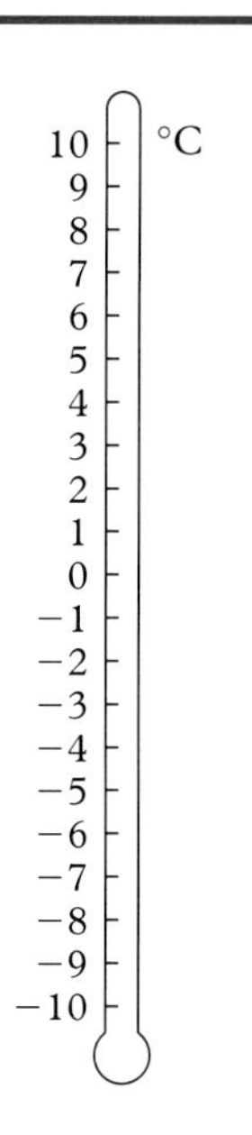

Examples

1 °C is lower than 4 °C
−2 °C is lower than 1 °C
−4 °C is lower than −1 °C

3 °C is higher than 2 °C
1 °C is higher than −2 °C
−1 °C is higher than −3 °C

2 Which temperature is lower?
a −2 °C or 4 °C **b** 0 °C or −5 °C **c** −2 °C or −5 °C

3 Which temperature is higher?
a −6 °C or 1 °C **b** −1 °C or 0 °C **c** −3 °C or −4 °C

4 Put these temperatures in order, lowest first.
a −4 °C, 5 °C, −2 °C, 3 °C
b 5 °C, −3 °C, 0 °C, −2 °C, 7 °C
c −6 °C, 1 °C, −1 °C, −3 °C, 0 °C, 4 °C

5 Put these temperatures in order, highest first.
a −1 °C, 2 °C, −3 °C
b −2 °C, 5 °C, 1 °C, −1 °C, 2 °C
c −11 °C, 8 °C, −5 °C, −9 °C, 2 °C, −1 °C

Example

Find the rule for this number pattern.
Write down the next two terms.
4, 2, 0, −2, −4, …, …

4, 2, 0, −2, −4, −6, −8

The rule is −2.
The next two terms are −6, −8

6 Find the rule for each number pattern.
Write down the next two terms.

a 3, 2, 1, 0, −1, ..., ...
b 8, 5, 2, −1, −4, ..., ...
c 10, 5, 0, −5, −10, ..., ...
d 30, 20, 10, 0, ..., ...

7 Copy these number patterns.
Find the rule for each one.
Use your rule to fill in the missing numbers.

a 5, 3, 1, ..., −3, ..., −7
b 9, 6, 3, ..., −3, ..., −9
c 100, 50, ..., −50, ..., −150

Less than <
Greater than >

We often use the signs < and > with numbers.
< means **'less than'** > means **'greater than'**

Examples

$-5\,°\text{C} < -2\,°\text{C}$ means −5 °C is less than −2 °C
$2\,°\text{C} > -4\,°\text{C}$ means 2 °C is greater than −4 °C

Exercise 6:2

1 Replace ? with < or >

a 4 °C ? 2 °C
b 0 °C ? −3 °C
c −5 °C ? −1 °C
d 6 °C ? −6 °C
e −2 °C ? 1 °C
f −3 °C ? −8 °C

2 Write down the temperatures in degrees Celsius (°C) on these thermometers.

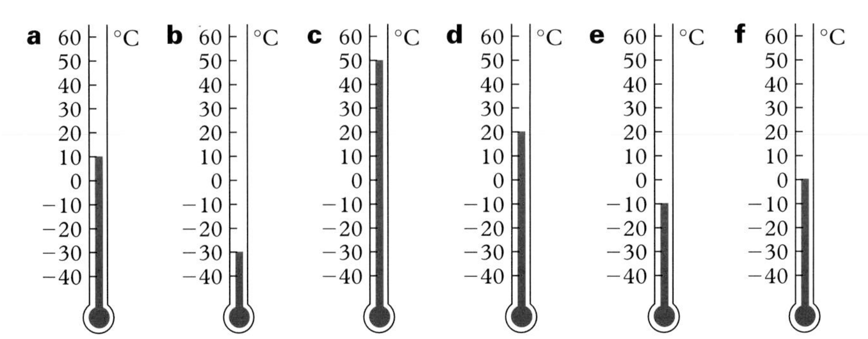

3 What is the difference between these day and night temperatures?

a day 8 °C, night −1 °C

b day 4 °C, night −7 °C

c day 6 °C, night 0 °C

d day 9 °C, night −3 °C

e day 10 °C, night 2 °C

f day 7 °C, night −9 °C

(Each thermometer scale is marked from −10 to 10.)

4 The temperature in a freezer is −20 °C.
A frozen hamburger is thawed to room temperature.
Room temperature is 21 °C.
How many degrees does the temperature of the hamburger rise?

5 Jane is standing on a cliff.
This picture shows what is above and below sea level.

a What is at about +60 m?

b How far below the fish is the top of the wreck?

c How far above the fish is the seagull?

d Estimate the distance of the seabed below sea level.

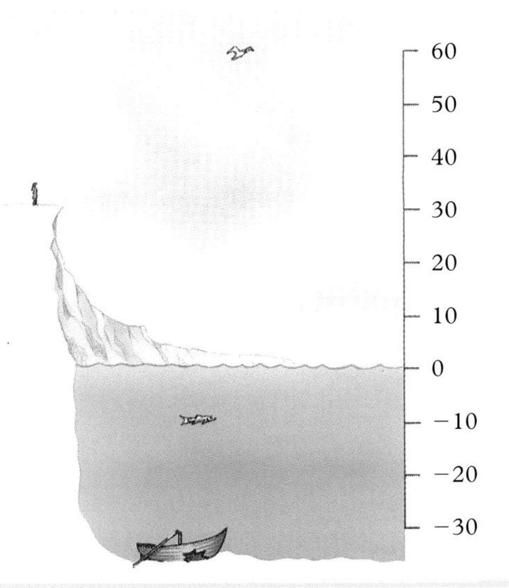

2 Using money

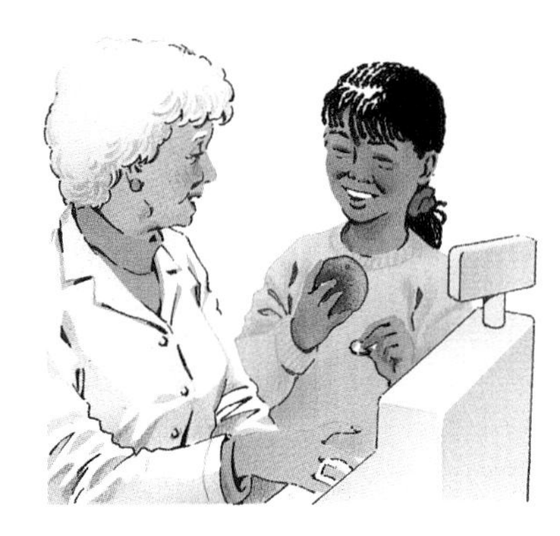

Charlene is buying a peach.
The peach costs 27 p.
Charlene has the correct money.
She gives the greengrocer a
20 p coin, a 5 p and a 2 p.

Example

Simon has 1 twenty pence, 2 ten pence and 1 two pence.
How much money has she got?

Write Simon's coins in figures.
Then add them up.
20 p + 10 p + 10 p + 2 p = 42 p

Exercise 6:3

Write these coins in figures.
Then add them up.

1 1 twenty pence, 1 ten pence, 2 five pence

2 2 twenty pence, 1 five pence, 1 two pence

3 1 fifty pence, 2 ten pence, 1 five pence

4 1 fifty pence, 1 twenty pence, 1 ten pence

5 2 twenty pence, 3 five pence, 2 two pence

6 2 fifty pence, 1 ten pence, 3 five pence

7 1 fifty pence, 1 twenty pence, 1 ten pence, 2 five pence

8 4 ten pence, 3 five pence, 3 two pence

9 3 twenty pence, 2 ten pence, 1 five pence

10 1 fifty pence, 3 ten pence, 2 five pence

11 1 fifty pence, 2 twenty pence, 1 ten pence

● **12** 1 pound, 1 fifty pence, 1 twenty pence, 1 ten pence, 1 five pence

'Shopkeepers' addition'

Example 1 Find the change when 16 p is paid using a 50 p coin.

Count on four units from 16 p to get to 20 p 17, 18, 19, 20
Count on three tens from 20 p to get to 50 p 30, 40, 50

The change is 34 p

Example 2 Find the change when 53 p is paid using a £1 coin.

Count on seven units from 53 p to get to 60 p 54, 55, 56, 57, 58, 59, 60
Count on four tens from 60 p to get to 100 p 70, 80, 90, 100

The change is 47 p

Exercise 6:4

1 Each of these is paid with a 50 p coin.
Find the change.

a 26 p	**c** 38 p	**e** 12 p	**g** 33 p	**i** 14 p
b 17 p	**d** 44 p	**f** 21 p	**h** 29 p	**j** 8 p

2 Each of these is paid with a 20 p coin.
Find the change.

a 15 p	**c** 11 p	**e** 16 p	**g** 18 p	**i** 9 p
b 13 p	**d** 4 p	**f** 5 p	**h** 7 p	**j** 14 p

3 Each of these is paid with a £1 coin.
Find the change.

a 38 p	**c** 27 p	**e** 22 p	**g** 32 p	**i** 76 p
b 53 p	**d** 64 p	**f** 85 p	**h** 69 p	**j** 84 p

4 Each of these is paid with a £1 coin.
Find the change.

a	14 p	**c**	47 p	**e**	71 p	**g**	17 p	**i**	34 p
b	36 p	**d**	29 p	**f**	63 p	**h**	6 p	**j**	9 p

● **5** Each of these is paid with a £5 note.
Find the change.

a	£1.20	**c**	£3.40	**e**	£1.35	**g**	£3.24	**i**	£1.63
b	£2.60	**d**	£4.10	**f**	£2.75	**h**	£4.18	**j**	£2.37

◀◀ REPLAY ▶

Example £5.35 × 4
On a calculator we get the display 21.4
We need two figures after the decimal point.
Answer £21.40

Exercise 6:5

Write the answers with two figures after the decimal point.

1 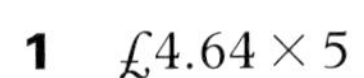 £4.64 × 5

2  £5.27 + £1.43

3 £6 ÷ 5

4 £10.56 − £6.06

5 £1.35 × 8

6 £5.20 ÷ 4

7 £4.45 × 2

8 £5.19 − £3.49

9 £3.46 + £4.84

● **10** £3 ÷ 5

Example John has £1.35. His sister Sally has 84 p.
How much do they have altogether?

84 p is the same as £0.84
£1.35 + £0.84 = £2.19

Exercise 6:6

Work out the answers to these.

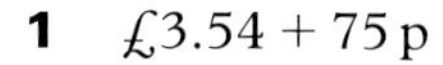

1 £3.54 + 75 p

2 £2.65 + 88 p + 43 p

3 £3.20 − 56 p

4 65 p + £1.72

5 £1.15 − 83 p

6 £5 + £1.25 + 47 p

7 £4.32 + 74 p

8 £3 − £2.30

9 56 p + £2 + 76 p

10 90 p + 55 p + £1.80

● **11** £1.03 − 9 p

● **12** £1.20 + 34 p + 8 p

Exercise 6:7

These questions are all about money.
Make sure you write the answers correctly.

1 Hannah has a £10 note.
She buys a T-shirt that costs £7.20.
How much change does Hannah get?

2 Alan has £2.42 and his brother Michael has £3.28.
How much do the brothers have altogether?

3 Four friends share a prize of £18.
How much does each friend get?

4 Kiwi fruit cost 22 p each.
How much do five kiwi fruit cost?

5 Jason buys a cheese jacket potato and a can of cola for his lunch.
The potato costs £1.25 and the cola costs 35 p.
How much does Jason's lunch cost?

6 Sarah pays 58 p bus fare each day to go to and from school.
How much does Sarah need for bus fares for five days?

7 Melanie is saving up to buy a new pair of jeans.
The jeans cost £22.50. Melanie has saved £14.80.
How much more does Melanie need?

8 A pack of four pizzas costs £5.40.
How much does one pizza cost?

9 One portion of fish and chips is £2.35.
How much do four portions cost?

10 Pritesh uses a £5 note to buy a ring binder costing £1.70.
How much change does Pritesh get?

11 Leroy has six weeks to save for a football shirt.
The shirt costs £19.20.
How much should Leroy save each week?

12 A multipack of eight bags of crisps costs £1.60.
How much does each bag of crisps cost?

13 Katrina buys a melon for £1.25 and a lettuce for 45 p.
How much does Katrina spend altogether?

14 Robert buys a bag of six oranges for £1.20.
How much does one orange cost?

15 Carpet tiles cost £4.95 each.
Mrs Ellis needs 30 carpet tiles for her office.
How much do 30 tiles cost?

16 Jill buys a pencil case for £1.45 and nine coloured pencils at 25 p each.
How much does Jill pay altogether?

17 Alice buys a cup of coffee and a sandwich.
- **a** How much does Alice pay altogether?
- **b** Alice pays with a £5 note.
How much change does Alice get?

MENU	
tea	60 p
coffee	80 p
sandwiches	£1.40
cakes from	90 p

• **18**
- **a** A pack of four chicken portions costs £2.20.
How much does one portion cost?
- **b** Mrs Patel buys a whole chicken for £1.80.
She cuts it into four portions herself.
How much does one of Mrs Patel's chicken portions cost?
- **c** How much does Mrs Patel save on each chicken portion?

3 The calculator

REPLAY

Examples Write these amounts of money correct to the nearest penny.

1 £7.458 **2** £1.3729 **3** £17.025

We need **two** figures after the decimal point.
Look at the **third** figure.
£7.458 is closer to £7.46
£1.3729 is closer to £1.37
£17.025 is halfway, so round up to £17.03

Exercise 6:8

Round these amounts of money correct to the nearest penny.

1	£2.418	**4**	£2.041	**7**	£5.2139	**10**	£12.0471
2	£1.324	**5**	£8.716	**8**	£6.8431	**11**	£5.629
3	£0.615	**6**	£0.125	**9**	£14.5254	• **12**	£3.3666…

Dean finds this very hard.
He can use the calculator to help.

The Fix mode

Press these keys on your calculator: **2nd F** **FSE** **2nd F** **TAB** **2**
The calculator will now round to **2** decimal places.

Dean keys in: **2** **.** **4** **1** **8**

The calculator displays 2.418

Dean presses the **=** key.

The calculator displays 2.42

Use your calculator to check your answers to Exercise **6:8**.

To change the calculator back to normal press these keys

2nd F **FSE** **2nd F** **FSE** **2nd F** **FSE**

Exercise 6:9

Use your calculator to do these questions.
Make sure it is in the correct mode before you start each question.

1 A packet of sausages costs £1.09
There are 8 sausages in the pack.
How much does one sausage cost?

2 Gita has picked 8 kg of plums from her garden.
She is going to sell them at the school Autumn Market.
She puts them into bags. Each bag holds 200 g.
a How many bags can she fill?
b She sells each bag for 45 p.
How much money does she make?

3 A television licence costs £84.50 for 12 months.
How much does the licence cost for one month?

4 Here are the number of school dinners sold in one week.
Monday 431, Tuesday 357, Wednesday 429, Thursday 337, Friday 388
a How many school dinners were sold altogether?
b The total amount of money taken was £1694.30
What is the cost of one school dinner?

- **5** Alan does not have enough money to buy this scarf.
He decides to knit a scarf in the same colours.
He needs 80 stitches on each row.
He works out that he needs to knit 390 rows.

a How many stitches does he have to knit?
b He can only knit 10 stitches every minute.
How many minutes does it take him to knit the scarf?
How many hours is this?
c His mother can knit 40 stitches every minute.
How many hours does his mother take to knit the same scarf?

6 This table shows the attendance at classes in a Leisure Centre for four weeks.

	Week 1	Week 2	Week 3	Week 4
squash	10	8	9	13
badminton	16	19	18	14
aerobics	23	25	21	22

a How many played badminton over the four weeks?
b How many went to classes in week 3?

7 Mary designs and makes jewellery. She sells her jewellery at markets.
The table shows her sales for one week.

	Rings	Earrings	Brooches
Monday	12	16	3
Tuesday	9	21	7
Wednesday	11	19	8
Thursday	8	15	4
Friday	9	23	5
Saturday	29	36	11

a How many rings did she sell during the week?
b How many pieces of jewellery did she sell on Wednesday?
c On what day did she sell 8 brooches?

This is Mary's price list.

ring	£4.50
earrings	£3.25
brooch	£3.75

d Mary wants to work out how much money she took on Monday.
Copy this and fill in the gaps:

Monday

12 rings at £4.50	...
16 earrings at £3.25	...
3 brooches at £3.75	...
Total	

e How much money did she take on Saturday?
Make a table like the one in part **d**.

You can store numbers in a calculator. You use the memory keys.
To store a number in the memory use the **STO** key.

Key in: **5** **STO** **M**

Press **ON/C**. The screen shows 0

Press **RCL** **M**. The screen shows 5

The **RCL** key tells the calculator to show the number stored in the memory. There are three to choose from M, X and Y.

You can add another number to the number stored in memory, M.
You use the **M+** key. This only works with memory M.

Press **ON/C**

Key in: **3** **M+** This adds 3 to the 5 already in the memory.

Press **ON/C**. Press **RCL** **M**. The screen shows 8

The 3 has been added to the 5.

At the beginning of a question you must always clear the memory.
To do this press **ON/C** **STO** **M**

If you now press **RCL** **M** the calculator will show 0. This means that nothing is stored in this memory.

Exercise 6:10

Remember to clear the memory before you start each question.

1 **a** Store the number 6 in the memory by keying in: **6** **STO** **M**

b Clear the screen by pressing **ON/C**
Add 4 to the number stored in the memory by keying in: **4** **M+**

c Clear the screen.

d Press **RCL** **M**
Write down the number on the screen.

2 **a** Store the number 10 in the memory.
b Add 18 to this number using the **M+** button.
c Clear the screen.
d Press **RCL** **M**
Write down the number on the screen.

3 **a** Store the number 26 in the memory.
b Add 75 to the memory.
c Clear the screen.
d Press **RCL** **M**
e Write down the number on the screen.

4 Store 245 in the memory.
Add 39 to it.
Write down the number now stored in the memory.

5 Store the first number in the memory.
Add the second number to it.
Press **RCL** **M** and write down the new number stored in the memory.
a 49 62 **b** 96 67 **c** 396 78 **d** 835 426

6 John has to do some shopping for his dad.
a At the butcher's he buys sausages for £1.38 and a chicken for £2.86
How much does he spend at the butcher's?
Store this number in the memory.
b At the baker's he buys 5 cakes for £1.70
and 2 loaves for £1.46
How much does he spend at the baker's?
Add this number to the memory.

c At the supermarket he buys 3 tins of soup
for £1.23, a packet of ham at £1.45 and
3 peaches for £0.75
How much does he spend at
the supermarket?
Add this number to the memory.
d Press **RCL** **M**. Write down the number on the screen.
What does this number tell you?
e Switch off the calculator.
Now switch it on again.
Check to see if there is a number in the memory.
Is it the same number as in part **d**?

7 Copy this shopping bill.
Work out the cost of the first item.
Store this in the memory.
Write down the cost in the last column.

Add the cost of the other items to the memory as you work out each line.
Use the number stored in the memory to fill in the TOTAL COST at the end.

Item	Number bought	Cost
bicycle tyres	2 at £7.24 each	
speedometer	1 at £23.50	
spokes	12 at 18 p each	
paint	1 tin at £3.25	
	TOTAL COST	

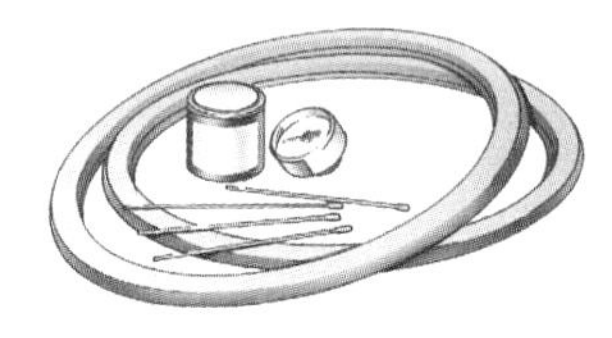

8 Copy this shopping bill.
Work out the cost of the first item.
Store this in the memory.
Write down the cost in the last column.

Add the cost of the other items to the memory as you work out each line.
Use the number stored in the memory to fill in the TOTAL COST at the end.

Item	Number bought	Cost
melons	2 at £1.75 each	
oranges	5 at 16 p each	
potatoes	3 kg at 32 p per kg	
carrots	2 packs at 55 p per pack	
lettuce	1 tin at 80 p	
	TOTAL COST	

1 Which temperature is lower?

a −7 °C or 14 °C **b** 0 °C or −9 °C **c** −6 °C or −7 °C

2 Which temperature is higher?

a −4 °C or 2 °C **b** −5 °C or 0 °C **c** −23 °C or −24 °C

3 Put these temperatures in order, lowest first.

a 4 °C, −9 °C, −3 °C, 3 °C
b 15 °C, −18 °C, 0 °C, −13 °C, 21 °C
c −7 °C, −1 °C, −4 °C, 11 °C, 0 °C, 7 °C

4 Find the rule for each number pattern.
Write down the next two terms.

a 4, 3, 2, 1, …, …
b 8, 4, 0, −4, …, …
c 19, 13, 7, 1, …, …
d 21, 12, 3, −6, …, …

5 Replace ? with $<$ or $>$

a 7 °C ? 1 °C
b 0 °C ? −6 °C
c −1 °C ? 2 °C
d 10 °C ? −9 °C
e −2 °C ? −3 °C
f −38 °C ? −35 °C

6 The picture shows the level indicator of a river.
On Monday the level of the water was 3 metres.
On Thursday the level of the water was −2 metres.

a Did the level of the water go up or down?
b By how much did it change?
c Between Thursday and Saturday the level went up by 3 metres.
What was the new level?

7 Write these coins in figures.
Then add them up.

a 1 fifty pence, 2 twenty pence, 3 ten pence
b 3 twenty pence, 1 ten pence, 4 five pence
c 1 fifty pence, 4 ten pence, 2 five pence, 2 two pence
d 3 ten pence, 6 five pence, 3 two pence
e 1 fifty pence, 2 ten pence, 3 five pence

8 Each of these is paid with a 50 p coin.
Find the change.

a 34 p **b** 39 p **c** 13 p **d** 23 p

9 Each of these is paid with a £1 coin.
Find the change.

a 17 p **b** 84 p **c** 88 p **d** 47 p

10 Write the answers with two figures after the decimal point.

a £8.45 × 4 **c** £2.27 − £1.87
b £2.34 + £3.16 **d** £4 ÷ 5

11 Use your calculator to round these sums of money to the nearest penny.

a £4.849 **c** £8.536 **e** £8.986
b £27.163 **d** £28.082 **f** £0.475

12 Write these amounts of money correctly.

a £1.8 **c** £12.7 **e** £6.34p **g** p86
b £4.75p **d** £3.5 **f** £10.0 **h** £5.46p

13 Work out the answers to these.

a £4.25 + 85p + £1.34 **d** £1.05 − 67p
b £7.30 − 95p **e** £3 + 65p + £2.46
c £5.32 + £4 + 76p **f** £5 − 75p

14 Store the first number in the memory.
Add the second number to it.
Press **RCL** **M** and write down the new number stored in the memory.

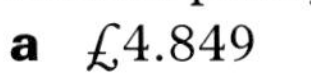

a 37 92 **b** 79 37 **c** 67 385 **d** 96 529

15 The table shows the charges at Stanthorne Leisure centre.

	Adults	Children
gym	£1.50	£0.50
squash	£2.75	£1.50
aerobics	£1.60	£0.80
badminton	£2.00	£1.00
swimming	£1.75	£1.25

Write down the cost for:

a 3 adults and 2 children to go swimming
b 4 children to play badminton
c 2 adults to play squash
d 5 adults to use the gym

16 Rani is shopping for her birthday party.

a At the supermarket she buys sausage rolls for £3.54 and crisps for £2.45.
How much does she spend at the supermarket?
Store this number in the memory of your calculator.

b At the baker's she buys 24 bread rolls for £2.88 and 3 cakes at £1.99 each.
How much does she spend at the baker's?
Add this number to the memory.

c At the toy shop she buys 3 packets of balloons for £1.35 and 2 boxes of party poppers at 99 p each.
How much does she spend at the toy shop?
Add this number to the memory.

d Which key do you press to tell the calculator to show the number stored in the memory?

e Write down the number stored in the memory.
What does this number tell you?

17 Copy this shopping bill.
Work out the cost of the first item.
Store this in the memory. Write down the cost in the last column.

Add the cost of the other items to the memory as you work out each line.
Use the number stored in the memory to fill in the TOTAL COST at the end.

Item	Number bought	Cost
tins of beans	2 at 26 p each	
packets of tea	2 at £1.89 each	
peaches	6 at 22 p each	
chicken	1 at £3.25	
bread	2 loaves at 56 p	
	TOTAL COST	

1 The calculator will round to any number of decimal places using the Fix mode. Set Fix mode by pressing **2nd F** **FSE** .

For **one** decimal place press:	**2nd F** **TAB** **1**
For **two** decimal places press:	**2nd F** **TAB** **2**
For **three** decimal places press:	**2nd F** **TAB** **3**
For **four** decimal places press:	**2nd F** **TAB** **4**
For the nearest whole number press:	**2nd F** **TAB** **0**

Remember: to change the calculator back to normal press

2nd **FSE** **2nd** **FSE** **2nd** **FSE**

a Set your calculator to 3 decimal places.
Round these numbers to 3 decimal places.
3.5694 6.0287 46.5589 30.3521 9.75853

b Set your calculator to 1 decimal place.
Round these numbers to 1 decimal place.
35.583 7.3495 21.947 8.091 50.607

c Set your calculator to 0 decimal places.
Round these numbers to the nearest whole number.
61.93 204.488 19.093 39.51 82.902

2 The table shows the tickets sold for a school play.

	Wednesday	Thursday	Friday	Saturday
adults £5	132	150	107	115
children £2.50	34	41	73	82
pensioners £1	36	22	18	13

a How many people attended the play on each night?
b How much money was taken on Wednesday night?
c How many adults saw the play during the week?
d What was the total amount of money taken from ticket sales?

3 On a quiz show contestants score 2 points for a correct answer. They lose a point for a wrong answer.
What is the final score for:
a 9 correct and 2 wrong answers?
b 4 correct and 8 wrong answers?
c 2 correct and 11 wrong answers?
In the same quiz these contestants all scored 11 points.
d Mark gave 5 wrong answers.
How many questions did he answer correctly?
e Jamila gave 7 correct answers.
How many questions did she get wrong?
f Luke got the same number of correct and wrong answers.
How many questions did he answer?

- **Negative** numbers — Numbers with minus signs in front are called **negative** numbers.

  Positive numbers — Other numbers except nought are **positive**. Positive numbers are sometimes written with a plus sign in front. Nought is not positive or negative.

  Examples — Negative numbers -2, -5, -32.
  Positive numbers 7, +3, 25.

- **Less than <**
  Greater than > — We often use the signs < and > with numbers.
  < means **'less than'** > means **'greater than'**

  Examples — $-5\,°C < -2\,°C$ means $-5\,°C$ is less than $-2\,°C$
  $2\,°C > -4\,°C$ means $2\,°C$ is greater than $-4\,°C$

- **Shopkeepers' addition**

  Example — Find the change when 16 p is paid using a 50 p coin.

  Count on four units from 16 p to get to 20 p 17, 18, 19, 20
  Count on three tens from 20 p to get to 50 p 30, 40, 50

  The change is 34 p

- *Examples*

  1 £5.35 × 4
  On a calculator we get the display 21.4
  We need two figures after the decimal point.
  Answer £21.40

  2 John has £1.35. His sister Sally has 84 p.
  How much do they have altogether?

  84 p is the same as £0.84
  £1.35 + £0.84 = £2.19

- **The Fix mode** — Press these keys on your calculator.
  2nd **FSE** **2nd F** **TAB** **2**
  The calculator will now round to **2** decimal places.

- **Memory** — Use the keys **STO** **RCL** **M** to store and recall numbers in the memory of the calculator.
  The number stays in the memory even when the calculator is switched off.

6 TEST YOURSELF

1 Put these temperatures in order, lowest first.
6 °C, −5 °C, −3 °C, 2 °C, 1 °C, −1 °C, 0 °C

2 Replace ? with $<$ or $>$
a 5 °C ? 3 °C **b** −6 °C ? −8 °C **c** −4 °C ? 0 °C

3 The temperature in the desert at night is −9 °C.
During the day it reaches 43 °C.
How many degrees does the temperature rise?

4 Write these coins in figures.
Then add them up.
1 fifty pence, 2 twenty pence, 3 ten pence, 1 five pence

5 Each of these is paid with a £1 coin.
Find the change.
a 40 p **b** 87 p **c** 24 p

6 Work out the answers to these.
a £5.72 + 69 p **c** £6.80 − £2.07
b 85 p + £4 + 78 p **d** £5 − 69 p

7 Judith has £7.48 in her Post Office account.
She pays in another £4.55.
How much does she now have in the account?

8 Tristan got £12 for his birthday.
He spent £5.75 on a calculator.
How much does he have left?

9 Use a calculator to round these to the nearest penny.
a £4.862 **b** £6.389 **c** £0.306

10 The insurance for Gavin's car is £452 for the year.
How much is this per month?
Give your answer correct to the nearest penny.

11 Copy this shopping bill.
Work out the cost of the first item.
Store the cost of the first item in the memory of your calculator.
Add the cost of the other items to the memory as you work out each line.
Use the number stored in the memory to fill in the TOTAL COST at the end.

Item	Number bought	Cost
pencils ruler files	5 at 38 p each 1 at 55 p 3 at £1.45 each	
	TOTAL COST	

7 Angles

CORE

QUESTIONS
EXTENSION
SUMMARY
TEST YOURSELF

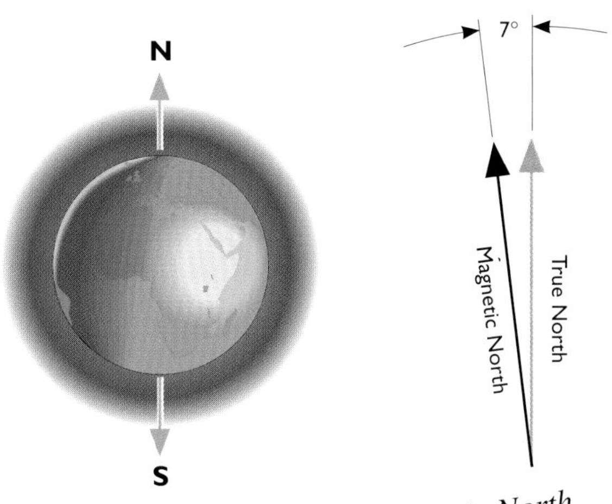

Compass needles point to *magnetic North*. This is slightly different from true North. Maps often have two arrows for North. One arrow is for true North and one is for magnetic North. Magnetic North should have a date by it because it varies from year to year! The angle between true North and magnetic North is around 7°.

1 ◀◀REPLAY▶

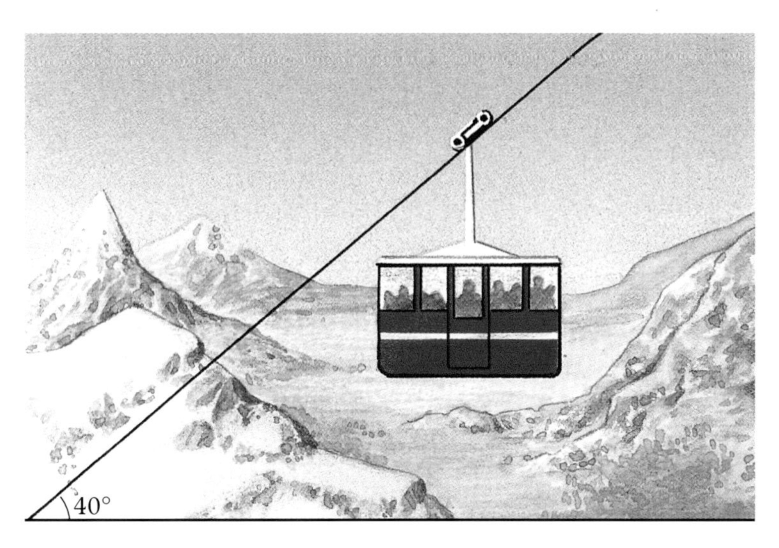

The cable car takes tourists up and down the mountain.
The cable is at an angle of 40° with the horizontal. It is dangerous for this angle to be too large.

Degree

We use degrees (written °) to measure angles.

Right angle
90°

Straight line
180°

Full turn
360°

Acute
Obtuse
Reflex

Acute angle
less than 90°

Obtuse angle
between 90° and 180°

Reflex angle
between 180° and 360°

Exercise 7:1

1 Write down the angles that are:

a straight lines **c** acute angles **e** reflex angles
b right angles **d** obtuse angles

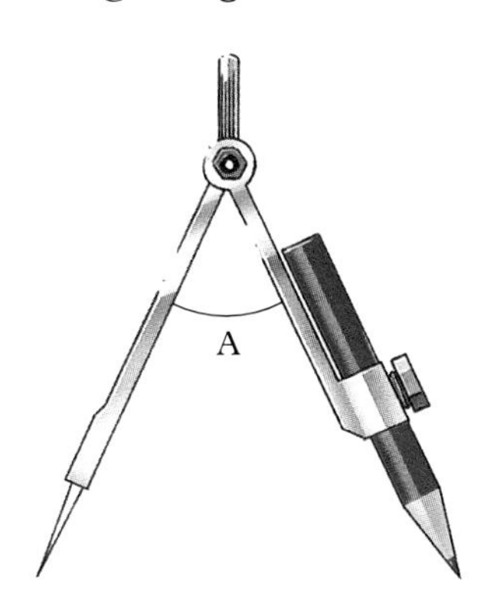

A pair of compasses

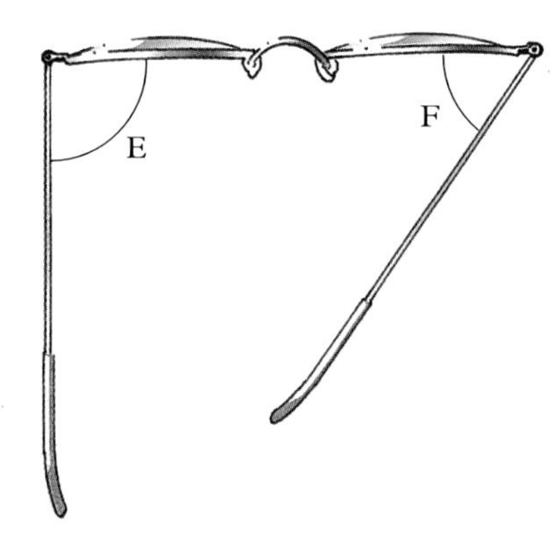

A pair of glasses

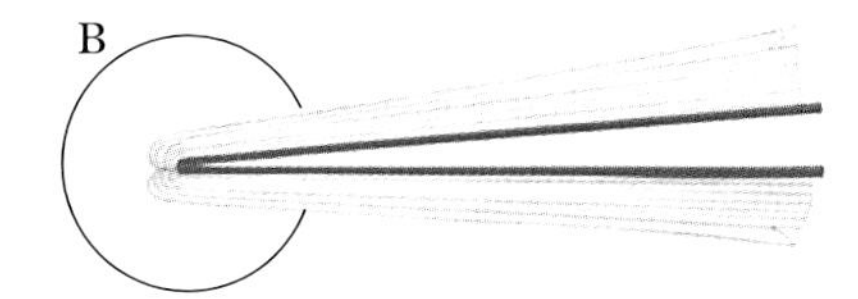

A book folded back on itself

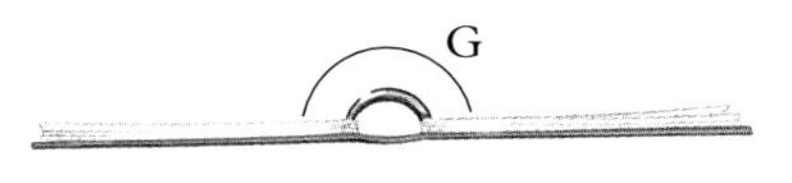

A ring binder open on a table

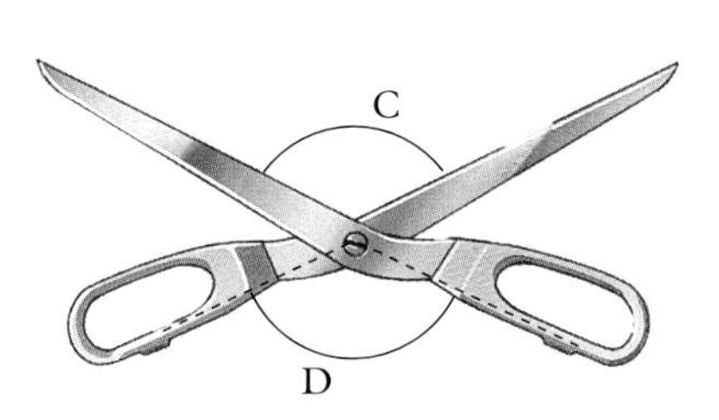

A pair of scissors

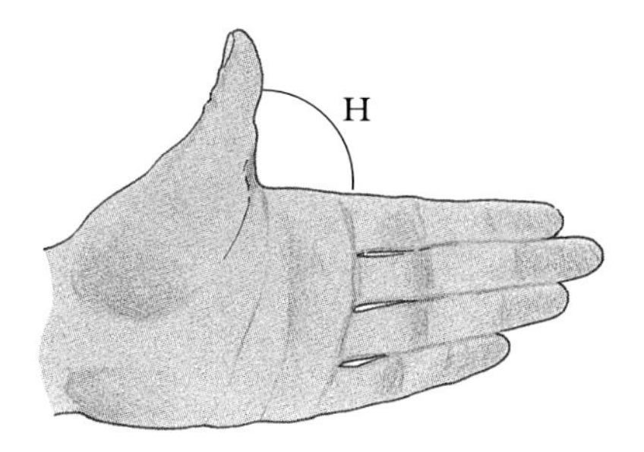

An outstretched thumb

2 Look at the angle in the cable car picture.
What type of angle is it?

• **3** Write down the name of each of these angles.
Choose from:
straight line, acute angle, reflex angle, right angle, obtuse angle

a 30° **c** 270° **e** 45° **g** 320° **i** 116°
b 125° **d** 180° **f** 90° **h** 170° **j** 6°

Exercise 7:2

1 Take a piece of rough paper.
  a Fold it to make a straight line.
  b Fold it again to make a right angle.
  Keep your right angle to use in the next question.

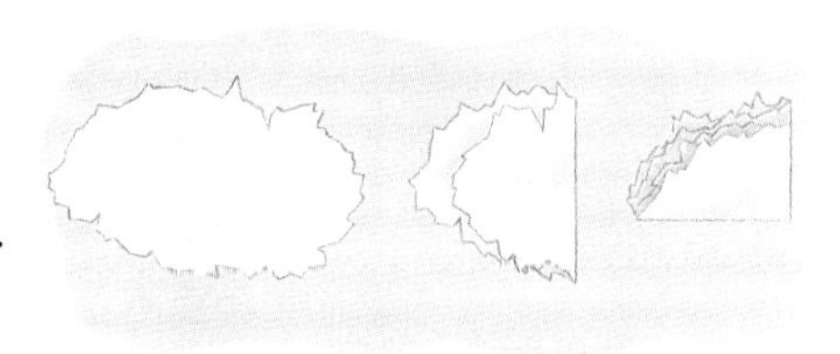

Example Estimate the sizes of these angles.

Fold 90° in half to get 45°

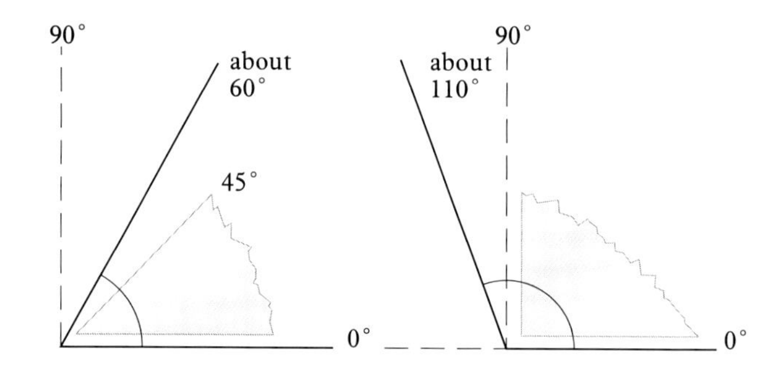

---

2 Estimate the size in degrees of each of these angles.
Use your folded right angle to help you.
Copy this table and fill in your estimates.
You will need the 'Actual' column for question **3**.

	Estimate	Actual
a		
b		
c		
d		
e		
f		
g		
h		

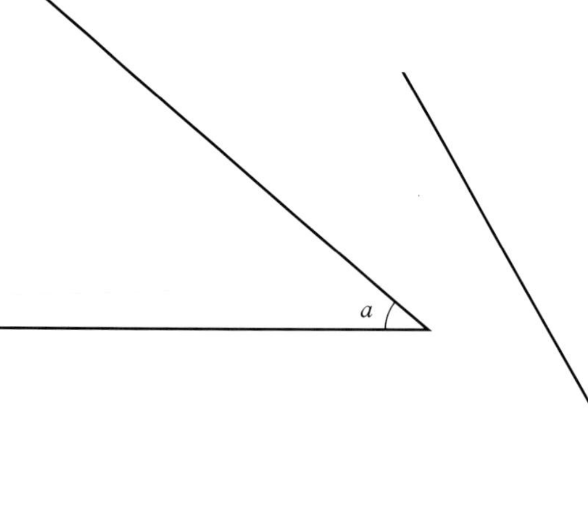

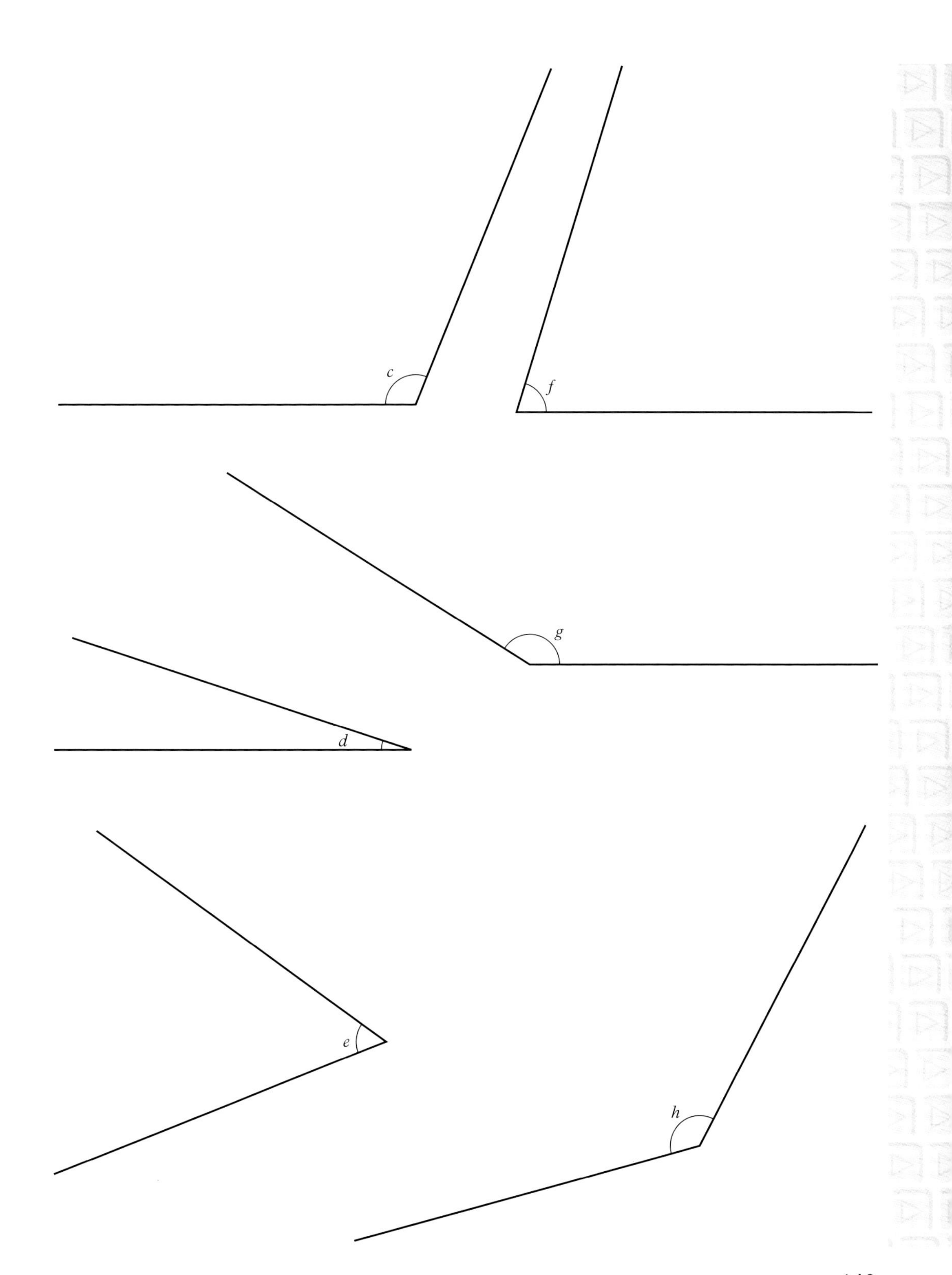
c
f
g
d
e
h

3 Use your protractor or angle measurer to measure the angles in question **2**.
Write your answers in the 'Actual' column in your table.

4 Use your protractor or angle measurer to draw these angles.
Label each angle like this:

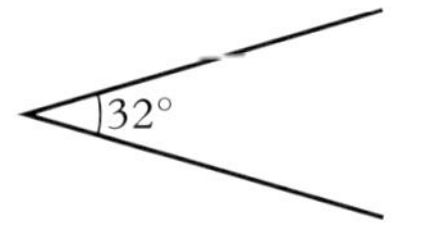

a	50°	**c**	120°	**e**	67°	**g**	113°	**i**	18°
b	35°	**d**	165°	**f**	42°	**h**	154°	**j**	96°

Examples

Calculate the angles marked with letters.

1 **Angles on a straight line** add up to 180°
$a = 180° - 50°$
$a = 130°$

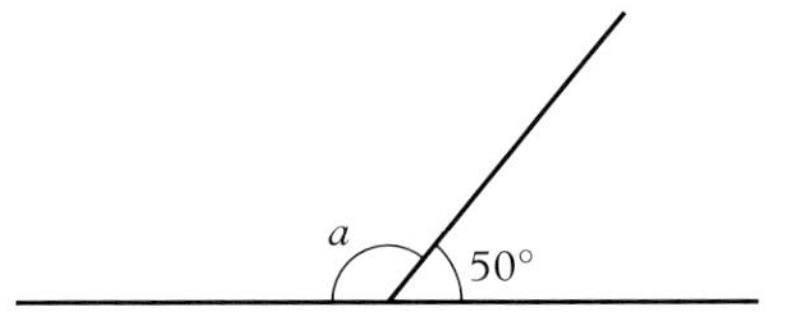

2 **Angles at a point** add up to 360°
$b = 360° - 330°$
$b = 30°$

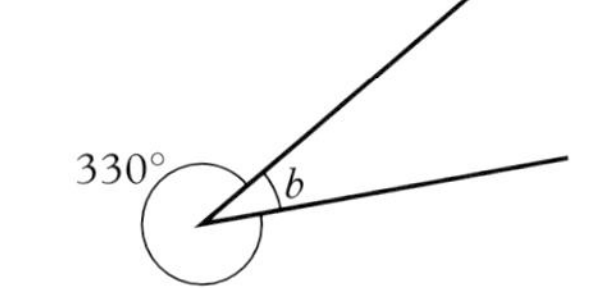

Exercise 7:3

Calculate the angles marked with letters.

1

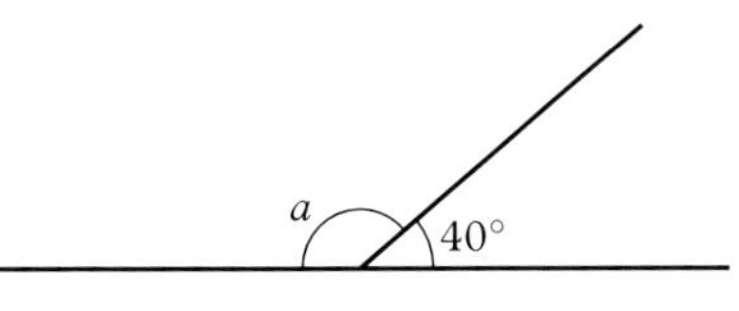

2

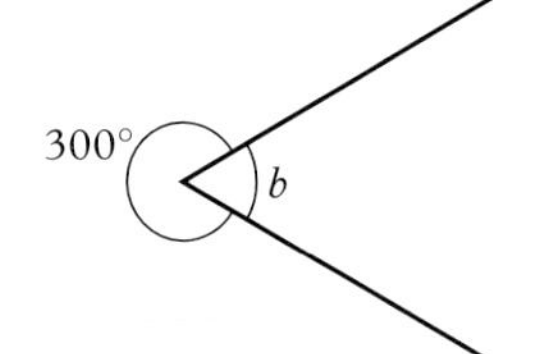

3

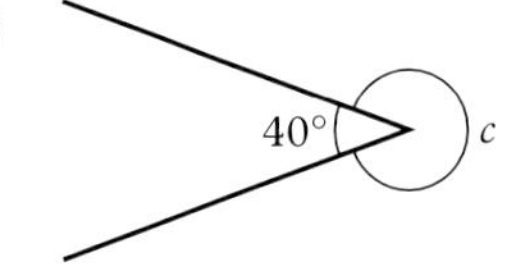

4

5

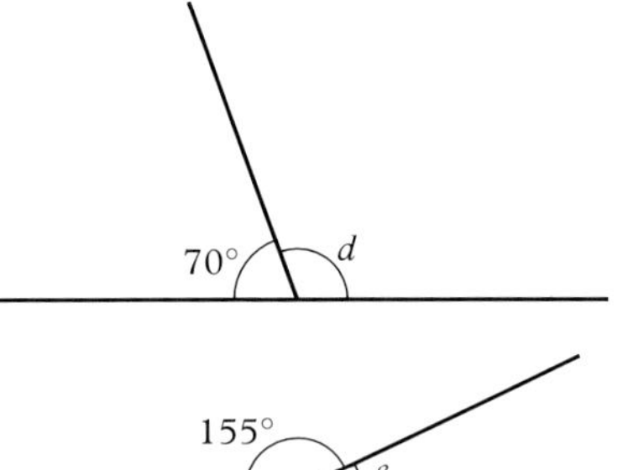

6

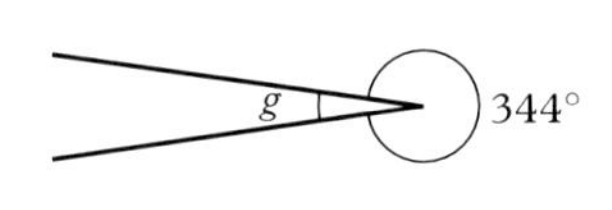

7

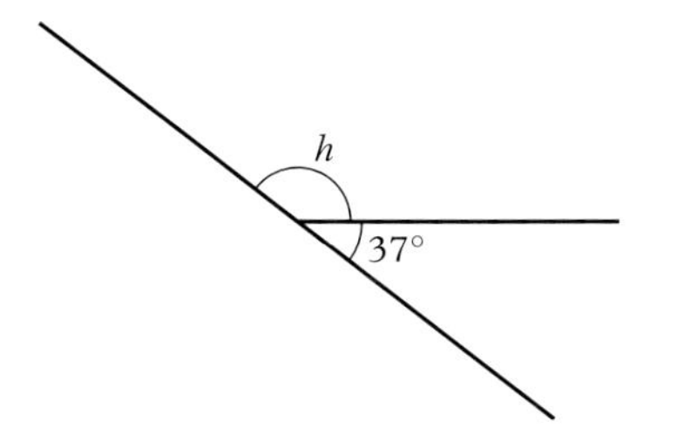

● **9**

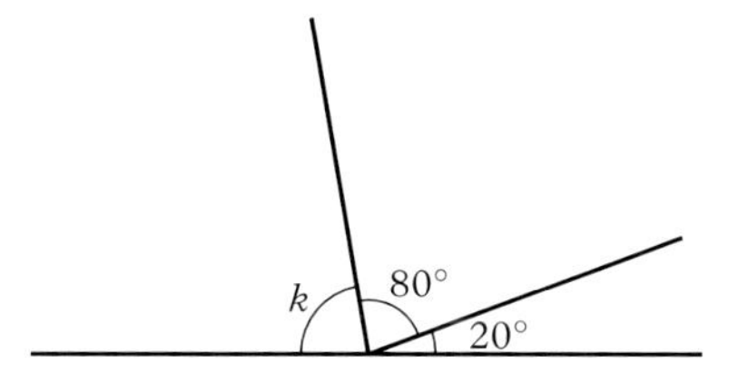

8

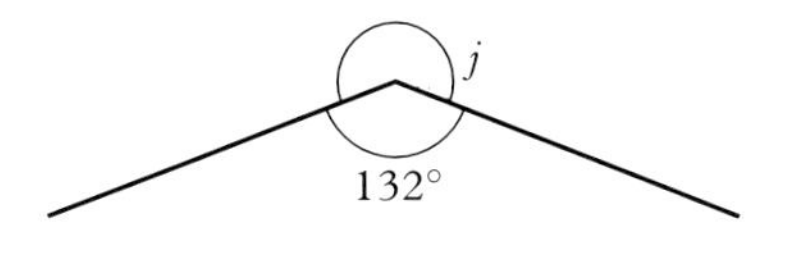

● **10**

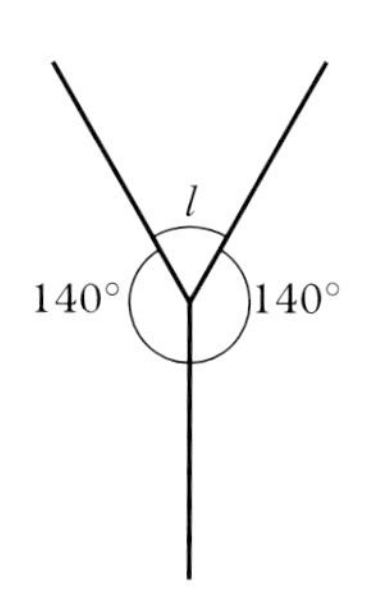

Exercise 7:4

Measure each angle of these triangles.
Measure each side.

1 Copy this list for triangle ABC.
Fill in the gaps.

$\angle A = \ldots°$ AB = … cm
$\angle B = \ldots°$ BC = … cm
$\angle C = \ldots°$ AC = … cm
Total = …°

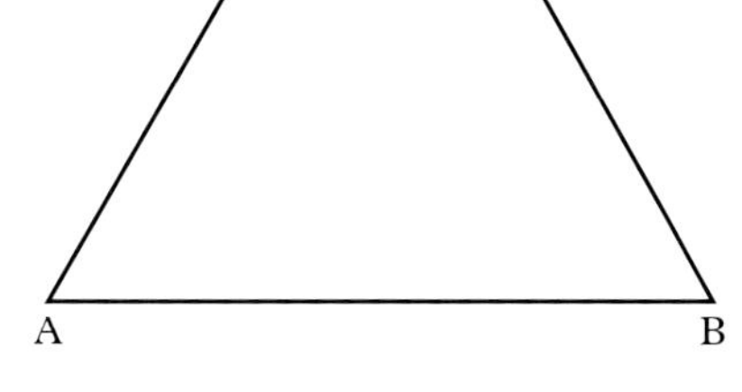

2 Copy this list for triangle DEF.
Fill in the gaps.

$\angle D = \ldots°$ DE = … cm
$\angle E = \ldots°$ EF = … cm
$\angle F = \ldots°$ DF = … cm
Total = …°

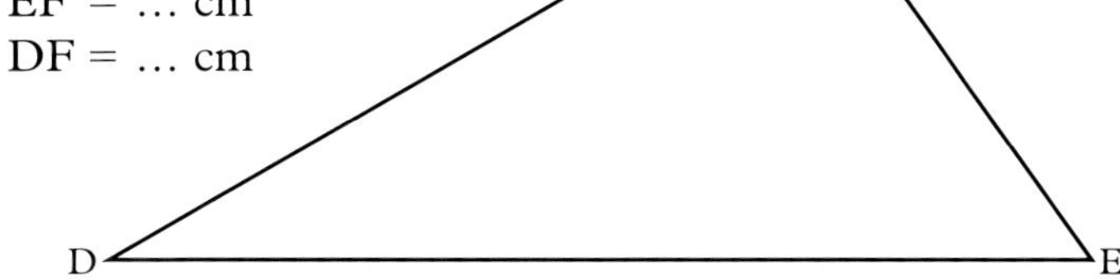

3 Copy this list for triangle GHI.
Fill in the gaps.

$\angle G = \ldots°$ GH = … cm
$\angle H = \ldots°$ HI = … cm
$\angle I = \ldots°$ GI = … cm
Total = …°

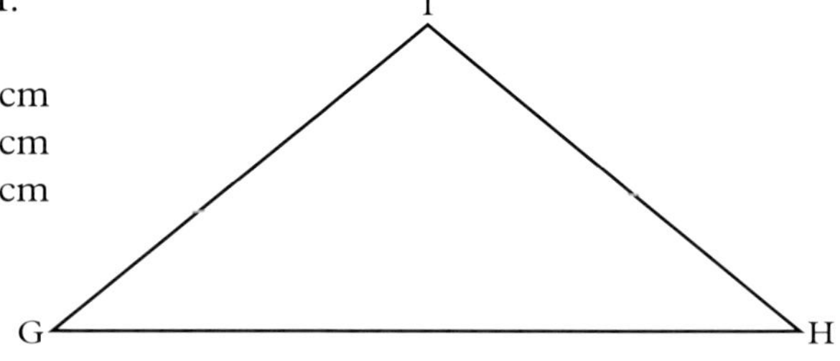

4 Look at the totals of the angles for questions **1–3**.
Write down what you notice.

● **5** **a** An equilateral triangle has three equal sides and three equal angles.
Which of the three triangles is equilateral?
b An isosceles triangle has two equal sides and two equal angles.
Which of the three triangles is isosceles?
c A scalene triangle has no equal sides and no equal angles.
Which of the three triangles is scalene?

Example Calculate angle c.

The angles of a triangle add up to 180°

$c = 180° - 30° - 40°$

$c = 110°$

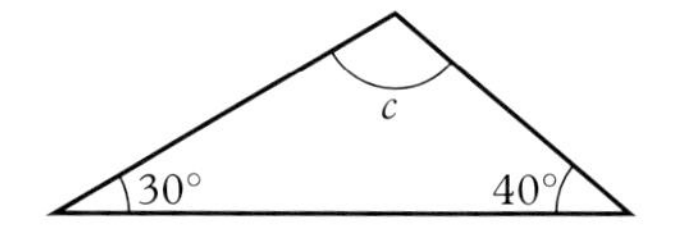

Exercise 7:5

Calculate the angles marked with letters.

1

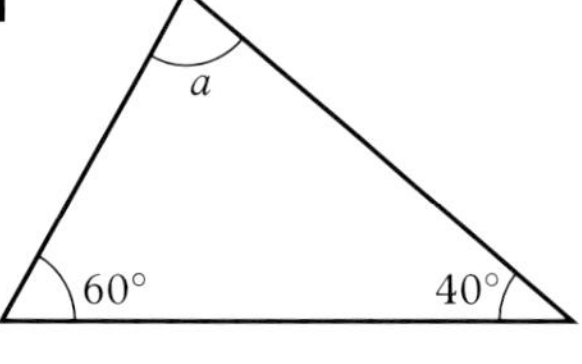

2

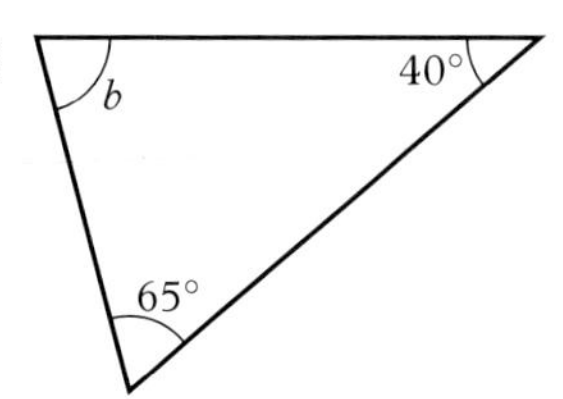

3

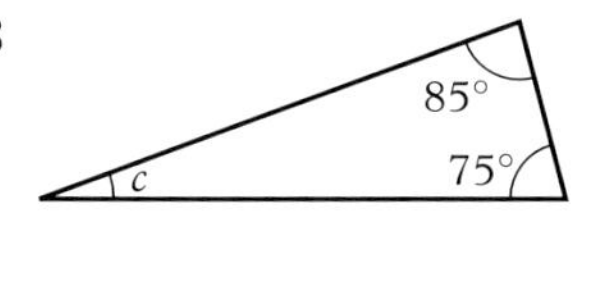

4

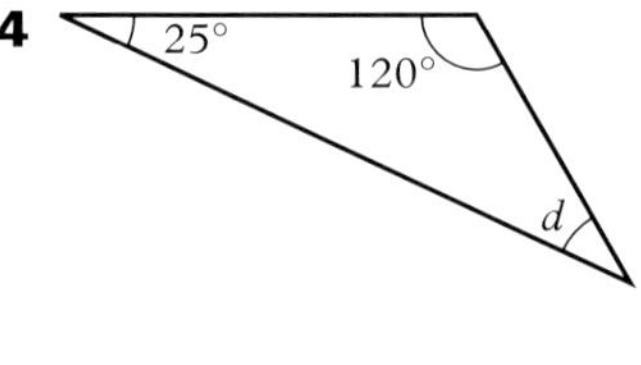

5

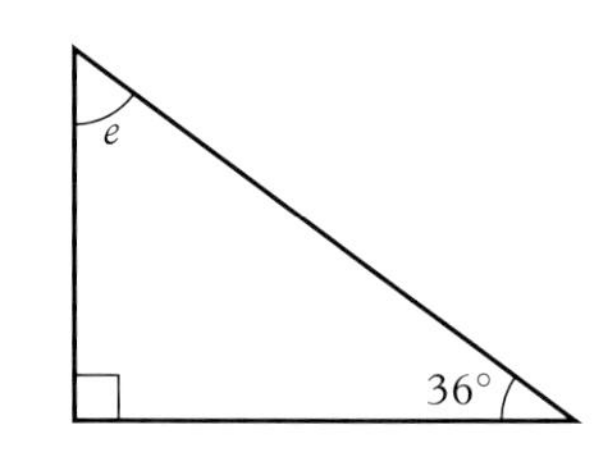

6

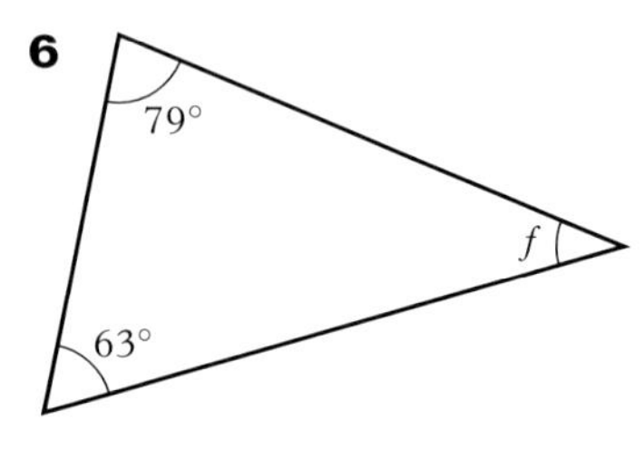

2 Parallel lines

Pairs of railway lines are parallel.
The two tracks on a railway line never meet. They always stay the same distance apart.

Different pairs of railway lines can cross. Sometimes a train can change from one pair of lines to another.
A system of moveable parts of lines is used. These are called points.

REPLAY

Examples

Parallel lines on diagrams are shown with arrows.

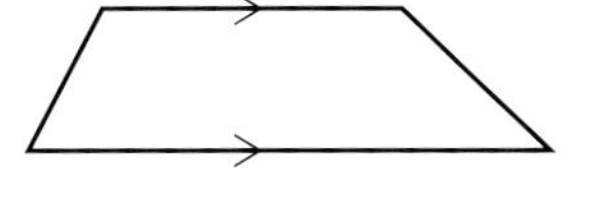

Two pairs of parallel lines need extra arrows.

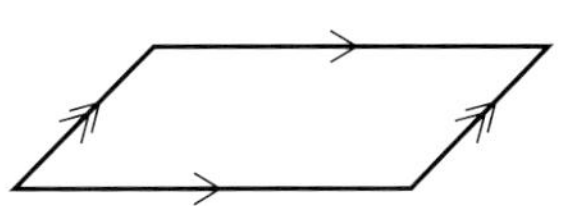

Exercise 7:6

1 a Copy these special quadrilaterals.

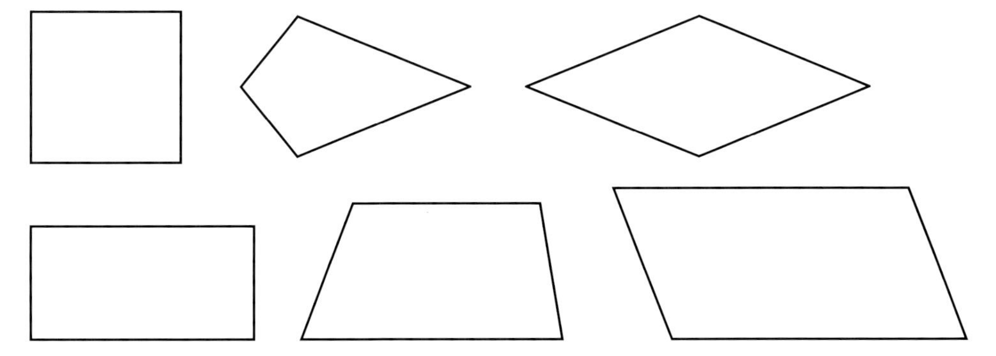

b Mark pairs of parallel sides with arrows like the examples.

c Label each quadrilateral with its name.
Choose from:
square, rectangle, rhombus, parallelogram, kite, trapezium.

Intersecting lines

Lines that cross are called **intersecting lines**.

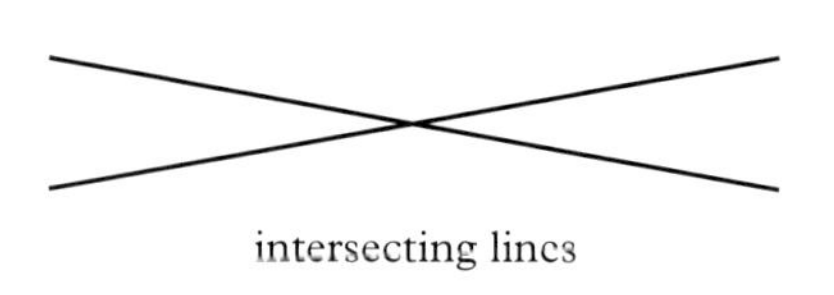

Exercise 7:7

1 **a** Draw a pair of intersecting lines like this.
b Measure and label all four of your angles.
Make your lines longer if you need to.
Turn your book round to help you.

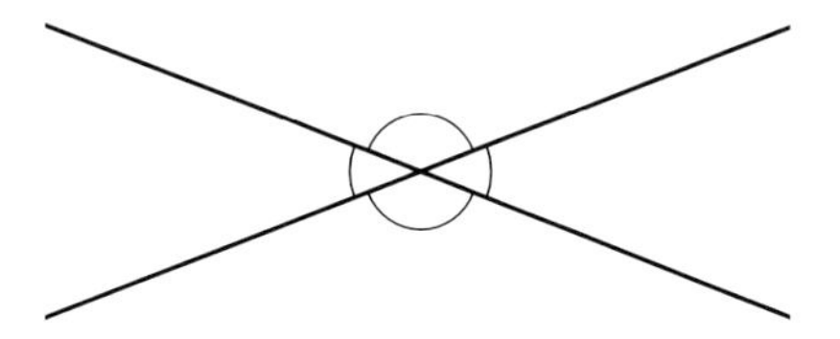

2 Do question **1** two more times.
Draw each pair of intersecting lines at a different angle.

3 Look at the angles you have measured.
Copy and fill in:
.... angles made by .... lines are equal.
Choose from: intersecting, opposite.

4 Draw another pair of intersecting lines.
Colour the pair of equal obtuse angles red.
Colour the pair of equal acute angles blue.

Example

Find the angles marked with letters.

p is opposite 120°
q is opposite 60°
$p = 120°$ $q = 60°$

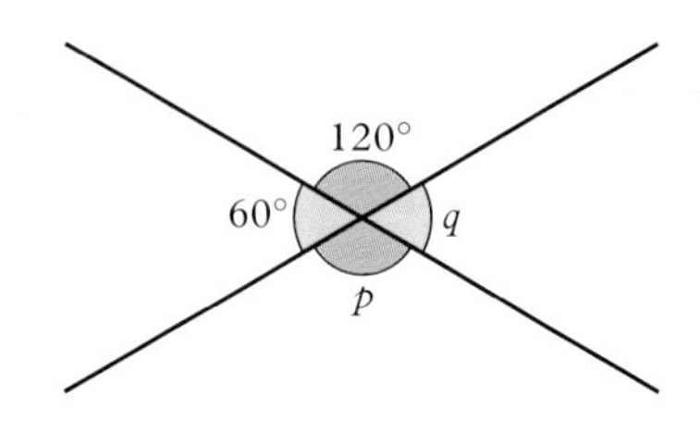

Exercise 7:8

Find the angles marked with letters.

1

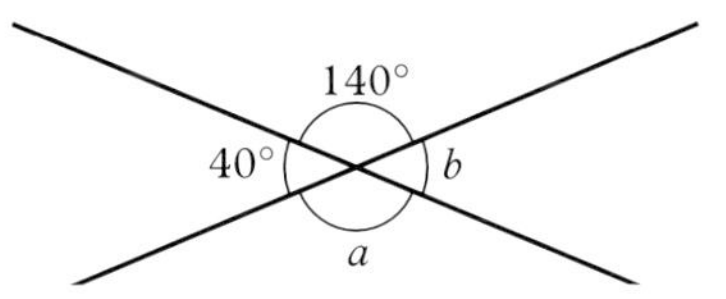

2

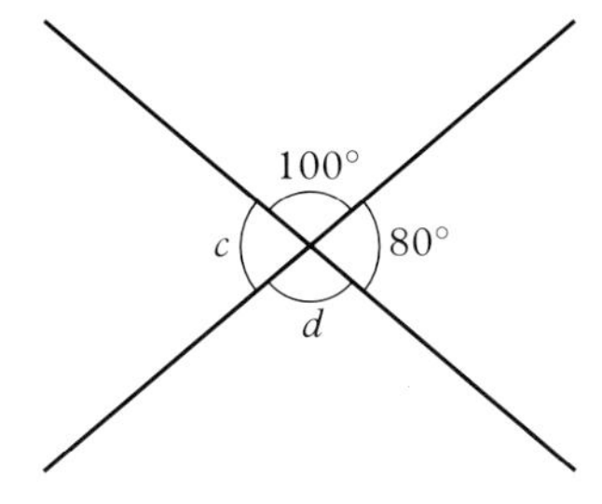

3

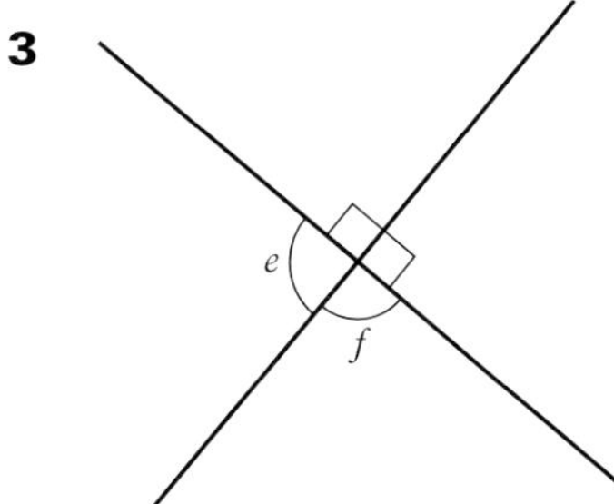

4

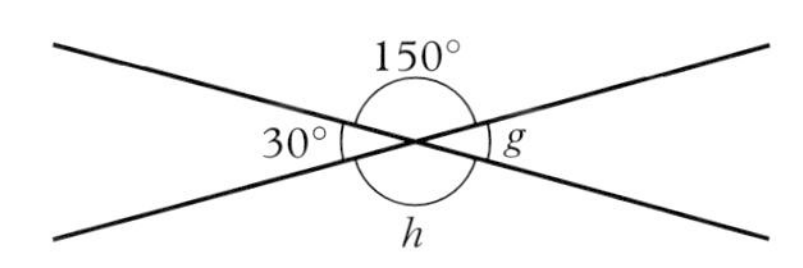

5

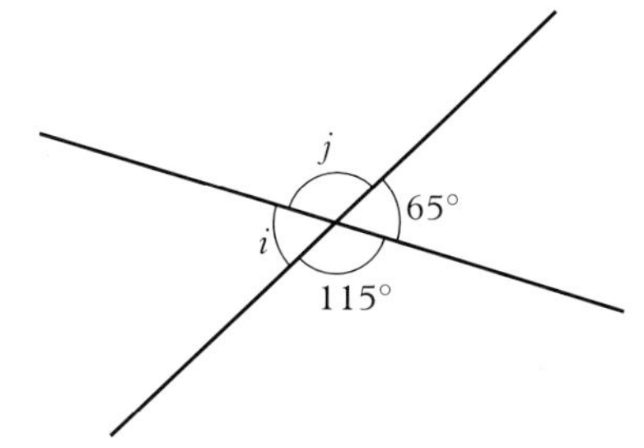

6

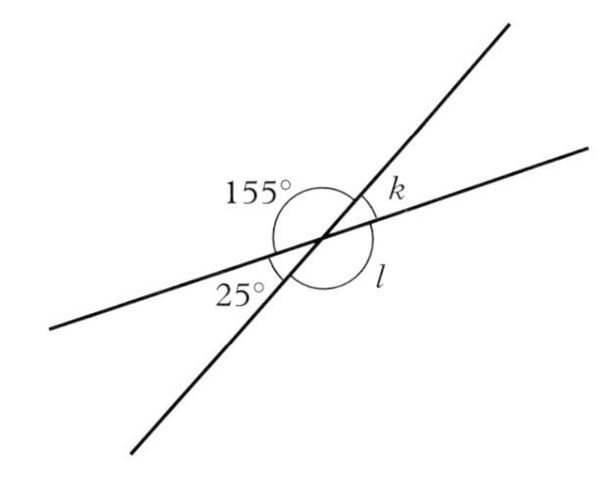

Exercise 7:9

1 **a** Draw a pair of parallel lines. Mark them with arrows.
b Draw a line intersecting both of your parallel lines.
c Measure and label all eight angles.

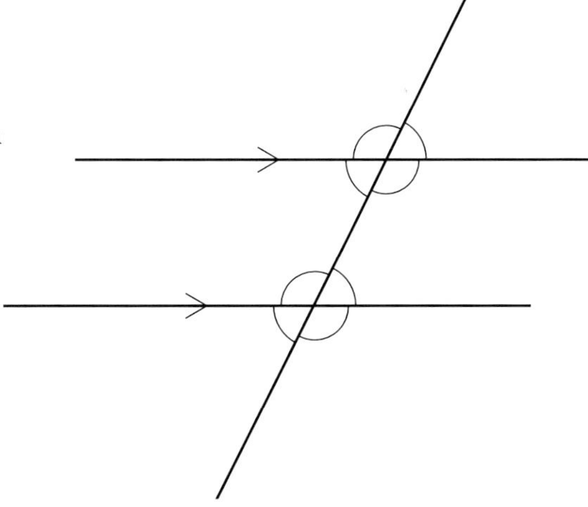

2 **a** Draw another pair of parallel lines.
Mark them with arrows.
b Draw a line intersecting both of your parallel lines at a different angle.
c Measure and label all eight angles.

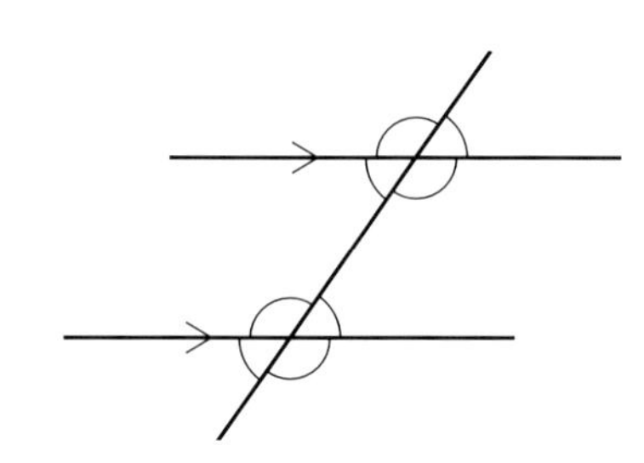

3 **a** Look at the angles you have measured.
What do you notice?
b Copy the diagram.
Colour the four equal obtuse angles red.
Colour the four equal acute angles blue.

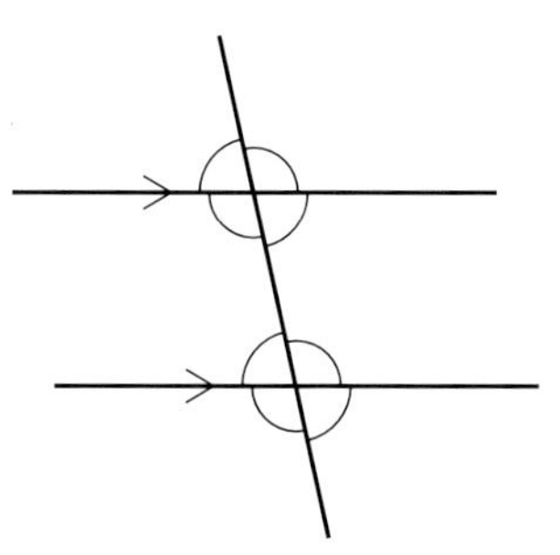

4 Copy the diagram.
Colour the four equal obtuse angles orange.
Colour the four equal acute angles green.

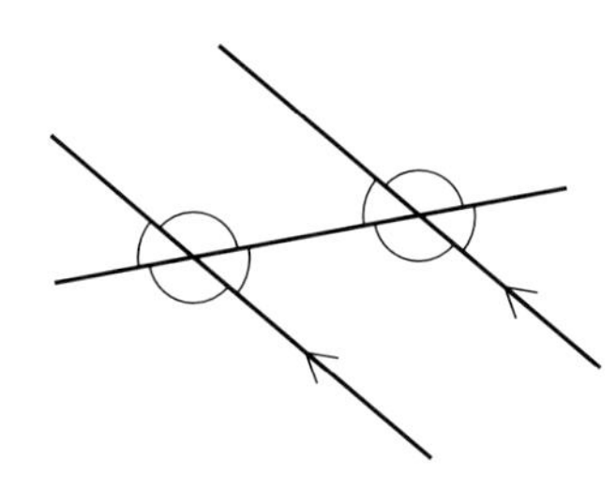

● **5** Copy the diagram.
Choose two colours.
Use them to colour equal angles.

Example Find the angles marked with letters.

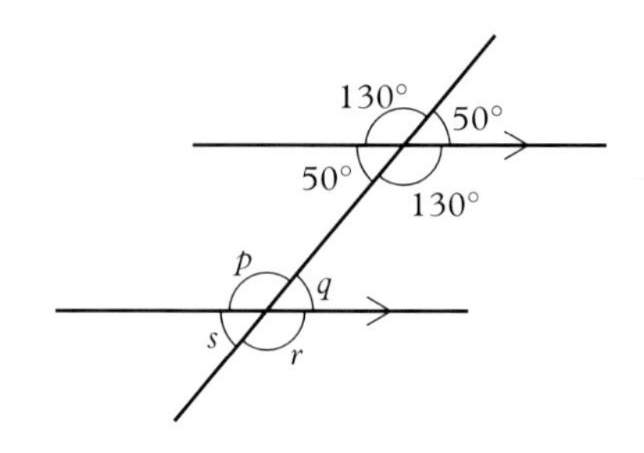

The 'bottom' set of four angles is the same as the 'top' set.
$p = 130°$ and $r = 130°$
$q = 50°$ and $s = 50°$

Exercise 7:10

Find the angles marked with letters.

1

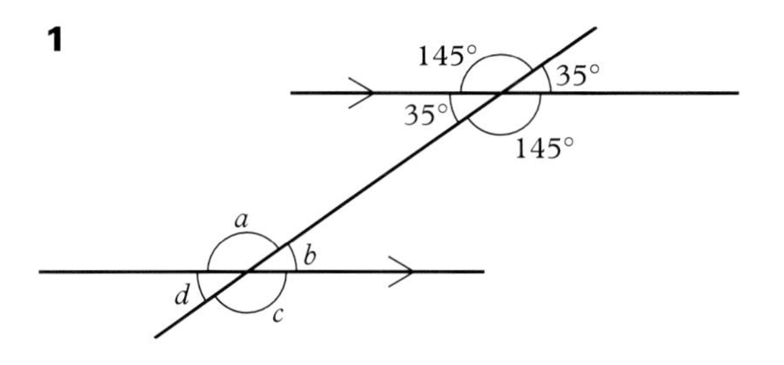

2

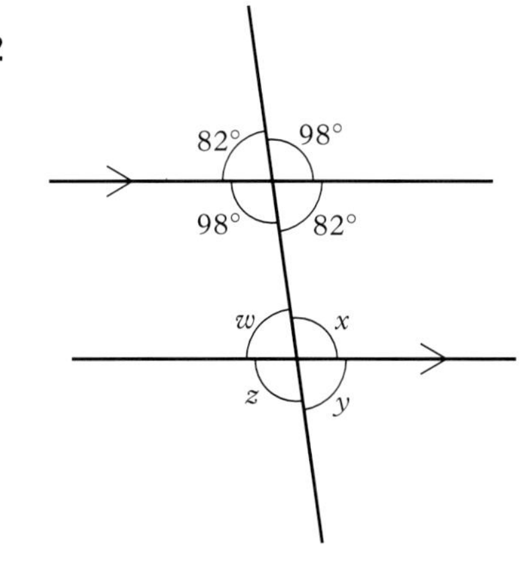

3

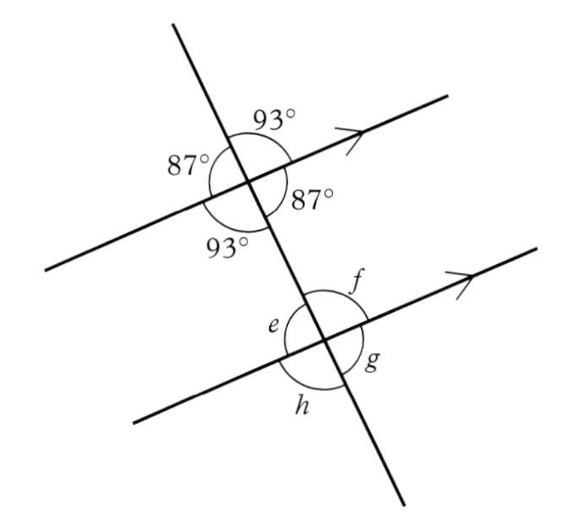

4

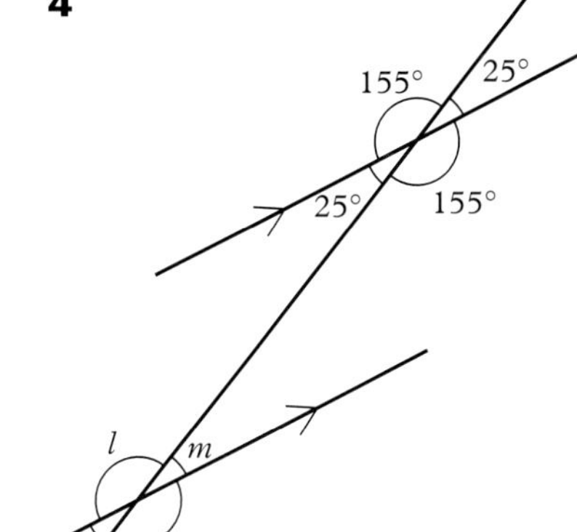

5

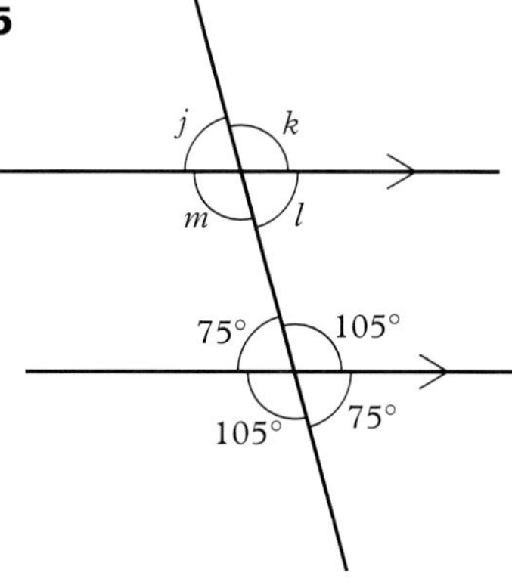

● **6**

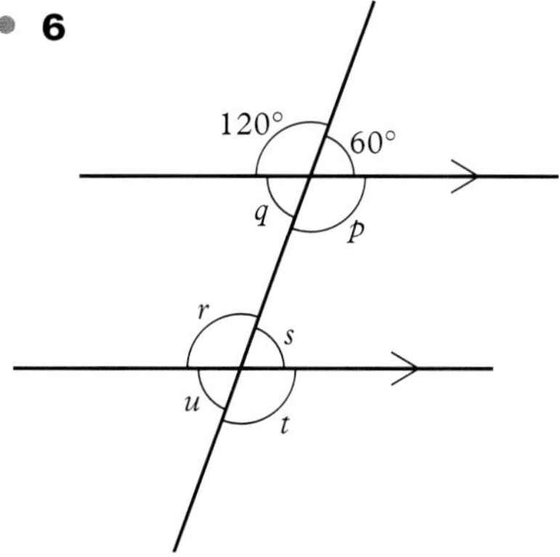

3 Polygons

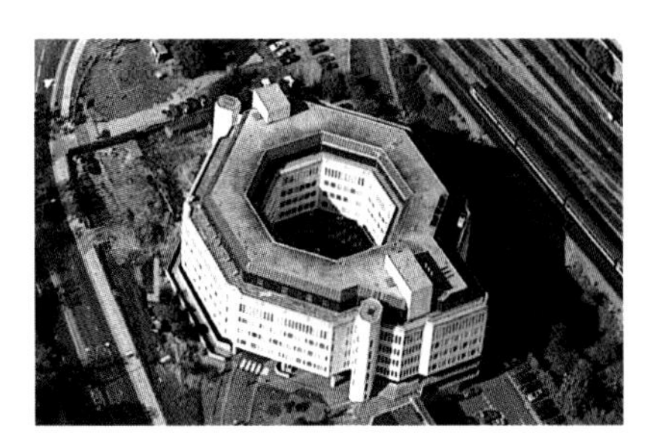

Most buildings are rectangular. Sometimes buildings use a different polygon in their shape. Can you see why this building is called the Octagon?

Polygon

A **polygon** is a shape with straight sides.

Number of sides	Name of polygon
3	triangle
4	quadrilateral
5	pentagon
6	hexagon
8	octagon

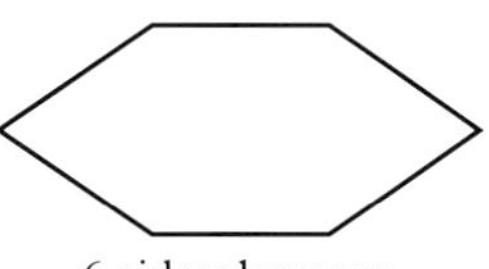

6 sides: hexagon

Regular polygon

Regular polygons have all their sides the same length. Also all the angles of a regular polygon are equal.

Equilateral triangles and squares are regular polygons.

a regular pentagon

Exercise 7:11

1

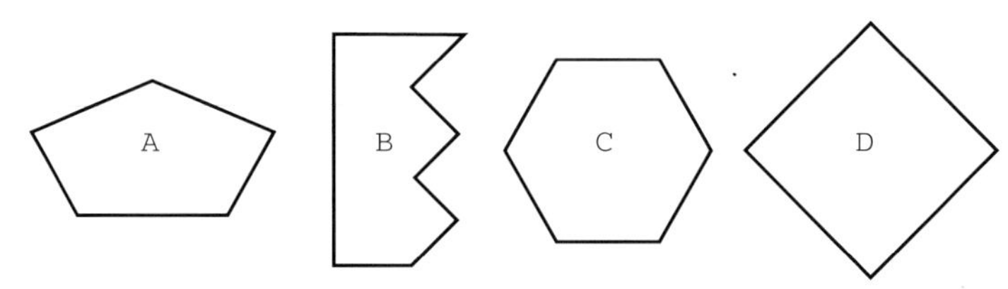

a Write down the names of these polygons.
b Which of the polygons are regular?

You need some paper fasteners and some geostrips for these questions.

2 **a** Choose three geostrips that are the same length.
Make a triangle using the strips and the paper fasteners.
You have made a regular polygon (an equilateral triangle).

b Can you change the shape of the triangle without undoing the paper fasteners?

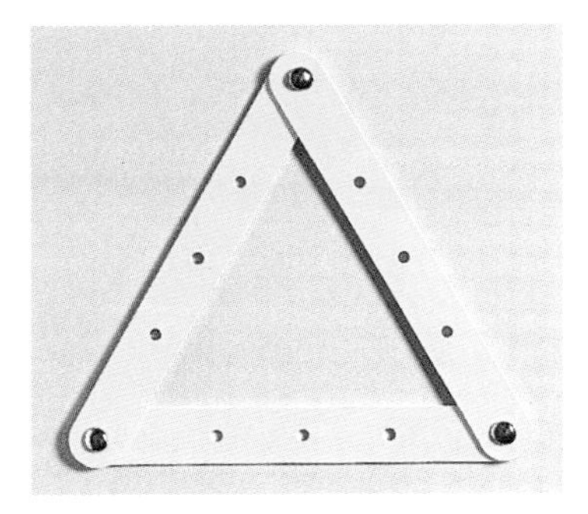

3 **a** Choose four geostrips that are the same length.
Join the four strips using the paper fasteners. Make a square.

b You can push the square out of shape without undoing the fasteners.
Write down the name of the new quadrilateral that you get.

c Take a new geostrip of any length.
Use it to join opposite corners of your quadrilateral.
Write down the name of a line that joins two vertices like this.
Keep this shape of five geostrips for question **4**.

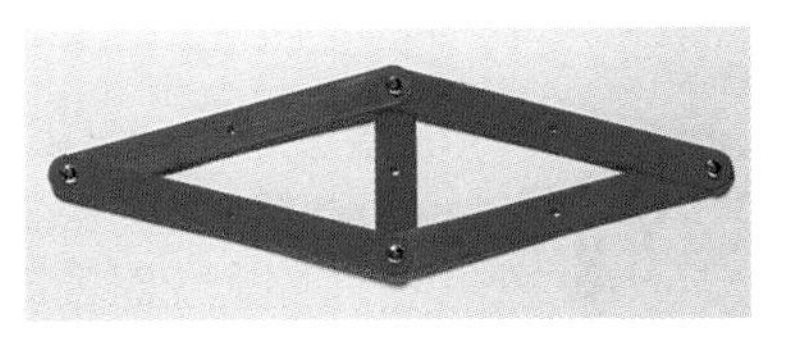

● **4** **a** Draw a square and mark the four right angles.

b Copy and fill in:

The four angles of a square are all r.......... angles.
They are all ...°
The angles of the square add up to 4 × ...° = ...°

c You need your shape made of five geostrips from question **3**.
How many triangles is your shape divided into?
Copy and fill in:

A quadrilateral can be divided into ... triangles.
The angles of one triangle add up to ...°
The angles of two triangles add up to 2 × ...° = ...°
The angles of a quadrilateral add up to ...°

Tessellation

A **tessellation** is a pattern made by repeating the same shape over and over again.
There are no gaps in a tessellation.

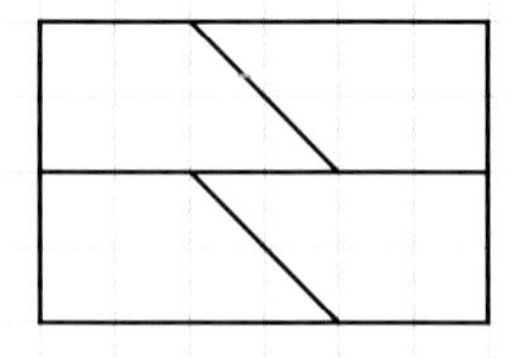

A tessellation of trapeziums

Exercise 7:12

You need a set of tiles in the shapes of regular polygons and some dotty isometric paper.

1 **a** Take some equilateral triangle shaped tiles.
Arrange them as a tessellation.
b Draw the tessellation on dotty isometric paper.
Stick the drawing in your book.
Label it 'A tessellation of equilateral triangles'.

2 **a** Take some square tiles.
Arrange them as a tessellation.
b Cut out a small piece of squared paper.
Stick the paper in your book and label it 'A tessellation of squares'.

3 **a** Take some regular pentagon shaped tiles.
Do they tessellate?
b Try hexagons and octagons.
Try any other regular polygon shaped tiles that you have.
Find out if any of them tessellate.
c One of these polygons does tessellate.
Draw the tessellation on dotty isometric paper.
Stick the drawing in your book.
Label it 'A tessellation of ....s'.

4 Bearings

Simon is orienteering. He has an orienteering map with checkpoints marked on it.
Simon is using a compass to find the direction or bearing of the next checkpoint.

Exercise 7:13

1 **a** Copy the compass diagram.

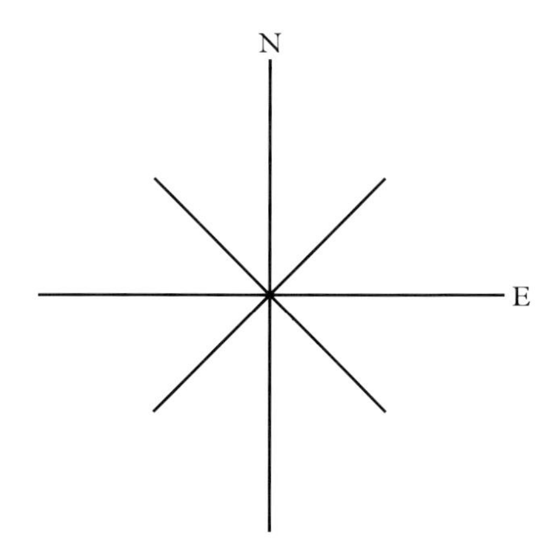

b The directions of North (N) and East (E) are marked.
Mark South (S) opposite North.
Mark West (W) opposite East.
c Mark North East (NE) between North and East.
d Complete the diagram by marking SE, SW, NW.

2 Sally and her family walk 5 km north.
Then they walk 7 km west.

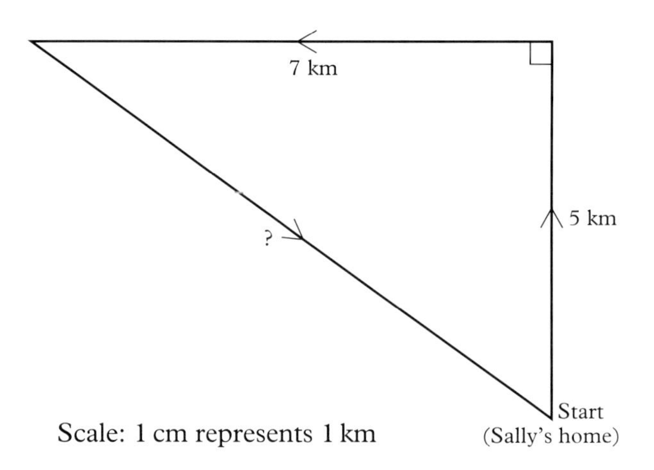

Scale: 1 cm represents 1 km

By measuring, find the distance Sally walks if she goes straight home.

3 The diagram (not to scale) shows a boat journey.
The boat sails 4.5 km south.
Then it sails 6 km east.

a Make an accurate drawing of the journey.
Use squared paper.
Use a scale of 1 cm to 1 km.

b The boat sails straight home on the way back.
By measuring, find the distance for the return journey.

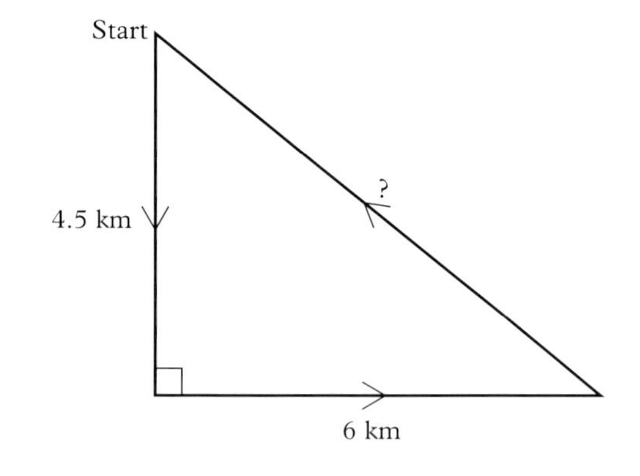

● **4** The diagram shows a Scout hike.
The Scouts walk 5 km east.
Then they walk 5 km north.

a Make an accurate drawing of the walk.
Use a scale of 1 cm to 1 km.

b The Scouts go straight home.

(1) By measuring, find the distance for the return journey.

(2) In what direction do the Scouts walk on the return journey?

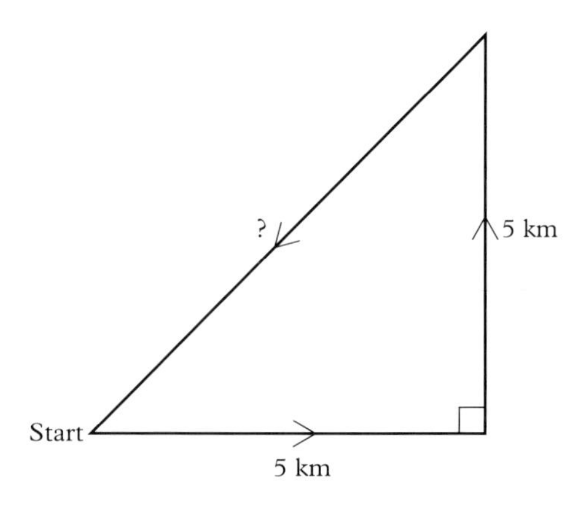

Bearing

A compass gives the **bearing** of an object. This is the direction you travel in to go straight to the object.
Bearings are measured clockwise from north in degrees.
Bearings always have three figures.

Example

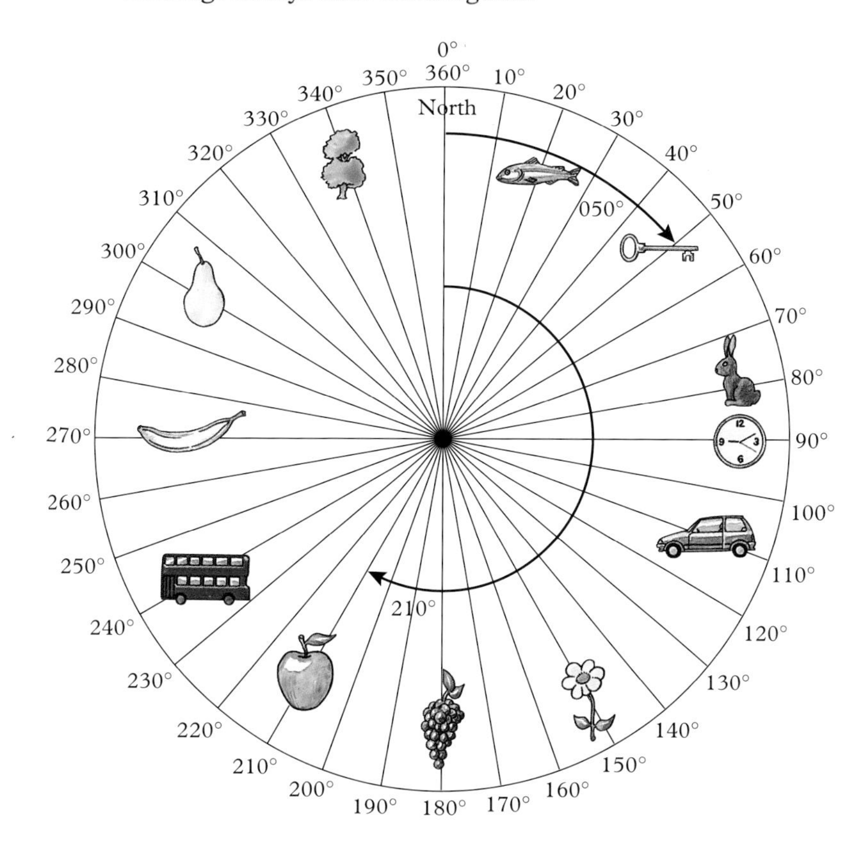

Write down the bearing of: **a** the key **b** the apple

a The key is on the 50° line.
Its bearing is 050°.

b The apple is on the 210° line.
Its bearing is 210°.

Exercise 7:14

1 Write down the bearing of these.

a flower	**c** rabbit	**e** tree	**g** fish	**i** grapes
b pear	**d** car	**f** banana	**h** bus	**j** clock

2 Ask your teacher for a copy of the 'Bearings' worksheet.

1 **a** Estimate the size in degrees of angles a and b.
b Measure angles a and b.
c Write down whether each angle is acute or obtuse.

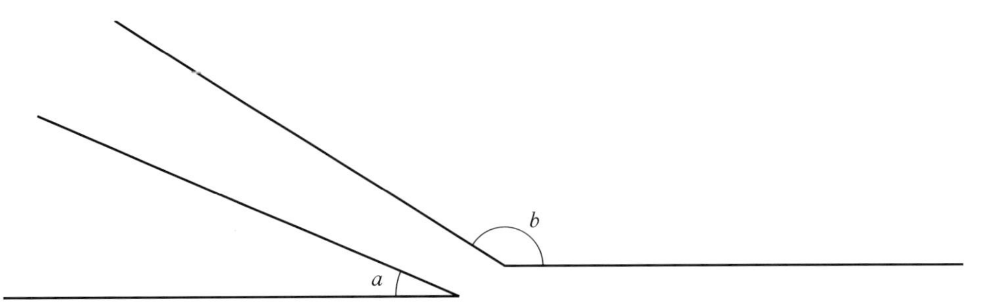

2 Calculate the angles marked with letters.

a

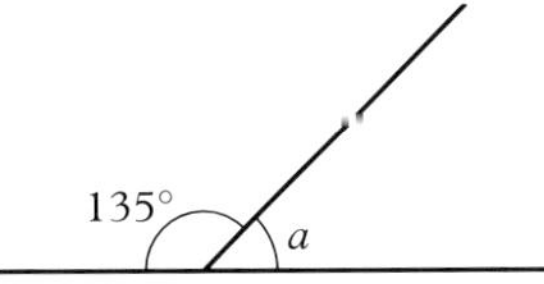

c

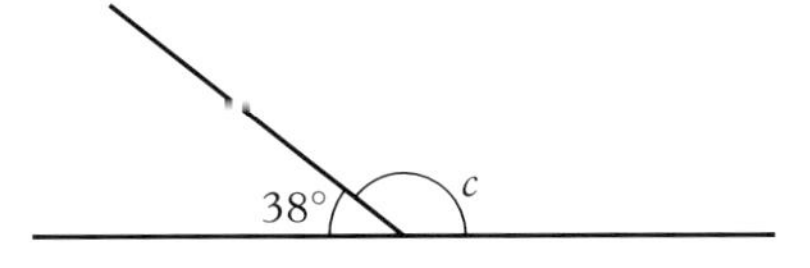

b

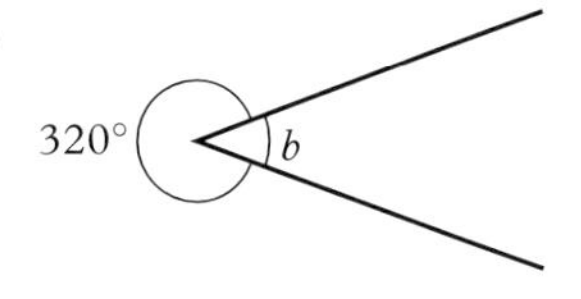

d

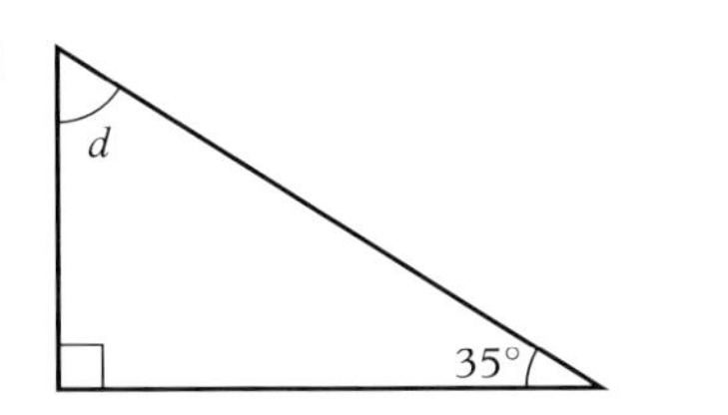

3 Find the angles marked with letters.

a

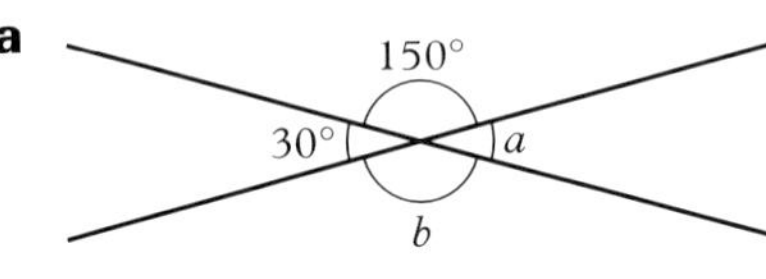

c

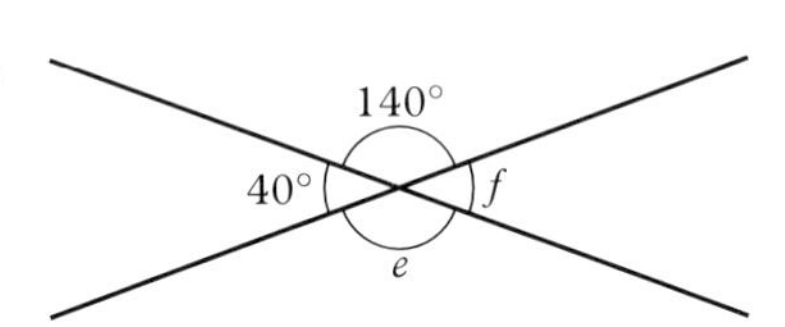

b

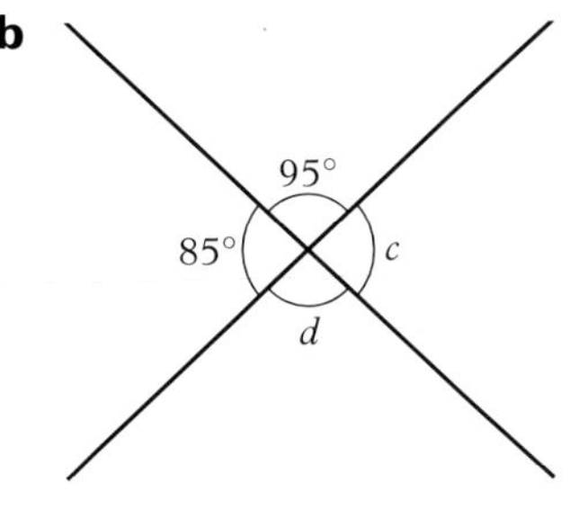

d

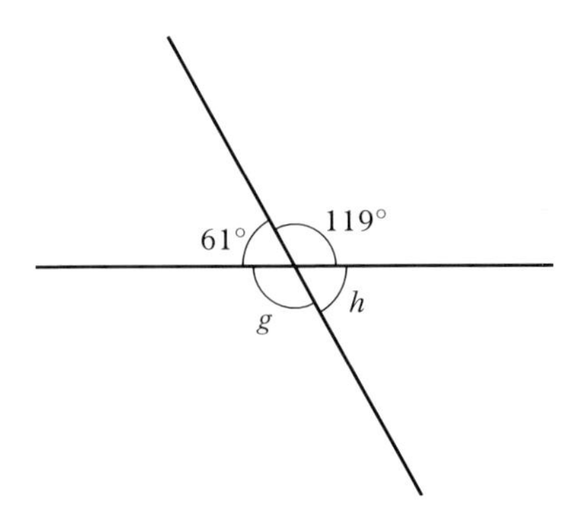

4 Find the angles marked with letters.

a

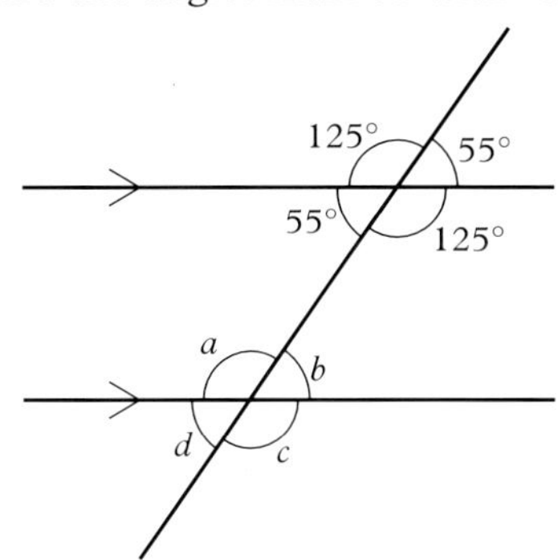

c

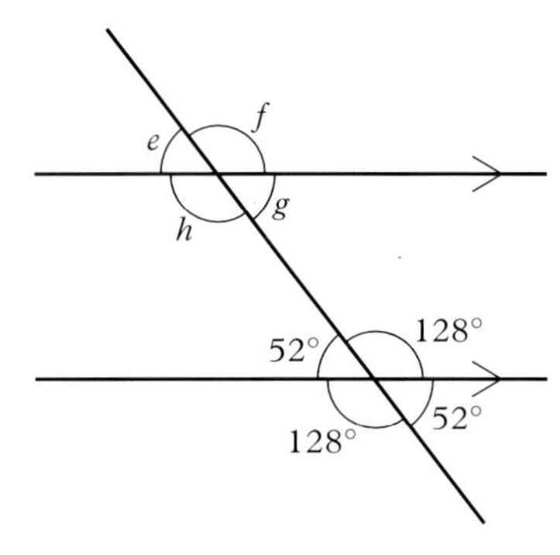

b

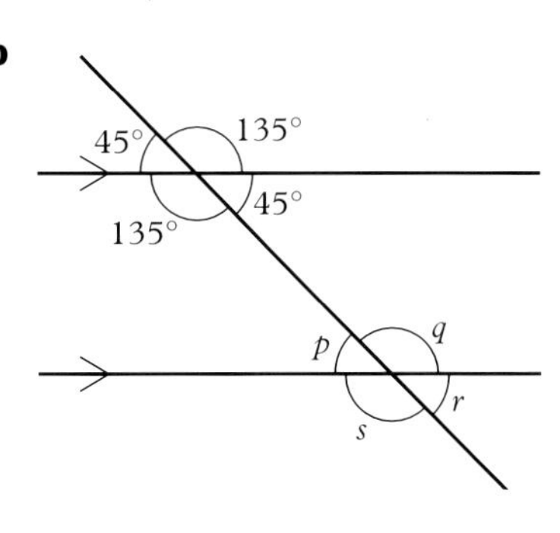

d

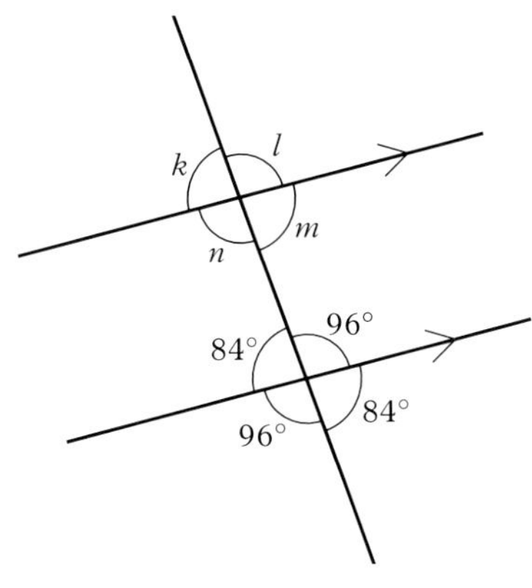

5 **a** Write down the names of these polygons.
b Which of the polygons is regular?

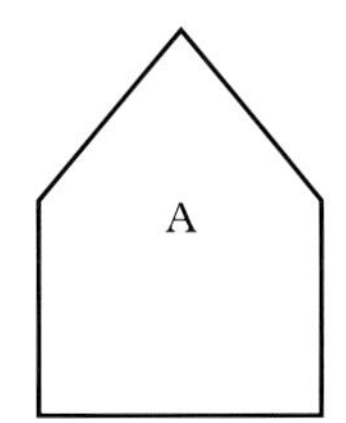

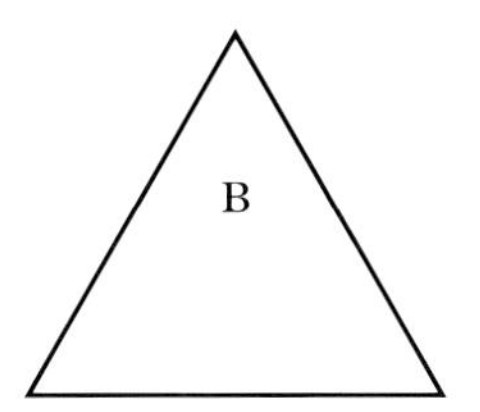

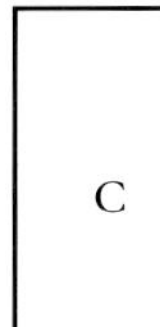

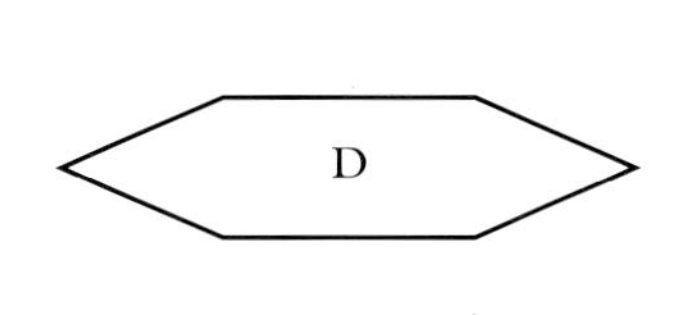

6 A boat sails 6.5 km east.
Then it sails 4 km south.

a Make an accurate drawing of the journey.
Use squared paper.
Use a scale of 1 cm to 1 km.

b The boat sails straight home on the way back.
By measuring, find the distance for the return journey.

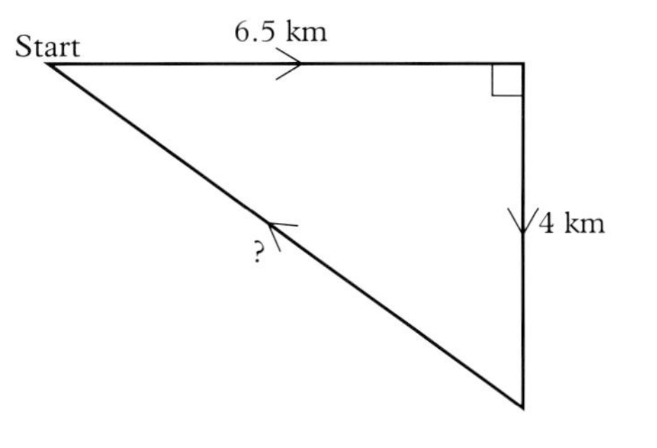

1 **a** Calculate the angles marked with letters.

(1)

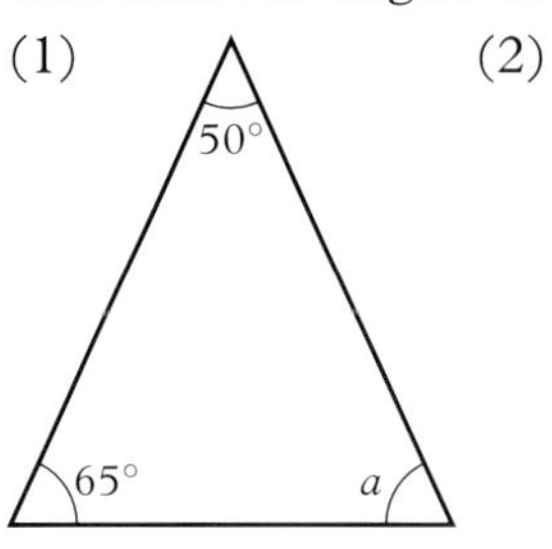

(2)

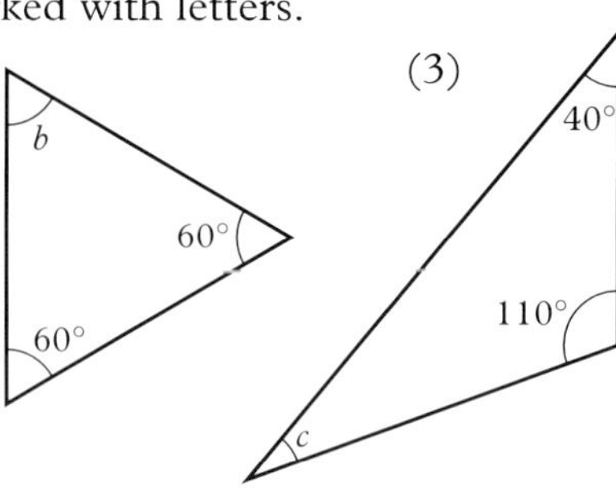

(3)

b Which of the triangles in part **a** is equilateral?
c Which of the triangles in part **a** is isosceles?
d Which of the triangles in part **a** is scalene?

2 **a** Calculate angle a.
b Now write down angle b and angle c.

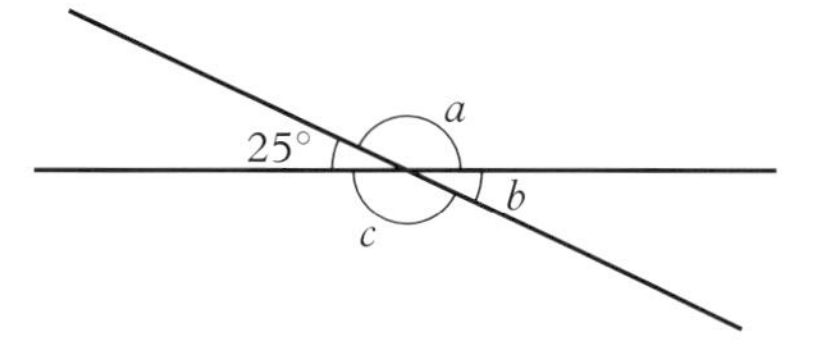

3 **a** Calculate angle p.
b Now write down angle q and angle r.
c Write down angles s, t, u, v.

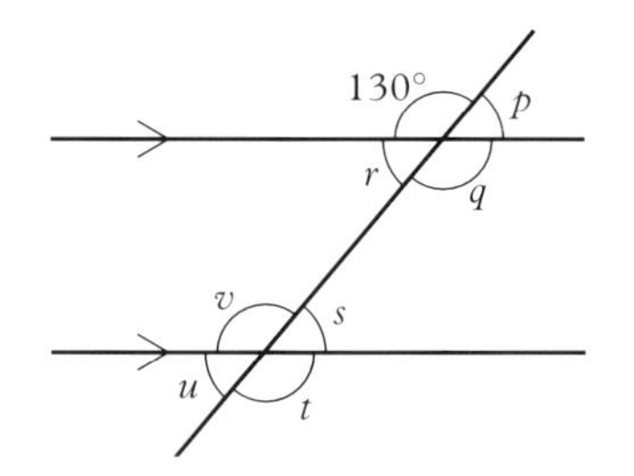

4 **a** Draw any quadrilateral. Use about half a page.
b Measure each angle.
c Add the angles together.
d Repeat parts **a** to **c** for a quadrilateral of a different shape.
e Write down what you notice about your answers to part **c** and part **d**.

5 Write down the bearing of B from A in each case.

a

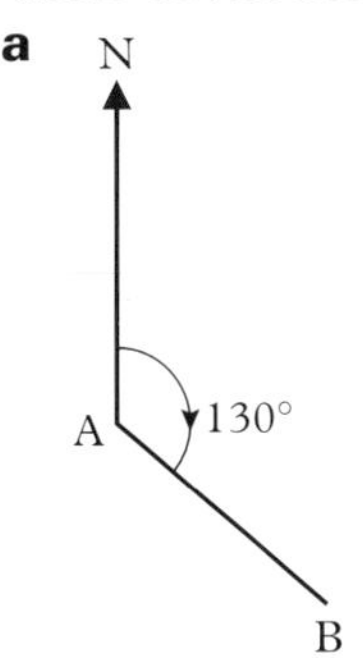

b

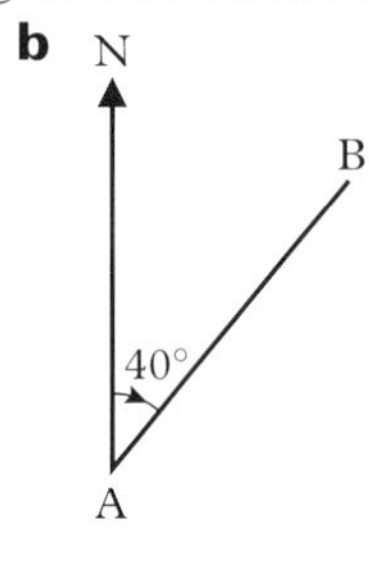

c

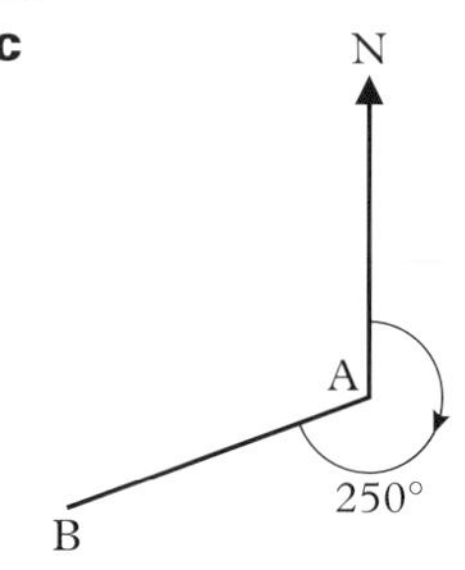

- **Acute angle:** less than 90° **Right angle:** 90° **Obtuse angle:** between 90° and 180°
  Straight line: 180° **Reflex angle:** between 180° and 360° **Full turn:** 360°

- **Angles on a straight line** add up to 180°
  Angles at a point make a full turn. They add up to 360°
  The angles of a triangle add up to 180°

- *Example* Find the angles marked with letters.

  p is opposite 120°
  q is opposite 60°
  $p = 120°$ $q = 60°$

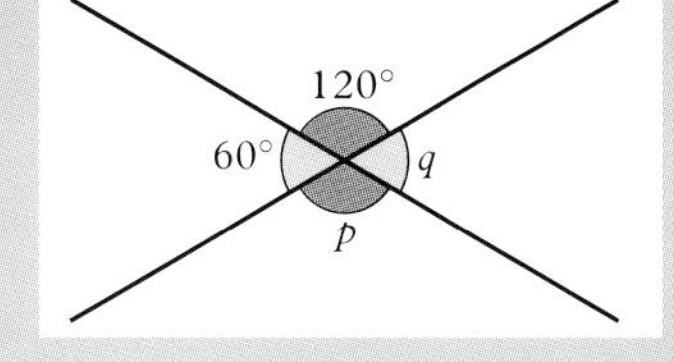

- *Example* Find the angles marked with letters.

  The 'bottom' set of four angles is equal to the 'top' set.
  $p = 130°$ and $r = 130°$
  $q = 50°$ and $s = 50°$

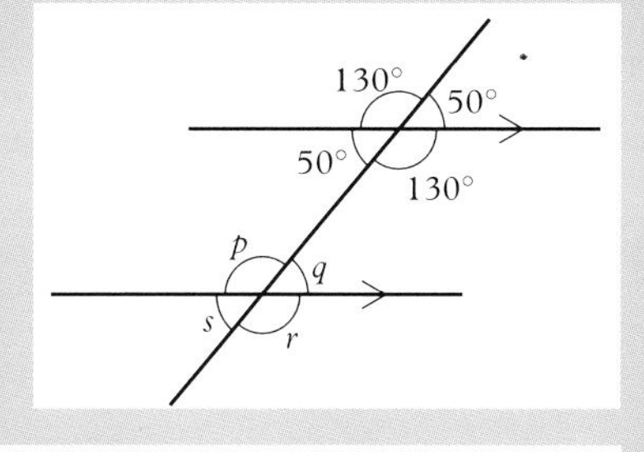

- **Polygon** A **polygon** is a shape with straight sides.

Number of sides	Name of polygon
3	triangle
4	quadrilateral
5	pentagon
6	hexagon
8	octagon

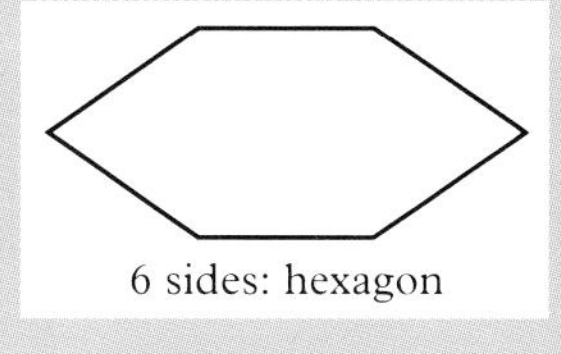
6 sides: hexagon

Regular polygon **Regular polygons** have all their sides the same length.
Also all the angles of a regular polygon are equal.
Equilateral triangles and squares are regular polygons.

- **Tessellation** A **tessellation** is a pattern made by repeating the same shape over and over again. There are no gaps in a tessellation.
  Regular polygons which tessellate are equilateral triangles, squares and regular hexagons.

- **Bearing** A compass gives the **bearing** of an object.
  Bearings are measured clockwise from north in degrees.
  Bearings always have three figures.

1 Which angle is: **a** acute **c** a right angle
b obtuse **d** reflex

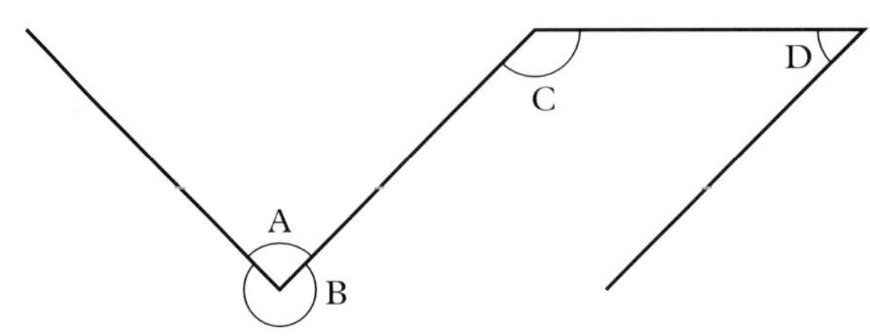

2 Calculate the angles marked with letters.

a

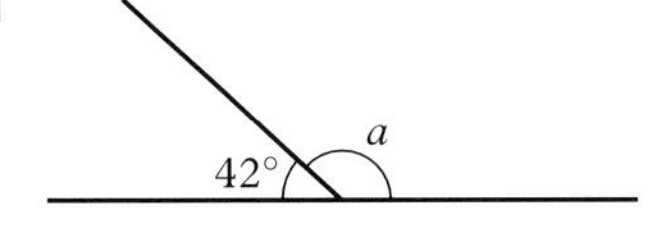

c

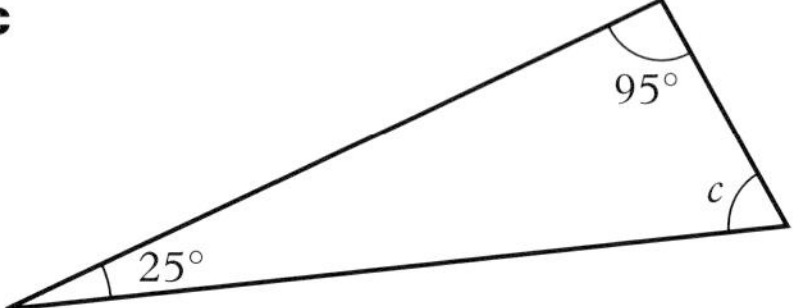

b

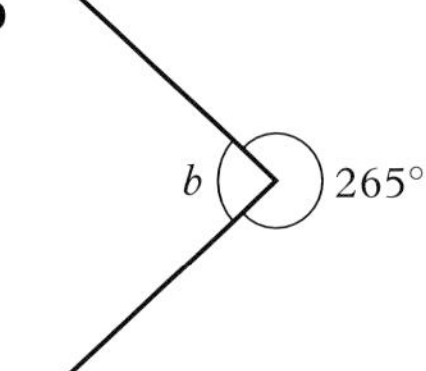

d

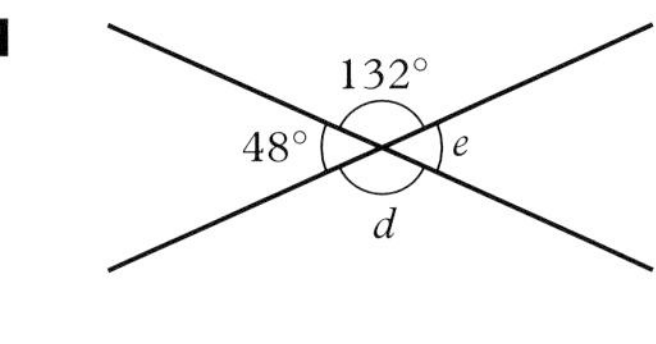

3 Find the angles marked with letters.

a

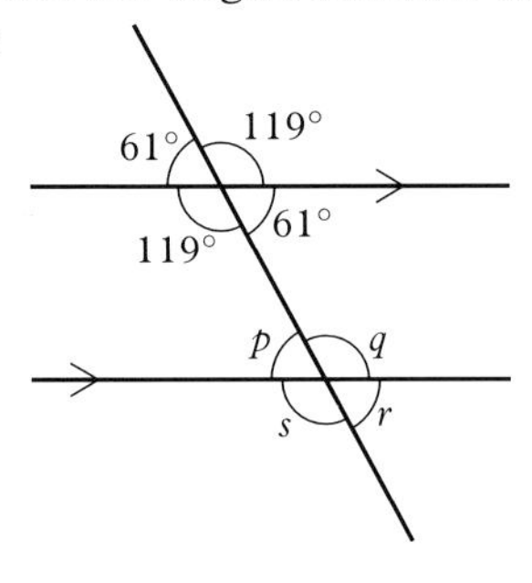

b

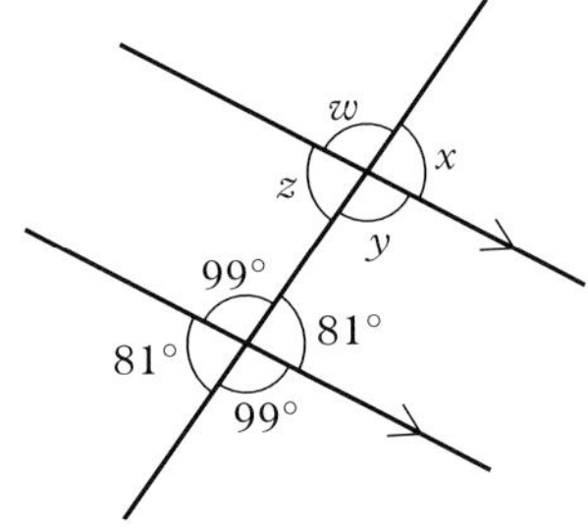

4 Copy the compass diagram.
Label all eight points with their directions.
North has been marked for you.

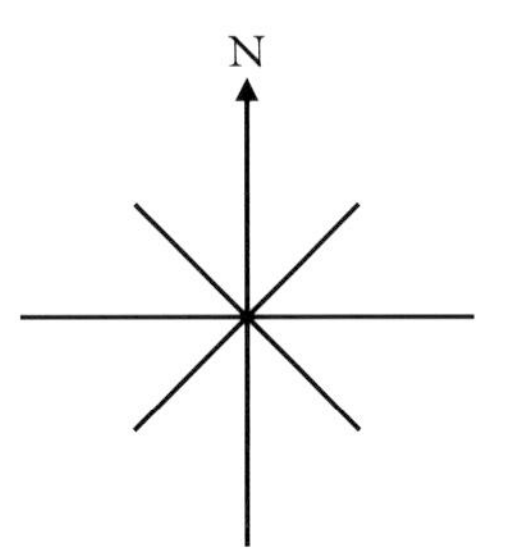

8 Probability

CORE

1 ◀◀REPLAY▶

2 It always adds up to 1

3 Probability diagrams

QUESTIONS

EXTENSION

SUMMARY

TEST YOURSELF

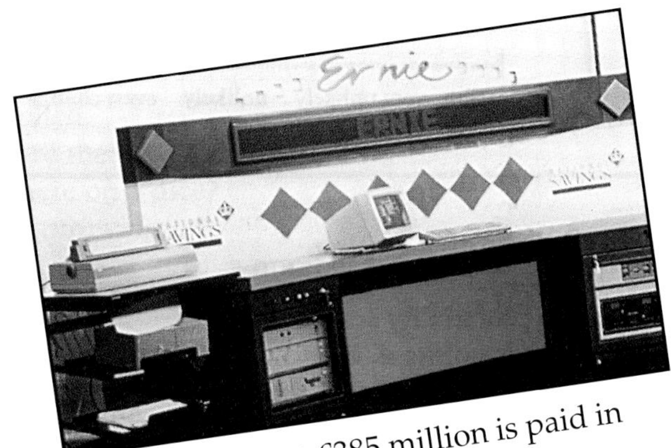

Every year about £385 million is paid in prizes by ERNIE.

ERNIE stands for Electronic Random Number Indicating Equipment.

ERNIE picks the numbers of the winning Premium Bonds each month.

Each Premium Bond costs £1 and every Bond has a 1 in 19 000 chance of winning a prize. Most prizes are £50 or £100 but there is a monthly prize of £1 million.

The chance of any Bond winning the £1 million prize in any month is about 1 in 8 billion!

1 REPLAY

Last year you used probability to help you decide what to say in the card game Higher or Lower.

Probability

Probability tells us how likely something is to happen.

We can show it on a probability scale:

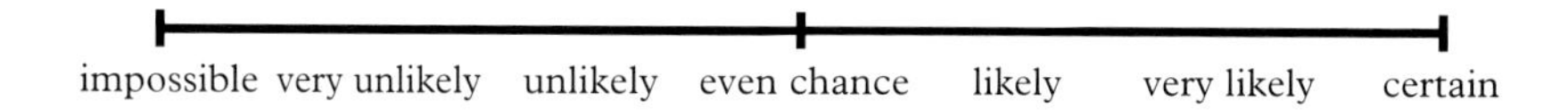

Exercise 8:1

1 Draw a probability scale.
Mark on it points **a**, **b** and **c** to show how likely you think each one is.
- **a** The next person you see will be over 2 metres tall.
- **b** There will be at least one sunny day in June in London.
- **c** You will pass your driving test before you are 18 years old.

Probability is written as a number.
We write 0 for impossible and 1 for certain.

We can draw our probability scale like this:

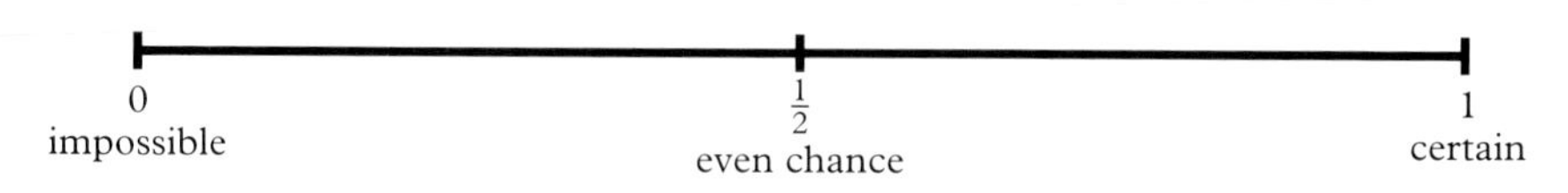

All probabilities must be between 0 and 1.

2 Draw a probability scale like this one:

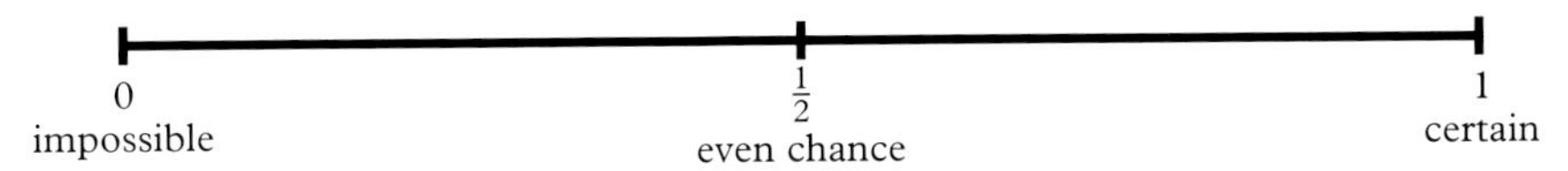

Mark on it points **a**, **b** and **c** to show how likely you think each one is.

a The next person you meet will be older than you.

b The next person you meet will have a twin.

c The next person you meet will be right-handed.

Probability is usually written as a fraction.

Sally bought 3 raffle tickets.
100 tickets were sold.

The probability that Sally wins the raffle is $\frac{3}{100}$.

Exercise 8:2

1 An ordinary fair dice is rolled.

a How many numbers are there on a dice?

b How many fives are there on a dice?

What is the probability of throwing

c a 5

d an even number

e a number less than 1

f a number less than 10?

2 Jamie bought 5 raffle tickets. A total of 100 tickets were sold.
What is the probability that Jamie will win first prize?

3 A letter is chosen at random from the word BOOK.

a How many letters are there to choose from?

What is the probability that the letter is

b B **c** O **d** W?

4 A tetrahedral dice is thrown.
The dice has 4 faces.
2 are red, 1 is yellow and 1 is blue.
What is the probability that the dice will land on a face that is

a yellow

b red

• **c** yellow or red?

5 A card is picked at random from an ordinary pack of 52 playing cards.

a How many cards are

(1) red (2) spades (3) a 9 (4) picture cards?

b What is the probability that the card will be

(1) red (2) a spade (3) a 9 (4) a picture card?

Remember: the picture cards are jack, queen, king and ace.

• **6** A bag contains 6 yellow counters and 5 green counters.
One counter is taken out at random.
Write down the probability that the counter is

a yellow **b** green **c** blue

A box contains 12 counters.
There are 8 red and 4 blue.

Rolf picks a counter from the box without looking.
He writes down the colour and puts it back in the box.

He does this 12 times.

Rolf *expects* to get 8 reds and 4 blues.

Exercise 8:3

1 Rolf picks a counter 24 times.

a How many reds does he expect to get?

b How many blues does he expect to get?

2 A fair coin is tossed.
Write down the number of heads you would expect to get in

a 2 throws **b** 10 throws **c** 100 throws

3 This spinner has 3 equal sections.
How many times would you expect to get a 2 if you spin it

a 3 times

b 6 times

c 30 times?

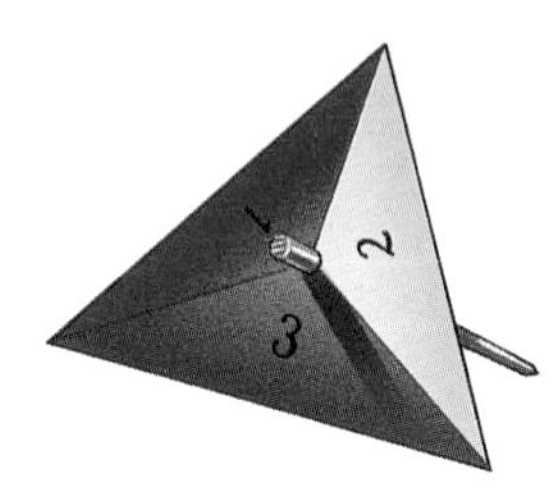

4 A box contains 10 blue pencils and 5 red pencils.
Sunita takes a pencil at random and writes down the colour.
She then puts the pencil back in the box.

a She does this 15 times.
Write down how many pencils she would expect to be
(1) blue (2) red

b She does this 30 times.
Write down how many pencils she would expect to be
(1) blue (2) red

5 A bag contains 5 blue balls, 4 yellow balls and 1 black ball.
Malcolm takes a ball at random and writes down the colour.
He then puts the ball back in the bag.

a He does this 10 times.
Write down how many balls he would expect to be
(1) blue (2) black (3) yellow

b He does this 50 times.
Write down how many balls he would expect to be
(1) blue (2) black (3) yellow

Game Holder of the box

You will need a box and
3 different colours of counters.
This is a game for 3–5 players.

One player is the 'Holder of the box'.
This player chooses 12 counters
of three different colours and puts
them in the box.
There must be at least one counter of each colour.
The other players must not see the counters.
The other players take turns to choose a counter at random from
the box, note the colour and return it to the box.

When a player returns a counter to the box he or she can guess
how many counters of each colour there are in the box.

You can only guess when you have just had your turn.
You will probably not want to guess until everyone has had
a couple of turns.

The first person to guess correctly wins.
The winner becomes the 'Holder of the box' for the next game.

Once you have played this game a few times you might like to make up
a new game of your own.
Write down the rules and explain how to play your game.

2 It always adds up to 1

Peter and Jane are going to the fair.
The weather forecast says that the probability of rain is 60%.

Peter does not want to get wet.
Jane is more cheerful.
She says that the probability of it not raining is 40%.

We usually write probabilities as fractions.
60% is $\frac{60}{100}$ and 40% is $\frac{40}{100}$.

$\frac{60}{100} + \frac{40}{100} = \frac{100}{100} = 1$

Probabilities always add up to 1.
We can show this on a probability scale.

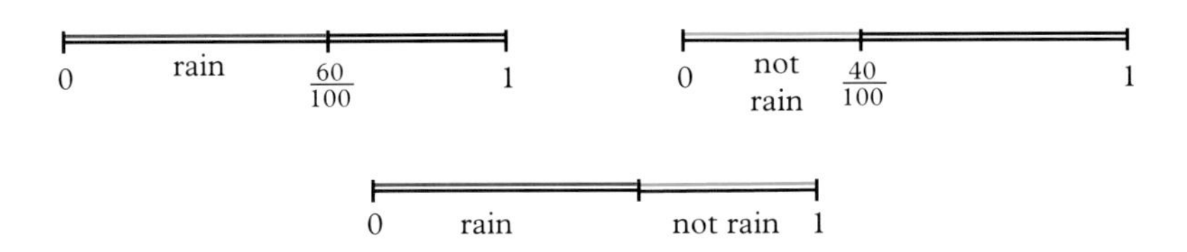

Exercise 8:4

1 Manzoor has a bag containing 3 red counters and 4 blue counters.
He picks 1 counter at random.

a Copy this probability scale. Draw a line 7 cm long.
Mark it like this in sevenths.

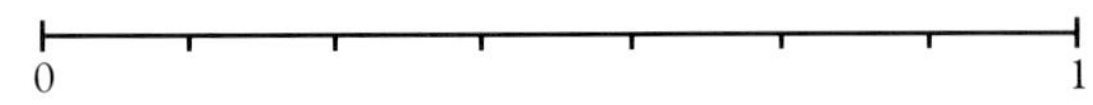

b The probability that Manzoor picks a red counter is $\frac{3}{7}$.
Colour the first three sevenths on your scale in red.
This shows the probability that the first counter is red.

c Colour the rest of the scale blue.
This shows the probability that the first counter is blue.

d What is the probability that the first counter is blue?

2 Manisha likes to plait her hair with beads.
She has a bag containing 6 green beads and
4 red beads.

a Copy this probability scale. Draw a line 10 cm long.
Mark it like this in tenths.

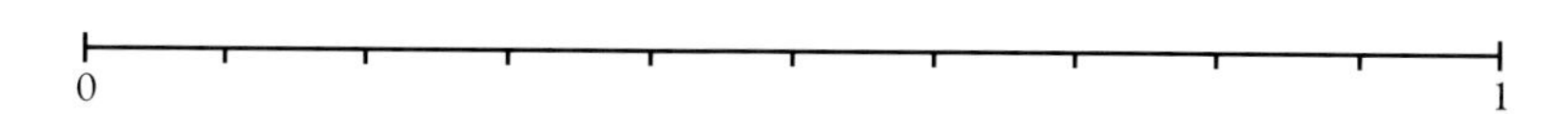

Manisha picks the first bead from the bag.

b Colour your scale to show the probability that the first bead will be green.

c What is the probability that the first bead will be green?

d Colour the rest of your scale to show the probability that the first bead will be red. Use a different colour.

e What is the probability that the first bead will be red?

3 Alice has 8 friends.
6 of them have brown hair and 2 of them have red hair.

a Copy this probability scale. Draw a line 8 cm long.
Mark it like this in eighths.

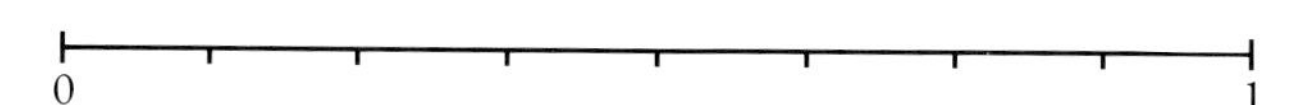

Alice picks one of her friends at random.

b Colour your scale to show the probability that Alice will pick someone with brown hair.

c What is the probability that Alice will pick someone with brown hair?

d Colour the rest of your scale to show the probability that she will pick someone with red hair. Use a different colour.

e What is the probability that she will pick someone with red hair?

4 To win a game you need to throw a 3 on a dice.
The probability of winning is $\frac{1}{6}$.

a Draw a probability scale. Split it into sixths.

b Colour part of your scale to show the probability of winning.

c Colour the rest of your scale to show the probability of losing.
Use a different colour.

d What is the probability of losing?

- **5** **a** The probability of taking a blue sock from a drawer containing 6 blue socks and 4 green socks is $\frac{6}{10}$.
  Write down the probability of *not* taking a blue sock.
  b The probability of picking a king from an ordinary pack of cards is $\frac{4}{52}$.
  Write down the probability of *not* picking a king.

Example

A box contains red, blue and green counters.
One counter is picked at random.
The probability that it is red is $\frac{5}{10}$ and
the probability that it is blue is $\frac{3}{10}$.
What is the probability that it is green?

This time we split the probability scale into tenths.
We have to colour 3 different sections to show the probabilities of the 3 colours.

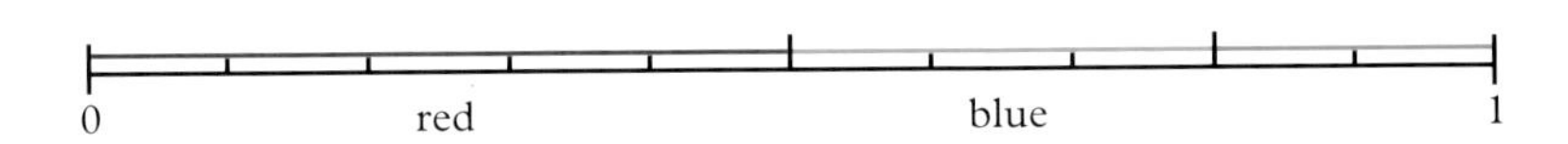

The part left over shows the probability of green.
The probability of green is $\frac{2}{10}$.

---

6 A box contains green, yellow and black counters.
One counter is picked at random.
The probability that it is green is $\frac{4}{10}$ and
the probability that it is yellow is $\frac{3}{10}$.
a Draw a scale to show the probabilities of green and yellow.
b What is the probability that the counter is black?
Show this probability on your scale.

7 Emma gets the bus to school each morning.
The probability that the bus is early is $\frac{3}{10}$.
The probability that the bus is exactly on time is $\frac{1}{10}$.
a Draw a scale to show the probabilities of the bus being early and on time.
b What is the probability that the bus is late?
Show this probability on your scale.

8 A box contains yellow, green and red counters.
One counter is picked at random.
The probability that it is yellow is $\frac{7}{20}$ and
the probability that it is green is $\frac{11}{20}$.
a Draw a scale to show the probabilities of yellow and green.
b What is the probability that the counter is red?
Show this probability on your scale.

• **9** The probability that Janice will go round to see her friend on any night is $\frac{7}{12}$. The probability that Janice will ring her friend is $\frac{3}{12}$.

Find the probability that Janice won't see or speak to her friend tonight.
You can draw a probability scale to help you if you wish.

◀◀ REPLAY ▶

Cancelling fractions

When we write probabilities as fractions, we should **cancel the fractions** to their simplest form.
We can do this using the $a^b/_c$ button on the calculator.

Example

To cancel the fraction $\frac{13}{52}$ we press:

The display shows 1 ⌐ 4 . This means $\frac{1}{4}$.

Exercise 8:5

1 Use the $a^b/_c$ button to cancel these fractions:

a $\frac{26}{52}$	**c** $\frac{6}{10}$	**e** $\frac{10}{20}$	**g** $\frac{4}{20}$	**i** $\frac{14}{22}$
b $\frac{4}{52}$	**d** $\frac{4}{10}$	**f** $\frac{5}{20}$	**h** $\frac{10}{12}$	**j** $\frac{6}{24}$

In the rest of this exercise give all probabilities as fractions in their simplest form.

2 Dale has a bag containing 10 sweets. There are 6 toffees and 4 fruit drops.
He takes a sweet out at random.
Find the probability that the sweet he gets is
a a toffee **b** a fruit drop **c** a chocolate raisin

3 Pritesh has 15 crayons in his pencil case. There are 4 blue, 6 green and 5 red.
He picks out a crayon at random.
Find the probability that the crayon he picks is

a green
b red
c pink
d blue

4 Sinead is not a tidy girl. She has all 20 of her exercise books in a heap in her room.
When she does her homework she picks them up at random until she gets the right one.
In her pile of books are 2 Maths, 6 English, 4 Science, 3 French, 2 History, 2 Geography and 1 Music.

What is the probability that the book she chooses first will be.

a Maths
b English
c Science
d French
e History
f Geography
g Music?

● **5** A bag contains a full set of 22 snooker balls. There are 15 reds, and 1 each of white, yellow, green, brown, blue, pink and black.

One ball is chosen at random.
Write down the probability that it is

a black
b red
c pink
d white
e grey
f not black
g not red
h not pink
i not white
j not grey

3 Probability diagrams

Sarah and Gavin are choosing their meal.

Sarah wants to know how many different meals she can choose. She can have soup and fish fingers, soup and sausages, soup and veggie burger, juice and fish fingers, juice and sausages or juice and veggie burger.

There are 6 possibilities. These can be shown in a table like this:

Starter	Main course
soup	fish fingers
soup	sausages
soup	veggie burger
juice	fish fingers
juice	sausages
juice	veggie burger

Exercise 8:6

1 Copy this table to show all of the possible meals from this menu. Fill it in.

Main course	Dessert

2 Rapinder is choosing his breakfast.
He can choose from 3 cereals: Cornflakes, Coco Pops and Weetabix.
He can drink either tea or coffee.

Draw a table to show all the possibilities for his breakfast.

3 Jennifer is deciding what to wear.
She has 2 T-shirts, one white and one red, and 3 pairs of shorts, one black, one grey and one blue.

Draw a table to show all the possible ways she can dress.

4 Philippa is on an adventure holiday.
In the morning she can choose from Sailing, Windsurfing and Canoeing.
In the afternoon she can choose from Climbing, Horse-riding and Archery.

Draw a table to show all the ways that Philippa can spend her day.

● **5** Write down the different breakfasts that you can choose from this menu.

Bill, Rudi and Keith decide to toss a coin to see who does the washing up.
As there are 3 of them they need 3 possible outcomes.
They decide to use 2 coins.

If the outcome is 2 heads Bill will wash up.

If the outcome is 2 tails Keith will wash up.

If the outcome is 1 head and 1 tail Rudi will wash up.

Is this fair?

Here are the possible outcomes. There are four.

We can use a table to show these.

		20 p coin H	T
2 p coin	H	H, H	H, T
	T	T, H	T, T

1 outcome gives 2 heads.
1 outcome gives 2 tails.
2 outcomes give 1 head and 1 tail.

Probability of 2 heads = $\frac{1}{4}$

Probability of 2 tails = $\frac{1}{4}$

Probability of 1 head and 1 tail = $\frac{2}{4}$

So this is not fair. 1 head and 1 tail will happen the most.

Exercise 8:7

1 David tosses the coin at the same time as Kelly spins the spinner.

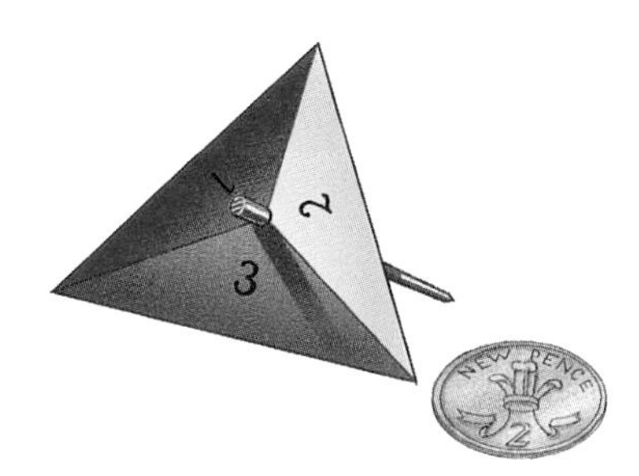

a Copy the table to show the possible outcomes.
Fill it in.

		Spinner 1	2	3
Coin	H	H, 1		
	T			T, 3

b Write down the number of possible outcomes.

c How many ways can you get a tail on the coin and a 3 on the spinner?

d What is the probability of getting a tail on the coin and a 3 on the spinner?

● **e** What is the probability of getting an odd number and a head?

2 Saleem throws a coin and rolls a dice.

a Copy this diagram to show the possible outcomes.
Fill it in.

		Dice					
		1	2	3	4	5	6
Coin	H	H, 1					
	T			T, 3			

b What is the total number of possible outcomes?

c What is the probability of getting a head and a 6?

d What is the probability of getting a tail and a 4?

● **e** What is the probability of getting a head and an even number?

3 The picture shows two tetrahedral dice.

They both have four faces.
The faces are numbered 1, 2, 3 and 4.
The score is on the face that the dice lands on.

Copy this table to show the possible outcomes.
Fill it in.

		Second dice			
		1	2	3	4
First dice	1	1, 1		1, 3	
	2				2, 4
	3		3, 2		
	4			4, 3	

a What is the total number of possible outcomes?

b What is the probability of getting a 1 on both dice?

● **c** What is the probability of getting the same number on both dice?

Game It's not fair

This is a game for two players
A and B.
Take turns to roll the dice.
Multiply the two numbers scored.
In this picture the score is
$4 \times 3 = 12$

For each roll:
player A gets a point if the answer is even
player B gets a point if the answer is odd

The first player to 10 points wins.

Play the game with a partner.
Who should win?
Can you change the rules of the game to make it fair?

Chinese dice

For this investigation, you need 3 dice.

Dice A has faces labelled	2	2	2	2	6	6
Dice B has faces labelled	1	1	5	5	5	5
Dice C has faces labelled	3	3	3	4	4	4

Two players play like this.

The first player chooses a dice.
The second player chooses a dice from the remaining two.

Each player rolls their dice and the player with the higher number scores 1 point.

This is done 12 times. The player with the most points wins.

Using these rules it is possible for one player to win nearly all the time.
Should this player choose the dice first or second?
How should they choose? Investigate.

1 Draw a probability scale like this:

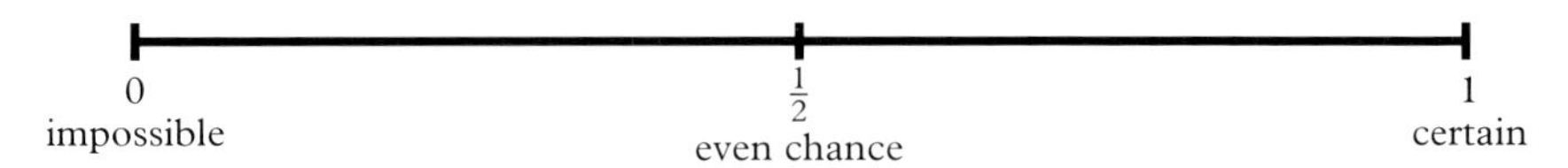

Mark on it points **a**, **b** and **c** to show how likely you think each one is.

a You will forget to do your Maths homework at least once this term.

b You will watch TV sometime over the weekend.

c You will eat chips tomorrow.

2 Janet buys 3 raffle tickets. 300 are sold altogether.
What is the probability that Janet will win first prize?

3 A box of chocolates has 4 plain chocolates and 6 milk chocolates.
Paul chooses a chocolate at random.

a How many chocolates are there?

Write down the probability that he gets

b a plain chocolate **c** a milk chocolate

4 A mixed football team has 5 girls and 6 boys. The captain is chosen at random.

a How many players are there in the team?

Write down the probability that the captain will be

b a girl **c** a boy

5 Sophie has 8 marbles in a bag. 3 are yellow and 5 are blue.
She takes out a marble at random.
She writes down the colour and puts the marble back in the bag.
She does this 16 times.

Write down the number of times she expects to get

a a yellow marble **b** a blue marble

6 A box contains 6 blue, 4 red and 2 green counters.
A counter is taken at random from the box.
The colour is noted and the counter is put back in the box.

a This is done 12 times.
Write down how many counters you would expect to be
(1) blue (2) red (3) green

b This is done 60 times.
Write down how many counters you would expect to be
(1) blue (2) red (3) green

7 This table shows the number of each flavour in a bag of toffees.

Flavour	Number
mint	5
chocolate	3
plain	7

One toffee is chosen at random.

a Which flavour is it most likely to be?

b What is the probability that it will be mint?

8 Danielle has a set of 20 cards numbered 1 to 20.
She picks out one card at random and then replaces it in the pack.

a Write down the probability that the number on the card is

(1) a 4 (2) even (3) bigger than 15

b Write down the probability that the number on the card is *not*

(1) a 4 (2) even (3) bigger than 15

9 Jason is choosing a pencil and a ruler.
He can have a pencil which is blue, red or brown.
He can have a ruler which is made of plastic or wood.

Write a list of all the possible choices that he can make.

10 Michael wants to buy a pack of sandwiches and a drink for his lunch.
He has to choose from this selection.

Sandwiches	Drinks
cheese	cola
tuna	lemonade
egg	milk

Write down all the possible lunches that he can have.

1 Manisha rolls an ordinary dice.
What is the probability that she will get

a a 4
b an odd number
c an 8
d a number less than 3?

2 This table shows the membership of a youth club.

	Under 13 years old	13 years old and over
boys	20	15
girls	18	22

a How many boys are there in the club?
b How many of the members are 13 or older?
c How many members are there in the club?

One person is chosen at random from the club.
Write down the probability that the person will be

d a boy
e 13 or older
f a girl who is 13 or older

3 Pat's piggy bank contains four £1 coins, three 50 p coins and five 20 p coins.
She shakes out a coin at random.
Write down the probability that the coin will be

a 50 p
b £1
c worth less than £1

4 A factory making calculators expects 1 in every 100 calculators to be faulty.

a How many faulty calculators would you expect to find in a batch of 1000?
b In a batch of 3420 calculators, 41 are found to be faulty.
Is this more or less than the number of faulty calculators you would expect?

5 The probability that George will win the 100 m race is $\frac{3}{5}$.
What is the probability that he will not win the race?

6 The probability that a bus will be late is $\frac{1}{3}$.
What is the probability that the bus will not be late?

- Probability tells us how likely something is to happen.
  We write it as a number.
  We write 0 for impossible and 1 for certain.

  We can show it on a probability scale:

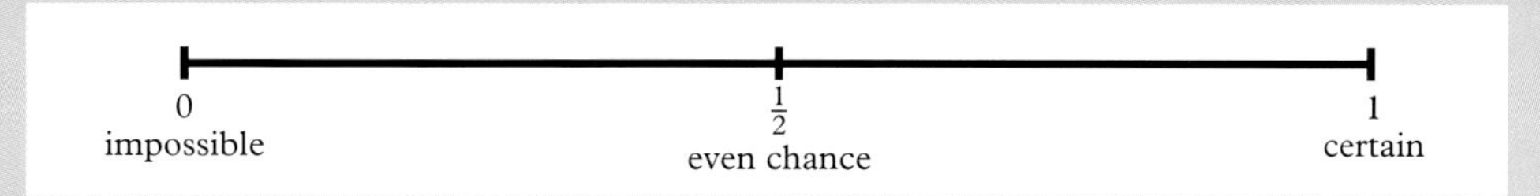

All probabilities must be between 0 and 1.

- Probability is usually written as a fraction.

Example Sally bought 3 raffle tickets.
100 tickets were sold.
The probability that Sally wins the raffle is $\frac{3}{100}$.

Example A box contains 12 counters. There are 8 red and 4 blue.
Rolf takes a counter from the box without looking.
He writes down the colour and puts it back in the box.
He does this 12 times.
Rolf expects to get 8 reds and 4 blues.

- Probabilities always add up to 1.
  We can show this on a probability scale.

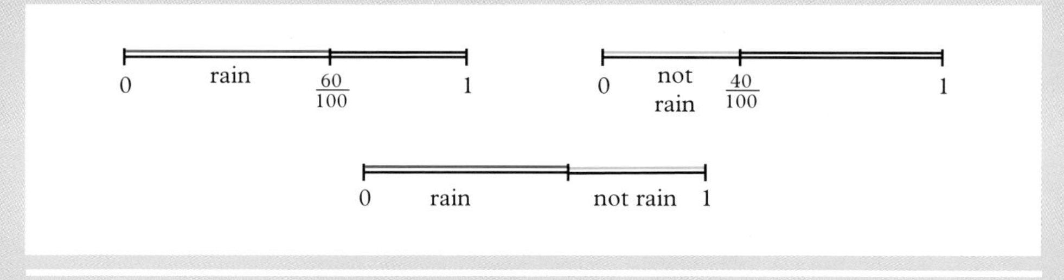

1 A letter is chosen at random from the word SCHOOL.
What is the probability that the letter is
a S **b** O **c** A?

2 A bag of sweets contains 4 toffees and 10 fruit drops.
Francis takes 1 sweet at random from the bag.
Write down the probability that the sweet is
a a toffee **b** a fruit drop

3 Lucy has 1 red, 1 green and 3 black pencils in her pencil case.
She takes 1 pencil out at random.
She writes down the colour and puts the pencil back in the case.
a She does this 10 times.
Write down how many pencils she expects to be
(1) red (2) green (3) black
b She does this 30 times.
Write down how many pencils she expects to be
(1) red (2) green (3) black

4 Use the $a^b/_c$ button to cancel these fractions:
a $\frac{6}{36}$ **b** $\frac{25}{75}$ **c** $\frac{45}{50}$

5 Yasmin has to colour a picture in her Art lesson.
She is only allowed to use 2 colours.
She has green, red and blue crayons.
Write a list of the different ways that she can colour her picture.

9 Percentages and fractions

CORE

QUESTIONS

EXTENSION

SUMMARY

TEST YOURSELF

Emily owns shares worth £200.
The share value rises by 10%.
Then the value falls by 10%.

True or False?
Emily's shares are now worth £200.

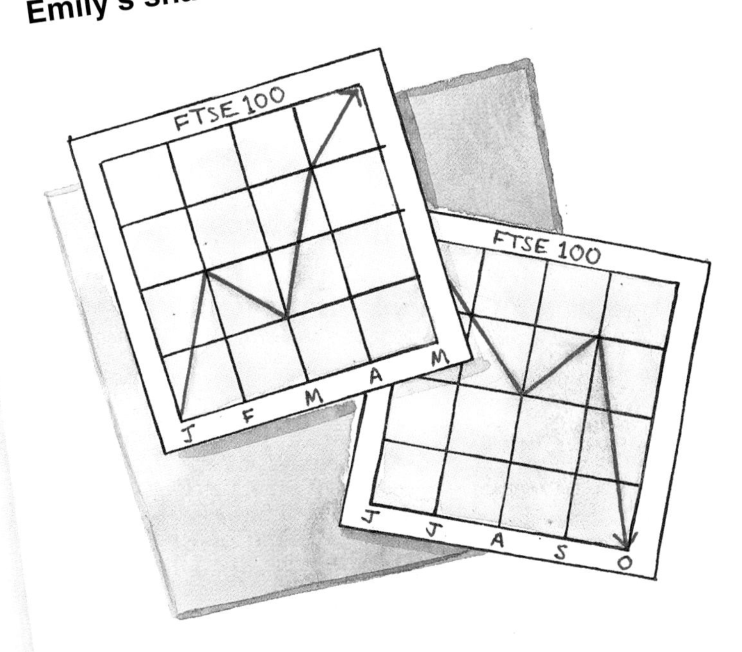

1 Simple percentages

82 out of these 100 children have blue eyes.

This is the same as saying that 82% have blue eyes.

16 out of these 100 children are left-handed.

This is the same as saying that 16% of them are left-handed.

Exercise 9:1

1 Pupils who are right-handed are shaded blue.
What percentage are right-handed?

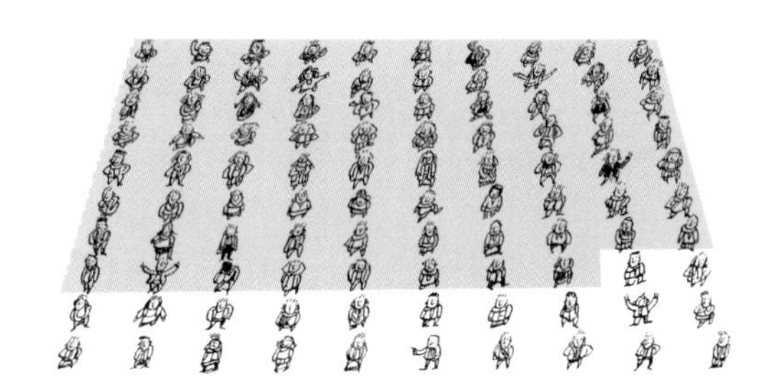

2 Pupils who stay at school for lunch are shaded red.
What percentage stay for lunch?

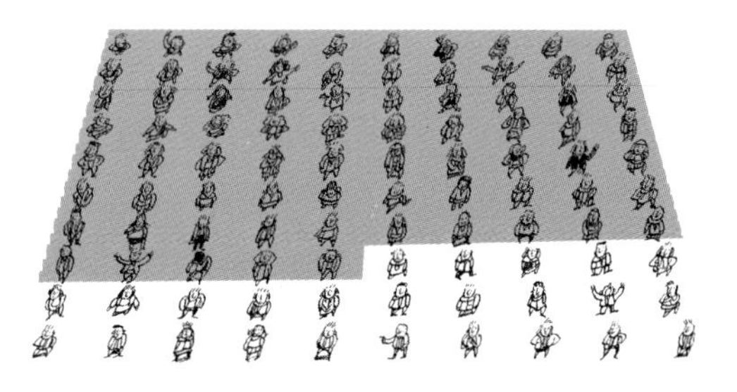

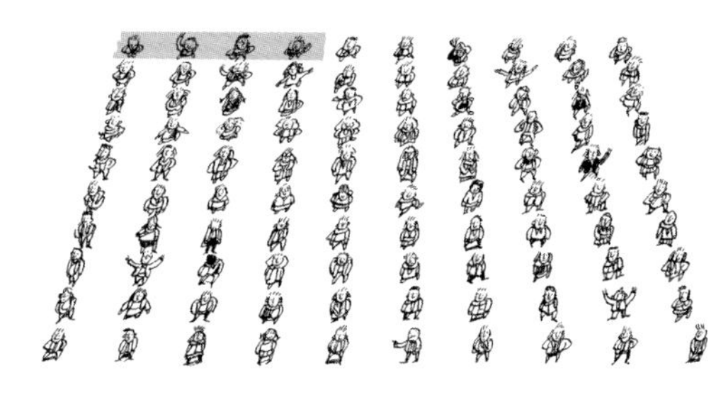

3 Pupils who did not do their homework are shaded green.

a What percentage did not do their homework?

b What percentage *did* do their homework?

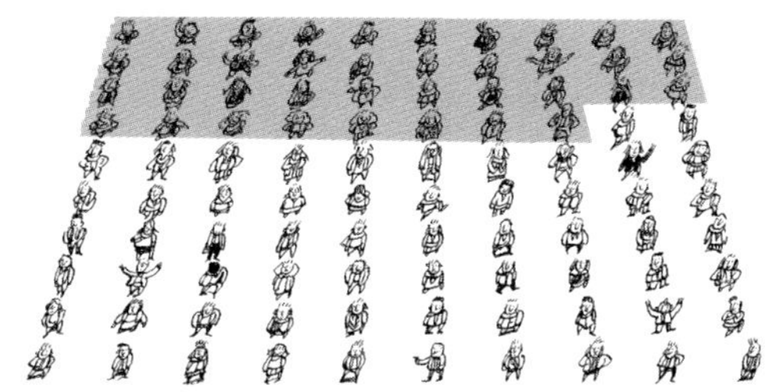

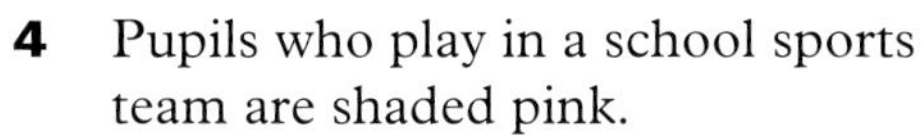

4 Pupils who play in a school sports team are shaded pink.

a What percentage of the pupils play for a school team?

b What percentage do *not* play for a school team?

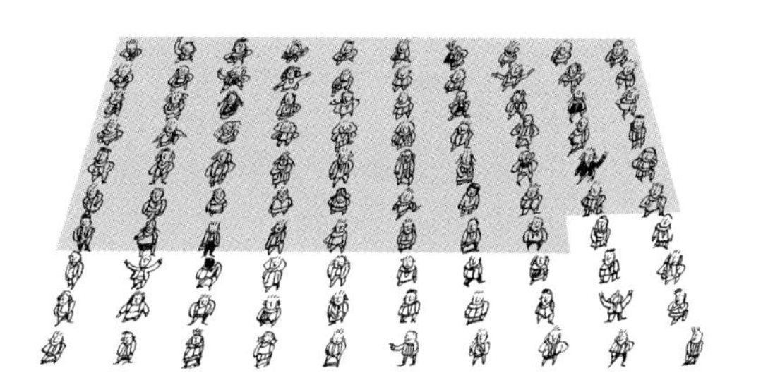

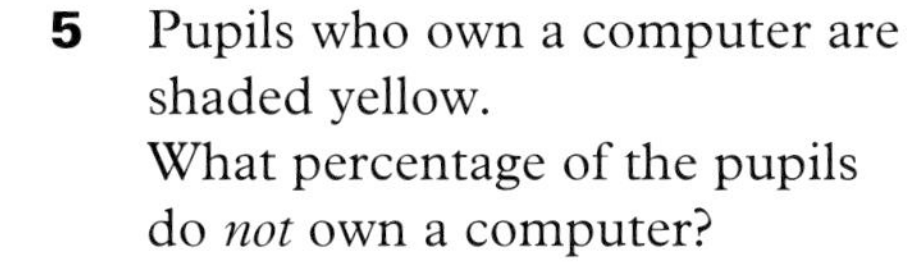

5 Pupils who own a computer are shaded yellow.
What percentage of the pupils do *not* own a computer?

You can also work out percentages when there are not 100 children.

82 out of 100 is 82%

41 out of 50 is still 82%

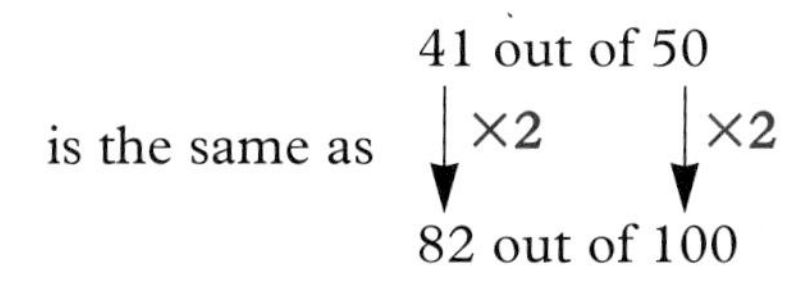

41 out of 50

is the same as ↓ ×2 ↓ ×2

82 out of 100

Exercise 9:2

1 Pupils who have a part-time job are shaded red.

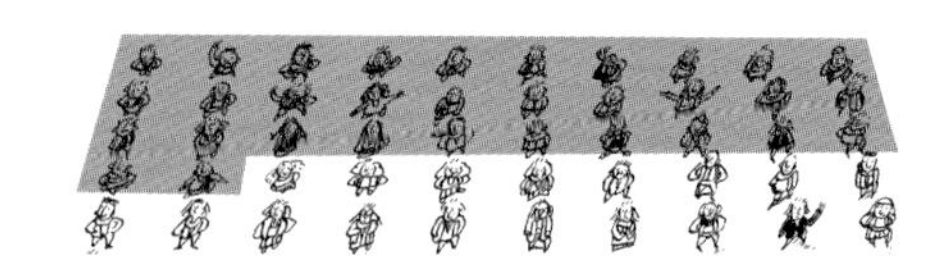

a How many of the 50 have a part-time job?

b What percentage have a part-time job?

2 Pupils who read a daily newspaper are shaded green.

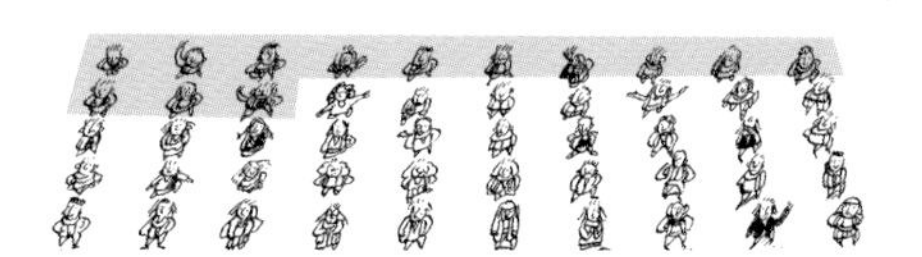

a How many of the 50 read a newspaper?

b What percentage read a newspaper?

3 Pupils who own a cat are shaded brown.

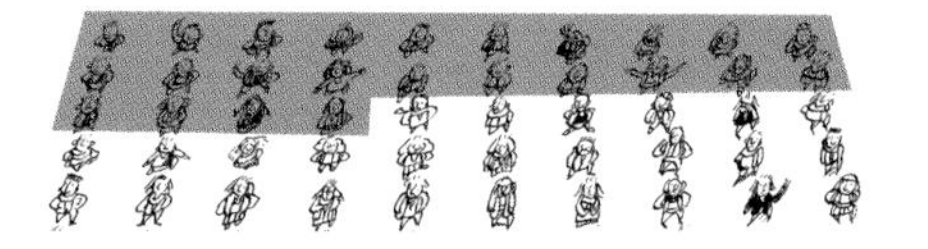

a How many of the 50 own a cat?

b What percentage own a cat?

4 Pupils who support Liverpool Football Club are shaded orange.

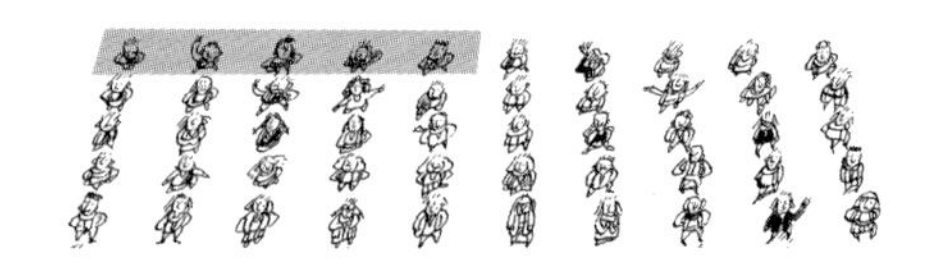

a How many of the 50 are shaded orange?

b What percentage support Liverpool?

c What percentage do *not* support Liverpool?

● **5** Pupils who go swimming regularly are shaded blue.

a How many pupils out of the 25 are shaded blue?

b How many groups of 25 make 100?

c What percentage go swimming?

d What percentage do *not* go swimming?

Shops often have special sale days.
They mark some items with a blue cross.
This means that there is 10% off the price.

They do not change the price on the ticket because the sale only lasts a few days.

You have to work out the sale price for yourself.

10% means 10 in every 100.

This is the same as 10 p in every £1

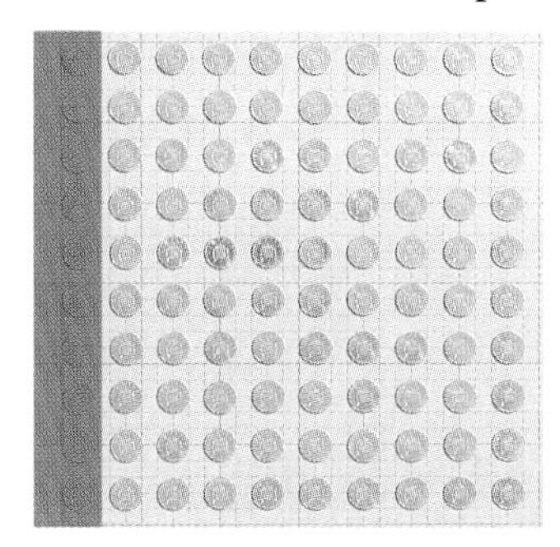

This is the same as 1 p in every 10 p

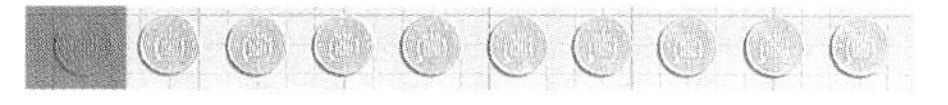

This makes it easy to find 10% of an amount of money.
You divide the amount by 10.

To divide by 10, move all the numbers one place to the right.

Example A T-shirt costing £6.50 is in the blue cross sale.
Work out how much you would save.

10% of £6.50 = £6 . 5 0 ÷ 10

(each digit moves one place to the right: ÷10)

= £0 . 6 5
= 65 p

You would save 65 p

Exercise 9:3

All these items are in the blue cross sale.
This means take 10% off.

1 Work out how much you would save on each of these.
- **a** A T-shirt costing £7.50
- **b** Shorts costing £9.50
- **c** Socks costing £3.50
- **d** A sweatshirt costing £8.50

2 Work out how much you would save on each of these.
- **a** A T-shirt costing £5.20
- **b** A board game costing £7.40
- **c** A pen costing £1.20
- **d** A diary costing £4.90

3 Work out how much you would save on each of these.
- **a** Jeans costing £22.50
- **b** A jacket costing £35.90
- **c** A jumper costing £12.80
- **d** Trainers costing £89.90

4 A personal stereo costs £24.90
- **a** How much would you save with 10% off?
- **b** How much would the stereo cost?

5 A pair of jeans costs £35.50
- **a** How much would you save in the blue cross sale?
- **b** How much would the jeans cost?

6 A computer game costs £26.90
Work out its new price in the sale.

7 A pair of shoes costs exactly £25
Work out how much they would cost in the sale.

8 A CD costs £12.90
How much would it cost in the sale?

Once you have worked out 10% it is quite easy to work out other percentages.

On the last day of the blue cross sale the discount is increased to 20%.

Everything marked with a blue cross now has 20% off.
To work out 20% of an amount:
First work out 10% of the amount.
Then multiply by 2.
$10\% \times 2 = 20\%$

Example

A pair of jeans costs £35.90
Work out the new price with 20% off.

10% of £35.90 = £3.59
20% of £35.90 = £3.59 × 2 = £7.18

The jeans would cost £35.90 − £7.18 = £28.72

Exercise 9:4

1 A pair of jeans costs £27.90
The price is reduced by 20%.
a Work out 10% of £27.90
b Work out 20% of £27.90

2 A portable TV costs £90
a Work out 10% of £90
b Work out 20% of £90
c Work out the cost of the TV if it is reduced by 20%.

3 A box of computer disks costs £8.50
The price is reduced by 20% in the sale.
a Find 20% of £8.50
b How much does the box of disks cost in the sale?

4 A ski jacket costs £120
The price is reduced by 20% in the sale.
Work out the cost of the jacket in the sale.

You can make up other percentages from 10%.

If you want to work out 40%, find 10% and then multiply by 4.
70% is 10% multiplied by 7.

Examples

1 Find 40% of £24

10% of £24 = £2.40
40% of £24 = £2.40 × 4 = £9.60

2 Find 60% of £50

10% of £50 = £5
60% of £50 = £5 × 6 = £30

Exercise 9:5

1 Find these percentages. You will need to work out 10% first.

a 30% of £24
b 40% of £30
c 40% of £45
d 60% of £150

2 A pair of jeans is reduced by 30% in a sale.
They normally cost £33
a Work out 30% of £33
b How much do the jeans cost in the sale?

3 There are 220 pupils in Year 8.
20% have brown eyes.
a Find 10% of 220.
b How many pupils have brown eyes?

4 In an election 22 000 people voted.
40% of them voted Labour.
a Find 10% of 22 000.
b Find 40% of 22 000.
This is the number of people who voted Labour.
c How many people did not vote Labour?

5 In a trial of 2000 cats, 60% preferred Kitidins.
a How many cats preferred Kitidins?
b What percentage preferred another brand?
c How many cats preferred another brand?

50% of something is half of it. You can divide by 2 to find 50%.
This is easier than finding 10% and then multiplying by 5.

You can find 25% by finding 50% and then dividing this by 2.

Examples

1 Find 50% of £70

50% of £70 = £70 ÷ 2 = £35

2 Find 25% of £130

50% of £130 = £130 ÷ 2 = £65
25% of £130 = £65 ÷ 2 = £32.50

6 Find:
a 50% of £60 **b** 50% of £46

7 Work out these percentages. Find 50% first.
a 25% of £40 **b** 25% of £180 ● **c** 25% of £170

8 There are 700 pupils at Habnor School.
50% have school meals.
25% take a packed lunch.
25% go home.
a How many pupils have school meals?
b How many pupils take a packed lunch?

9 Here are 6 question cards and 6 answer cards.
Work out each question.
Match it with its answer.
Write the questions and answers in your book.

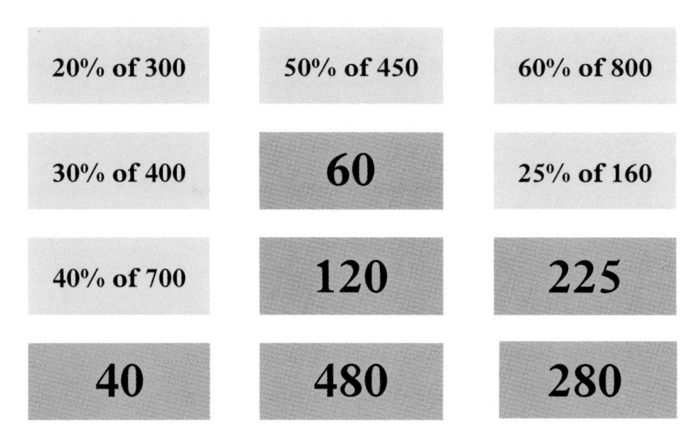

2 Calculating percentages

These opinion poll results are given as percentages.
We can work them out with a calculator.

To work out a percentage on a calculator:

(1) Turn the percentage into a decimal.
To do this, divide it by 100.

(2) Multiply by the decimal.

Examples

1 Find 38% of 1200 people.

38% = 38 ÷ 100 = 0.38
38% of 1200 = 0.38 × 1200 = 456 people

2 Find 47% of 1200 people.

47% = 47 ÷ 100 = 0.47
47% of 1200 = 0.47 × 1200 = 564 people

Exercise 9:6

1 Copy and fill in:

a $56\% = \ldots \div 100 = 0.56$
b $76\% = 76 \div 100 = \ldots$
c $32\% = \ldots \div 100 = \ldots$
d $98\% = \ldots \div 100 = \ldots$
e $\ldots\% = 12 \div 100 = 0.12$
f $\ldots\% = 85 \div 100 = \ldots$

2 1200 people take part in a survey about banks.
They are asked which bank they use.

23% say Nat West
17% say Lloyds
18% say Barclays
15% say Midland
27% say another bank

a Add up the percentages.
Write down the total.

b Copy and fill in:
(1) 23% of 1200 = $0.23 \times 1200 = \ldots$
(2) 17% of 1200 = $0.17 \times 1200 = \ldots$
(3) 18% of 1200 = $\ldots \times 1200 = \ldots$
(4) 15% of 1200 = $\ldots \times 1200 = \ldots$
(5) 27% of 1200 = $\ldots \times 1200 = \ldots$

c Add up your answers to part **b**.
Write down the total.

3 Class 8J have a Maths test. The total mark is 40.
The teacher gives them their marks as percentages.
They want to know how many marks they got.

Copy this table.
Fill it in.

Name	Percentage	Working	Mark
Terry	35%	0.35×40	
Sian	65%	0.65×40	
Alan	85%		
Lindsey	95%		

4 Look at this advertisement.

a Pritesh buys a Chart CD. It normally costs £13
(1) Work out 15% of £13 (0.15×13)
(2) How much does the CD cost in the sale?

b Glenn also buys a Chart CD. It normally costs £13.80
(1) Work out 15% of £13.80
(2) How much does the CD cost in the sale?

c Michelle buys a Rock CD. It normally costs £11
There is 26% off in the sale.
(1) Work out 26% of £11
(2) How much does the CD cost?

d Anne buys a Classical CD. It normally costs £15
(1) Work out 12% of £15
(2) How much does the CD cost in the sale?

Rob's Records

CD Sale

15% off Chart CDs
Up to 33% off Rock CDs
12% off all Classical CDs

Exercise 9:7 Four in a row

This is a game for two players.
You will need two colours of counters.
Each player uses a different colour.
You need one calculator between you.

Underneath the number 650 you can see a list of 36 percentages.
If you work out these percentages of 650 you get the answers shown in the board underneath.

Player 1:
(1) Choose a square on the board.
(2) One percentage from the list will give the answer in the square.
Choose the percentage that you think is correct.
(3) Calculate the percentage.
(4) Cover up the calculator answer on the board with a counter.

Player 2:
You do the same thing using your counters.

The winner is the first person to get four counters in a straight line.
The line can be in any direction.
The better you are at predicting the answers, the more likely you are to win!

650

23% 57% 68% 24% 12% 45% 97% 81% 27%

39% 42% 17% 15% 47% 25% 84% 71% 55%

66% 10% 13% 54% 93% 61% 49% 60% 80%

22% 43% 74% 99% 24% 33% 58% 17% 75%

149.5	110.5	305.5	214.5	357.5	442
390	162.5	156	292.5	110.5	396.5
526.5	643.5	604.5	461.5	175.5	520
97.5	429	370.5	143	318.5	630.5
78	481	253.5	65	487.5	546
84.5	396.5	279.5	273	377	351

3 Fractions

Bill is ordering some new stock.
Three-quarters of the ice creams that he sells are cornets.
One-quarter are lollies.

Bill has sold 1200 ice creams this week.
He wants to work out how many lollies he has sold.

Example Find one-quarter of 1200.

To split something into quarters, divide by 4.
$1200 \div 4 = 300$
One quarter of 1200 is 300. He has sold 300 lollies

Exercise 9:8

1 Find one-quarter of:
a 400 **b** 600 **c** 560 **d** 24 **e** 36

2 To find one-third of something, divide by 3.
Find one-third of:
a 300 **b** 123 **c** 51 **d** 84 **e** 111

3 To find one-sixth of something, divide by 6.
Find one-sixth of:

a 300 **b** 72 **c** 108 **d** 162 **e** 1542

4 Copy this table. Fill it in.

	Fraction	Divide by
one half		2
one-third	$\frac{1}{3}$	3
one-quarter		
one-fifth		5
one-sixth	$\frac{1}{6}$	
one-seventh		
		8
	$\frac{1}{9}$	
		10

5 Use your table to help you answer these questions.

a $\frac{1}{10}$ of 300 **c** $\frac{1}{5}$ of 240 **e** $\frac{1}{3}$ of 159

b $\frac{1}{7}$ of 252 **d** $\frac{1}{8}$ of 192 **f** $\frac{1}{9}$ of 333

Three-quarters of the ice creams Bill sells are cornets.
Once Bill had found $\frac{1}{4}$ of 1200 it was easy to work out $\frac{3}{4}$ of 1200.

Example Find $\frac{3}{4}$ of 1200.

We know that $\frac{1}{4}$ of 1200 is 300.

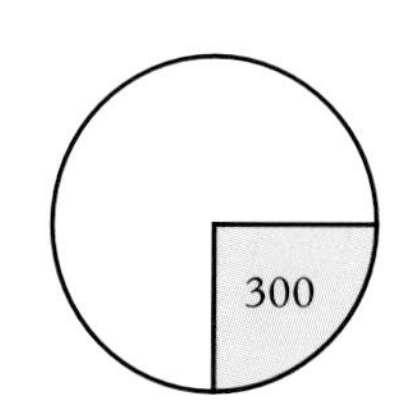

$\frac{3}{4}$ of 1200 is three times as much.
We multiply $\frac{1}{4}$ of 1200 by 3

$300 \times 3 = 900$

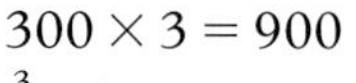

$\frac{3}{4}$ of $1200 = 900$
Bill has sold 900 cornets.

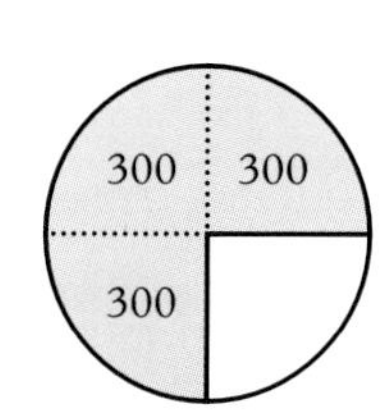

To find $\frac{3}{4}$ of something:
(1) Divide by 4 to find $\frac{1}{4}$
(2) Multiply by 3 to find $\frac{3}{4}$

Exercise 9:9

1 Find:
a $\frac{1}{4}$ of 240
b $\frac{3}{4}$ of 240

2 Find:
a $\frac{1}{5}$ of 240
b $\frac{2}{5}$ of 240
c $\frac{3}{5}$ of 240

3 Find:
a $\frac{1}{7}$ of 168
b $\frac{2}{7}$ of 168
c $\frac{5}{7}$ of 168

4 Find:
a $\frac{1}{8}$ of 192
b $\frac{3}{8}$ of 192
c $\frac{7}{8}$ of 192

5 Paul always saves $\frac{1}{4}$ of his pocket money.
He gets £3.60 each week.
a How much does he save each week?
b What fraction does he spend each week?
c How much does he spend each week?

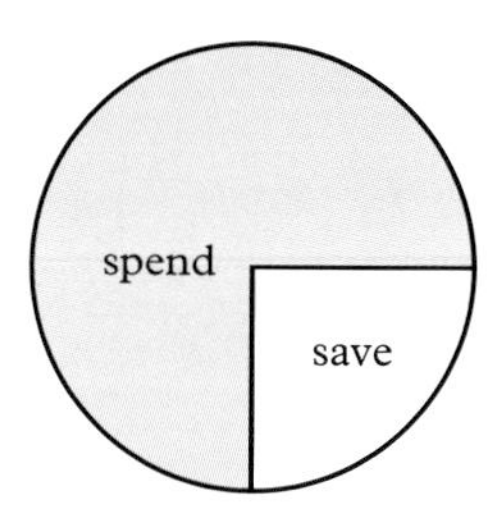

6 In a box of apples, $\frac{2}{7}$ have gone bad.
There are 35 apples in the box.
How many apples have gone bad?

7 $\frac{2}{5}$ of the cars sold by a garage are hatchbacks.
The garage sells 45 cars in August.
a How many hatchbacks do they sell?
b How many other cars do they sell?

You can do fractions questions on your calculator.
You use the button $a^b/_c$ to enter a fraction.

To enter $\frac{3}{4}$ press 3 $a^b/_c$ 4

To find $\frac{3}{4}$ of 240 press 3 $a^b/_c$ 4 × 2 4 0 =

You should get 180

Exercise 9:10

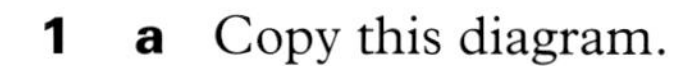

1 **a** Copy this diagram.

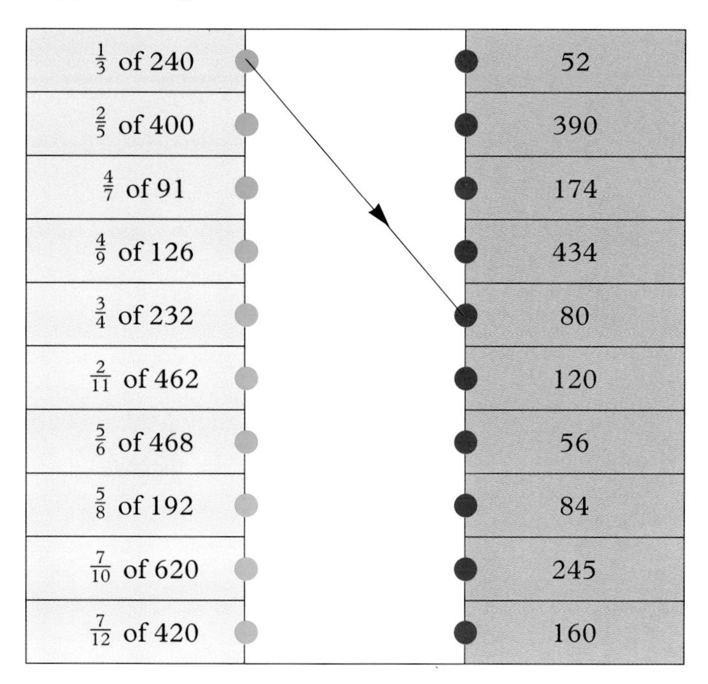

b Work out the answers to the questions.
Join each question to the correct answer with an arrow.
One has been done for you.

2 Josie has a herd of 225 cows on her farm.
At the market she sells $\frac{2}{5}$ of them.
a How many cows does she sell?
b How many cows has she got left?

3 Javed planted 60 seeds in his garden.
$\frac{5}{6}$ of the seeds grew. The others died.
a How many seeds grew?
b What fraction of the seeds died?

● **4** There are 1050 pupils in a school.
A survey showed that $\frac{2}{7}$ of them wear glasses.
How many pupils do *not* wear glasses?

1 There are 100 apples in a box.
13 of them are bad.
What percentage of the apples are bad?

2 There are 50 girls in the gym club at school.
24 of them like vaulting best.
What percentage of the girls like vaulting best?

3 Freda asked 50 pupils in Year 8 for their favourite sport.
Here are her results:
Football 34 Swimming 5 Running 4 Hockey 4 Netball 3
What percentage of pupils like each sport?

4 Work out how much you would save on each of these in the sale.
- **a** A shirt costing £15
- **b** A coat costing £25
- **c** A book costing £9.50
- **d** A CD costing £13.50
- **e** A watch costing £14.80

5 The basic rate of tax is 25%. This means that you have to pay 25% of what you earn in tax.
Work out the tax that you pay if you earn:
a £400 **b** £200 **c** £300 **d** £450

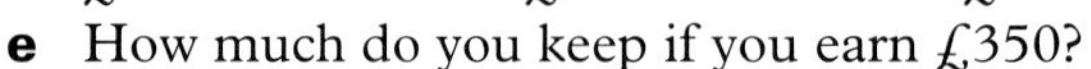

e How much do you keep if you earn £350?

6 There are 220 pupils in Year 8 at Stanthorne High.
- **a** 70% of them have chips every day.
How many pupils have chips every day?
- **b** 30% have a brother.
How many pupils have a brother?
- **c** 40% have a sister.
How many pupils have a sister?
- **d** 20% walk to school each day.
How many pupils walk to school each day?
- **e** What percentage of pupils *do not* walk to school each day?

7 Work these out.
a 20% of £500 **c** 30% of 340 girls **e** 25% of 5 metres
b 40% of £600 **d** 25% of 8 hours **f** 50% of 15 kilograms

8 Copy and fill in:

a 23% of 1300 = 0.23 × 1300 = …
b 47% of 1500 = 0.47 × 1500 = …
c 73% of 2300 = … × … = …
d …% of 4500 = 0.39 × … = …

9 Find:

a 64% of 3800 people
b 29% of £4600
c 52% of 450 grams
d 37% of £2479

10 1500 people take part in a shopping survey.
They are asked if they use a supermarket for all of their shopping.
47% say that they do use a supermarket.

a How many people use a supermarket for all of their shopping?
b What percentage of people *do not* use a supermarket for all of their shopping?

11 Stephen does a survey about favourite flavours of ice cream. He writes a report of his results. This is part of his report. How many people like each flavour of ice cream the best?

Favourite flavours of ice cream of 200 people

Vanilla 57%
Chocolate 23%
Strawberry 12%
Other 8%

12 In a class of 27 pupils $\frac{2}{3}$ are right-handed.

a How many pupils are right-handed?
b What fraction of pupils are left-handed?

13 Vanessa shares her 120 sweets with her friends.
She gives $\frac{1}{8}$ to Rebecca and $\frac{3}{8}$ to Fazia.
She keeps the rest herself.

a How many sweets does Vanessa give to Rebecca?
b How many sweets does Vanessa give to Fazia?
c What fraction of the sweets does Vanessa keep for herself?

14 Work these out.

a $\frac{4}{7}$ of 350
b $\frac{5}{8}$ of 640
c $\frac{7}{12}$ of 2448
d $\frac{5}{11}$ of 286

15 A bag contains 24 counters.
$\frac{1}{4}$ of them are blue, $\frac{2}{3}$ are green and the rest are yellow.
How many counters of each colour are in the bag?

1 There are 25 pupils in 8N.
12 of them come to school by bus.
What percentage of the pupils in 8N come to school by bus?

2 A computer game usually costs £38
In a sale the cost is reduced by 20%.
How much does the game cost in the sale?

3 22 000 people voted in a local election.
35% voted Conservative.

a Work out 10% of 22 000.

b Use your answer to **a** to work out 5% of 22 000.

c Use your answers to **a** and **b** to work out how many people voted Conservative.

d What percentage of people did *not* vote Conservative?

4 Mr Hussein can earn £3500 before he pays tax.
Then he pays 25% on the rest of his earnings.
In one year Mr Hussein earns £12 500
Copy and fill in:

a Mr Hussein pays tax on £12 500 − £3500 = £…

b Amount of tax = 25% of £… = £…

c Mr Hussein keeps £12 500 − £… = £…

5 VAT stands for Value Added Tax. You pay it on lots of things you buy.
VAT is charged at $17\frac{1}{2}\%$ on most things.
$17\frac{1}{2}\%$ is 0.175 as a decimal.
Work out the VAT on each of these items.

a A video costing £10 without VAT.

b A picture frame costing £30 without VAT.

c Training shoes costing £40 without VAT.

6 A bag contains 36 beads.
$\frac{1}{3}$ of them are red, $\frac{2}{9}$ are blue and the rest are green.

a How many beads of each colour are in the bag?

b What fraction of the beads are green?

7 There are 32 teeth in a full adult set.
$\frac{1}{8}$ are canines, $\frac{3}{8}$ are molars and $\frac{1}{4}$ are incisors.
The rest are called pre-molars.

a How many canines are there?

b How many molars are there?

c What fraction of the teeth are pre-molars?

- To find 10% of an amount divide the amount by 10.

Example 10% of £6.50 = £6 . 5 0 ÷ 10

(each digit moves ÷10)

= £0 . 6 5
= 65 p

- You can make up other percentages from 10%.

If you want to work out 40%, find 10% and then multiply by 4.
70% is 10% multiplied by 7.

50% of something is half of it. You can divide by 2 to find 50%.
This is easier than finding 10% and then multiplying by 5.

You can find 25% by finding 50% and then dividing this by 2.

Examples

1 Find 40% of £24

10% of £24 = £2.40
40% of £24 = £2.40 × 4 = £9.60

2 Find 25% of £70

50% of £70 = £70 ÷ 2 = £35
25% of £70 = £35 ÷ 2 = £17.50

- To work out a percentage on a calculator:

(1) Turn the percentage into a decimal.
To do this, divide it by 100.

(2) Multiply by the decimal.

Example Find 38% of 1200 people

38% = 38 ÷ 100 = 0.38
38% of 1200 = 0.38 × 1200 = 456 people

- To split something into quarters, divide by 4.

Example One-quarter of 1200 = 1200 ÷ 4 = 300

- To find $\frac{3}{4}$ of something:

(1) Divide by 4 to find $\frac{1}{4}$

(2) Multiply by 3 to find $\frac{3}{4}$

- You can do fractions questions on your calculator.

You use the button **a b/c** to enter a fraction.

To enter $\frac{3}{4}$ press **3** **a b/c** **4**

To find $\frac{3}{4}$ of 240 press **3** **a b/c** **4** **×** **2** **4** **0** **=**

You should get 180

1 There are 100 Revels in a bag.
23 of them are toffees.
What percentage of the Revels are toffees?

2 There are 50 bananas on a supermarket shelf.
12 of them are very ripe.
What percentage of the bananas are very ripe?

3 In a sale everything is reduced by 10%.
Work out how much you would save on each of these in the sale.
a A T-shirt costing £8
b A jacket costing £20
c A tape costing £9.50
d A CD costing £12.50
e A book costing £14.80

4 Work these out.
a 10% of £400
b 40% of £400
c 25% of £340

5 Copy and fill in:
a 46% of 1100 $= 0.46 \times 1100 = \ldots$
b 67% of 1700 $= 0.67 \times 1700 = \ldots$
c 73% of 8600 $= \ldots \times \ldots = \ldots$

6 Work these out.
a 48% of 6700 people
b 38% of 1200 metres
c 96% of 750 grams
d 7% of £1327

7 A bar of chocolate weighs 60 grams.
What is the weight of $\frac{1}{3}$ of the bar?

8 In a class of 28 pupils $\frac{2}{7}$ have blonde hair.
a How many pupils have blonde hair?
b What fraction of the pupils do *not* have blonde hair?

9 Paul eats a lot of sweets. He has fillings in $\frac{1}{4}$ of his 28 teeth.
a How many fillings has Paul got?
b What fraction of his teeth are *not* filled?

10 Straight lines

CORE

1 Lines of the grid

2 Patterns of lines

3 Curves from straight lines

QUESTIONS

EXTENSION

SUMMARY

TEST YOURSELF

The co-ordinates we use to draw graphs are called Cartesian co-ordinates. They were named after a Frenchman called René Descartes (1596–1650). In 1619 he had a dream in which he realised that all the sciences were connected and that physics could be expressed using the language of geometry. One of Descartes' famous sayings was: '*Cogito ergo sum*' which is Latin for '*Je pense, donc je suis*'.

1 Lines of the grid

Bill is on holiday in New York.
He wants to visit the World Trade Center Building.
It is at the intersection of Liberty Street with West Street.

◀◀REPLAY▶

Exercise 10:1

1 Look at the red line.
The co-ordinates of the point P are (2, 3).

Write down the co-ordinates of the points A, B, C and D.

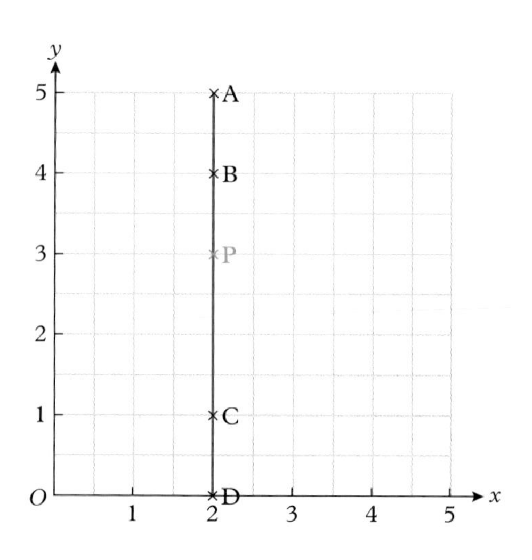

In question **1** all the points have $\boldsymbol{x}$ co-ordinate = **2**
In algebra this is $\boldsymbol{x} = \mathbf{2}$
The rule for the line is $\boldsymbol{x} = \mathbf{2}$

2 Write down the rules for these lines.
Copy and fill in:
a The rule is x = …
b The rule is x = …
c The rule is … = …
d The rule is … = …

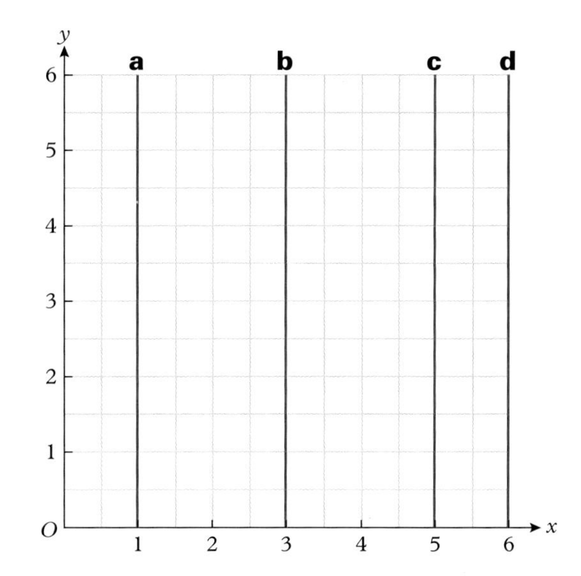

3 Look at the red line.
Write down the co-ordinates of the points A, B, C, D and E.

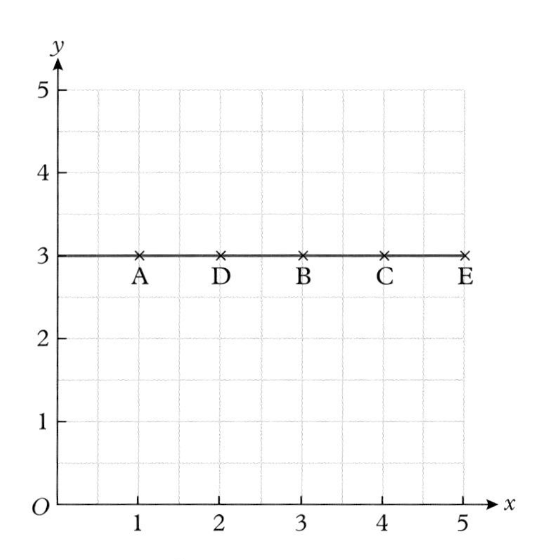

In question **3** all the points have $\boldsymbol{y}$ co-ordinate = **3**
In algebra this is $\boldsymbol{y} = \mathbf{3}$
The rule for the line is $\boldsymbol{y} = \mathbf{3}$

4 Write down the rules for these lines.
Copy and fill in:
a The rule is y = …
b The rule is y = …
c The rule is … = …
d The rule is … = …

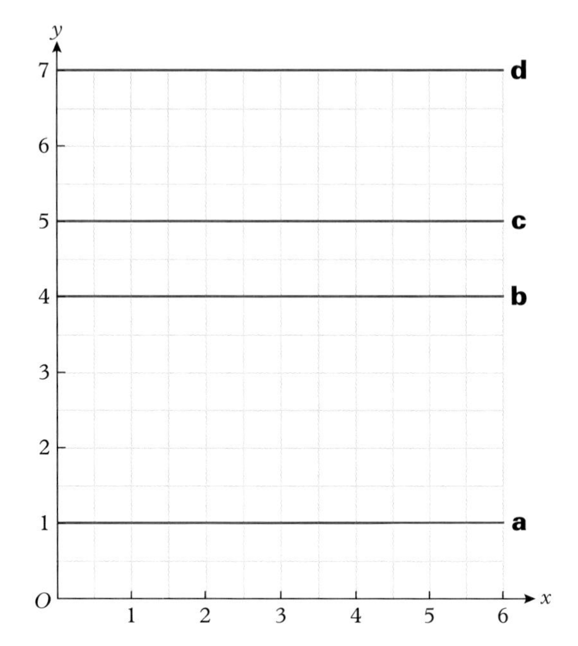

5 Write down the rules for these lines.

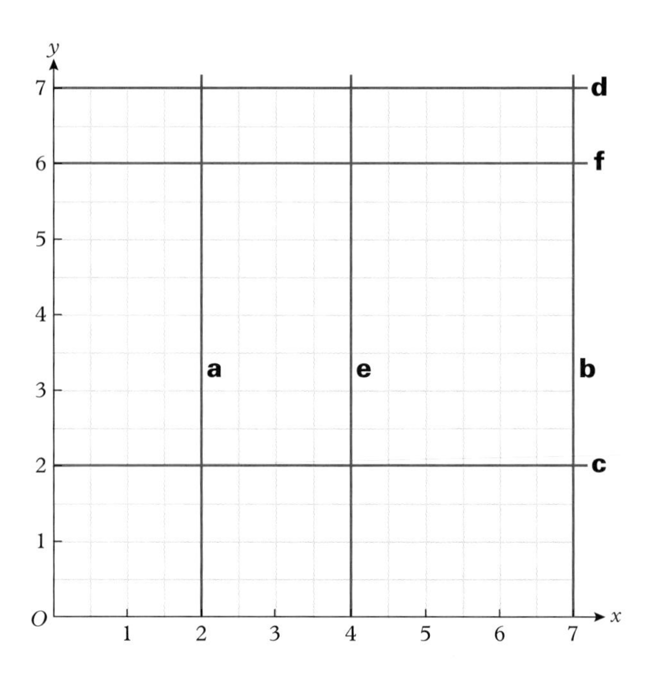

6 **a** Copy the axes on to squared paper.

b Draw the line $x = 3$
Label the line with its rule.

c Draw the line $y = 2$
Label the line.

d The lines cross at a point.
Write down the co-ordinates of this point.
Remember to use brackets (…, …)

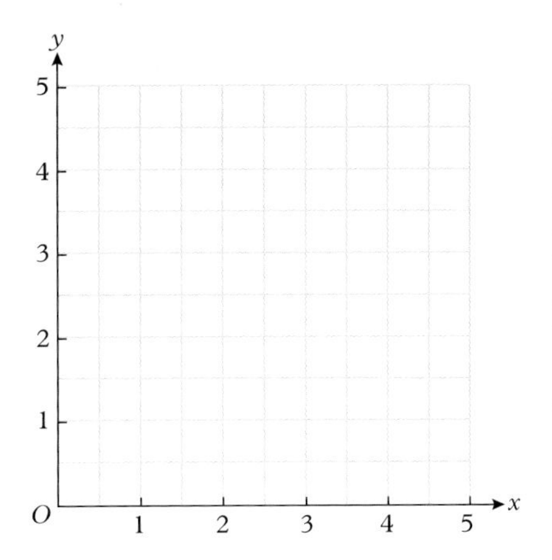

7 **a** Copy the axes on to squared paper.

b Draw the line $x = 4$
Label the line.

c Draw the line $y = 1$
Label the line.

d Write down the co-ordinates of the point where the lines cross.

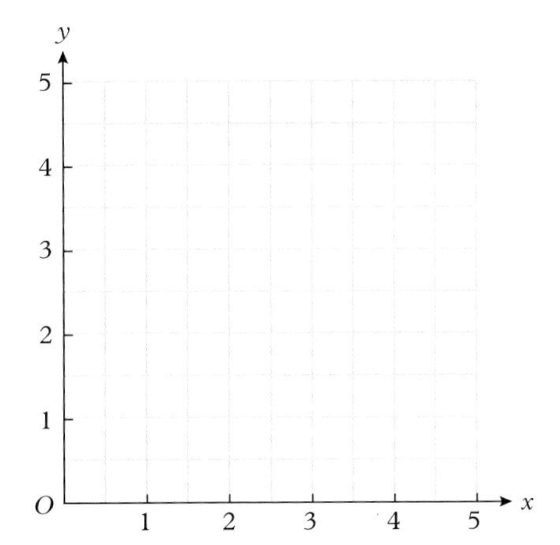

8 **a** Copy the axes on to squared paper.

b Draw two more lines:
one straight up and
one straight across.
They must cross at the point
(2, 5)

c Copy and fill in the rules for these two lines.

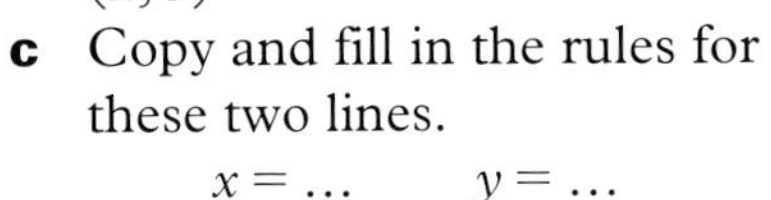
$x = \ldots \qquad y = \ldots$

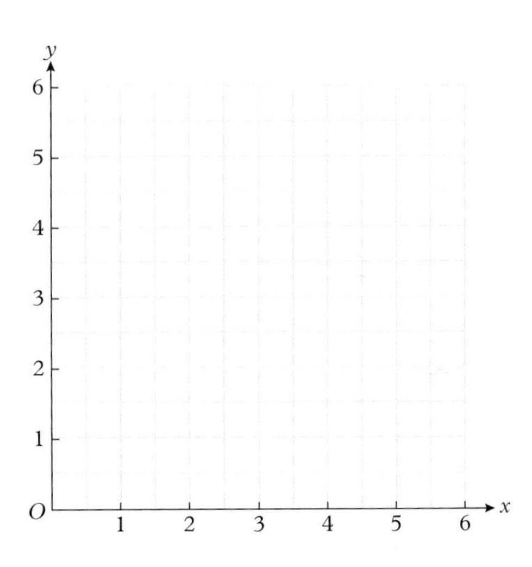

Point of intersection	The point where two lines cross is called a **point of intersection**.

Exercise 10:2

1 Write down the co-ordinates of the point of intersection of these lines.

a $x = 1$ and $y = 6$

b $x = 4$ and $y = 3$

c $x = 5$ and $y = 4$

d $x = 0$ and $y = 1$

2 Write down the rule for:

a the x axis

b the y axis

c Write down the co-ordinates of the point of intersection of these two lines.

d What do we call this point?

3 **a** Copy the axes on to squared paper.

b Plot these points:
(1, 2) (1, 5) (2, 3)
Join the points with a ruler to make a triangle.

c Draw the line $x = 3$ on your axes.

d Reflect the triangle in the line $x = 3$

e Write down the co-ordinates of the vertices of this new triangle.

Remember: 'vertices' means 'corners'

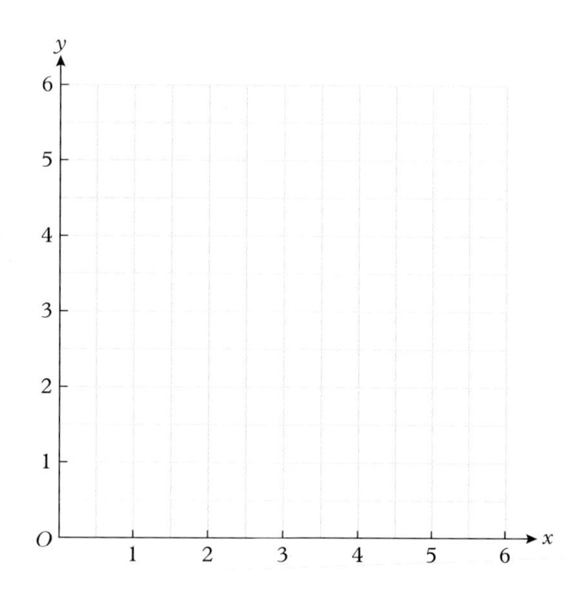

4 **a** Copy the axes for question **3** again.

b Draw the triangle whose vertices are (1, 0) (1, 3) (4, 1)

c Reflect this triangle in the line $y = 3$

d Write down the co-ordinates of the vertices of the new triangle.

2 Patterns of lines

Matthew and Katy are looking for patterns on a grid.

Exercise 10:3

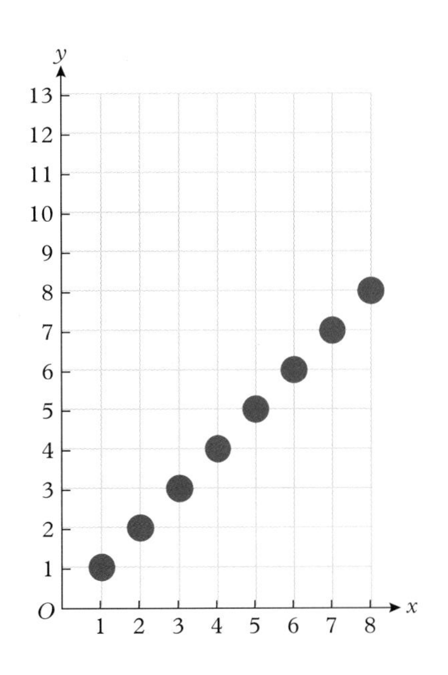

You will need some counters and a grid.

1 **a** Copy the axes on to the grid.
Use it for all the questions in this Exercise.

b Matthew has put counters on points of the grid. He wants the y co-ordinate to be the same as the x co-ordinate.
Katy sees that they are in a straight line.

Mark the points on your grid where the $\boldsymbol{y}$ co-ordinate = the $\boldsymbol{x}$ co-ordinate
Join the points with a straight line.
The rule for the line is $\boldsymbol{y = x}$

c Label the line with its rule $y = x$

Equation

The rule of a line is called the **equation** of the line.
The equation of this line is $y = x$

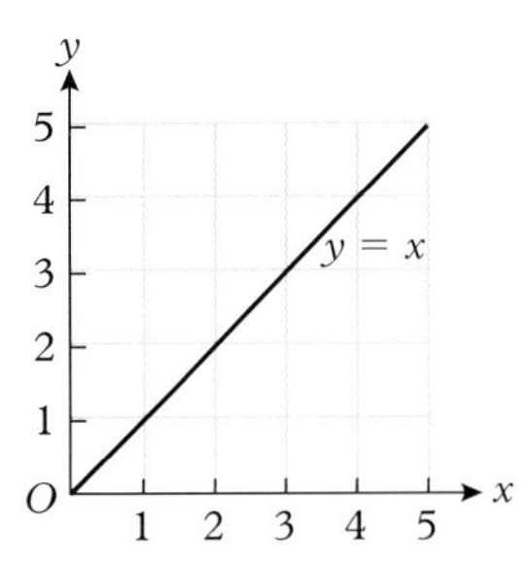

---

2 Katy puts counters on the grid where
the $\boldsymbol{y}$ co-ordinate = 2 × the $\boldsymbol{x}$ co-ordinate.
She marks the points on her grid.
She joins the points with a straight line.

a Put counters on your grid so that it looks like Katy's.
Mark the points.
Join the points with a straight line.

b Copy:
The equation of the line is $\boldsymbol{y} = 2 \times \boldsymbol{x}$
In algebra this is $\boldsymbol{y} = 2\boldsymbol{x}$

c Label the line with its equation $y = 2x$

3 **a** Put counters on your grid where the
$\boldsymbol{y}$ co-ordinate is 3 × the $\boldsymbol{x}$ co-ordinate.

b Mark the points.
Join them with a straight line.

c Copy and fill in the equation of the line.
$\boldsymbol{y} = \ldots \boldsymbol{x}$

d Label the line with its equation.

4 You have drawn the lines $y = x$
$y = 2x$
$y = 3x$

a Which line is the steepest?

b Which line is the least steep?

c Which part of the equation tells you how steep the line is?

5 **a** Which line do you think will be steeper:
$y = 3x$ or $y = 4x$

b Use counters on your grid to find three points where
the y co-ordinate is 4 × the x co-ordinate
Mark the points.
Draw the line $y = 4x$

c Was your answer to **a** correct?

6 Which line is the steeper in each of these pairs?

a $y = x$ or $y = 4x$

b $y = 2x$ or $y = 6x$

c $y = 5x$ or $y = 4x$

d $y = 3x$ or $y = 4x$

e $y = 8x$ or $y = 5x$

Marcus is looking at some patterns on a grid.
He has put his counters on the grid where
y co-ordinate = ***x*** co-ordinate + 1
The equation is:

$$\boldsymbol{y} = \boldsymbol{x} + 1$$

Exercise 10:4

You will need some counters.

1 **a** Make a new grid like the one that you used in Exercise 10.3.
Use it for all the questions in this Exercise.

b Use counters on your grid to help you draw the line $y = x$
Label the line with its equation.

c Now put the counters on the grid like Marcus did.
Remember:
y co-ordinate = x co-ordinate + 1
Your counters should be in a straight line.

d Mark the points.
Join them with a straight line.

e Copy and fill in the equation of the line.
$y = x + \ldots$

f Label the line with its equation.

2 **a** Put counters on your grid where
y co-ordinate = x co-ordinate + 2

b Mark the points.
Join them with a straight line.

c Copy and fill in the equation of the line.
$y = x + \ldots$

d Label the line with its equation.

3 You have drawn the lines $y = x$
$y = x + 1$
$y = x + 2$

a Copy and fill in:
The lines are all p..................
b Which line is higher up the grid?
c Where do you think the line $y = x + 3$ will go?
d Use counters to help you draw the line $y = x + 3$ on your grid.
Label the line with its equation.
e Was your answer to **c** correct?

4 Look at your grid. You have drawn four lines on it.
a Copy and fill in these sentences.
The line $y = x$ crosses the y axis at 0.
The line $y = x + 1$ crosses the y axis at 1.
The line $y = x + 2$ crosses the y axis at ...
The line $y = x + 3$ crosses the y axis at ...
b Where will the line $y = x + 4$ cross the y axis?
c Use counters to help you draw the line $y = x + 4$ on your grid.
Label the line with its equation.
d Was your answer to **b** correct?

5 Where will these lines cross the y axis?
a $y = x + 5$
b $y = x + 7$
c $y = x + 8$
d $y = x + 12$

Exercise 10:5 Patterns with co-ordinates

1 Here is a pattern of triangles.

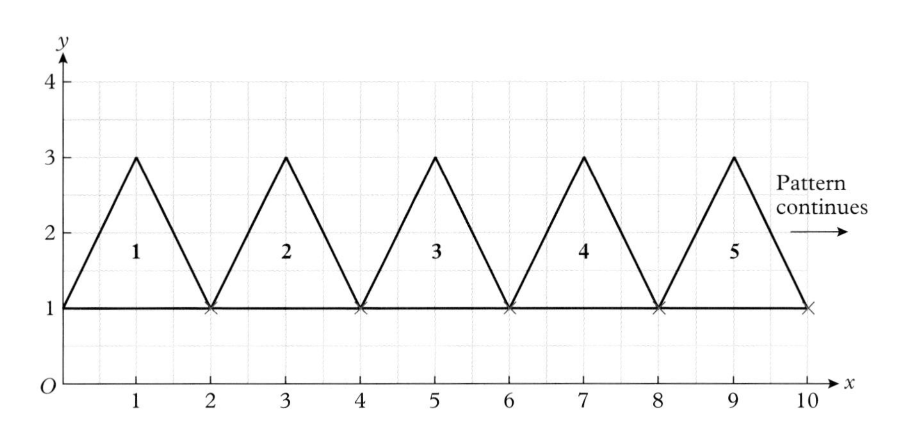

The pattern continues to the right.

a Write down the co-ordinates of the top of triangle 1.

b Write down the co-ordinates of the top of triangles 2 and 3.

c Copy this table.
Fill it in.

Triangle number	1	2	3	4	5
x co-ordinate of top	1	3	5		

d How many do you add to the x co-ordinate each time?

On the right of each triangle is a red cross.

e Write down the co-ordinates of the cross for triangle 1.

Here is a table of x co-ordinates for the cross for each triangle.

Number of triangle	1	2	3	4	5
x co-ordinate of cross	2				

f Copy the table.
Fill it in.

g How many do you add to the x co-ordinate each time?

• **2** Here is a pattern of squares.

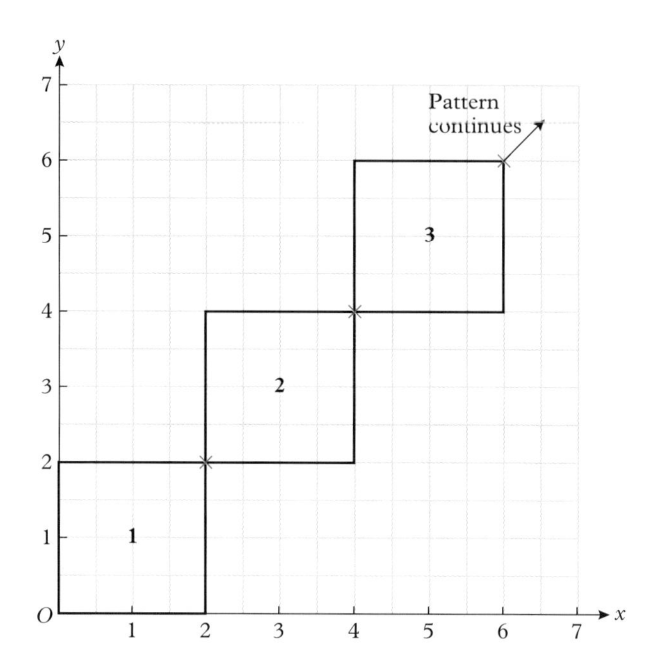

One corner of each square is marked with a red cross.

a Write down the co-ordinates of the cross at the top of square 1.

b Write down the co-ordinates of the cross at the top of square 2.

c What do you notice about the x and y co-ordinate of each cross?

Here is a table of the x co-ordinate of the cross at the top of each square.

Number of square	1	2	3
x co-ordinate of cross	2	4	

d Copy the table.
Fill it in.

e How many do you add to the x co-ordinate each time?

f Copy this and fill in the gaps.
x co-ordinate = … × $n$umber of square

g Write this formula in algebra.
$x = \ldots \times n$

h Use your formula to find the x co-ordinate of the 4th square.
Check that the answer is correct by looking at your table.

i Use your formula to find the x co-ordinate of the 25th square.

3 Curves from straight lines

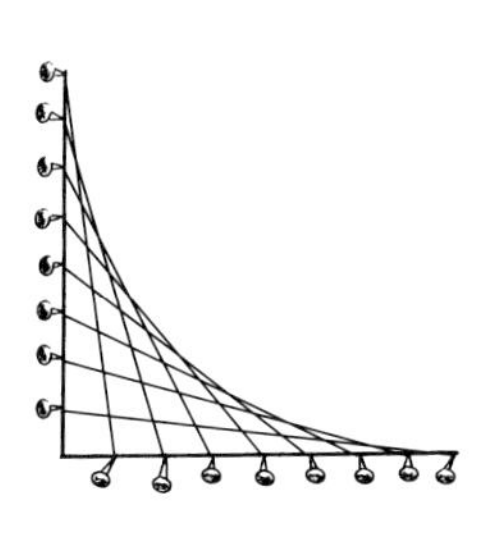

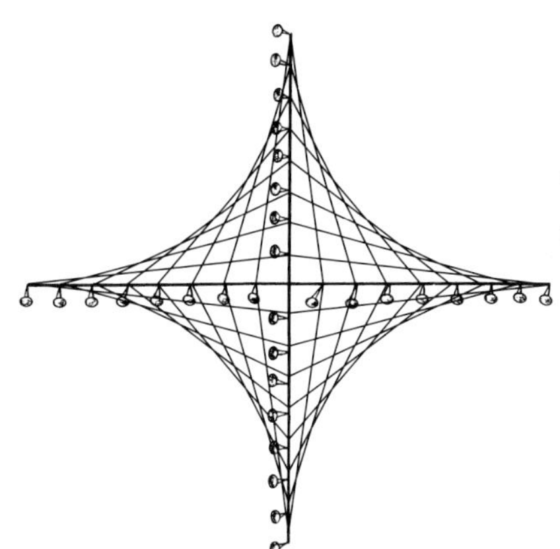

You can use straight lines to draw curves.

Exercise 10:6

1 Draw two lines 8 cm long like this.
Mark every centimetre along the line.
Number the marks like this.

Use a ruler to draw these straight lines.
Join the numbers **1** to 8
2 to 7
3 to 6 and so on.

Each pair of numbers adds up to 9.

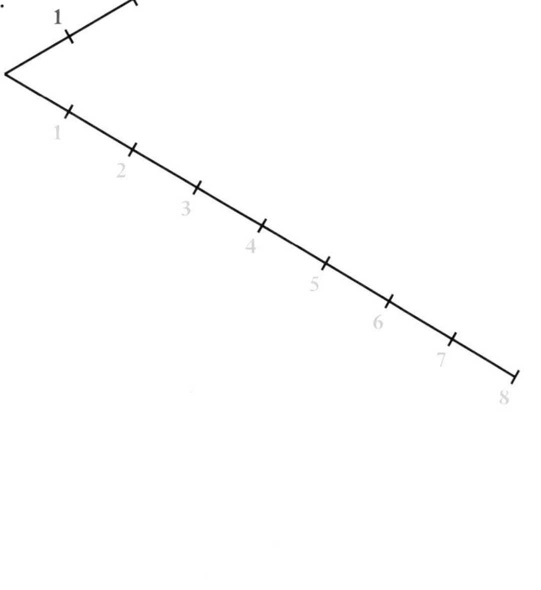

You should get a pattern like this.

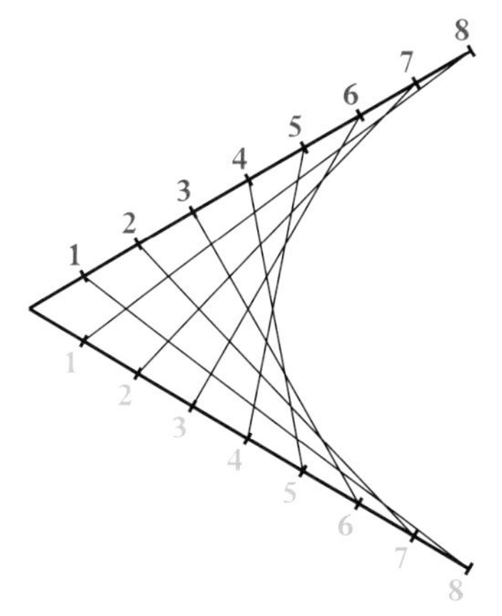

2 Draw another two lines 8 cm long as in question **1**.
This time make a mark every half centimetre along the lines.
Number the marks 1 to 16 like this.

Join the numbers **1** to 16
2 to 15
3 to 14 and so on.

Each pair of numbers adds up to 17.

You get a better curve when the marked points are closer together.

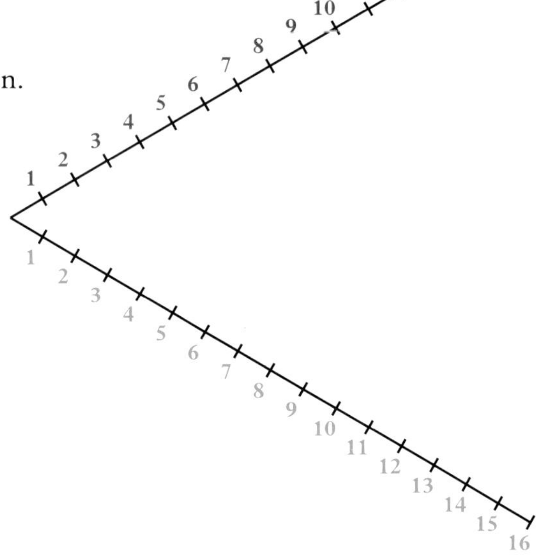

3 Copy this diagram on to squared paper.

a Join the black and blue numbers.
1 to 9, **2** to 8, and so on.
Each pair of numbers adds up to 10.

b Join the black and green numbers **1** to 9, **2** to 8, and so on.

c Join the blue and red numbers 1 to **9**, 2 to **8**, and so on.

d Join the green and red numbers 1 to **9**, 2 to **8**, and so on.

Your pattern should look like this.

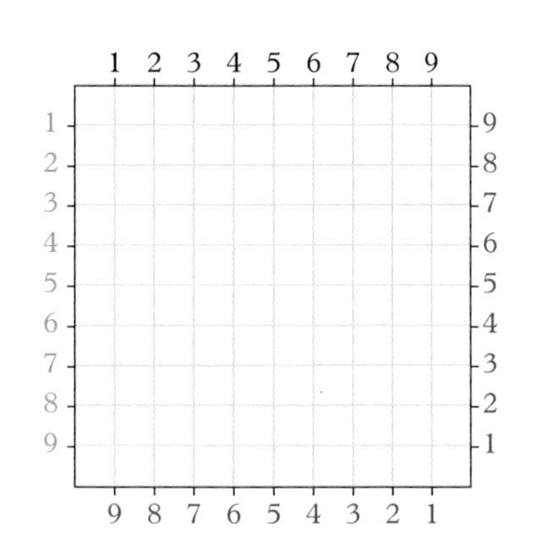

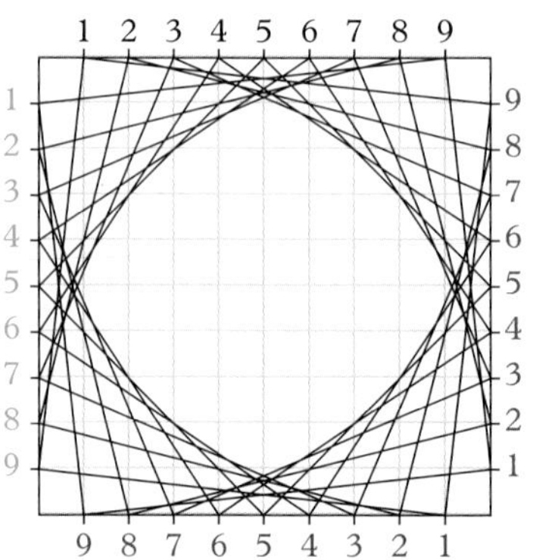

4 **a** Draw two lines like these. Make your lines 10 cm long. Make a mark every half centimetre. Number the marks like this.

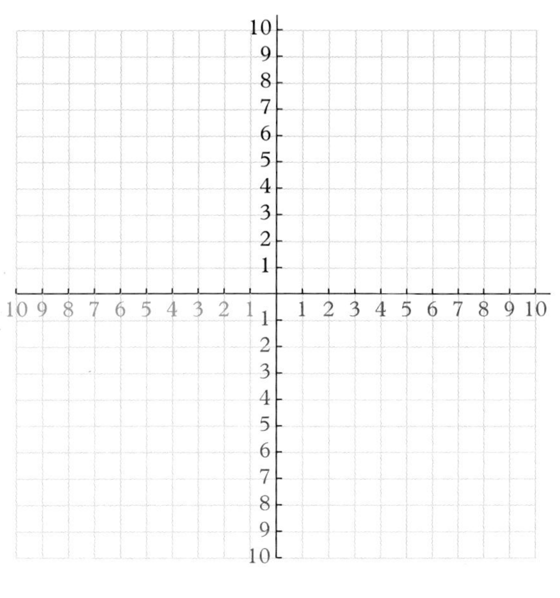

b Join the black and blue numbers first.
Join the numbers **1** to 10
2 to 9
3 to 8
and so on.
Each pair of numbers adds up to 11.

c Join the black and green numbers
1 to 10, **2** to 9, and so on.

d Next join the blue and red numbers.

e Then join the red and green numbers.

Your pattern should look like this.

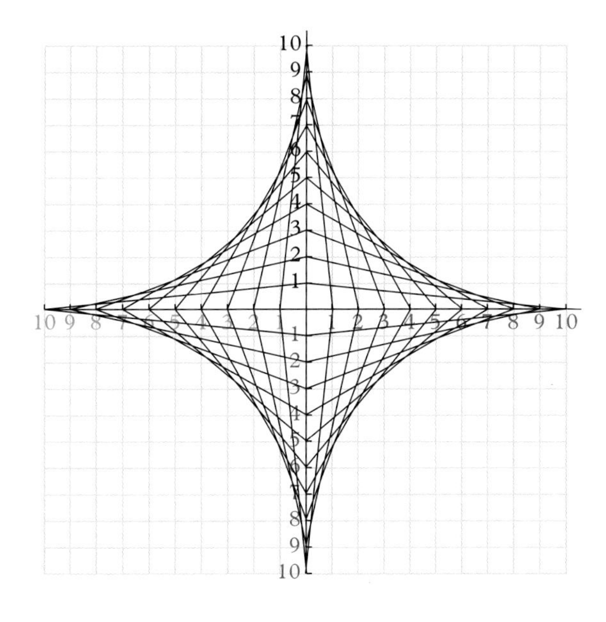

Exercise 10:7

Look at this diagram of a circle.
It is numbered 1 to 36.

The numbers continue round the circle a second time.
We now have numbers 37 to 72 on the marks.

We can join pairs of numbers using different rules.

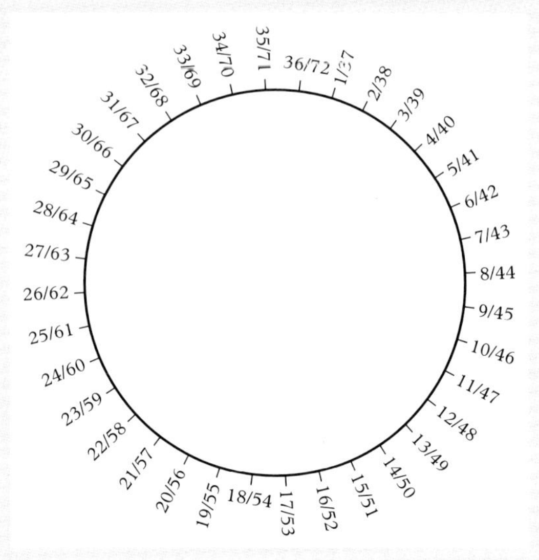

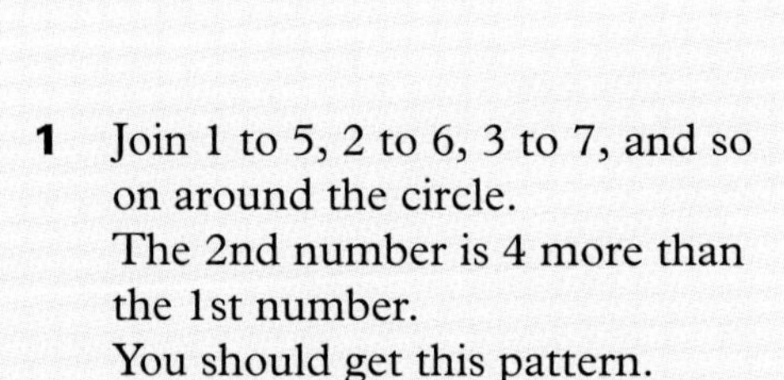

1 Join 1 to 5, 2 to 6, 3 to 7, and so on around the circle.
The 2nd number is 4 more than the 1st number.
You should get this pattern.

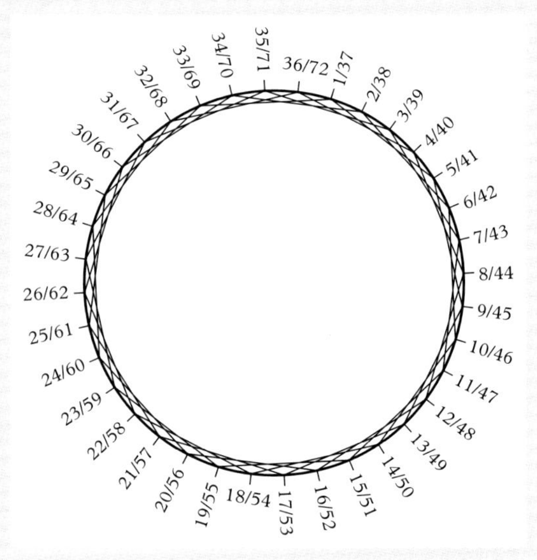

2 Join 1 to 11, 2 to 12, 3 to 13, and so on.
The 2nd number is 10 more than the 1st number.
You should get a different pattern.

3 Investigate the different patterns that you can get.
Describe what you think is happening.
What about patterns like 1 to 2, 2 to 4, 3 to 6, and so on?
The 2nd number is twice the 1st number.

1 Write down the rules for these lines.
Copy and fill in:
a The rule is $x = \ldots$
b The rule is $x = \ldots$
c The rule is $y = \ldots$
d The rule is $y = \ldots$

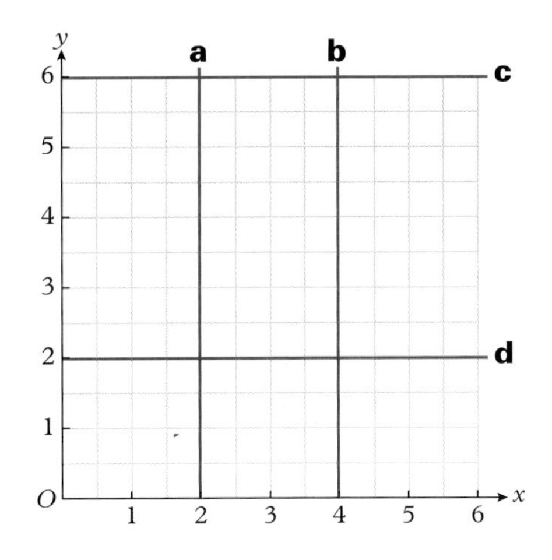

2 Write down the rules for these lines.

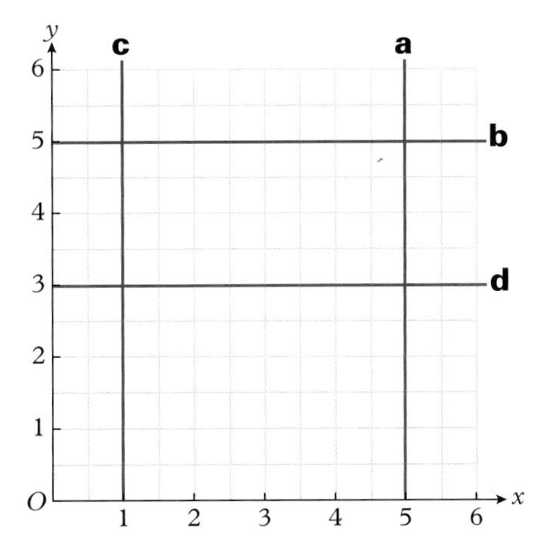

3 **a** Copy the axes on to squared paper.
b Draw the line $x = 2$
Label the line.
c Draw the line $y = 4$
Label the line.
d The lines cross at a point.
Write down the co-ordinates of this point.
Remember to use brackets $(\ldots, \ldots)$

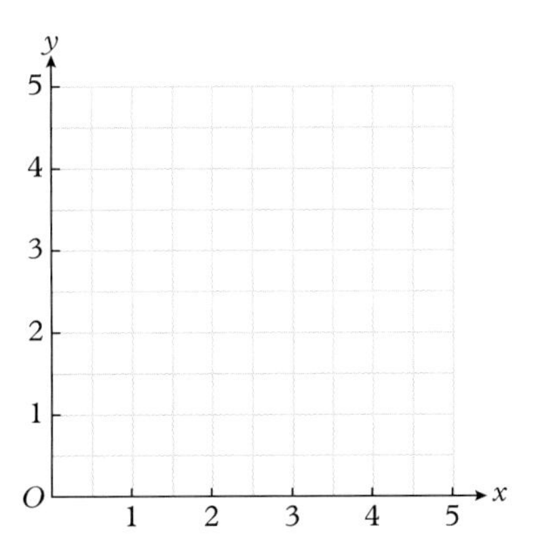

4 Copy these axes on to squared paper.

a Draw the line $x = 4$
Label the line.

b Draw the line $y = 2$
Label the line.

c The two lines cross at a point.
Write down the co-ordinates of this point.

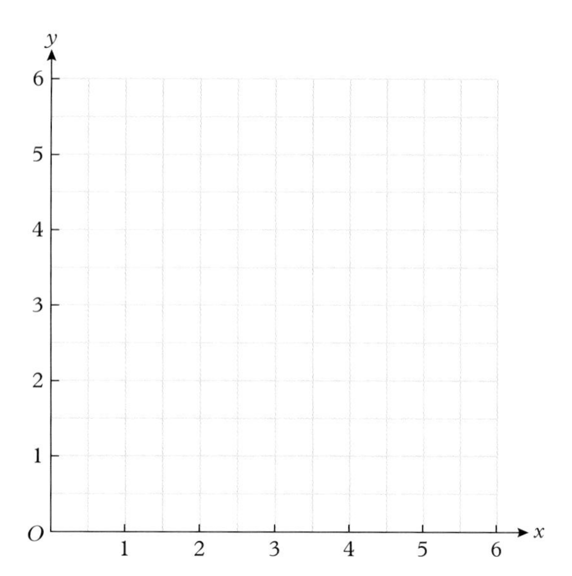

5 **a** Copy the axes in question **4**.

b Draw the line $x = 1$

c Draw the line $y = 5$

d The lines cross at a point.
Write down the co-ordinates of this point.

6 **a** Copy the axes in question **4** again.

b Draw two lines, one straight up and one straight across.
They must cross at the point $(3, 4)$.

c Copy and fill in the rules for these two lines.

$x = \dots \qquad y = \dots$

7 Write down the rules of the two lines that cross at the point.
One line is straight across and the other is straight up.

a $(2, 8)$ **b** $(5, 7)$ **c** $(6, 4)$

8 Write down the co-ordinates of the point of intersection of these lines.

a $x = 5$ and $y = 3$

b $x = 6$ and $y = 1$

c $x = 2$ and $y = 8$

d $x = 7$ and $y = 4$

9 Which line is the steeper in these pairs?

a $y = 3x$ and $y = 5x$

b $y = 7x$ and $y = 4x$

c $y = x$ and $y = 3x$

d $y = 9x$ and $y = 10x$

10 **a** Copy the axes on to squared paper.

b Plot these points in order
(1, 1) (2, 1) (2, 2) (3, 2)
(3, 5) (1, 3) (1, 1)
Join them with a ruler as you go.

c Draw the line $x = 3$ on your axes.

d Reflect the shape in the line $x = 3$

e Write down the co-ordinates of the vertices of the new shape.

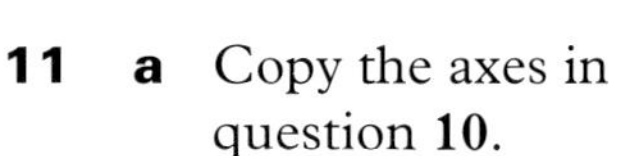

11 **a** Copy the axes in question **10**.

b Plot these points in order
(1, 4) (3, 6) (6, 6) (6, 5) (4, 5) (4, 4)
Join them with a ruler as you go.

c Draw the line $y = 3$ on your axes.

d Reflect the shape in the line $y = 3$

e Write down the co-ordinates of the vertices of the new shape.

12 Look at these three lines.

$y = x + 3$ $\qquad$ $y = x + 7$ $\qquad$ $y = x + 2$

a What can you say about the three lines?

b Geoff plots the three lines.
Which line is highest up the grid?

c Which line is lowest on the grid?

d Where does the line $y = x + 7$ cross the y axis?

13 Where will these lines cross the y axis?

a $y = x + 3$

b $y = x + 6$

c $y = x + 1$

d $y = x + 4$

1 The sides of a square have the rules

$x = 1 \qquad y = 2 \qquad x = 5 \qquad y = 6$

a Copy the axes on to squared paper.

b Draw the four lines on your axes. They should make a square.

c Write down the co-ordinates of the vertices of the square.

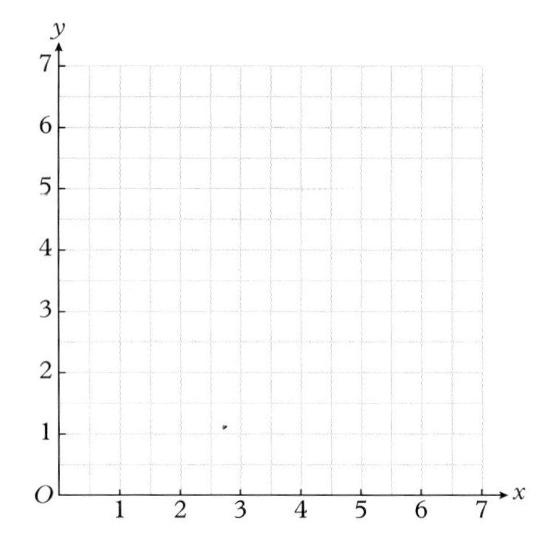

2 Copy the axes in question **1**.
The vertices of a rectangle have co-ordinates
$(1, 5)\ (7, 5)\ (7, 2)\ (1, 2)$
Plot these points and draw the rectangle.
Write down the rules for the four sides of the rectangle.

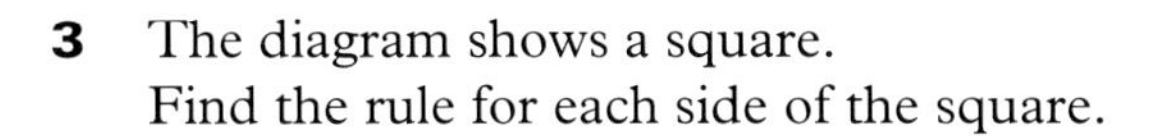

3 The diagram shows a square.
Find the rule for each side of the square.

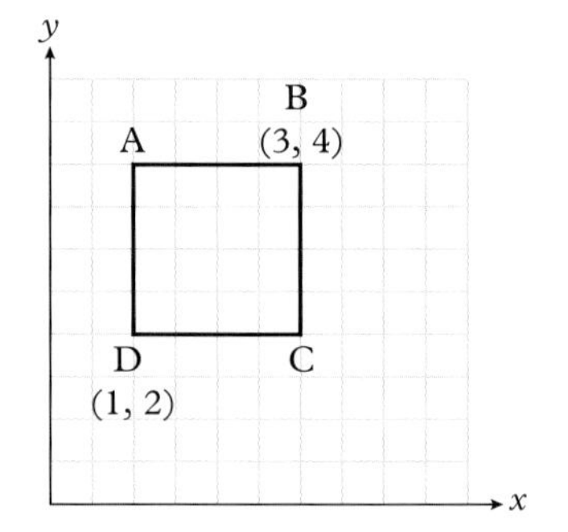

4 Copy these axes on to squared paper.

a Draw the line $y = 2x$

b Draw the line $y = x + 2$

c Write down the co-ordinates of the point of intersection of these two lines.

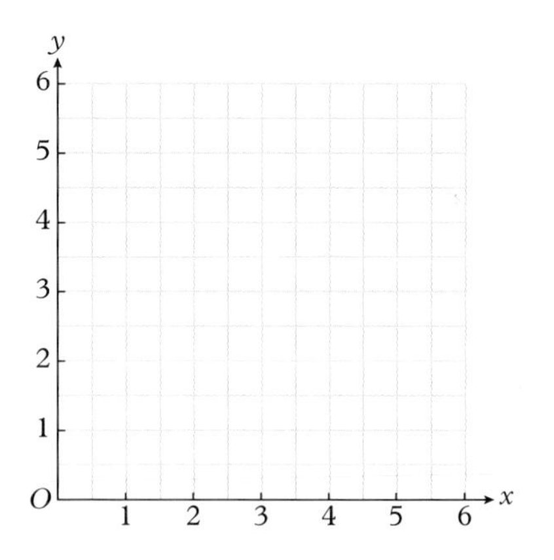

5 **a** Copy the axes in question **4**.

b Draw and label the lines

$y = 5 \qquad y = 2 \qquad x = 1 \qquad x = 6$

c Write down the co-ordinates of the four points where these lines intersect.

d The lines form a rectangle.
Write down the length of the rectangle.

e Find the area of the rectangle.

- All the points in this line have
  x co-ordinate = **2**

  The rule for the line is
  $\boldsymbol{x = 2}$

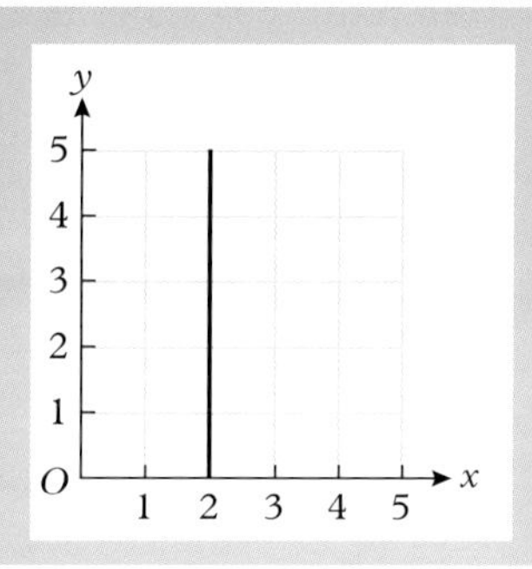

- **Point of intersection**
  The point where two lines cross is called a **point of intersection**.

  The point of intersection of these two lines is
  (3, 2)

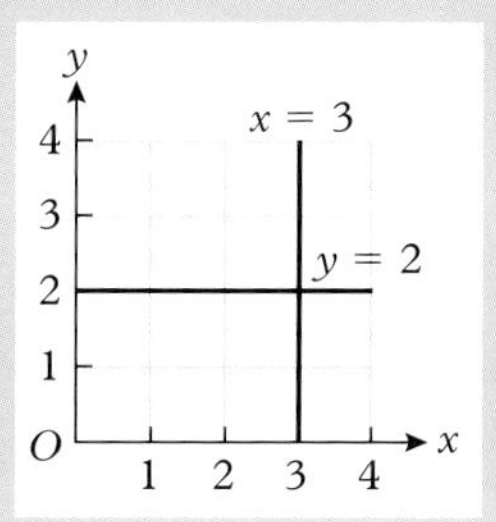

- **Equation**
  The rule of a line is called the **equation** of the line.

  The equation of this line is $y = x$

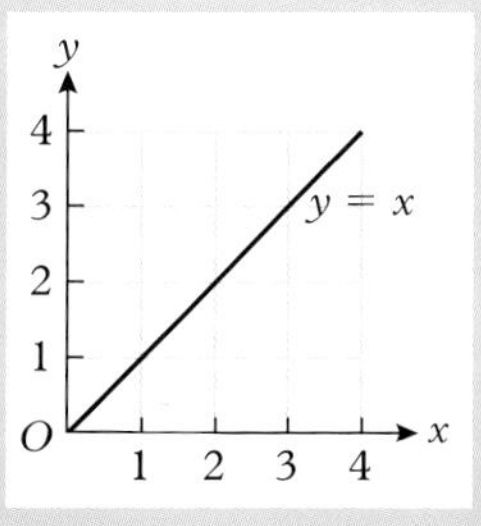

- Look at these lines.

  The red number tells us how steep the line is.
  The bigger the number the steeper the line.

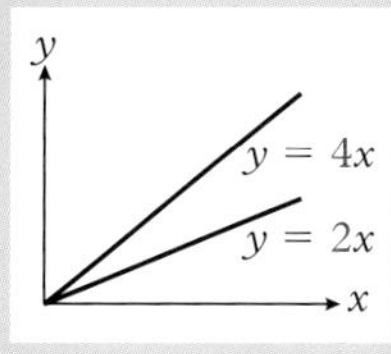

Look at these lines.
The blue number tells us where the line crosses the y axis.

The line $y = x + 2$ crosses the y axis at 2
The line $y = x + 5$ crosses the y axis at 5

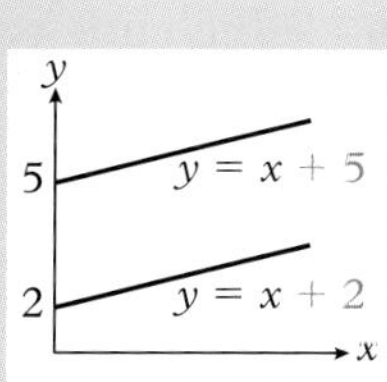

1 Match these rules to these lines.

$x = 4$ $\quad y = 2$

$x = 1$ $\quad y = 5$

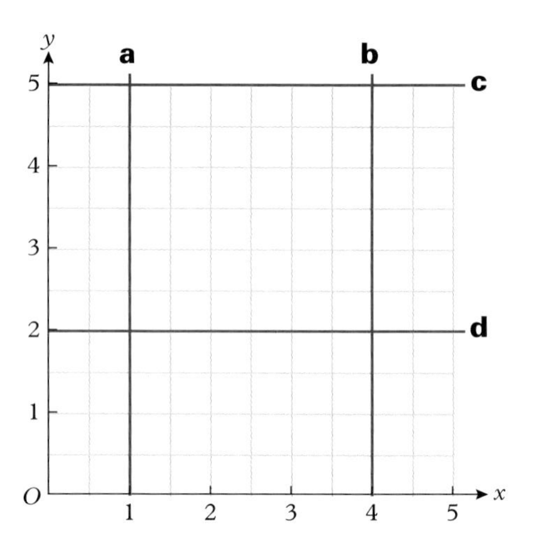

2 **a** Copy the axes in question **1** on to squared paper.

b Draw the line $x = 4$
Label the line.

c Draw the line $y = 2$
Label the line.

d The lines cross at a point.
Write down the co-ordinates of this point.

3 Two lines cross at the point $(5, 3)$
One is straight up and one is straight across.
Write down their rules.

4 Write down the co-ordinates of the point of intersection of the lines $y = 6$ and $x = 1$

5 Look at these equations of lines.

$y = 3x \qquad y = x \qquad y = 5x$

a Which line is the steepest?

b Which line is the least steep?

6 Where will these lines cross the y axis?

a $y = x + 3$ **b** $y = x + 5$ **c** $y = x$

7 Look at these equations of lines.

$y = x + 4 \qquad y = x + 7 \qquad y = x$

a What can you say about these lines?

b Which line is highest up the grid?

c Which line is lowest on the grid?

d Which two lines would the line $y = x + 2$ be between?

11 Ratio

CORE

1 The metric system

2 Changing sizes

3 Proportion

4 Maps and scales

QUESTIONS

EXTENSION

SUMMARY

TEST YOURSELF

Most maps of the UK are produced from the Ordnance Survey. The Board of Ordnance used to be in charge of defending Britain. (Ordnance means military supplies.) They wanted good maps for soldiers to use so they began the Ordnance Survey.

The Ordnance Survey put 'bench marks' in places like the stone of bridges or on the tops of hills. They use these points to measure from.

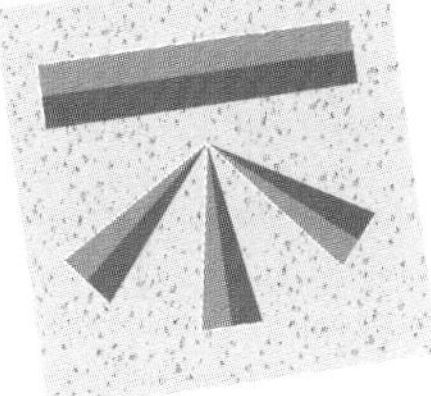

A bench mark

A large-scale Ordnance Survey map

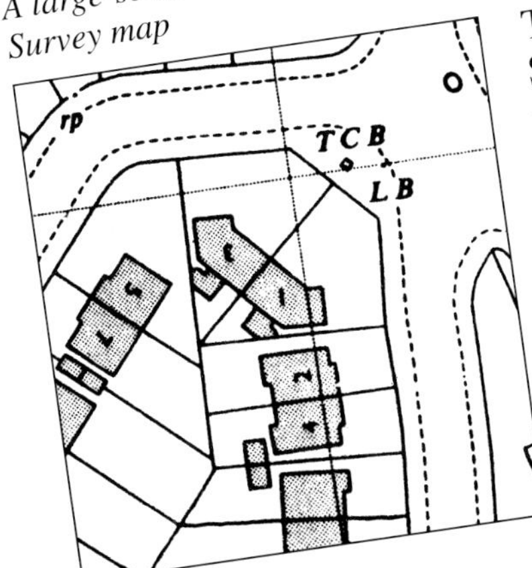

The Ordnance Survey bring maps up to date from time to time. They mark new buildings and roads.

They produce large-scale maps and smaller-scale maps.

1 The metric system

Jane and Andy have broken a window.
Their father is measuring to find the size of glass that is needed to repair the window.
His tape measure has one side marked in feet and inches. The other side is marked in metric units.

Jane has a pencil and paper to write down the measurements.
Jane asks her father what units he is using.
He says he is using millimetres.

◀◀REPLAY▶

Units of length

10 millimetres (mm) = 1 centimetre (cm)
100 centimetres = 1 metre (m)
1000 metres = 1 kilometre (km)

Example

0mm 10 20 30 40 50 60 70 80
0cm 1 2 3 4 5 6 7 8

This line measures 5.7 cm (or 57 mm).

Converting units within the metric system

Examples

1 Convert 6.75 m to cm

$6.75\text{ m} = 6.75 \times 100\text{ cm}$
$= 675\text{ cm}$

2 Convert 6400 m to km

$6400\text{ m} = 6400 \div 1000\text{ km}$
$= 6.4\text{ km}$

Exercise 11:1

1 Convert the units in each of these.
Copy and fill in:

a 4 cm = 4 × 10 mm
= ... mm

b 5 m = 5 × 100 cm
= ... cm

c 7 km = 7 × 1000 m
= ... m

d 3.9 cm = 3.9 × 10 mm
= ... mm

e 15 m = 15 × 100 cm
= ... cm

f 0.5 km = 0.5 × 1000 m
= ... m

2 Convert the units in each of these.
Copy and fill in:

a 60 mm = 60 ÷ 10 cm
= ... cm

b 8000 m = 8000 ÷ 1000 km
= ... km

c 350 cm = 350 ÷ 100 m
= ... m

d 42 mm = 42 ÷ 10 cm
= ... cm

e 7500 m = 7500 ÷ 1000 km
= ... km

f 800 cm = 800 ÷ 100 m
= ... m

3 Convert the units in each of these.
Think carefully whether you need to multiply or divide.

a 50 mm to cm (10 mm = 1 cm)
b 3000 m to km (1000 m = 1 km)
c 9 m to cm (100 cm = 1 m)
d 7 cm to mm (10 mm = 1 cm)
e 4.5 cm to mm (10 mm = 1 cm)
f 12 000 m to km (1000 m = 1 km)
g 0.5 m to cm (100 cm = 1 m)
h 56 mm to cm (10 mm = 1 cm)

• **4** Convert the units in each of these.
Think carefully whether you need to multiply or divide by 10, 100 or 1000.

a 4 km to m
b 400 cm to m
c 20 mm to cm
d 6 cm to mm
e 15 km to m
f 2 m to cm
g 30 mm to cm
h 5000 m to km

5 Copy these and fill them in.
Choose from mm, cm, m, km.

a A paperclip is about 30 ... long.
b A door is about 2 ... high.
c A teaspoon is about 13 ... long.
d The distance from London to Cardiff is about 240 ...
e A filing cabinet is about 45 ... wide.
f A football pitch is about 70 ... wide.
g A fingernail is about 10 ... wide.
h The English Channel is about 33 ... across.

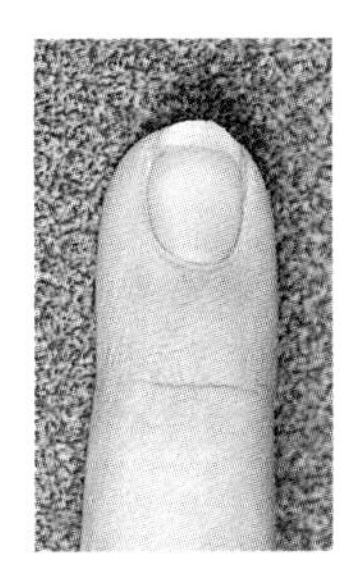

Converting Imperial units of length to metric units

1 in = 2.5 cm   1 yd = 0.9 m   1 mile = 1.6 km

Examples

1 Convert 3 in to cm
1 in = 2.5 cm
3 in = 3 × 2.5 cm
= 7.5 cm

2 Convert 3.5 yd to m
1 yd = 0.9 m
3.5 yd = 3.5 × 0.9 m
= 3.15 m

3 Convert 4 miles to km
1 mile = 1.6 km
4 miles = 4 × 1.6 km
= 6.4 km

Exercise 11:2

1 Convert the units in each of these.
Copy and fill in:

a 2 in = 2 × … cm
= … cm

b 6 yd = 6 × … m
= … m

c 7 miles = 7 × … km
= … km

d 10 yd = 10 × … m
= … m

e 20 miles = 20 × … km
= … km

f 12 inches (1 foot) = 12 × … cm
= … cm

2 Convert the red lengths into metric units.

a Julie's book is 8 in by 6.5 in.
b Deepal's bedroom door is 30 in wide.
c A cricket pitch is 22 yd long.
d Allison has a 1 foot ruler.
She also has a smaller ruler 6 in long.
e Paul runs the London marathon, which is 26.2 miles.
f Stanthorne High's tennis court is 26 yd by 12 yd.

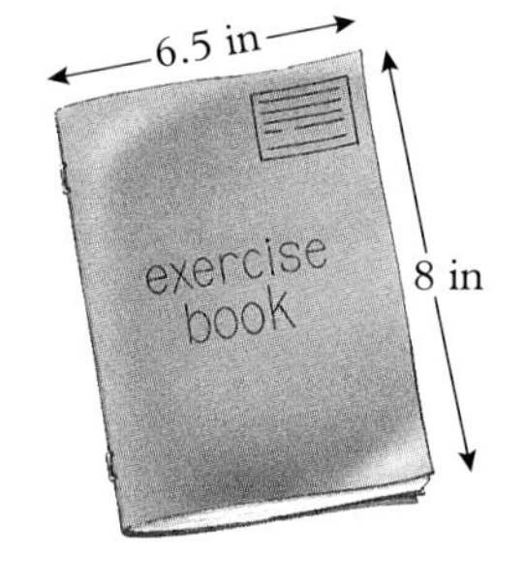

1 inch is about $2\frac{1}{2}$ cm.
1 yard is a bit less than 1 metre.
1 mile is a bit more than $1\frac{1}{2}$ km.

Example

Estimate these lengths in metric units.

a 4 inches **b** 18 yd **c** 12 miles

a 1 inch is about $2\frac{1}{2}$ cm
$2 \times 4 = 8$
$\frac{1}{2}$ of 4 is 2
4 inches is about $8 + 2 = 10$ cm

b 1 yard is a bit less than 1 metre
18 yd is a bit less than 18 m
18 yd is about 16 or 17 m

c 1 mile is a bit more than $1\frac{1}{2}$ km
$\frac{1}{2}$ of 12 is 6
$12 + 6 = 18$
12 miles is a bit more than 18 km
12 miles is about 19 or 20 km

3 Estimate these in metric units.

a	6 inches	**e**	2 yd	**i**	2 miles
b	8 inches	**f**	12 yd	**j**	30 miles
c	10 inches	**g**	25 yd	**k**	1000 miles
d	20 inches	**h**	100 yd	**l**	16 miles

4 **a** 1 in = 2.5 cm, 1 yd = 0.9 m, 1 mile = 1.6 km
Use these and multiplication to convert the lengths in question **3** into metric units.

b Use your answers to **a** to check your estimates in question **3**.

Units of mass

Units of mass have similar names to units of length.

1000 milligrams (mg) = 1 gram (g)
1000 grams = 1 kilogram (kg)
1000 kg = 1 tonne (t)

A quarter teaspoon of sugar weighs about 1 gram.
An ordinary bag of sugar weighs 1 kilogram.

Converting units within the metric system

Examples

1 Convert 2.5 kg to g

$2.5\text{ kg} = 2.5 \times 1000\text{ g}$
$= 2500\text{ g}$

2 Convert 5000 g to kg

$5000\text{ g} = 5000 \div 1000\text{ kg}$
$= 5\text{ kg}$

Exercise 11:3

Convert the units in each of these.
Think carefully whether you need to multiply or divide.

1 **a** 4 kg to g (1000 g = 1 kg)
b 6 kg to g
c 55 kg to g
d 2000 g to kg
e 7500 g to kg
f 900 g to kg

2 **a** 3 g to mg (1000 mg = 1 g)
b 1250 mg to g
c 7000 mg to g

3 **a** 8000 kg to t (1000 kg = 1 t)
b 5 t to kg
c 1.5 t to kg

Converting Imperial units of mass to metric units

1 ounce is about 30 grams. (16 ounces = 1 pound)
1 pound is a bit less than half a kilogram. (14 pounds = 1 stone)
1 ton is a bit more than 1 tonne.

4 Estimate the red amounts in metric units.
a A newborn baby boy weighs about 8 pounds.
b An egg weighs about 2 ounces.
c A woman weighs about 140 pounds.
d A small car weighs about 2 tons.
e An orange weighs about 6 ounces.
f A large roast turkey weighs about 20 pounds.

Sometimes we need to be more accurate.
1 ounce (oz) = 28 g   1 pound (lb) = 450 g = 0.45 kg

Examples

1 Convert 3 ounces to g

1 oz = 28 g
3 ounces = 3 × 28 g
= 84 g

2 Convert 5 pounds to kg

1 pound = 0.45 kg
5 pounds = 5 × 0.45 kg
= 2.25 kg

5 Convert the units in each of these.
Copy and fill in:

a 4 ounces = 4 × 28 g
= ... g

b 0.5 ounces = 0.5 × ... g
= ... g

c 3 pounds = 3 × 0.45 kg
= ... kg

d 6.5 pounds = 6.5 × ... kg
= ... kg

● **6** Convert the units in each of these.

a 8 ounces to g   **b** 14 pounds to kg   **c** 100 pounds to kg

Units of capacity

Units of capacity have similar names to units of length.

1000 millilitres (m*l*) = 1 litre (*l*)
100 centilitres (c*l*) = 1 litre

5 m*l*

75 c*l*

1 litre

The plastic medicine spoon holds 5 m*l*.
The bottle holds 75 c*l*.
The carton of fruit juice holds 1 litre.

We can convert units of capacity in the same way as units of length or mass.

Exercise 11:4

1 Convert the units in each of these.

a 3000 ml to l (1000 ml = 1 l)
b 75 cl to l (100 cl = 1 l)
c 7 l to ml
d 4.5 l to ml
e 0.5 l to ml
f 9000 ml to l
g 800 ml to l
h 5600 ml to l
i 0.25 l to ml

Converting Imperial units of capacity to metric units

One pint is a bit more than half a litre.
One gallon is about $4\frac{1}{2}$ litres.

---

2 Estimate the red quantities in metric units.

a A washing-up bowl holds about 12 pints of water.
b A household bucket holds about 2 gallons of water.
c A dustbin would hold about 20 gallons of water.
d A classroom waste bin would hold about 7 gallons of water.

Sometimes we need to be more accurate.
1 pint = 0.57 l 1 gallon = 4.5 l (8 pints = 1 gallon)

Examples

1 Convert 4 pints to litres.

1 pint = 0.57 l
4 pints = 4 × 0.57 l
= 2.28 l

2 Convert 3 gallons to litres.

1 gallon = 4.5 l
3 gallons = 3 × 4.5 l
= 13.5 l

---

3 Convert each of these quantities to litres.
Copy and fill in:

a 7 pints = 7 × 0.57 l
= ... l

b 0.5 pints = 0.5 × ... l
= l

c 15 gallons = 15 × 4.5 l
= ... l

d 5.6 gallons = 5.6 × ... l
= ... l

● **4** Convert each of these quantities to litres.

a 5 pints **b** 9 gallons **c** 3.5 pints **d** 1.4 gallons

2 Changing sizes

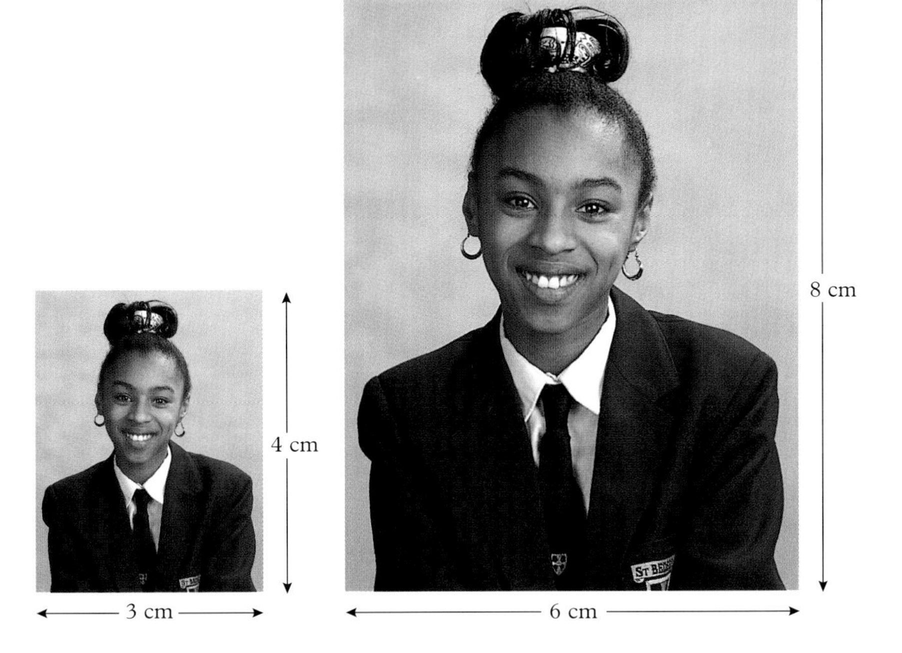

Year 8 have had their photographs taken.
Sonya has bought the large size for her mother.
The small size is for her school record.

The width of the small photograph is half the width of the large photograph.
Also, the length of the small photograph is half the length of the large one.

Exercise 11:5

1 **a** Measure this square.
Copy it into your book.
b Draw a new square with sides twice as long.
c Draw another new square with sides half as long.
(Divide by 2 to get half of something.)

2 **a** Measure this rectangle.
Copy it into your book.
b Draw a new rectangle with sides twice as long.
c Draw another new rectangle with sides three times as long.

● **3** Here are two sizes of the same photograph.

A

B

a (1) Measure the width of A.
(2) Measure the width of B.
(3) How many times larger is the width of B than the width of A?

b (1) Measure the length of A.
(2) Measure the length of B.
(3) How many times larger is the length of B than the length of A?

c What do you notice about your answers to **a** and **b**?

Example

A car-hire company has 8 cars and 4 vans for hire.
How many *times* more cars are there than vans?

$8 \div 4 = 2$
There are 2 times as many cars as vans.

Exercise 11:6

1 Alan is 12 years old. His little sister Claire is 6 years old.
How many *times* older is Alan than Claire?

2 Gurjeet has £9 pocket money. His friend Dale has £3.
How many *times* more money does Gurjeet have than Dale?

3 Laura works 15 hours a week. Nancy works 3 hours.
How many *times* longer does Laura work than Nancy?

• **4** There are 30 pupils in 8L. 10 of them are girls.

a How many boys are there in 8L?

b How many *times* more boys are there than girls?

5 Here are some counters.

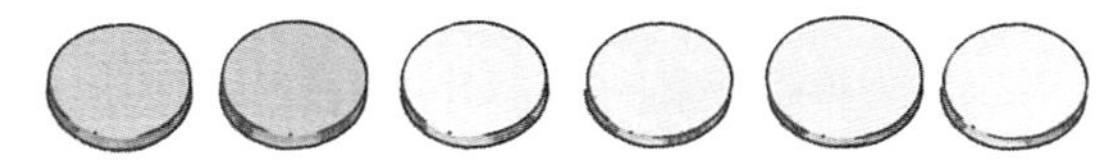

How many *times* more yellow counters are there than green counters?

6 Here are some chocolates.
Some of them are in coloured wrappers.
How many *times* more chocolates are there without coloured wrappers than with coloured wrappers?

7 How many *times* more girls are there than boys?

8 **a** (1) Make this pattern with cubes.

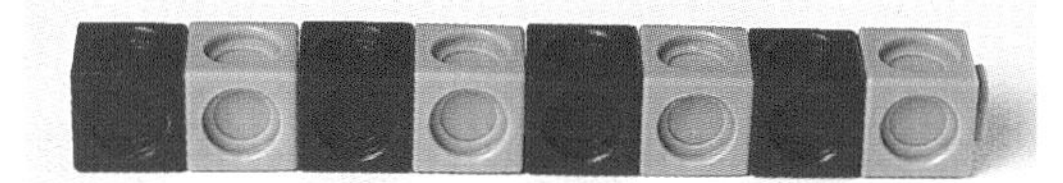

(2) Separate the cubes into two groups.
Make a group of red cubes and a group of blue cubes.

(3) How many *times* more blue cubes are there than red cubes?

Repeat part **a** for these two patterns of cubes.

b

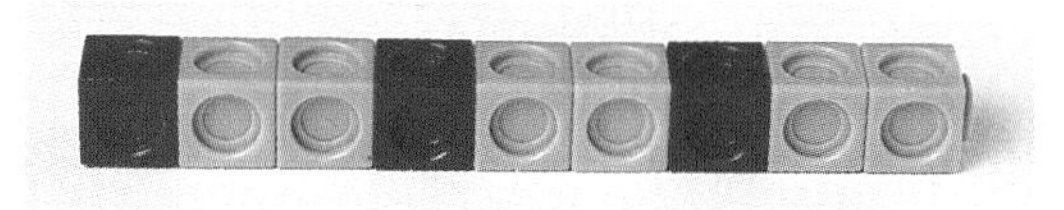

c

d Make up a pattern that has twice as many red cubes as blue ones.

e Make up a pattern that has three times as many red cubes as blue ones.

3 Proportion

Robert is cooking some fruit buns.
The recipe is for 20 buns but
Robert only wants to make 10.
He needs to change the amounts
in the recipe.

Exercise 11:7

1 Here are the ingredients to make 20 fruit buns.

14 oz self-raising flour
4 oz sultanas
2 oz raisins
6 oz sugar
7 oz margarine
1 teaspoon mixed spice
2 small eggs

a Write down the ingredients that you need to make 10 buns.
b Write down the ingredients that you need to make 40 buns.

Example The instructions on a bottle of car shampoo say 'one part shampoo to ten parts water'.
The bottle contains 500 m*l* of shampoo.

a Mr Patel uses the whole bottle of shampoo.
How much water does he add?

b How much diluted shampoo does he make altogether?

a Mr Patel adds ten times as much water as shampoo.

$500 \times 10 = 5000$ m*l*

b The total of water and shampoo is 5000 m*l* + 500 m*l* = 5500 m*l*

---

2 The instructions on a bottle of orange squash say 'one part squash to five parts water'.
Louise is making a jug of the orange drink.

a Louise uses 200 m*l* of the squash.
How much water does she use?

b How much of the orange drink does Louise have in her jug?

3 The instructions on a bottle of carpet shampoo say 'One part shampoo to 30 parts water.'

a The bottle of shampoo contains 500 m*l*.
How much water do you add if you use the whole bottle?

b How much diluted shampoo will you have altogether?

4 Mr Bean uses three parts sand to one part cement to make mortar.

a (1) How much sand does Mr Bean mix with 6 kg cement?
(2) How much mortar does this make altogether?

b (1) How much cement does Mr Bean mix with 30 kg of sand?
(2) How much mortar does this make altogether?

5 The instructions on a medicine bottle are 'Dilute with two parts water.'
A nurse measures 10 m*l* of the medicine.
How much water does she need?

6 Hannah is making this bracelet.
She has seven more orange beads.

a How many more green beads does she need?

b Hannah has only eight green beads left.
How many orange beads can she use?

7 Mrs Ellis plants red roses and yellow roses in this pattern.

a If she plants four red roses, how many yellow roses does she need?

b If she plants 20 yellow roses, how many red roses does she need?

8 This bronze axe head is one part tin and nine parts copper.
The axe head contains 30 g of tin.
How much copper does it contain?

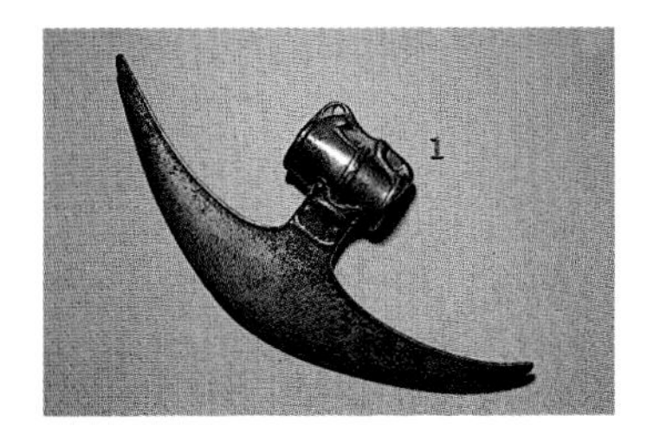

4 Maps and scales

Tony wants to draw a plan of his room.
Denis helps Tony measure the room.
Tony has to choose a scale before he can draw his plan.

◀◀ REPLAY ▶

Scale — The **scale** of a drawing gives the relative size of the actual length to the drawn length.

Exercise 11:8

1 Tony makes a scale drawing of his room. He uses a scale of 1 cm to 1 metre.

a (1) Measure the length of the drawing in centimetres.
(2) Write down the actual length of the room in metres.

b (1) Measure the width of the drawing in centimetres.
(2) Write down the actual width of the room in metres.

Scale: 1 cm to 1 m

2 Tony decides his drawing is too small.
He draws a new rectangle twice as big.

a Draw Tony's new rectangle.

b Label your rectangle with the new scale: *Scale:* 2 cm to 1 m

We can find the length of a curved line.
We use a piece of string.
Place the string on top of the curved line.
Mark the length of the line on the string.
Measure the marked length of the string with a ruler.

We can use this method for estimating distances on maps.

3 You will need a piece of string to help you with this question.

This map shows some places in North Wales.

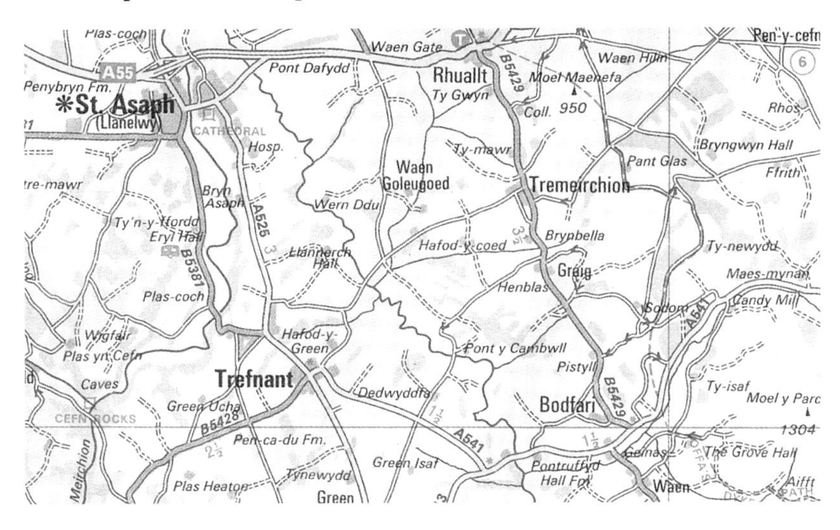

Scale: 1 cm to 1 km

a (1) Estimate the distance on the map from St Asaph to Rhuallt.
(2) Write down this distance in kilometres.

b (1) Estimate the distance on the map from Trefnant to Waen Gate along the minor road. Use your string to help you.
(2) Write down this distance in kilometres.

c A seagull flies straight from St Asaph to Bodfari.
(1) Measure this distance on the map.
(2) Write down this distance in kilometres.

d Mr Williams drives south from St Asaph to Trefnant.
He takes the road past the caravan site.
He then drives to Bodfari.
At Bodfari he turns north to Tremeirchion and Rhuallt.
From Rhuallt he drives back to St Asaph.
(1) Estimate the distance on the map that Mr Williams drives. Use your string to help you.
(2) Write down the distance Mr Williams drives in kilometres.

● **4** You will need a piece of string to help you with this question.

This map shows part of the north coast of Norfolk.

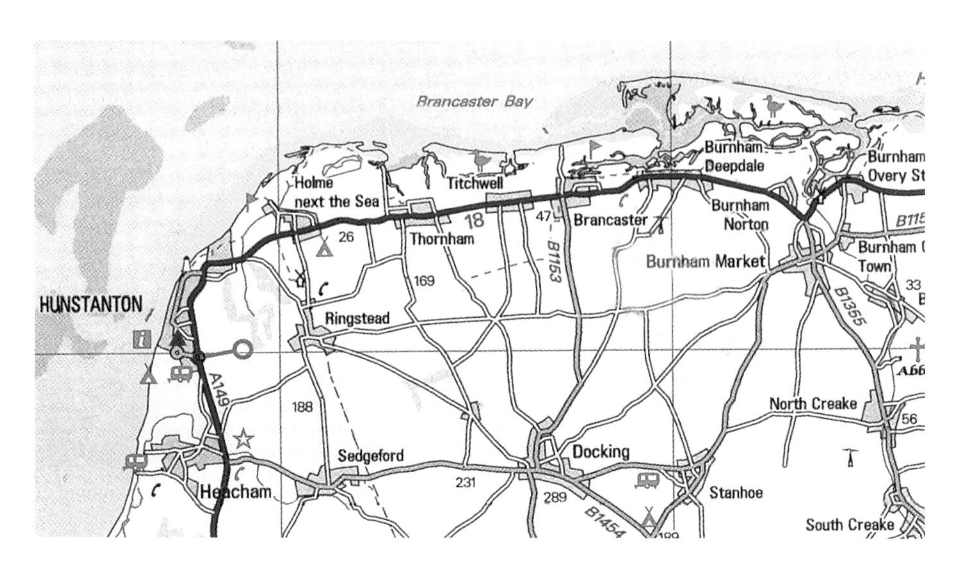

Scale: 1 cm to 2 km

a Copy this table.
Fill it in.

Distance on map	1 cm	2 cm	3 cm	4 cm	5 cm
Actual distance	2 km	4 km			

b (1) Estimate the distance on the map along the minor road from Ringstead to Burnham Market.
(2) Work out this distance in kilometres.

c (1) Estimate the distance on the map from Burnham Deepdale to Docking.
Use your string to help you.
(2) Work out this distance in kilometres.

d Shona and Rowan go for a cycle ride.
They start from Stanhoe and go west to Heacham.
Then they turn north to Hunstanton.
They go along the coast through Titchwell to Burnham Market.
Then they go straight back to Stanhoe.
(1) Estimate the length of their cycle ride on the map in centimetres.
Use your string to help you.
(2) Work out the actual distance in kilometres.

QUESTIONS

1 Convert the units in each of these.

a 380 cm to m
b 1.7 kg to g
c 0.6 *l* to m*l*
d 1900 mg to g
e 7250 g to kg
f 8.6 km to m
g 50 000 m*l* to *l*
h 14.7 m to cm
i 17.9 cm to mm
j 0.35 g to mg
k 95 cm to m
l 0.25 m to mm

2 Give an estimate of these Imperial quantities.
Use the metric unit given.

a 12 inches or 1 foot (cm)
b 5 miles (km)
c 20 yd (m)
d 4 ounces (g)
e 2 pounds (kg)
f 1 pound (g)
g 4 pints (*l*)
h 2 gallons (*l*)

3 Use multiplication to convert these quantities accurately to metric units.
Use the metric unit given.

a 11 inches (cm)
b 14 yards (m)
c 45 miles (km)
d 7 ounces (g)
e 4 pounds (kg)
f 15.7 pounds (kg)
g 8 pints (*l*)
h 2.5 gallons (*l*)
i 55 gallons (*l*)

4 **a** Measure the sides of this rectangle.
b Draw a larger rectangle with sides four times as long.

5 How many *times* more cats are there than dogs?

6

How many *times* more red counters are there than green?

7 **a** How many *times* more yellow squares are there than blue in this grid?
b Draw a grid of 12 squares like the one in **a**.
Colour it red and yellow.
Make it have twice as many red squares as yellow ones.

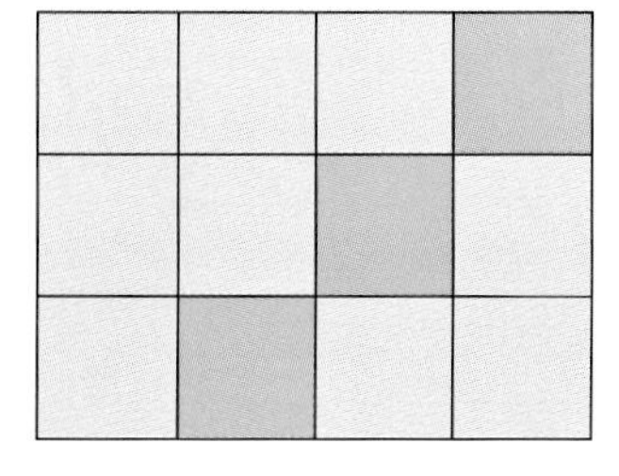

8 A cake recipe uses one part sugar to four parts flour.

a How much flour do you need when you use 150 g of sugar?

b How much flour do you need when you use 1 kg of sugar?

9 Louise is threading beads in a pattern.

a She has ten more red beads.
How many more blue beads does she need?

b Louise only has six blue beads left.
How many red beads can she use?

10 The instructions on a bottle of lemon squash say 'one part squash to four parts water'.
Paul is making a jug of the lemon drink.

a Paul uses 300 m*l* of the lemon squash.
How much water does he use?

b How much of the lemon drink does Paul have in his jug?

11 Each line is drawn to the scale shown.
Measure each line.
Write down the length that each line represents.

a ________________________ *Scale:* 1 cm to 1 km

b __________________________________ *Scale:* 1 cm to 3 km

c ______________ *Scale:* 1 cm to 5 km

d _____________________ *Scale:* 1 cm to 10 km

e _______________________________ *Scale:* 1 cm to 4 km

f ___________________ *Scale:* 2 cm to 1 km

12 You will need string to help you with this question.

a (1) Estimate the distance on the map along Hadrian's Wall from Stanwix to Newtown.

(2) Work out this distance in kilometres.

b Mrs Graham drives from Carlisle to Longtown. Then she goes from Longtown to Brampton and back to Carlisle through Warwick.

(1) Estimate the distance on the map that Mrs Graham drives in centimetres.

(2) Work out the actual distance in kilometres.

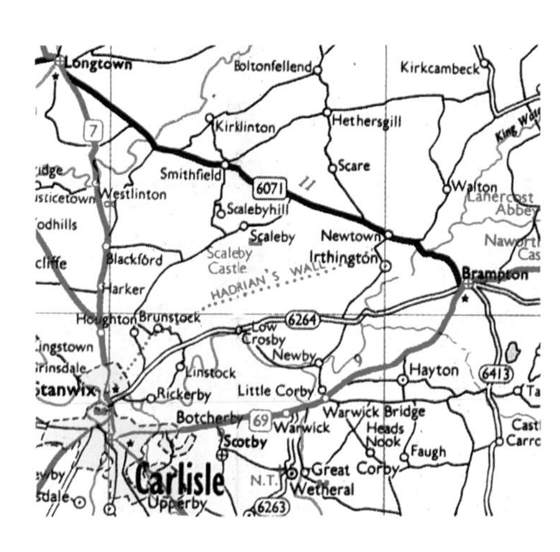

Scale: 1 cm to 3 km

1 Learn these to help you remember the size of some Imperial units.

- Two and a quarter pounds of jam weigh about a kilogram.
- A litre of water's a pint and three quarters.
- A metre measures three foot three, it's longer than a yard you see.

Can you think of any more helpful rhymes?

2 These are sayings, phrases and names of people.
The words that complete the sayings have been converted to metric units.
Write down the correct words.

a 30 cm in the grave
b 45 *l* hat
c Sharon 6.4 kg
d New Scotland 0.9 metres
e 0.57 *l* sized
f 0.45 kg of flesh
g Give him 2.5 cm and he will take 1.6 km
h A miss is as good as 1.6 km
i It went down like 1016 kg of bricks
j She hasn't got 28 g of common sense

Can you make up some more of these yourself?

3 Look at the patterns of counters.

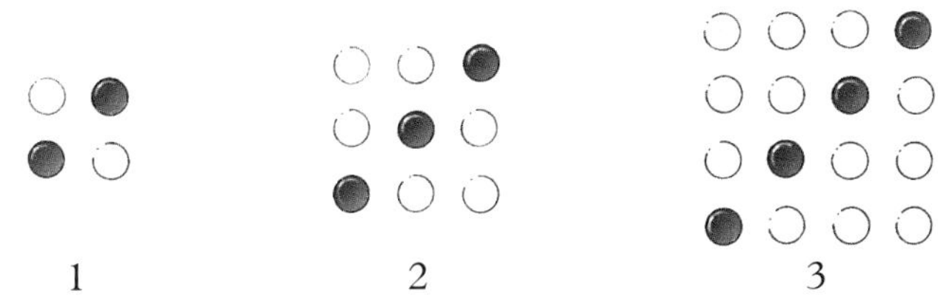

1 2 3

a How many times more white counters than black counters are there in the first pattern?
b How many times more white counters than black counters are there in the second pattern?
c How many times more white counters than black counters are there in the third pattern?
d Predict the answer for the fourth pattern.
Draw the fourth pattern to see if you are right.
e Copy this table.
Use the pattern to fill it in.

Number of pattern	1	2	3	4	5	6
Number of black counters	2	3	4	5	6	7
Number of white counters	2	6				

f (1) How many black counters will there be in the 10th pattern?
(2) How many white counters will there be in the 10th pattern?
g How many white counters will there be in the 20th pattern?
h Copy and fill in:
To get the number of white counters you add ... to the number of the pattern and multiply the answer by the number of the pattern.

4 **a** (1) Measure this rectangle.
Copy it into your book.
(2) Measure a diagonal.

b (1) Draw a new rectangle with sides twice as long as the first one.
(2) Measure a diagonal.

c How many times larger is the diagonal of the second rectangle than the diagonal of the first rectangle?

d (1) Work out the perimeters (distances all the way round the outside) of the two rectangles.
(2) How many times larger is the perimeter of the second rectangle than the perimeter of the first rectangle?

5 The instructions on a bottle of lemon squash say 'Dilute with six parts water.'
Gemma makes a jug of the drink.

a (1) Gemma measures 150 m*l* of squash.
How much water does she need?
(2) How much diluted squash does Gemma have altogether?

b Gemma makes a second jug of the drink. She dilutes the squash the same as before.
If she uses 1200 m*l* of water, how much squash does she use?

6 You will need a piece of string to help you with this question.

The map has a scale of 2 cm to 1 km. It shows three villages which all have churches shown like this ✝

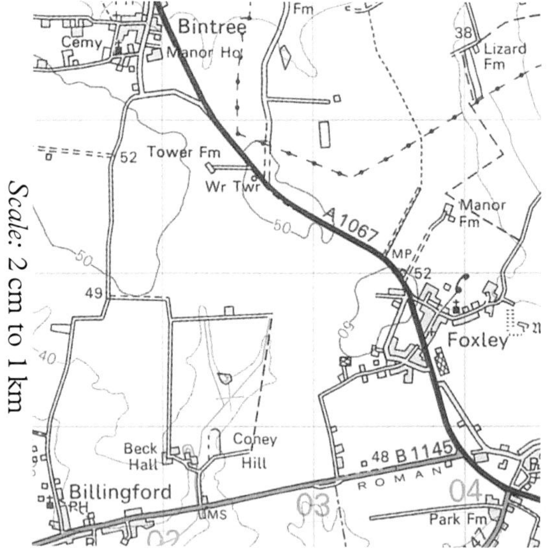

Scale: 2 cm to 1 km

a How many kilometres does 1 cm on the map represent?

b A bird flies from Billingford church to Foxley church.
(1) Measure the distance it flies on the map in centimetres.
(2) Work out how far it actually flies.

c The vicar drives from Billingford church to Bintree church.
Then he goes to Foxley church and back to Billingford on the main road.
(1) Use your string to estimate the length of the vicar's journey on the map.
(2) How far does the vicar actually drive?

SUMMARY

- **Length** $10\,mm = 1\,cm$ $100\,cm = 1\,m$ $1000\,m = 1\,km$
  1 inch is about $2\frac{1}{2}$ cm. 1 in = 2.5 cm
  1 yard is a bit less than 1 metre. 1 yd = 0.9 m
  1 mile is a bit more than $1\frac{1}{2}$ km. 1 mile = 1.6 km

- **Mass** $1000\,mg = 1\,g$ $1000\,g = 1\,kg$ $1000\,kg = 1\,t$
  A quarter teaspoon of sugar weighs about 1 gram.
  An ordinary bag of sugar weighs 1 kilogram.
  1 ounce is about 30 grams. 1 ounce (oz) = 28 g
  1 pound is a bit less than half a kilogram. 1 pound (lb) = 450 g = 0.45 kg
  1 ton is a bit more than 1 tonne 1 kg = 2.2 pounds

- **Capacity** $1000\,ml = 1\,l$ $100\,cl = 1\,l$
  A plastic medicine spoon holds 5 m*l*.
  The carton of juice holds one litre.
  One pint is a bit more than half a litre. 1 pint = 0.57 *l*
  One gallon is about $4\frac{1}{2}$ litres. 1 gallon = 4.5 *l*

- **Converting units within the metric system**

Examples **1** Convert 6.75 m to cm

$6.75\,m = 6.75 \times 100\,cm$
$= 675\,cm$

2 Convert 5000 g to kg

$5000\,g = 5000 \div 1000\,kg$
$= 5\,kg$

- **Proportion**

Examples **1** A car-hire company has 8 cars and 4 vans for hire.
How many *times* more cars are there than vans?

$8 \div 4 = 2$
There are 2 times as many cars as vans.

2 The instructions on a bottle of car shampoo say 'one part shampoo to ten parts water'.
The bottle contains 500 m*l* of shampoo.
a Mr Patel uses the whole bottle of shampoo.
How much water does he add?
b How much diluted shampoo does he make altogether?

a Mr Patel adds ten times as much water as shampoo.
$500 \times 10 = 5000\,ml$
b The total of water and shampoo is $5000\,ml + 500\,ml = 5500\,ml$

- **Scale** The **scale** of a drawing gives the relative size of the actual length to the drawn length.
  Examples of scales are 1 cm to 1 m or 1 cm to 2 km

1 Convert the units in each of these.

a 300 cm to m
b 25 mm to cm
c 7 km to m
d 8.6 m to cm
e 4500 g to kg
f 7.2 kg to g
g 0.4 tonnes to kg
h 3000 m*l* to *l*
i 4.8 *l* to m*l*

2 Convert the red quantities to the metric unit given in brackets.

a Your middle finger is about 3 inches long. (cm)
b The Tyne bridge in Newcastle is 177 yd long. (m)
c The speed limit in towns is 30 miles an hour. (km)
d A medium sized apple weighs about 4 ounces. (g)
e A man weighs about 165 pounds. (kg)
f A large watering can holds about 3 gallons. (*l*)
g Two mugs of coffee make about a pint. (*l*)

3 **a** Measure this rectangle.
Copy it into your book.
b Draw a new rectangle with sides twice as long.

4 Melanie is 6 years old. Her brother Keith is 18 years old.
How many times older than Melanie is Keith?

5 The instructions on a tin of concentrated orange juice say 'add three parts water to one part orange juice'.
a A tin holds 250 m*l* of juice.
How much water do you add?
b How much orange drink does this make altogether?

6 The map shows the position of three towns.
The scale is 1 cm to 2 km.
a (1) Measure the distance from Aytown to Beetown on the map.
(2) Write down the actual distance in kilometres.
b (1) Measure the distance from Beetown to Ceetown on the map.
(2) Write down the actual distance in kilometres.
c (1) Measure the distance from Ceetown to Aytown on the map.
(2) Write down the actual distance in kilometres.

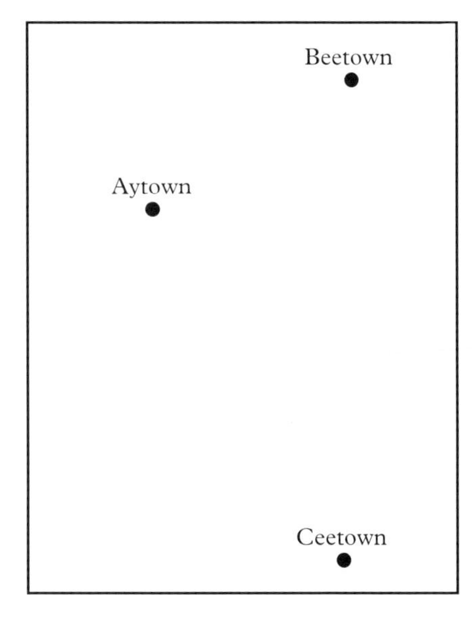

12 Area

CORE

1 **Perimeter and area**

2 **Compound shapes**

3 **Areas of triangles**

QUESTIONS

EXTENSION

SUMMARY

TEST YOURSELF

The surface area of a human lung is approximately the same as the area of a tennis court.

1 Perimeter and area

REPLAY

This is a picture of York.
It shows the old perimeter wall.
This goes all the way round the outside of the old part of the city.

Perimeter

The total distance around the outside of a shape is its **perimeter**.

The red line is the perimeter of this shape.
The perimeter is
$2 + 2 + 1 + 1 + 1 + 3 = 10$ cm

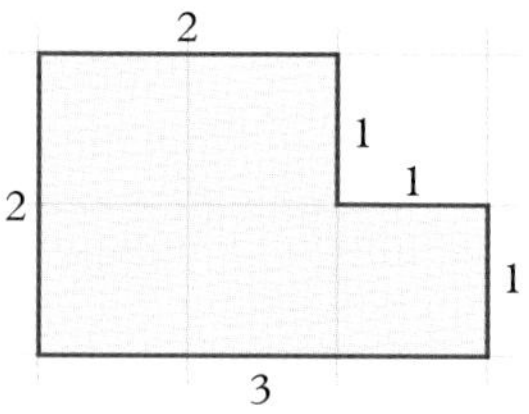

Each square has an area of 1 cm^2

Area

The amount of space inside the shape is called its **area**.

The area of this shape is shaded green.
We use squares to measure area.
There are 5 squares inside this shape.

The area of this shape is 5 cm^2.

Exercise 12:1

Copy these shapes on to 1 cm squared paper.
Fill in the gaps.

1

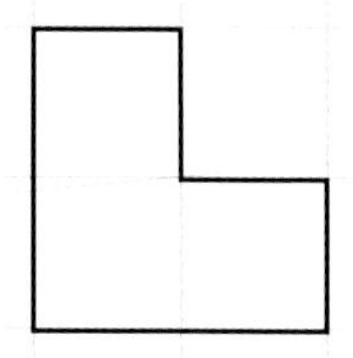

perimeter = … cm
area = … cm^2

2

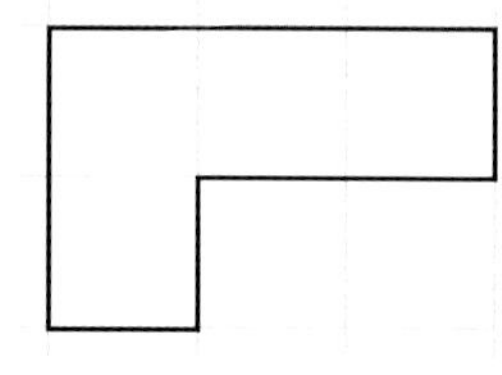

perimeter = … cm
area = … cm^2

3

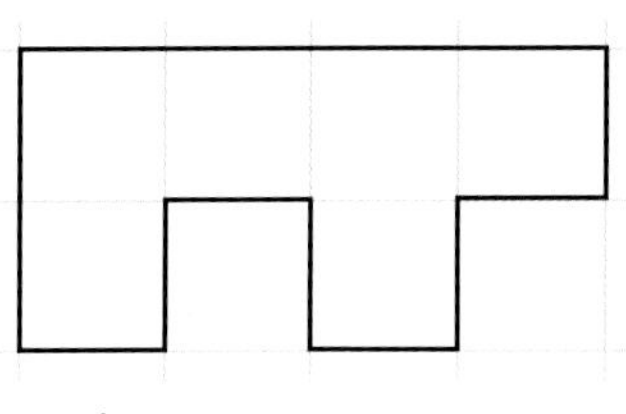

perimeter = … cm
area = … cm^2

5

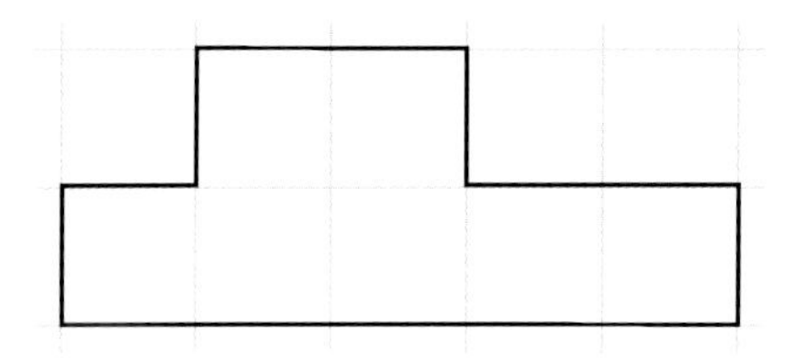

perimeter = … cm
area = … cm^2

4

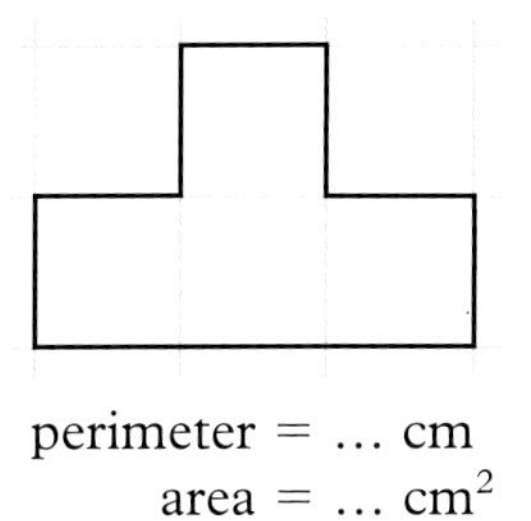

perimeter = … cm
area = … cm^2

6

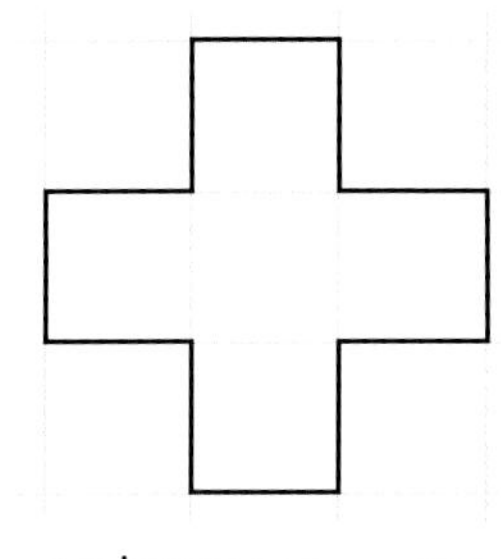

perimeter = … cm
area = … cm^2

Area of a rectangle

Area of a rectangle = ***l***ength × ***w***idth
$= l \times w$

Example

Calculate the area of this rectangle.

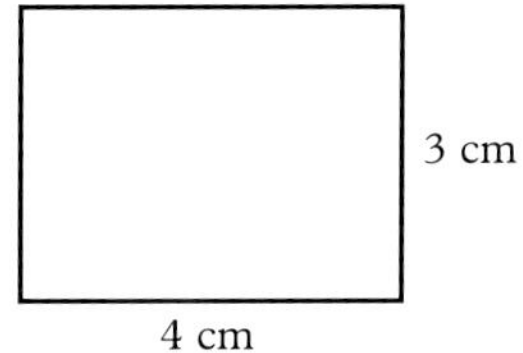

Area = length × width
$= 4 \times 3$
$= 12\ cm^2$

Exercise 12:2

Find the areas of these rectangles.

1

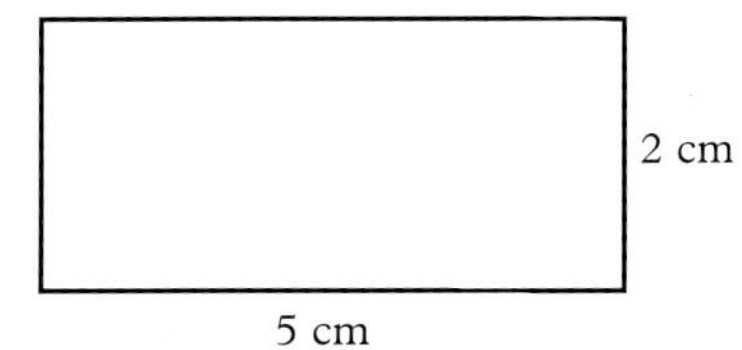

2

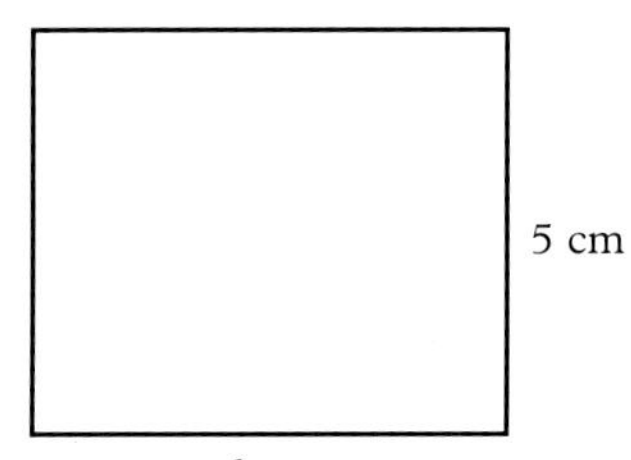

3 Rectangle: 8 cm by 1 cm

4 Rectangle: 11 cm by 3 cm

5 Find the perimeter of each rectangle in questions **1**, **2**, **3** and **4**.

6 A dining room measures 4 m by 3 m.
What is the area of the room?

7 A picture measures 30 cm by 25 cm.
What is the area of the picture?

8 The front of a Bran Flakes packet measures 190 cm by 270 cm.
Find its area.

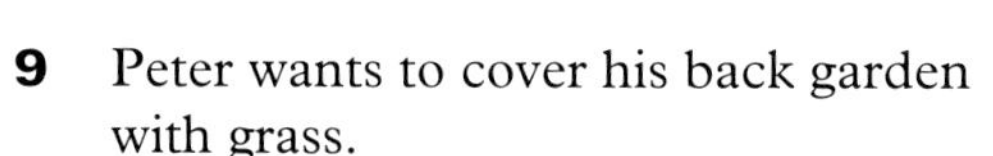

9 Peter wants to cover his back garden with grass.
- **a** What is the area of his back garden?
- **b** Grass seed costs 25 p for every m^2.
  How much will the grass seed cost?

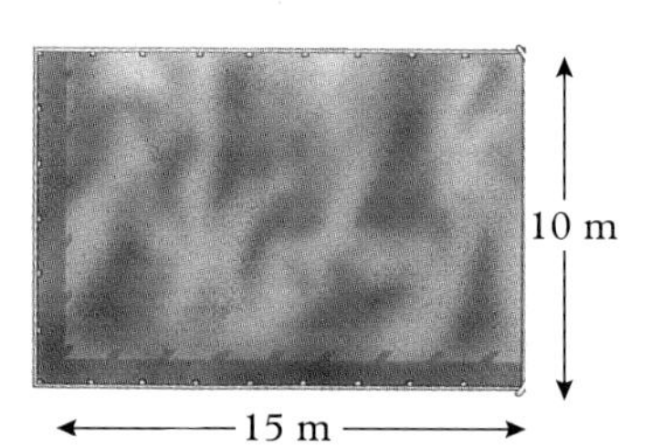

10 Sara wants a new carpet for her bedroom.
Her room looks like this.
- **a** What is the area of Sara's room?
- **b** The carpet Sara chooses is £6 per m^2.
  How much will the carpet cost?

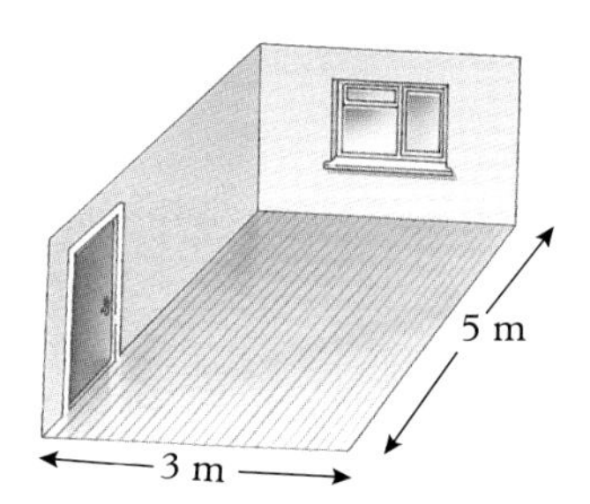

11 Sinita is making new curtains for her bedroom.
The material is 2 metres wide.
She buys a length of 6 metres.
- **a** What area of material does she buy?
- **b** The material costs £5 per m^2.
  How much does Sinita's material cost?

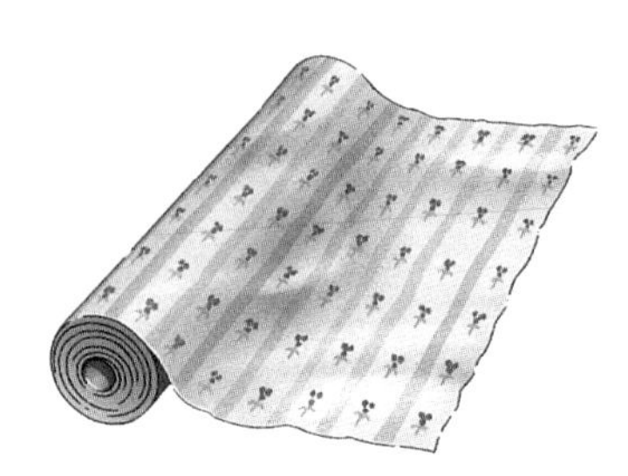

Example

Estimate the area of this leaf.

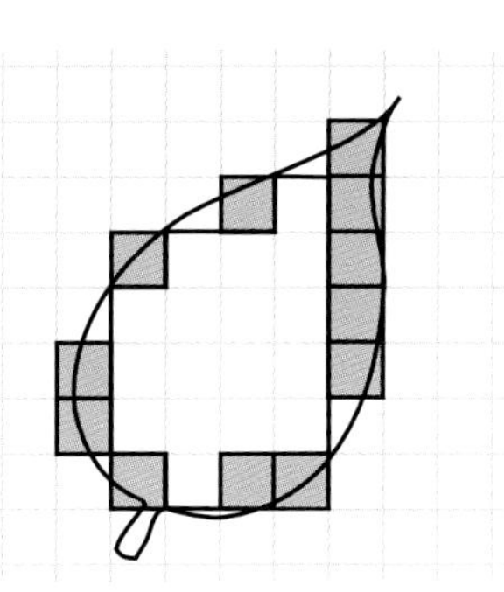

Count whole squares first.
There are 17 whole squares.

Now count squares which lie more than half inside the outline.
There are 12 of these.

An estimate of the area of the leaf is:
$17 + 12 = 29$ squares.

Exercise 12:3

Estimate the areas of these leaves.

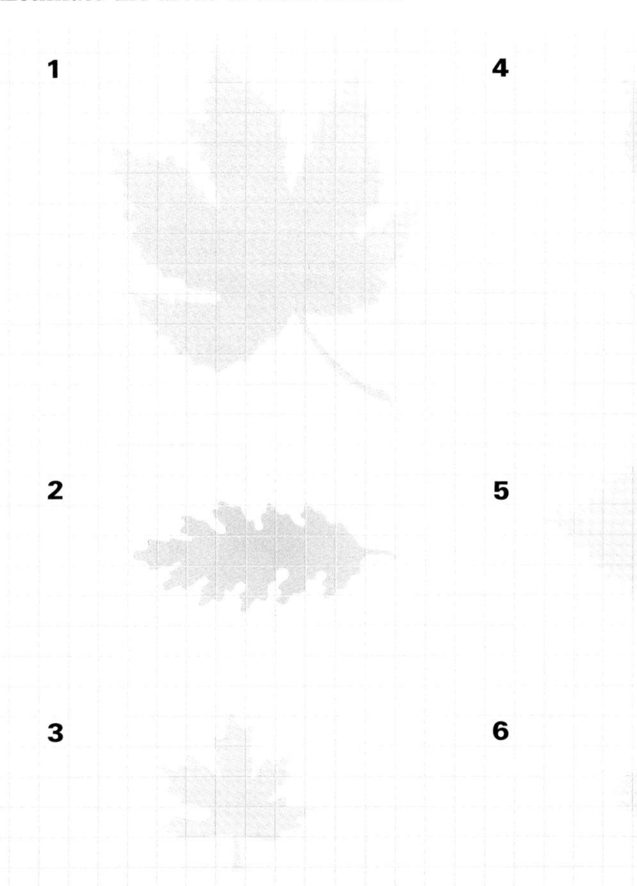

2 Compound shapes

Most rooms are rectangles.
Some rooms are two rectangles put together to make an L shape or a T shape.

Walls of rooms are rectangles with rectangular holes for doors and windows.

REPLAY

Example Find the area of this L shape.

The shape is made of two rectangles A and B.
The dashed line shows the join.

The length of A is 10 cm.
We need to find the width.
blue line + red line = green line
blue line + 3 = 7
so blue line = 4 cm

Area of A = $4 \times 10 = 40\ \text{cm}^2$
Area of B = $3 \times 5 = 15\ \text{cm}^2$

Area of shape = $40 + 15$
$= 55\ \text{cm}^2$

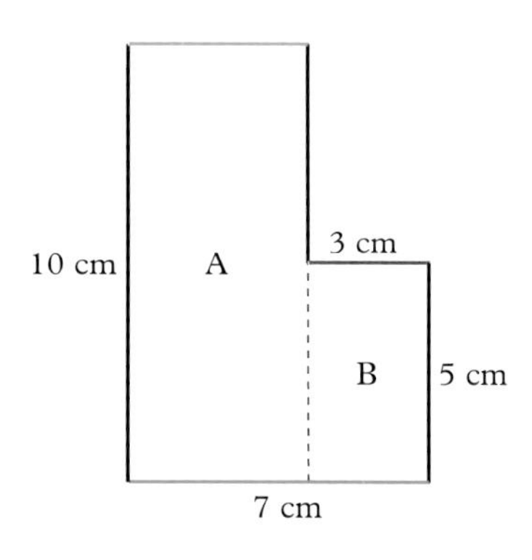

Exercise 12:4

Find the area of each of these shapes.
When the shape has a blue line, find this first.

1 Copy and fill in:

blue line + 3 = 8
blue line = … cm

Area of A = $9 \times \ldots = \ldots\ \text{cm}^2$
Area of B = $3 \times 6 = \ldots\ \text{cm}^2$

Area of shape = $\ldots + \ldots\ \text{cm}^2$
$= \ldots\ \text{cm}^2$

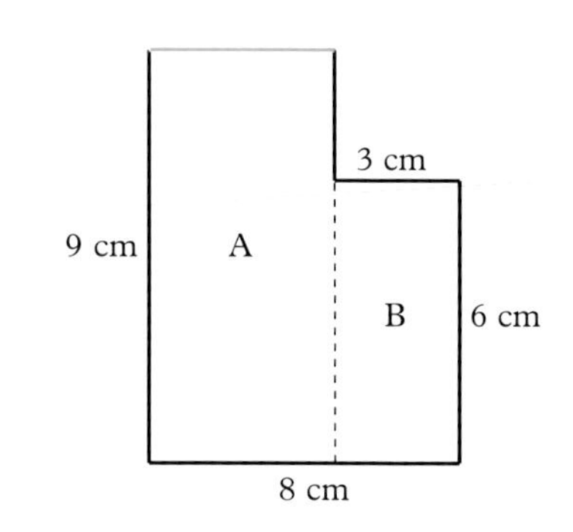

2 Copy and fill in:

blue line + … = …
blue line = … cm

Area of A = $14 \times … = …\ \text{cm}^2$
Area of B = $10 \times … = …\ \text{cm}^2$

Area of shape = … + …
= … cm^2

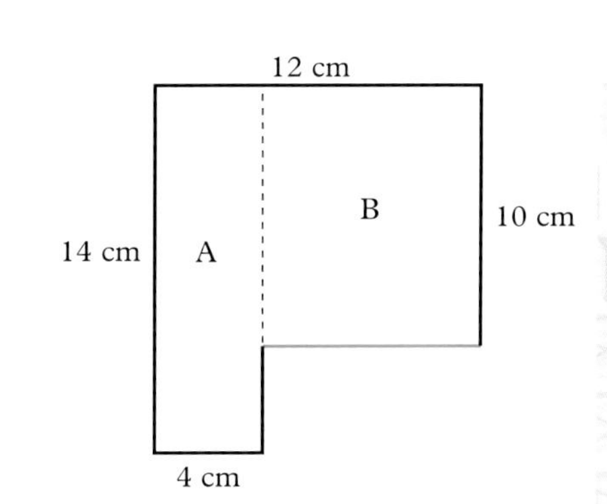

3

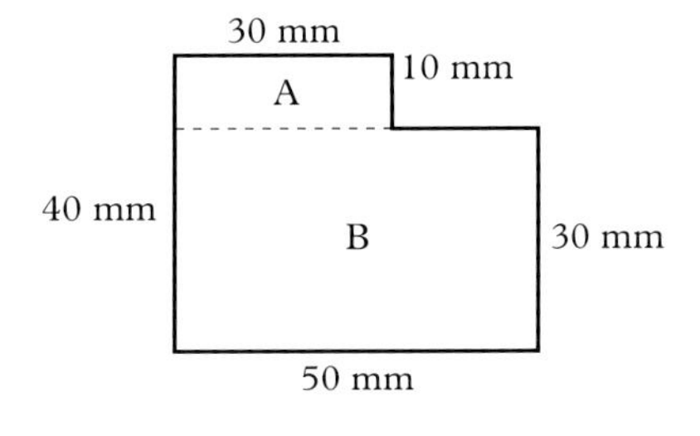

4

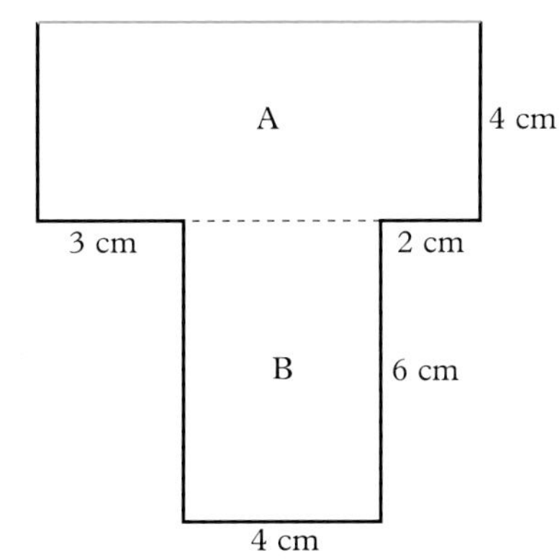

● **5** This is a plan of an L shaped classroom. The scale is 1 cm to 1 m.

a Make the measurements that you need.
Find the area of the plan.

b Write down the area of the classroom in m^2.

c The classroom is to have a carpet. 1 m^2 of carpet costs £12.
How much will it cost to carpet the room?

Scale: 1 cm to 1 m

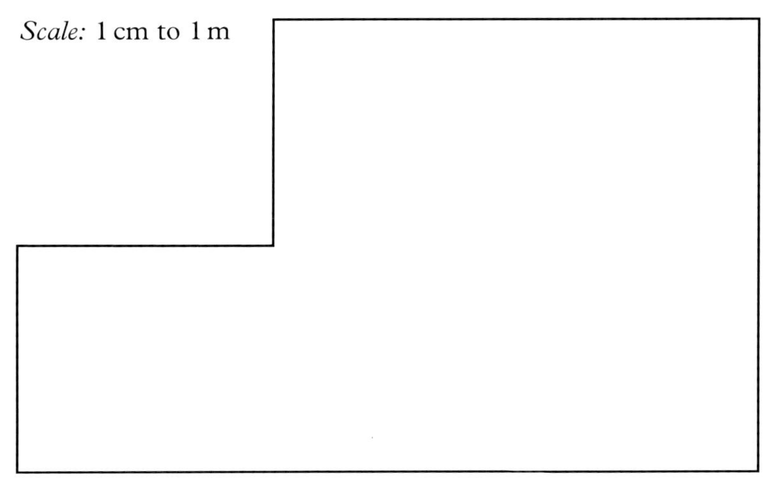

Example This shape has the middle cut out.
Find the area of the piece that is left.

Area of whole $= 10 \times 5$
$= 50\ \text{cm}^2$

Area of piece cut out $= 5 \times 2$
$= 10\ \text{cm}^2$

Area of piece left $= 50 - 10$
$= 40\ \text{cm}^2$

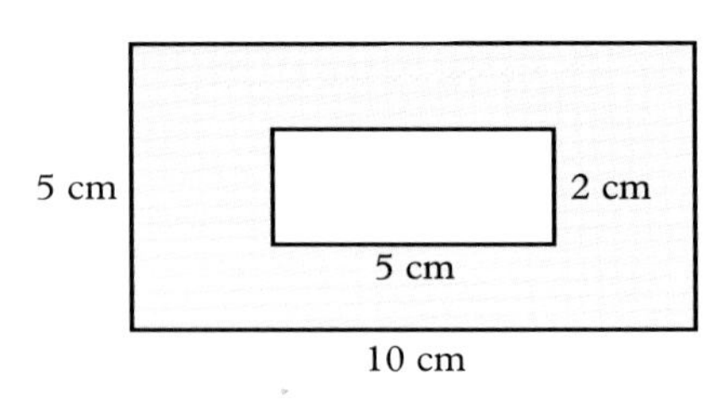

Exercise 12:5

Each of these shapes has a piece cut out.
Find the area of the piece that is left.

1 Copy and fill in:

Area of whole $= \ldots \times \ldots$
$= \ldots\ \text{cm}^2$

Area of piece cut out $= \ldots \times \ldots$
$= \ldots\ \text{cm}^2$

Area of piece left $= \ldots - \ldots$
$= \ldots\ \text{cm}^2$

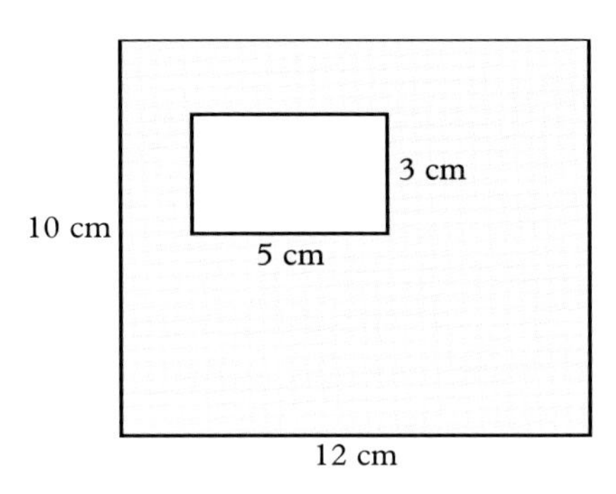

2

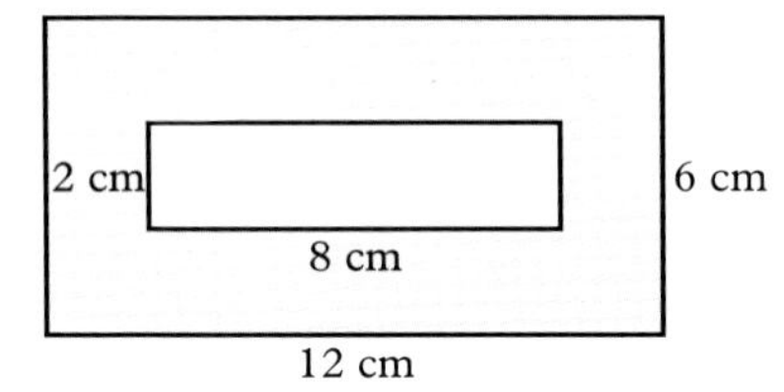

3

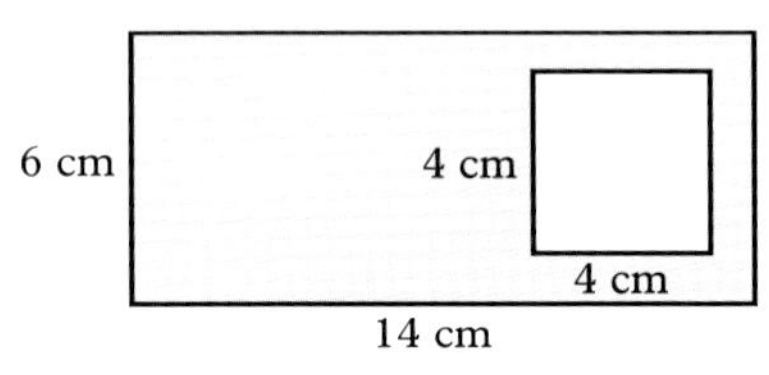

● **4** Here is a classroom wall.
It has two windows.

a Find the area of the small window.
b Find the area of the large window.
c Find the total area of the wall, including the windows.
d The wall is going to be painted.
Use your answers to **a**, **b** and **c** to work out the area to be painted.

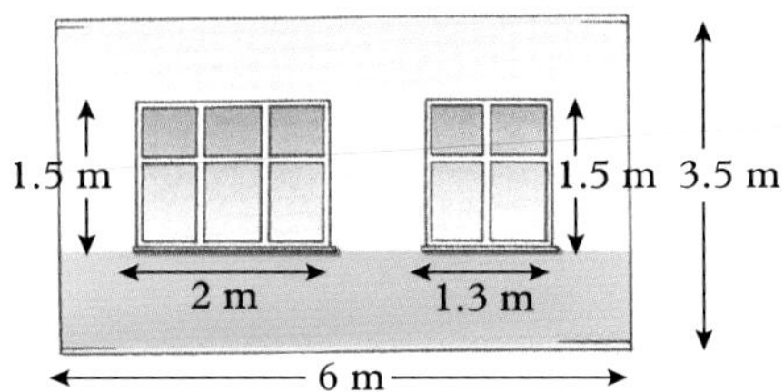

3 Areas of triangles

The sail of this yacht is a triangle. There is a formula to find the area of triangles.

REPLAY

Here is a triangle.
We use **base** and **height** instead of length and width.

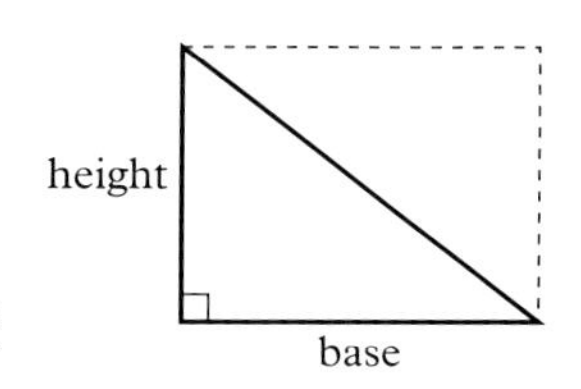

Area of a triangle

Area of a triangle $= \dfrac{\text{area of rectangle}}{2}$

$= \dfrac{\text{base} \times \text{height}}{2}$

Example Find the area of this triangle.

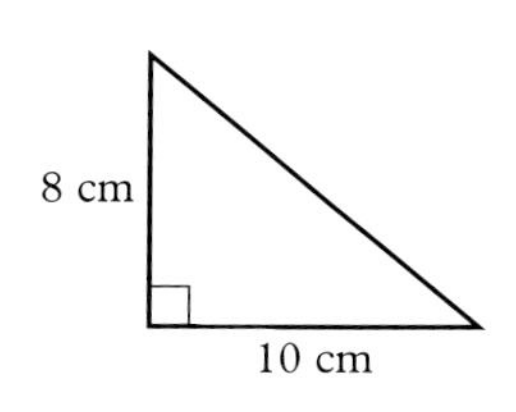

Area of triangle $= \dfrac{\text{base} \times \text{height}}{2}$

$= \dfrac{10 \times 8}{2}$

$= 40\ \text{cm}^2$

Exercise 12:6

Find the areas of the triangles in questions **1**–**7**.

1 Copy and fill in:

Area of triangle $= \dfrac{\text{base} \times \text{height}}{2}$

$= \dfrac{\ldots \times \ldots}{2}$

$= \ldots\ \text{cm}^2$

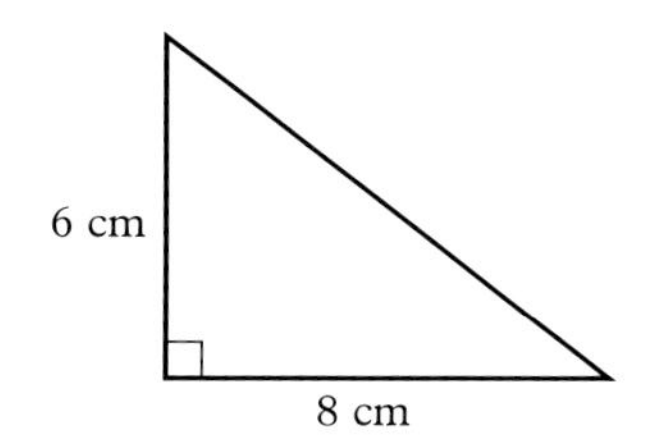

2

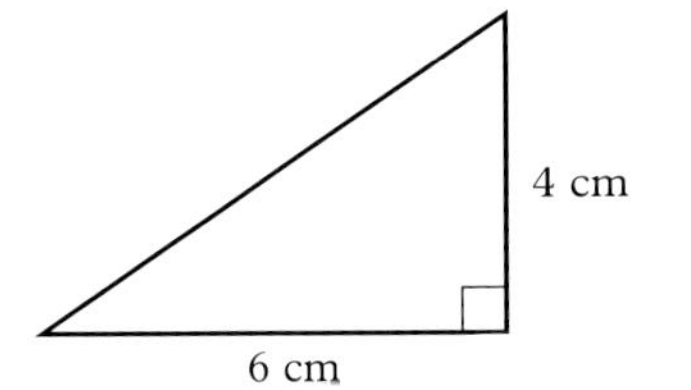

3

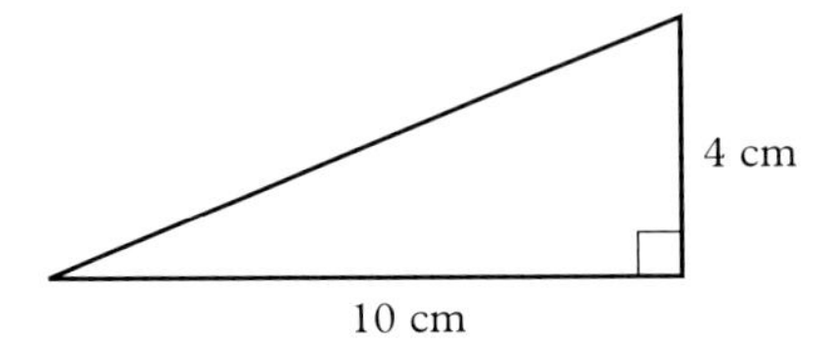

4

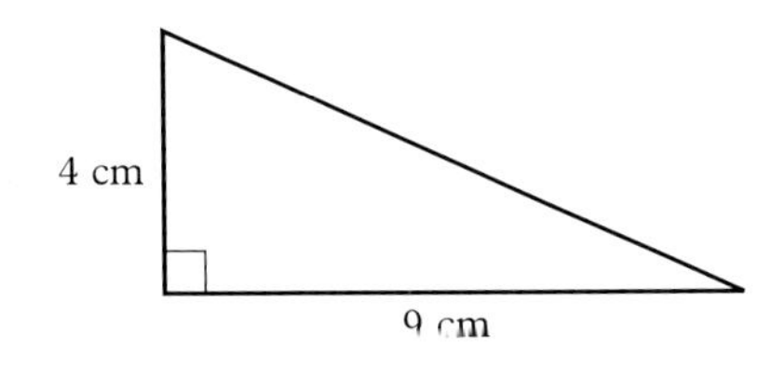

5

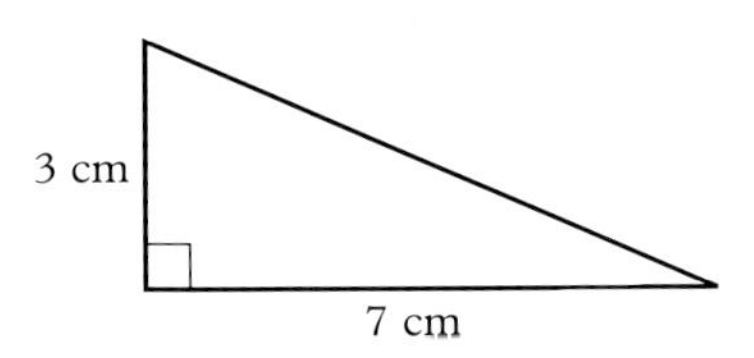

6

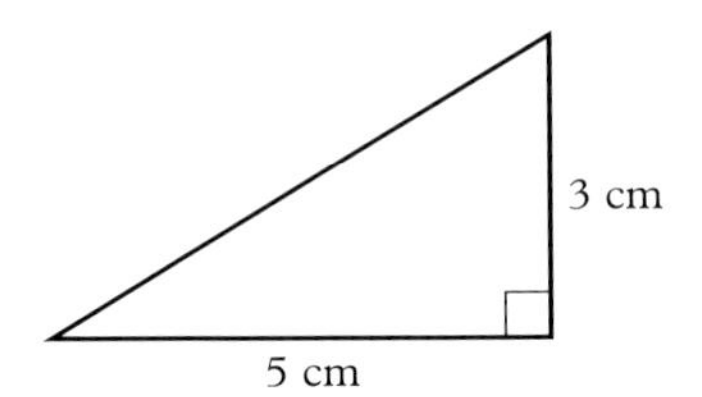

7

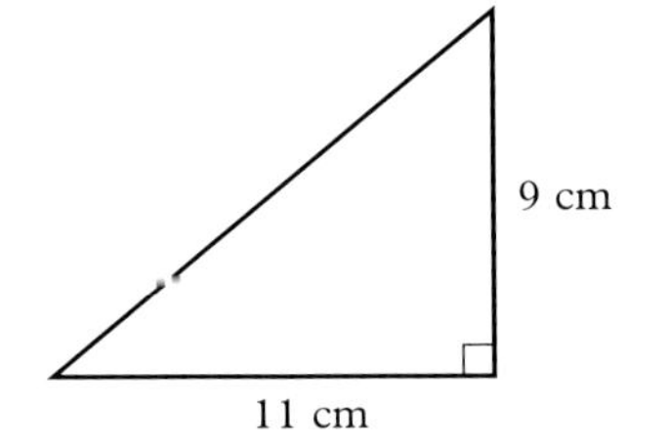

8 **a** Use Area of triangle = $\frac{\text{base} \times \text{height}}{2}$ to find the areas of these triangles.

(1)

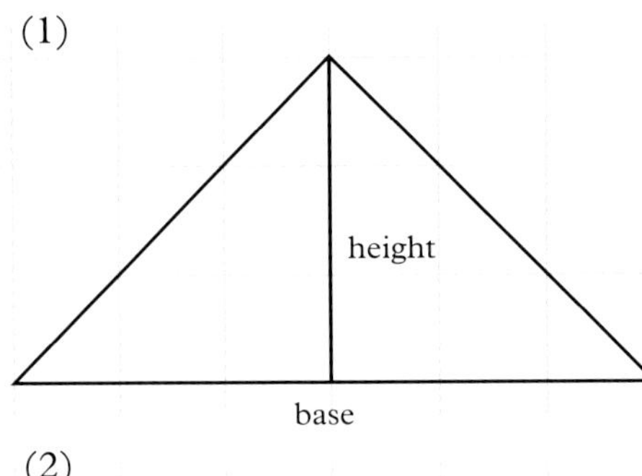

(2)

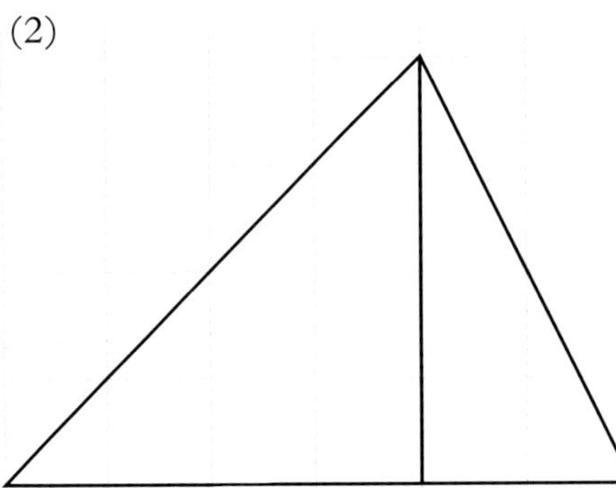

b Check your answers by counting squares.

9 Use Area of triangle = $\dfrac{\text{base} \times \text{height}}{2}$ to find the areas of these triangles.

a

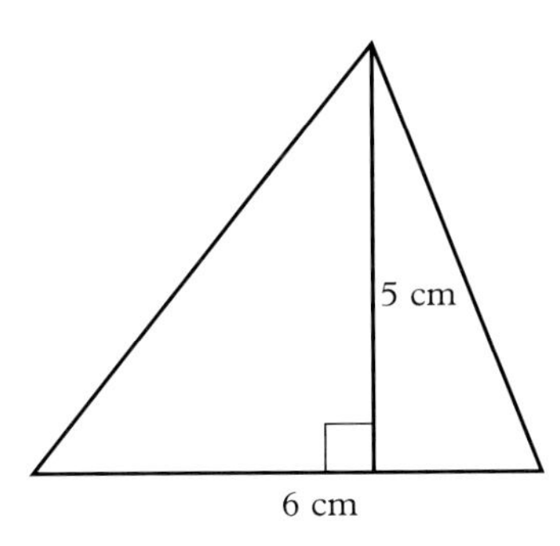

c

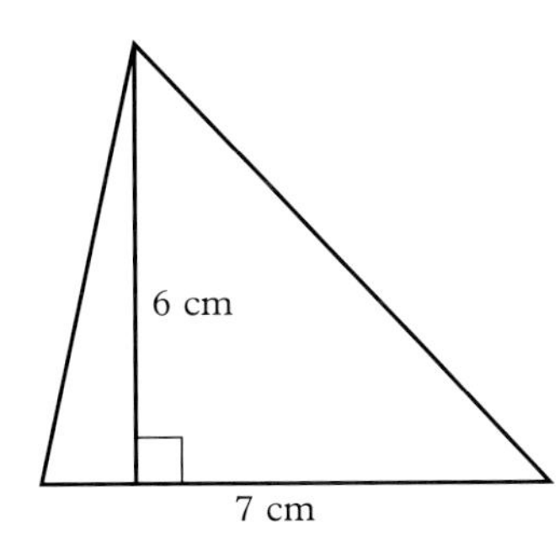

b

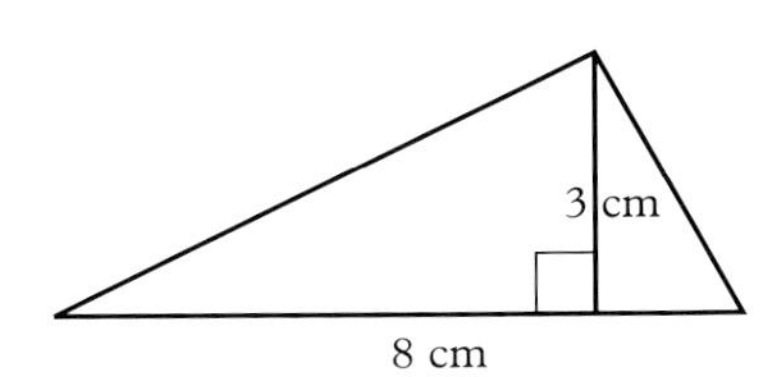

d

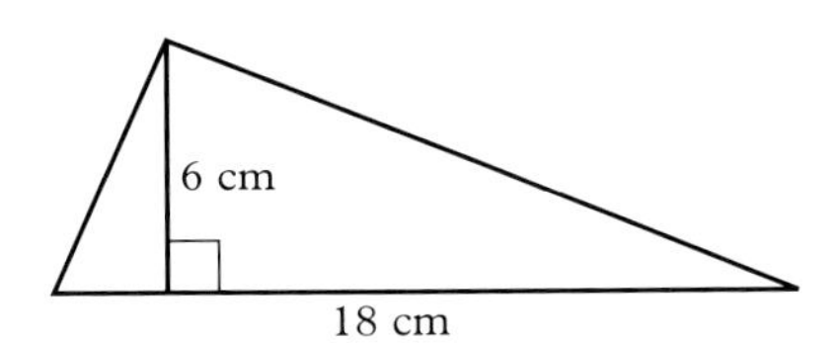

10 The height can be outside the triangle.
Find the areas of these triangles.

a Copy and fill in:

$$\text{Area of triangle} = \frac{\text{base} \times \text{height}}{2}$$
$$= \frac{\ldots \times 10}{2}$$
$$= \ldots \text{ cm}^2$$

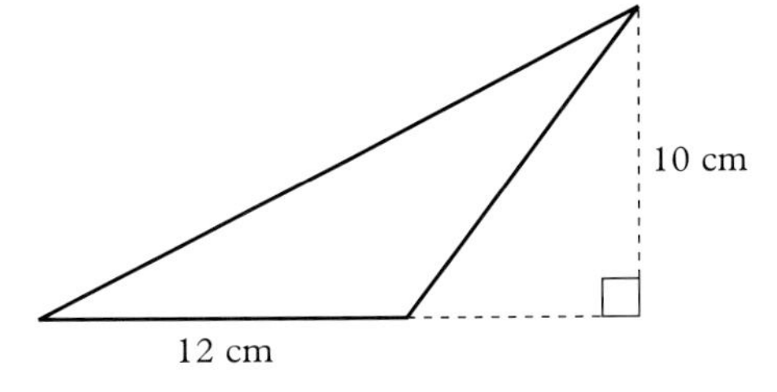

b

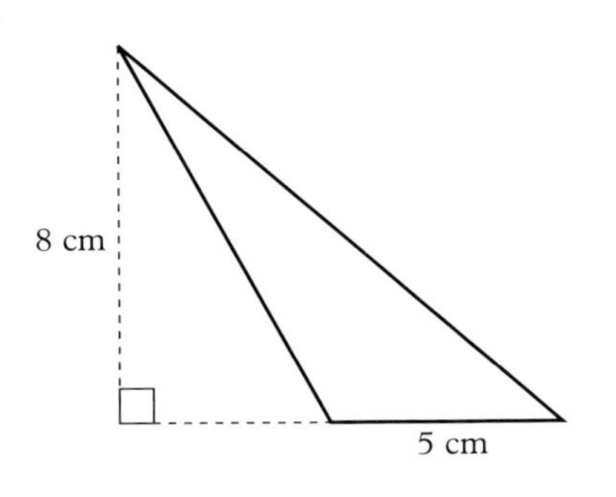

c

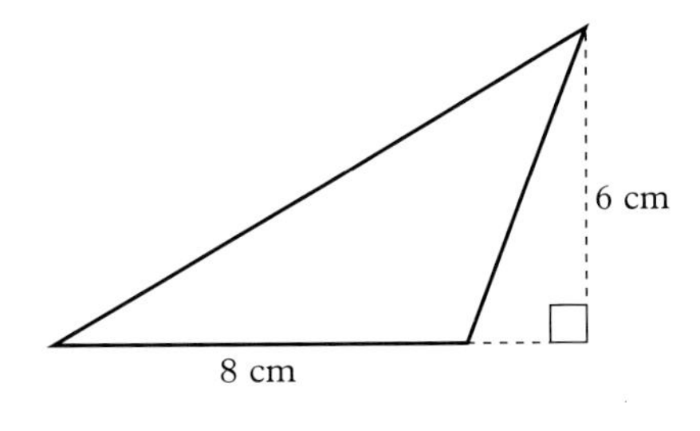

11 Sometimes the triangle can be on its side or even upside down.
Find the areas of these triangles.

a Copy and fill in:

$$\text{Area of triangle} = \frac{\text{base} \times \text{height}}{2}$$
$$= \frac{\ldots \times \ldots}{2}$$
$$= \ldots \text{ cm}^2$$

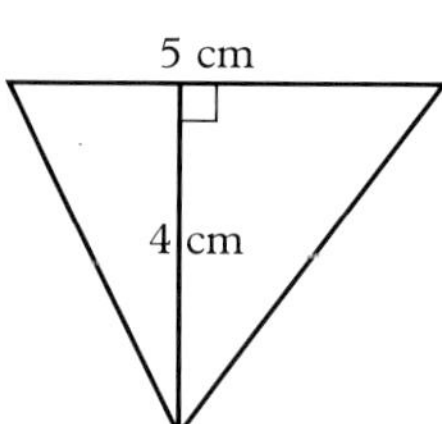

b

15 cm

20 cm

c

6 cm

6 cm

d

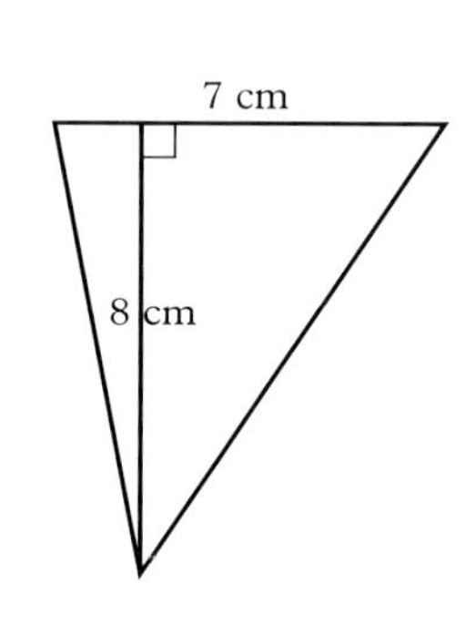

12 These triangles are drawn accurately.
Find the area of each triangle.
You will need to measure the base and height.

a

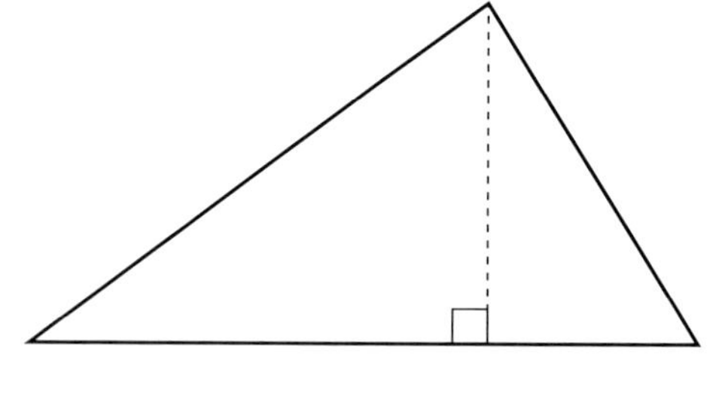

c

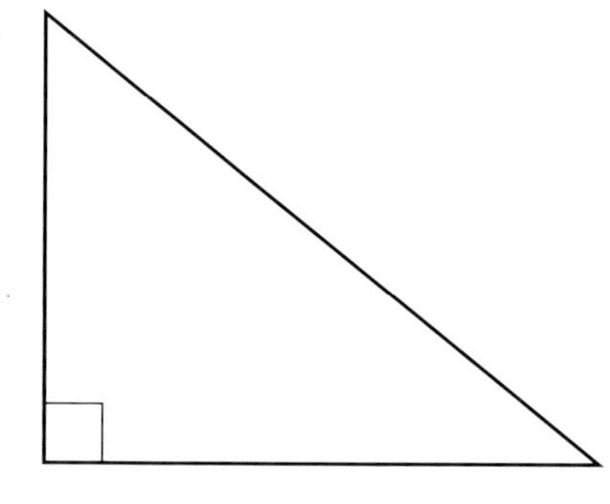

b

● **d**

Exercise 12:7

1 The sail of a yacht is a triangle.
The base of the triangle is 3 m
and the height is 4 m.
Find the area of the sail.

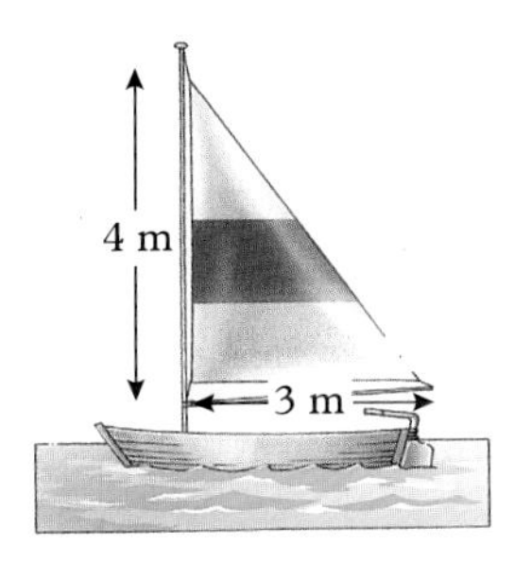

2 This silk scarf is a triangle.
The two short sides are each 70 cm long.
Work out the area of the scarf.

3 The front of this tent is a triangle.
The tent is 2 m wide and
1.5 m high.
Work out the area of the front of
the tent.

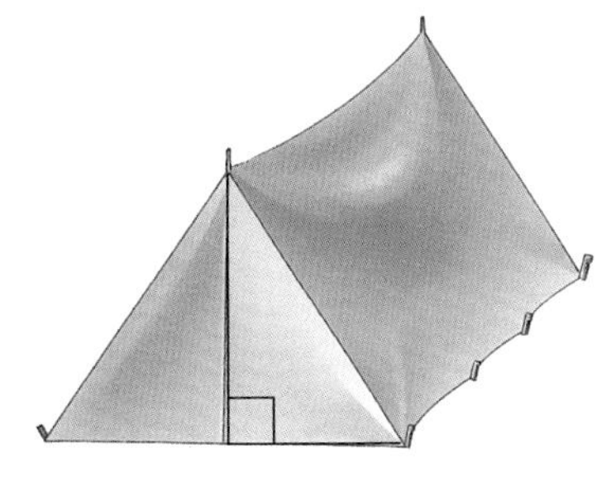

• **4** The picture shows the end wall of
a shed.
The wall can be divided into a
triangle and a rectangle.
Copy and fill in:

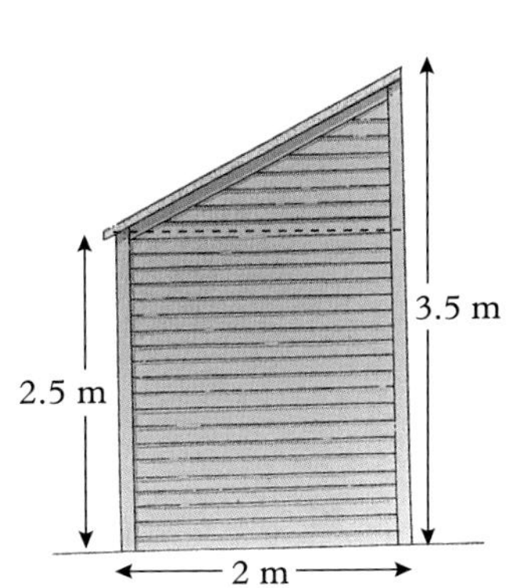

Height of triangle = … − … = … m

Area of triangle = $\dfrac{\ldots \times \ldots}{2}$ = … m^2

Area of rectangle = … × … = … m^2

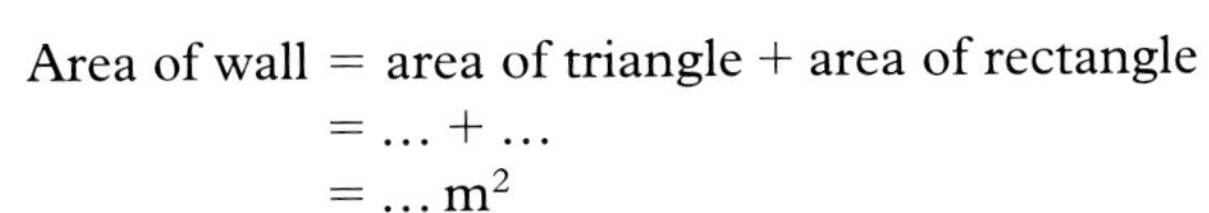

Area of wall = area of triangle + area of rectangle
= … + …
= … m^2

1 **a** Write down the perimeter of each shape.

(1)

(2)
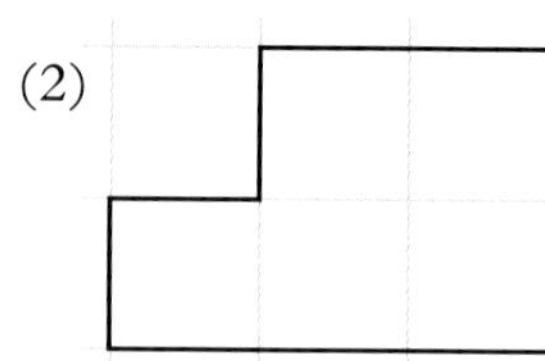

(3)
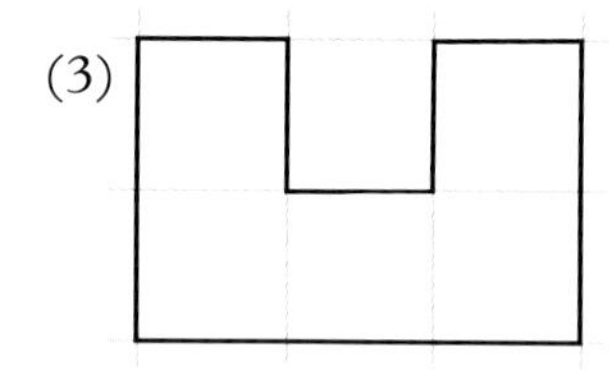

b Write down the area of each shape.

c Answer true or false to each of these:

(1) Shapes with the same perimeter always have the same area.

(2) Shapes with the same area always have the same perimeter.

2 Work out the areas of these rectangles.

a

20 mm

40 mm

b

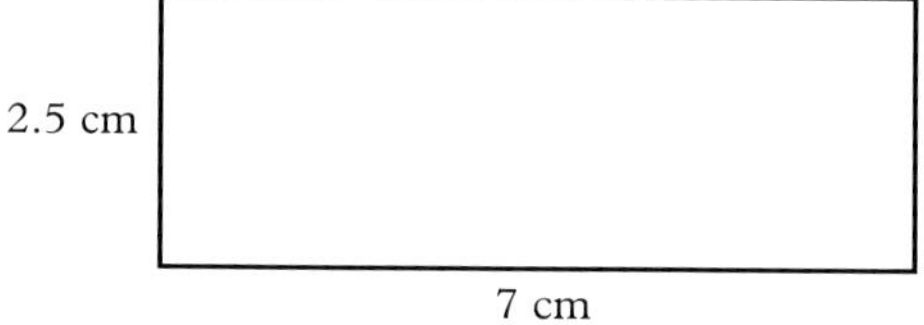

3 Find the perimeters of the rectangles in question 2.

4 Work out the area of each of these shapes.
Find the blue length in each shape first.

a

11 cm

4 cm

3 cm

2 cm

8 cm

b

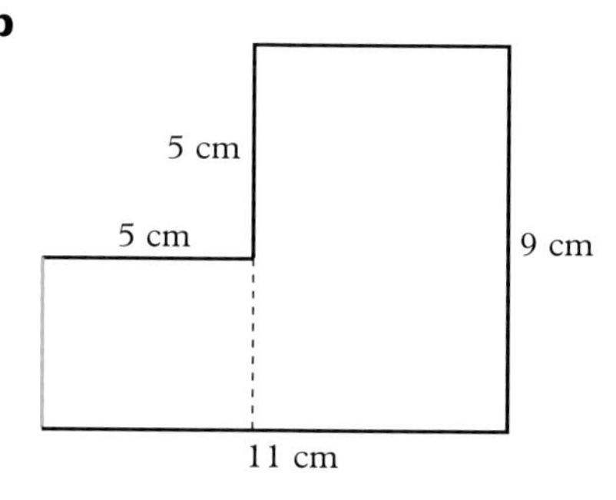

5 **a** Work out the area of the whole shape.

b Work out the area of the piece cut out.

c Work out the area of the piece that is left.

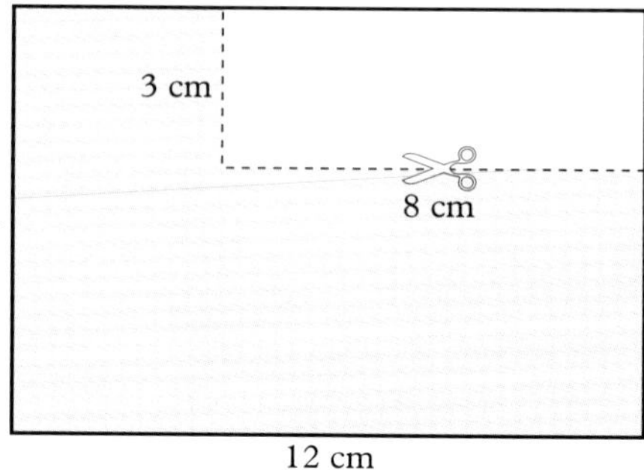

6 Find the areas of these triangles.

a

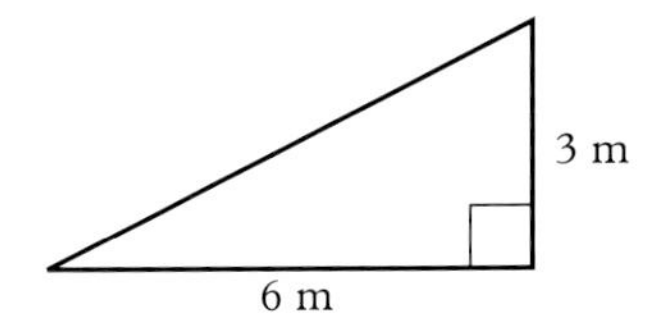

c

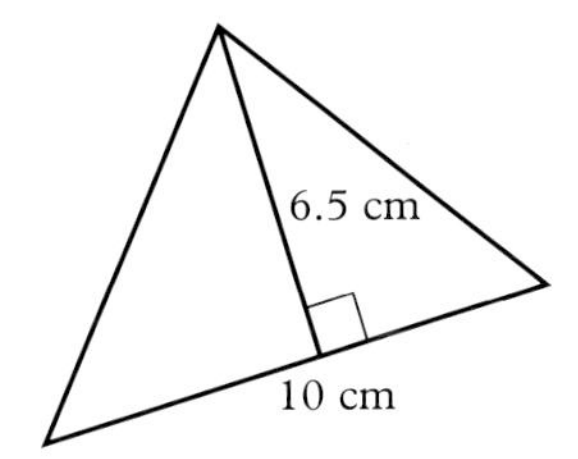

b

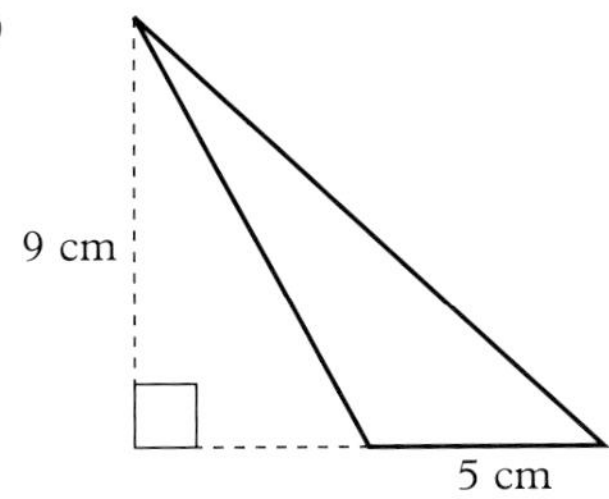

d

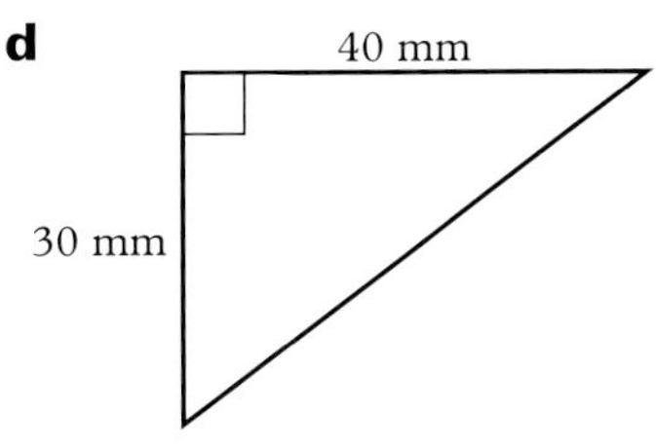

7 **a** A rug is in the shape of a rectangle.
The rug is 2.5 m wide and 4 m long.
Find the area of the rug.

b The rug has a red edge.
Find the length of the edge.

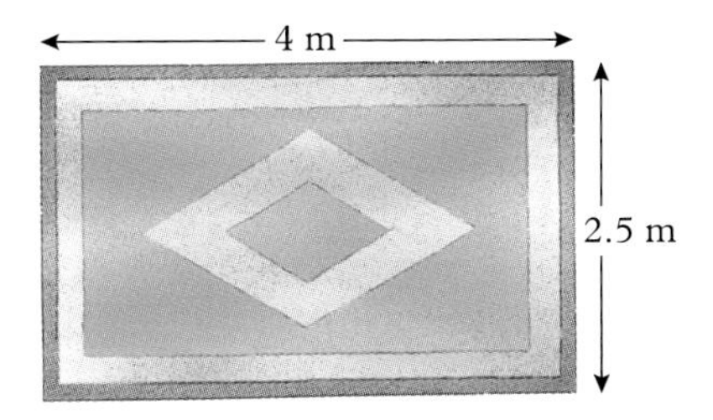

8 Colin has a rectangle of card 30 cm by 20 cm.
Colin cuts a rectangular hole 20 cm by 10 cm in the card to frame a picture.

a Find the area of the whole sheet of card.

b Find the area of the rectangle that Colin cuts out.

c Find the area of the piece of card that is left.

9 The diagram shows an L shaped lawn.

a Find the area of the lawn.

b Mr Green puts fertiliser on the lawn.
He uses 25 g per m^2.
How much fertiliser does Mr Green use?

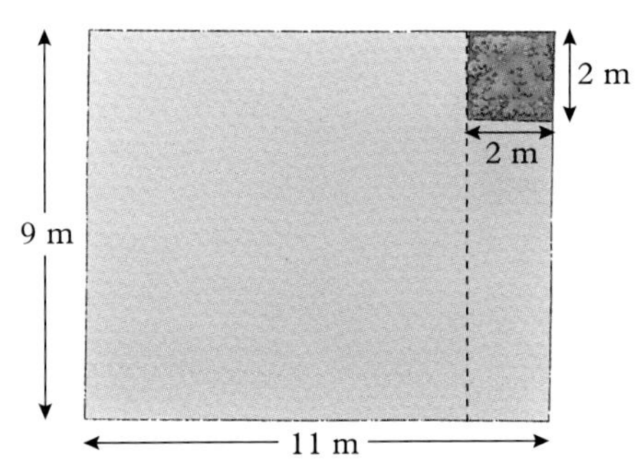

1 The diagram shows a kitchen worktop.
Find the area of the worktop.

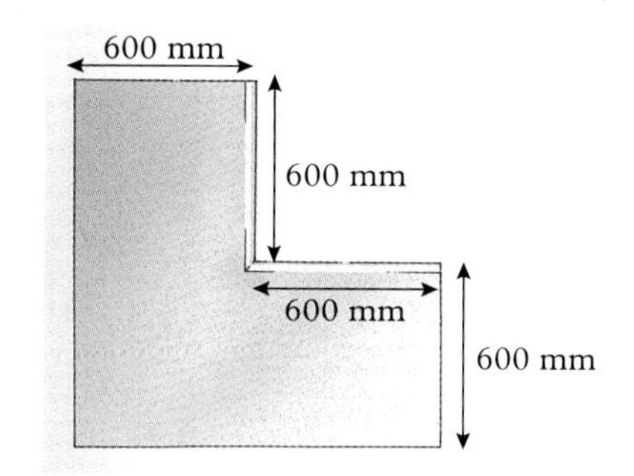

2 **a** Work out the area of:
(1) the red triangle
(2) the blue triangle

b Write what you notice about your answers to **a**.

c Copy the diagram on to squared paper.
Use a different colour to draw another triangle with the same area as the red and blue triangles.

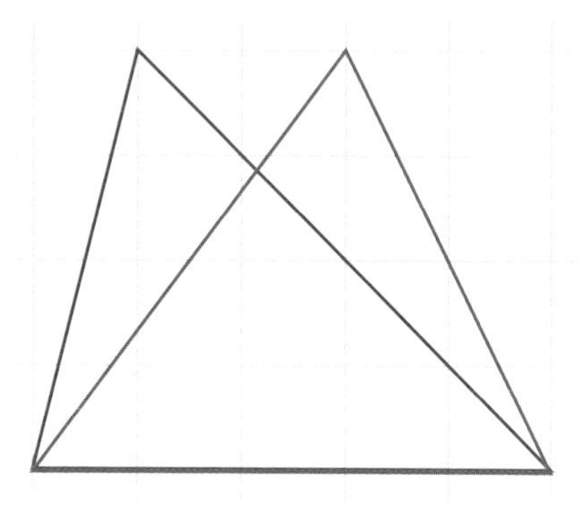

3 **a** Here is a scale drawing of a bedroom in a motel. It has a bathroom opening out of the bedroom.
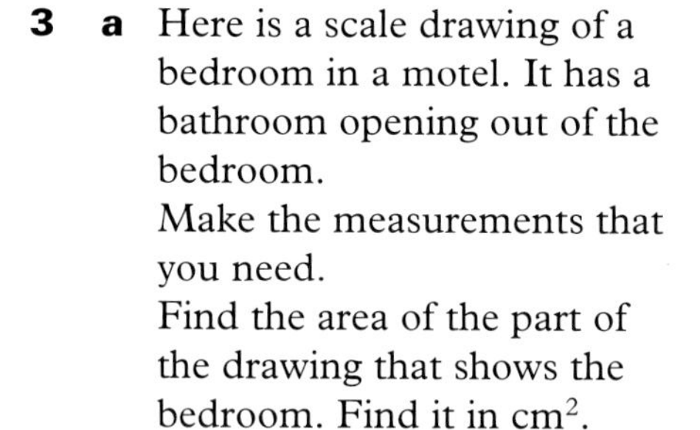
Make the measurements that you need.
Find the area of the part of the drawing that shows the bedroom. Find it in cm^2.

b The scale of the plan is 1 cm to 1 m.
Write down the area of the bedroom in m^2.

c Four carpet tiles cover 1 m^2.
How many tiles do you need to carpet the bedroom?

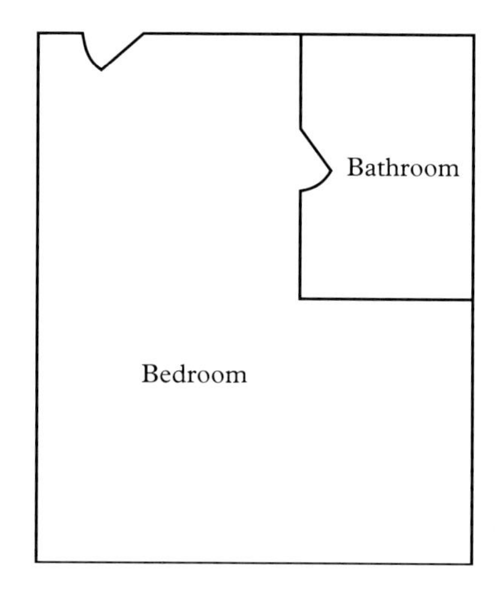

4 Here is the wall of a house.
The wall is going to be painted.
Find the area to be painted.

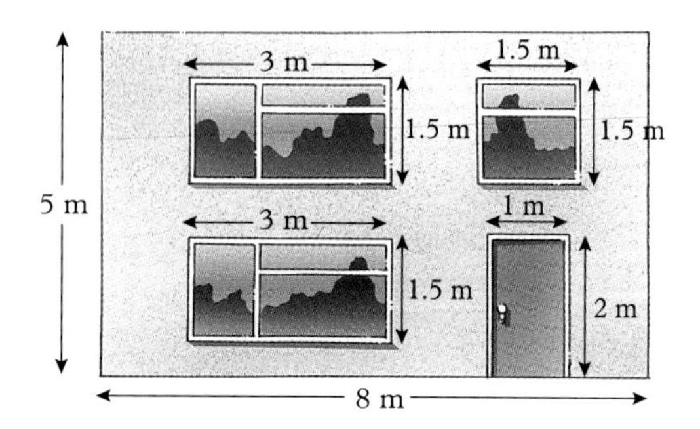

- **Perimeter** The total distance around the outside of a shape is called its **perimeter**.
  The red line is the perimeter of this shape.
  The perimeter is
  $2 + 2 + 1 + 1 + 1 + 3 = 10\,\text{cm}$

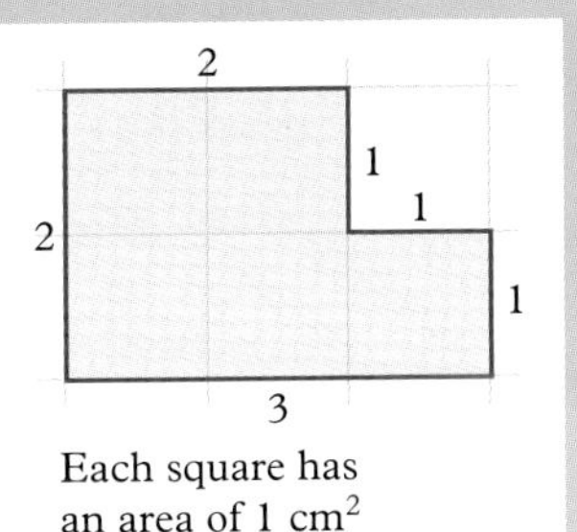

Each square has an area of 1 cm^2

Area The amount of space inside the shape is called its **area**.

The area of this shape is shaded green.
We use squares to measure area.
There are 5 squares inside this shape.
The area of this shape is 5 cm^2.

- **Area of a rectangle** **Area of a rectangle** = ***l***ength × ***w***idth
  $= l \times w$

Example Calculate the area of this rectangle.
Area = length × width
$= 4 \times 3$
$= 12\,\text{cm}^2$

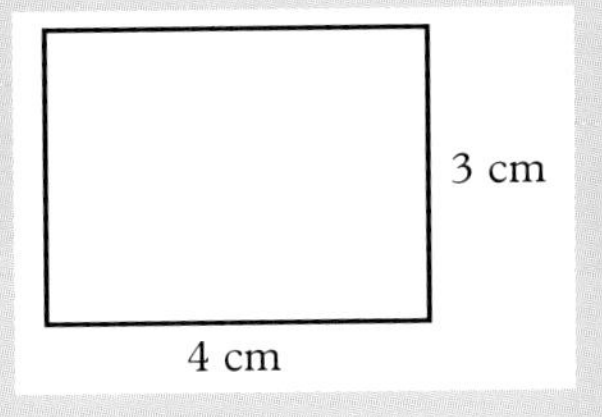

- *Example* Find the area of this L shape.

The shape is made of two rectangles A and B.
The dashed line shows the join.

The length of A is 10 cm.
We need to find the width.
blue line + red line = green line
blue line + 3 = 7
so blue line = 4 cm

Area of A $= 4 \times 10 = 40\,\text{cm}^2$
Area of B $= 3 \times 5 = 15\,\text{cm}^2$

Area of shape $= 40 + 15$
$= 55\,\text{cm}^2$

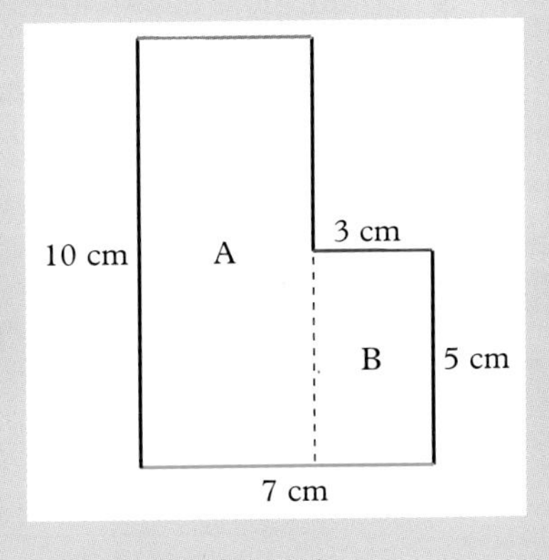

- **Area of a triangle** $\textbf{Area of a triangle} = \dfrac{\text{base} \times \text{height}}{2}$

Example Find the area of this triangle.

$$\text{Area of triangle} = \frac{\text{base} \times \text{height}}{2}$$
$$= \frac{10 \times 8}{2}$$
$$= 40\,\text{cm}^2$$

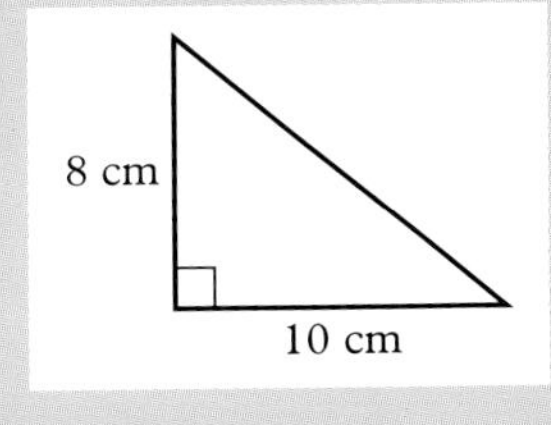

1 **a** Find the perimeter of this shape.
b Find the area of this shape.

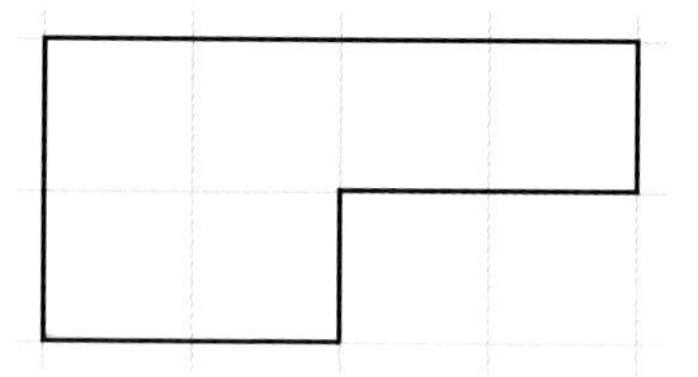

2 **a** Work out the area of this rectangle.
b Find the perimeter of this rectangle.

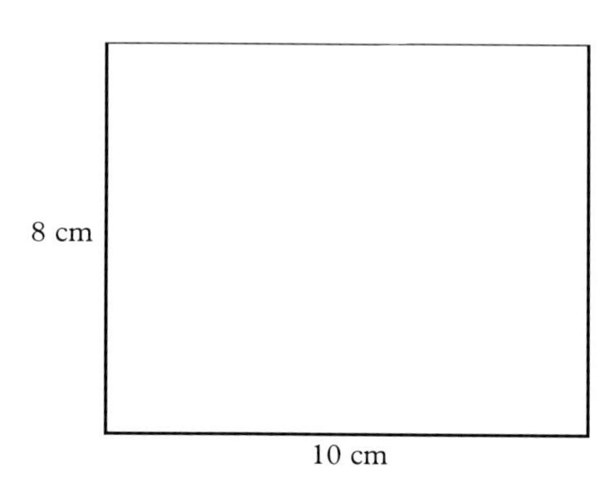

3 Find the areas shaded green in these shapes.

a

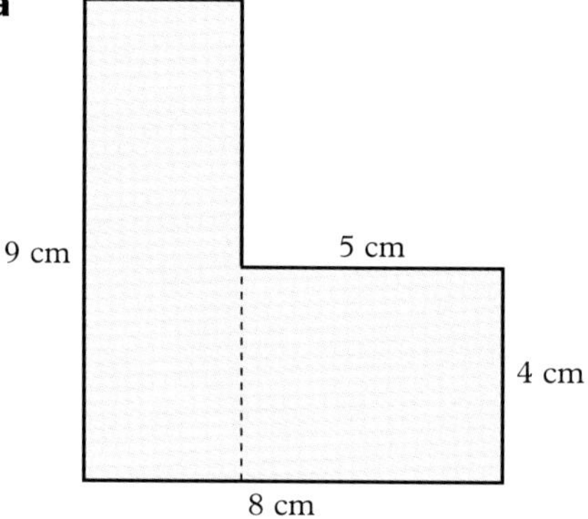

b

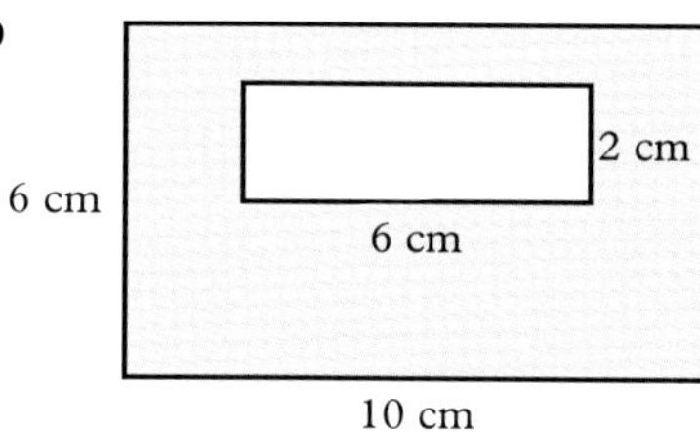

4 Find the areas of these triangles.

a

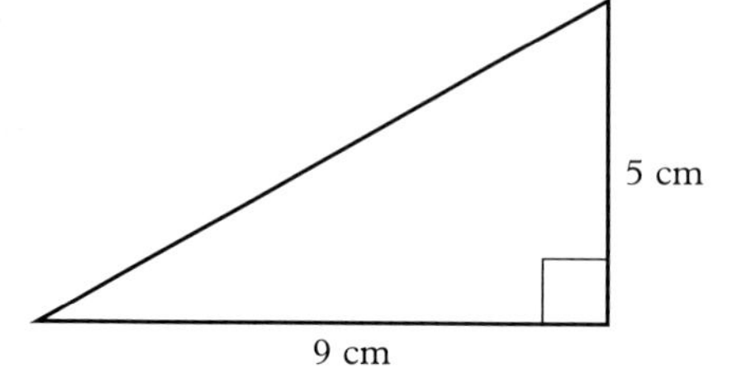

b

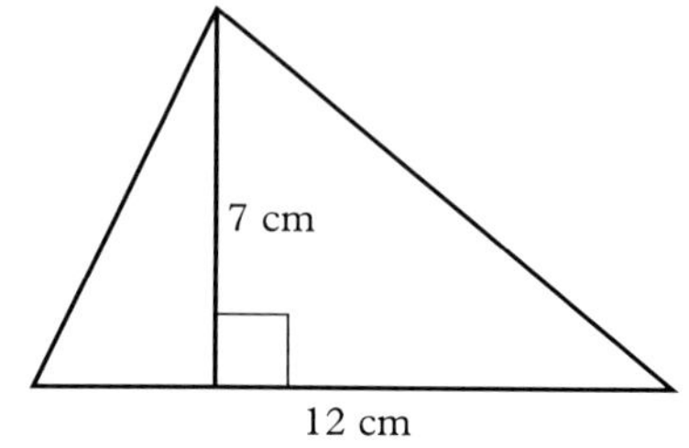

13 Statistics: getting it together

CORE

QUESTIONS

EXTENSION

SUMMARY

TEST YOURSELF

Crazy Cricket Calculations

Frank and Paul play for the same cricket team.

In the first half of the season, Frank averaged more runs per innings than Paul. He hoped he might win the trophy for the best batting average of the season.

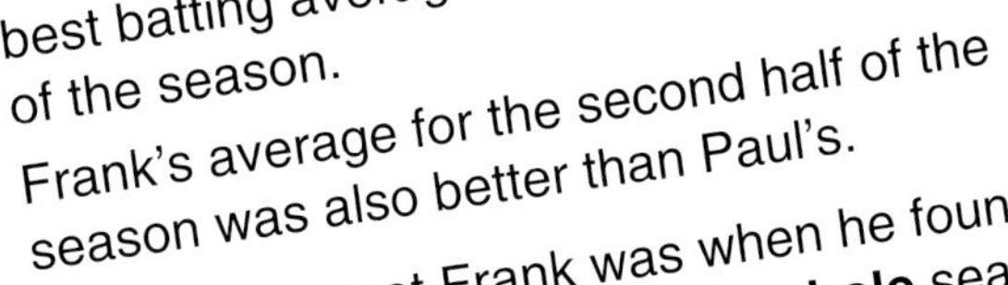

Frank's average for the second half of the season was also better than Paul's.

Think how upset Frank was when he found out that Paul's average for the **whole** season was the best, so Paul won the trophy!

How could this happen?

1 Averages and range

◀◀ REPLAY ▶

Year 8 pupils are in eight forms at Stanthorne High.
The forms do not all have the same number of pupils.
One form has 25 pupils, three have 27, two have 28 and two have 29.

Mean

To find the **mean** of a set of data:
(1) Find the total of all the data values.
(2) Divide by the number of data values.

Example

Find the mean number of pupils in a Year 8 form at Stanthorne High.

The total is:
$$25 + 27 + 27 + 27 + 28 + 28 + 29 + 29 = 220$$
The mean is $220 \div 8 = 27.5$

You cannot really have 27.5 people in a form! You must not round the mean to a whole number even if you think the answer is silly.

Exercise 13:1

1 Stanthorne High has a school nurse. She counted the number of pupils with bad asthma every day for two weeks.
Here are her results:

3 15 0 3 1 0 4 3 1 4

Work out the mean number of pupils with asthma.

2 Tony timed his journeys to and from school for a week.
Here are his times in minutes:

25 21 24 26 21 24 26 27 21 27

Find the mean time for Tony's journeys.

3 The amounts collected for *Children in Need* by the eight Year 8 classes were:

£15 £12 £20 £17 £15 £13 £15 £17

a Find the total amount collected.
b Find the mean amount collected.

4 These are the amounts that Joanne spent on her school lunches in one week.

85 p 90 p 75 p 98 p 92 p

Find the mean amount Joanne spent.

5 Some children were weighed and measured as part of a medical examination.
Here are the results.

Height (cm)	148	136	130	127	137	143	139	141	144	129
Weight (kg)	65	55	46	41	51	61	58	61	59	49

a (1) Find the total of all the heights.
(2) Find the mean height.
b (1) Find the total of all the weights.
(2) Find the mean weight.

● **6** These are the monthly rainfall figures in millimetres for South Wales for one year.

Jan	115.8	Apr	63.5	Jul	85.4	Oct	114.3
Feb	76.2	May	76.2	Aug	99.1	Nov	116.8
Mar	58.4	Jun	55.8	Sep	91.4	Dec	109.1

a Find the total rainfall for the year.
b Work out the mean rainfall per month.
c Write down the months that had a rainfall lower than the mean.
d Write down the months that had a rainfall higher than the mean.

Mode The **mode** is the most common or the most popular data value. This is sometimes called the **modal value**.

Example Find the modal number of pupils in a Year 8 form at Stanthorne High.

The numbers in the forms are:

25 27 27 27 28 28 29 29

The most common number is 27.

The modal value is 27 pupils.

7 Here are the school nurse's results on bad asthma.
She wrote down the number of cases every day for two weeks.

3 15 0 3 1 0 4 3 1 4

Write down the modal number of asthma cases.

8 Here are Tony's times in minutes for his journeys to and from school.

25 21 24 26 21 24 26 27 21 27

Write down the modal time for Tony's journeys.

9 Mrs Brown gets cross if 8B forget their maths exercise books. She counts the number of forgotten books for eight lessons.
Here are her results:

0 1 3 1 2 0 1 1

Write down the mode.

10 The mode does not have to be a number.
Here is a pie-chart of the ways 8M and their teacher come to school.

a What is the mode?

b Explain how you can find the mode from the pie-chart.

Pie-chart of the ways 8M come to school

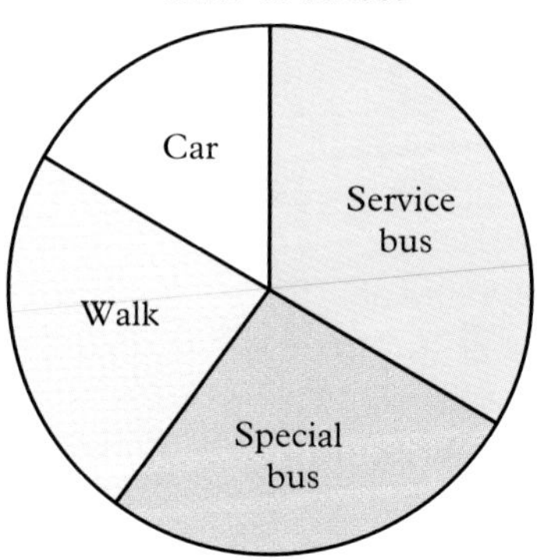

Median

There is a third type of average called the **median**.
The median is the middle value of the data.
You must make sure that your data is in order from smallest to largest.

Example

These are the amounts that Manisha spent on her school lunches in one week.

75 p 92 p 95 p 88 p 98 p

Find the median amount Manisha spent.

Write the numbers in order:

75 p 88 p **92 p** 95 p 98 p

The middle value is 92 p so this is the median.

11 Find the the median of each of these sets of numbers.
Remember to put the numbers in order first.

a	7	5	6	7	4	8	3		
b	14	16	17	12	13				
c	35	37	29	21	38	36	32		
d	0	4	0	2	8	5	1	7	9

Example

Find the median number of pupils in a Year 8 form at Stanthorne High.

The numbers in the forms are:

25 27 27 27 28 28 29 29

There are two middle values.

The median is $\frac{27 + 28}{2} = 27.5$

Like the mean, the median does not have to be one of the data values.

12 Find the median of each of these sets of numbers.

a	3	5	6	6	7	8		
b	12	14	15	17	18	18		
c	7	9	6	6	9	10	11	7
d	31	35	34	31	33	36	34	38
● **e**	6	4	5	7	3	8	9	2

13 Here are the school nurse's results on bad asthma.
She wrote down the number of cases every day for two weeks.
3 15 0 3 1 0 4 3 1 4
Work out the median.

● **14** Here are Tony's times in minutes for his journeys to and from school.
25 21 24 26 21 24 26 27 21 27
Work out the median time for Tony's journeys.

Range

For any set of data, the **range** is the biggest value take away the smallest value.

Example

Find the range of the number of pupils in Year 8 forms at Stanthorne High.

The numbers in the forms are:
25 27 27 27 28 28 29 29
The biggest value is 29. The smallest value is 25.
The range is $29 - 25 = 4$

Exercise 13:2

1 Here are the school nurse's results on bad asthma.
She wrote down the number of cases every day for two weeks.
3 15 0 3 1 0 4 3 1 4
Find the range.

2 Here are Tony's times in minutes for his journeys to and from school.
25 21 24 26 21 24 26 27 21 27
Find the range of his times.

3 The amounts collected for *Oxfam* by the eight Year 8 classes were:
£12 £19 £20 £16 £14 £13 £18 £11
Find the range.

4 These are the amounts Jude spent on his school lunches in one week.
95 p 80 p 75 p 88 p 95 p
Find the range.

5 Some children were weighed and measured as part of a medical examination.

Height (cm)	148	136	130	127	137	143	139	141	144	129
Weight (kg)	65	55	46	41	51	61	58	61	59	49

a Find the range of the heights.
b Find the range of the weights.

Tally-table When there is a lot of data we make a **tally-table**. We use tally marks.

Tally marks **Tally marks** are done in groups of five. The fifth tally mark goes across the other four: ~~||||~~

Exercise 13:3

1 These are the numbers of pupils in each form for Years 7 to 11 at Stanthorne High.

Year 7	30	27	26	28	29	30	28	29
Year 8	25	27	28	27	29	27	28	29
Year 9	28	27	29	27	26	29	25	27
Year 10	28	24	27	28	26	27	28	27
Year 11	25	26	27	29	27	28	26	28

a Find the range.
b Copy this tally-table. Fill it in.

Number of pupils in a form	Tally	Total
24		
25		
26		
27		
28		
29		
30		
	Total	

c Use the table to find the mode.
d Explain how you found the mode.

2 We can find the mean number of pupils in a form at Stanthorne High.
We use a table like this.

a Copy the table.
Fill it in.

Number of pupils in a form	Number of forms	Total number of pupils
24	1	$24 \times 1 =$
25	3	$25 \times 3 =$
26	5	$26 \times 5 =$
27	12	$27 \times 12 =$
28	10	$28 \times 10 =$
29	7	$29 \times 7 =$
30	2	$30 \times 2 =$
Total	40	

b Copy and fill in:
Mean number of pupils
= total number of pupils ÷ total number of forms
= ... ÷ 40
= ...

3 Some pupils at Stanthorne High come to school by car.
One morning 8J did a survey of how many pupils arrived in each car.

They found the mean from a table like this.

a Copy the table.
Fill it in.

Number of pupils in a car	Number of cars	Total number of pupils
1	38	$1 \times 38 =$
2	27	$2 \times 27 =$
3	12	$3 \times 12 =$
4	3	$4 \times 3 =$
Total	80	

b Copy and fill in:
Mean number of pupils
= total number of pupils ÷ total number of cars
= ... ÷ 80
= ...

2 Grouping data

Children's books are often given a reading age.
This measures how difficult a book is to read.

There are a few ways of measuring reading age.
One way is to count the length of the words. Books for older children may have longer words.
Another way is to count the number of words in each sentence.

Word length and sentence length are examples of discrete data.

Discrete data When data can only be certain individual values it is called **discrete**.

Example Shoe size is an example of discrete data.
The values can only be 1, $1\frac{1}{2}$, 2, $2\frac{1}{2}$, etc. There are no shoe sizes in between these.

Exercise 13:4

W **1** **a** Look at the two pages from children's books.
Copy this tally-table for Book A.
Fill it in.

Word length (letters)	Tally	Total
1		
2		
3		
4		
5		
6		
7		
8		
9		
10		

b Now make a tally-table for Book B.

To compare the two books it is best to draw some diagrams.

2 **a** Copy the axes on to graph paper.

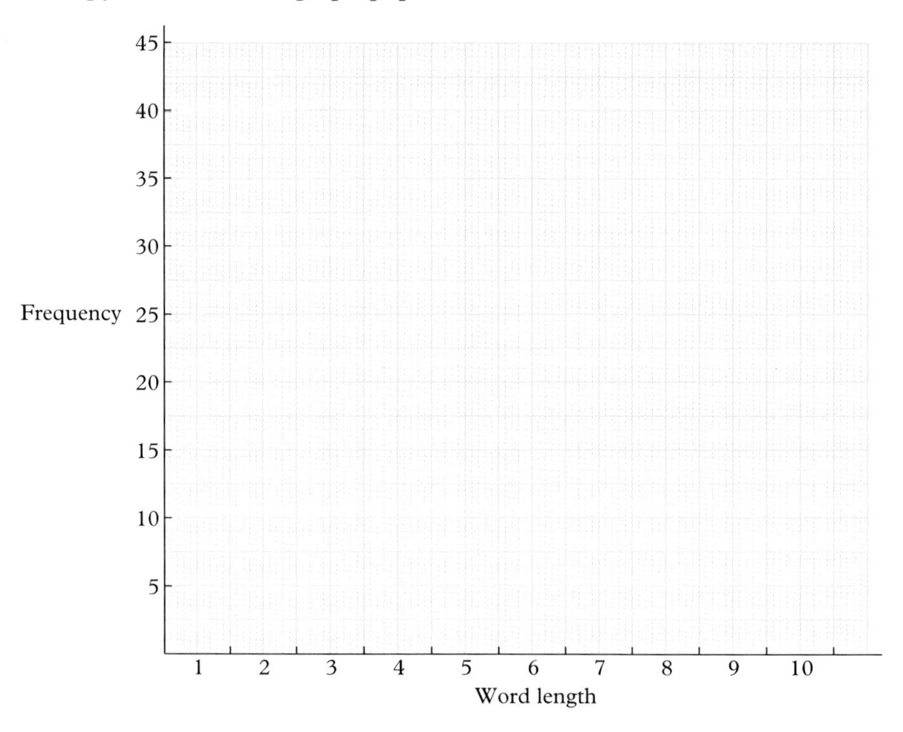

b Use your tally-table for Book A to draw a bar-chart.
c Copy the axes again.
d Use your tally-table for Book B to draw another bar-chart.

3 Use your two bar-charts to answer these questions.
a Which book has the most 2-letter words?
b Which book has the most 6-letter words?
c Copy and fill in:
Choose from **short** **long** **A** **B**
Book A has more … words than Book B.
Book B has more … words than Book A.
I think that Book … is easier to read.
d Why do you think this book is easier to read?

4 **a** Which is the most common length of word in Book A?
b Copy and fill in:
The modal word length for Book A is … letters.
c Which is the most common length of word in Book B?
d Copy and fill in:
The modal word length for Book B is … letters.

5 **a** Add the red column to your tally-tables.

Word length (letters)	Tally	Number of words	Total number of letters (= word length × total)
1			

b Fill in this column.
Add up the numbers in the column.
This is the total number of letters.

c Divide your answer to **b** by the total number of words.
This is the mean word length.

There is another way of measuring how difficult books are to read.
You can count the number of words in a sentence.
This is called the sentence length.

Exercise 13:5

1 **a** Go back to your page from Book A.
Count the number of words in each sentence.
Write down each sentence length in your book.

b Count the length of the sentences in the page from Book B.
Write down each sentence length in your book.

Sentences can be lots of different lengths.
It is sensible to put these in groups before you make a tally-table.

Length of sentence (in words)	Tally	Total
1–5		
6–10		
11–15		
16–20		
21–25		
26–30		
31–35		

Sentences with 1, 2, 3, 4 or 5 words go into the 1–5 group.
Sentences with 6, 7, 8, 9 or 10 words go into the 6–10 group
and so on.

Then you can draw a bar-chart from the grouped data.

2 **a** Copy the tally-table.
b Tally the sentence lengths from Book A.
Use the numbers you wrote down in question **1**.
c Copy the tally-table again.
Tally the sentence lengths from Book B.

3 **a** Copy these axes on to squared paper.

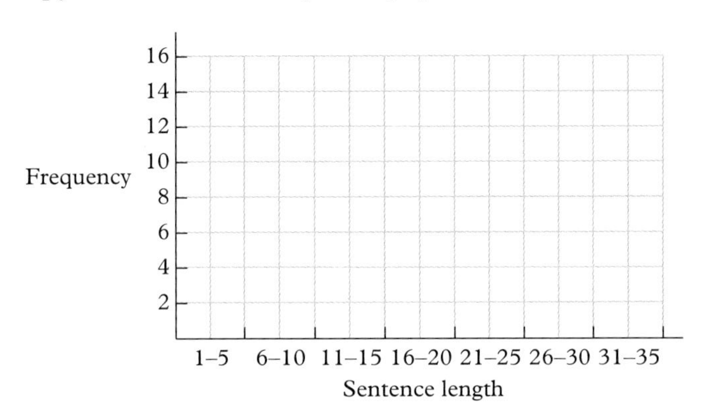

b Use your tally-table for Book A to draw a bar-chart.
Don't leave gaps between the bars.
c Copy the axes again.
d Use your tally-table for Book B to draw another bar-chart.

4 **a** Which group has the most sentences in it for Book A?
b Copy and fill in:
The modal sentence length for Book A is … words.
c Which group has the most sentences in it for Book B?
d Copy and fill in:
The modal sentence length for Book B is … words.
● **e** Think about your answers to **b** and **d**.
Which book do you think is easier to read?

● **5** You can work out the mean sentence length.
a Write down the total number of words on the page from Book A.
b Write down the total number of sentences on the page from Book A.
c Copy and fill in:
mean sentence length
= total number of words ÷ total number of sentences
= … ÷ …
= …
d Write down the total number of words on the page from Book B.
e Write down the total number of sentences on the page from Book B.
f Work out the mean sentence length for Book B.

Sometimes you have to decide on your own groups.

Example

Class 8P take a Maths test. Their marks are given to them as percentages.

56	48	79	70	45	16	89	91	25	78
67	58	94	47	26	34	85	67	14	35
36	96	75	37	58	94	34	65	67	48

Their teacher groups the marks in 10s.

Mark	11–20	21–30	31–40	41–50	51–60	61–70	71–80	81–90	91–100
Pupils	2	2	5	4	3	5	3	2	4

He then groups the marks in 30s.

Mark	11–40	41–70	71–100
Pupils	9	12	9

He draws bar-charts of both sets of data.

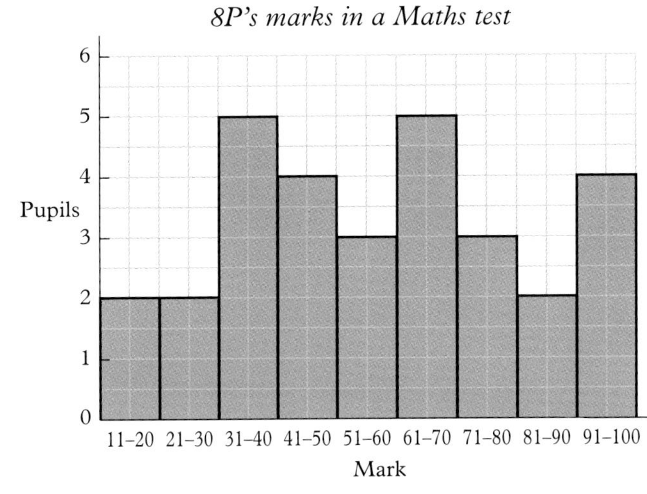

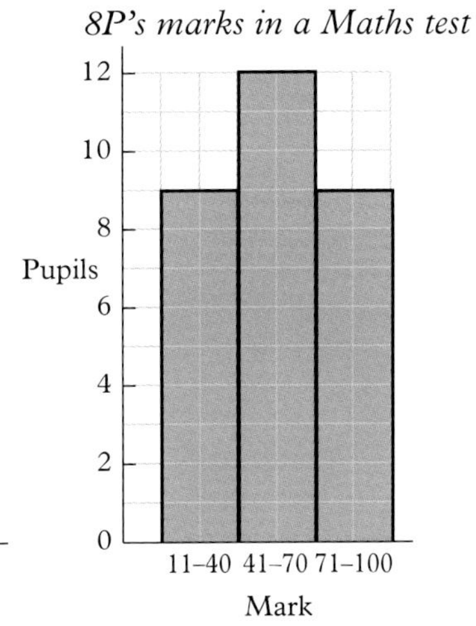

He decides that grouping in 10s is the best because it shows more detail.

Exercise 13:6

1 Class 8P also take a Science test.
Here are their marks in percentages.

63	52	58	63	56	19	84	93	27	71
56	51	52	24	26	41	78	68	18	32
92	96	80	27	64	99	25	59	68	40

a Decide how to group the data.
Make a tally-table and fill it in.

b Draw a bar-chart for your tally-table.

2 In a Science lesson Davinder has to measure the lengths of 30 earthworms.
His measurements are to the nearest centimetre.

12	16	18	9	5	7	15	14	12	13
12	10	8	5	16	19	20	11	17	8
9	13	11	11	12	17	18	15	14	14

a Decide how to group the data.
Make a tally-table and fill it in.

b Draw a bar-chart for your tally-table.

c Double the size of your groups. Make a new tally-table.

d Draw a bar-chart for your new tally-table.

● **e** Which groups do you think work best?
Explain your answer.

3 This table shows the number of people visiting a hospital on each day in June.

Number of people	31–50	51–70	71–90	91–110	111–130	131–150
Number of days	1	1	3	4	5	4

Number of people	151–170	171–190	191–210	211–230	231–250	251–270
Number of days	4	3	2	1	1	1

a Join the groups up in pairs so that there are just 6 groups.
Make a new table for the data.
Your groups will be 31–70, 71–110, 111–150 and so on.

b Draw a bar-chart for your new table.

c Which groups do you think are the most sensible?

3 Frequency polygons

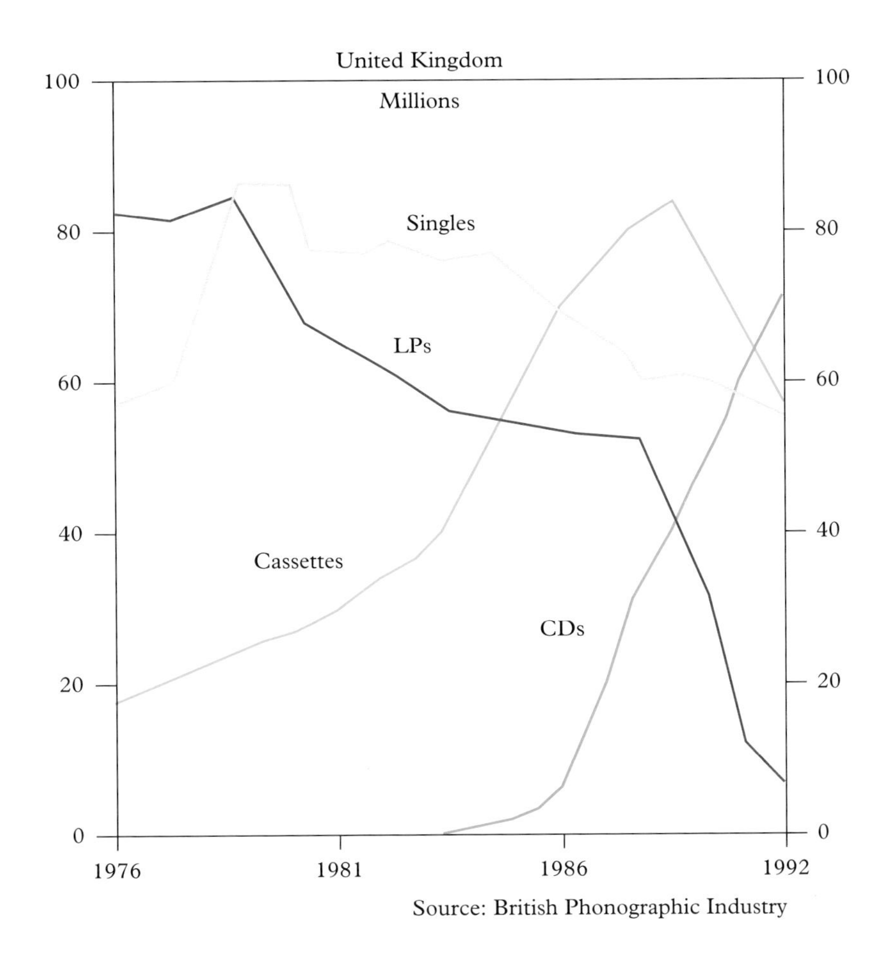

These frequency polygons show the sales of LPs, cassettes, CDs and singles since 1976.

Frequency polygon — **Frequency polygons** are often used to compare two sets of data.

Trend — The points are joined together to show the **trend**.
The trend shows how the data is changing.
You do not read information from the lines in between the points.

Exercise 13:7

1 Look at this table.
It shows the total number of goals scored in 40 football matches played one Saturday.

Number of goals	0	1	2	3	4	5	6
Number of matches	5	9	12	5	7	1	1

a Look at the figures in red.
How many matches had 2 goals in them?

b Look at the figures in green.
How many matches had 6 goals in them?

c Write down all the possible final scores that have 6 goals in them.
Start with 6–0, 5–1, 4–2, …

Here is a frequency polygon showing this information.

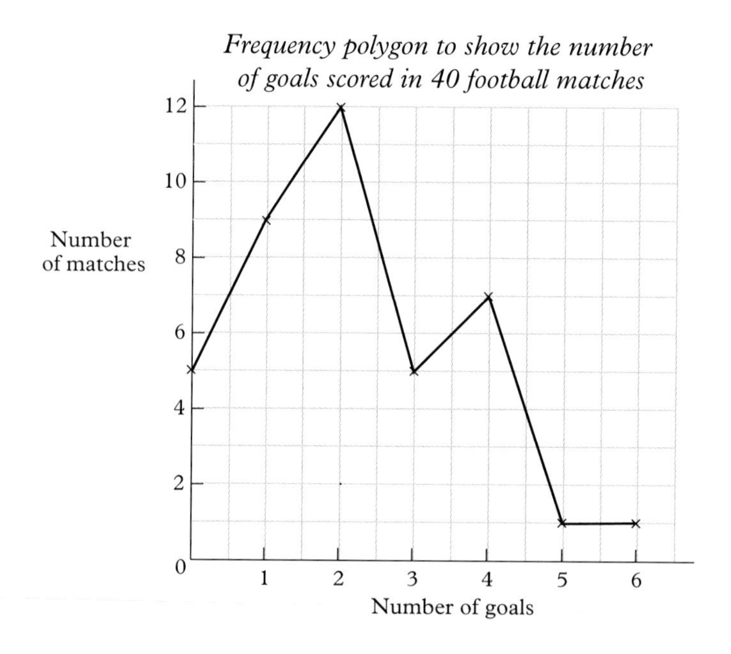

d How many matches had 5 goals in them?
Is this the same as in the table?

e How many matches had 2 goals in them?

2 Look at this frequency polygon.
It shows the number of pupils in each year at a boys' secondary school.

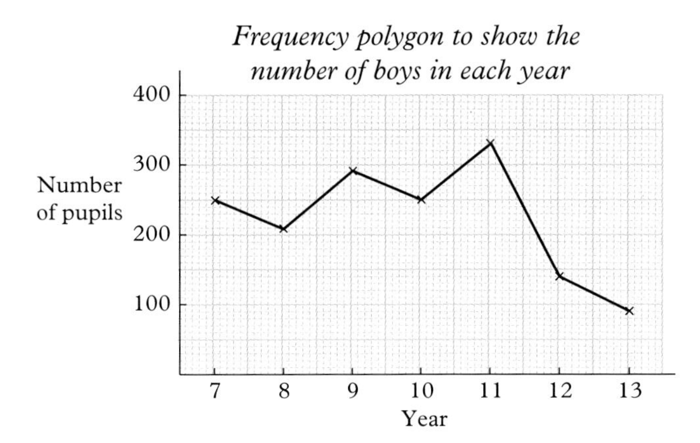

Copy this table.

Year	7	8	9	10	11	12	13
Number of pupils							

Fill in the table. Get the information from the frequency polygon.

3 This frequency polygon shows the number of pupils at the nearby girls' school.

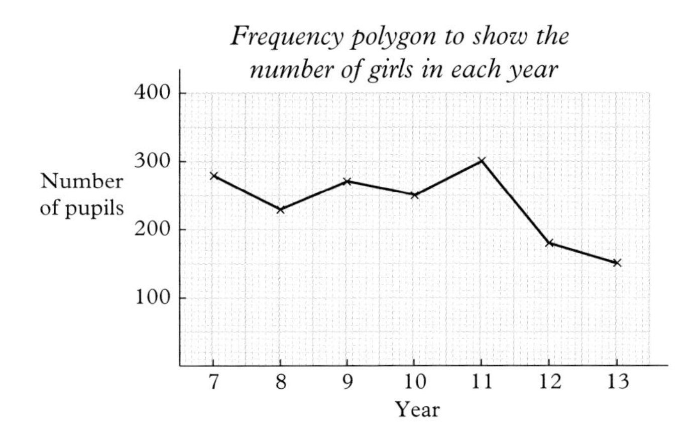

Copy the table from question **2** again.
Fill it in. Get the information from the frequency polygon.

The frequency polygons from question **2** and question **3** can be drawn on the same diagram.
This makes them easier to compare.

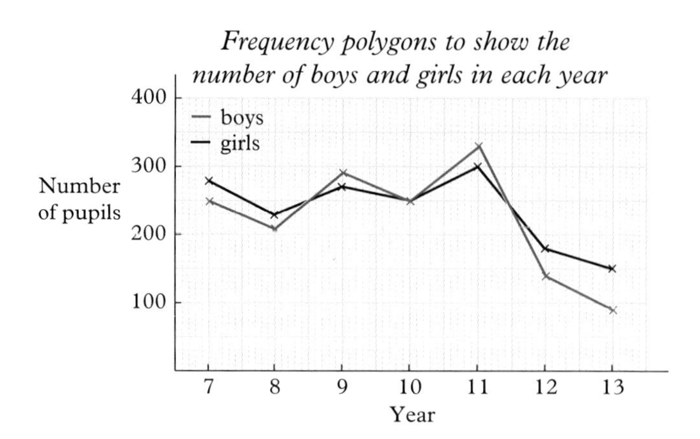

4. Look at the diagram with both frequency polygons on it.
   a Which school has the most Year 7 pupils?
   b Which school has more pupils in Year 9?
   c In which year do both schools have the same number of pupils?
   d How many more boys are there in Year 9 than girls?
   e How many more girls are there in Year 8 than boys?

5. Look at these frequency polygons.
   They show the number of pupils at two schools.

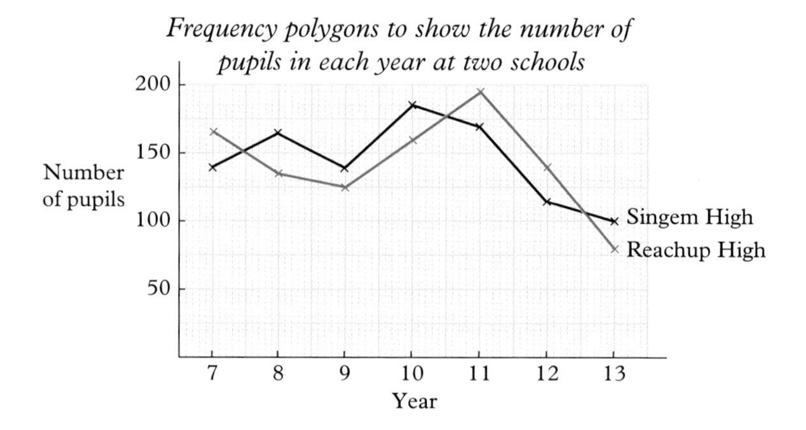

   a Which school has the most Year 7 pupils?
   b Which school has the most Year 9 pupils?
   How many more Year 9 pupils has it got?
   c Make a list of the number of pupils in each year at Singem High.
   How many pupils does it have altogether?
   d How many pupils are there at Reachup High?

6 Here is a frequency polygon showing lengths of words in a book.

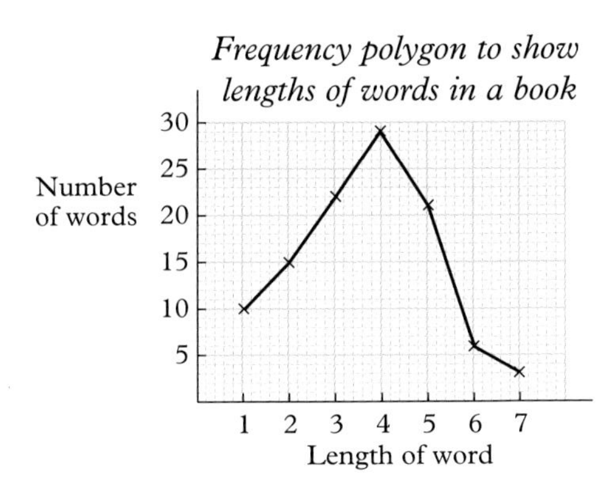

a Copy this table.

Length of word	1	2	3	4	5	6	7
Number of words							

b Fill in the table from the frequency polygon.
c Which length of word is the most common?
d Which length of word is the least common?

7 Here is a copy of the frequency polygon from question **6**.
This time there is another frequency polygon shown in red.

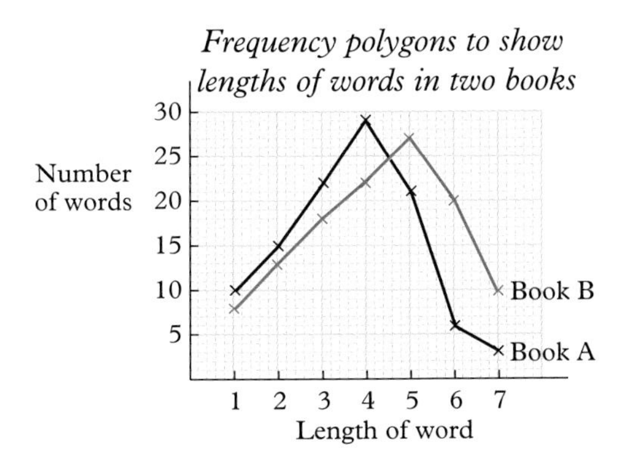

a Copy the table from question **6** again.
Fill it in.
b Which book has more 3-letter words, Book A or Book B?
c Which book has more 6-letter words?
d Which book do you think is easier to read?
Explain your answer.

8 8P have been comparing two reading books. The books are for pupils in junior school.
8P have counted the numbers of letters in the first 50 words of each book.
Here are two tables showing their results.

Number of letters in a word	1	2	3	4	5	6	7
Number of words in *Read for fun*	3	5	14	17	6	4	1

Number of letters in a word	1	2	3	4	5	6	7
Number of words in *Reading made easy*	4	5	9	13	10	7	2

a Copy the axes on to squared paper.

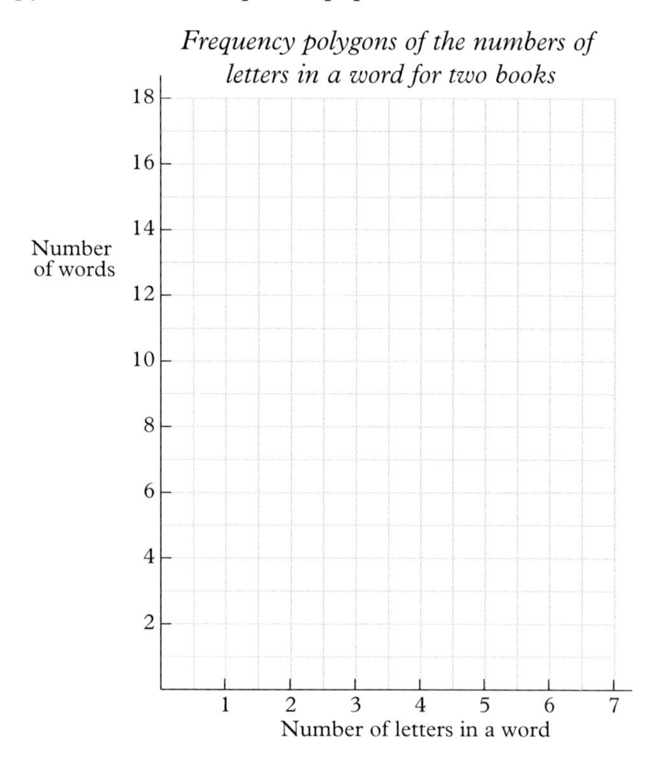

b Plot the points for *Read for fun.*
Join them with straight lines.

c On the same diagram, plot the points for *Reading made easy.*
Join the points with straight lines. Use a different colour.

d Which book do you think is easier to read?
Explain your answer.

1 The owner of a launderette kept a record of the number of people using the machines every day for a month.
Here are his results:

31	37	9	49	21	47	25	39	35	32
45	30	16	26	41	33	50	22	40	14
34	43	21	28	42	17	31	36	53	41

a Copy this tally-table.
Fill it in.

Number of people	Tally	Total
1–10		
11–20		
21–30		
31–40		
41–50		
51–60		
	Total	

b Draw a bar-chart of the data.
c Make a new tally-table with the data in three groups: 1–20, 21–40, 41–60.
d Draw a bar-chart from your new tally-table.
e Explain which bar-chart you think is better.

2 A gardener counted the number of peas in 50 pods for two varieties of pea.
The frequency polygons show her results.

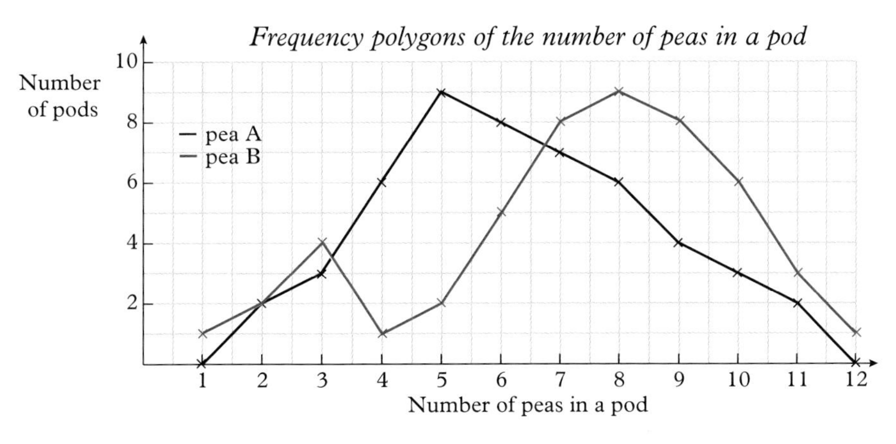

a Which pea had the most pods with four peas?
b Which pea had the most pods with ten peas?
c Write down the modal number of peas in a pod for pea A.
d Write down the modal number of peas in a pod for pea B.
e Use the graphs to decide which pea usually has more peas in its pods.

1 Elmtown Council is trying to get people to share cars when they go to work. This helps to reduce the traffic.
The council do regular surveys to see if more people are sharing.
Here is a set of their results for 50 cars.

Number of people in a car	Number of cars	Total number of people
1	15	1 × 15 =
2	18	2 × … =
3	11	… × … =
4	4	… × … =
5	2	… × … =
Total	**50**	

a Copy the table.
Use the table to work out the total number of people in the 50 cars.
b Work out the mean number of people in a car.
c Write down the mode.
d How many cars contain more than one person?
e Draw a bar-chart of the data.

2 Here is a table showing the numbers of pupils in two schools.

Number of pupils	Year 7	Year 8	Year 9	Year 10	Year 11
The Burton School	170	160	180	200	150
The Bravo School	150	160	140	120	150

a Copy the axes on to squared paper.

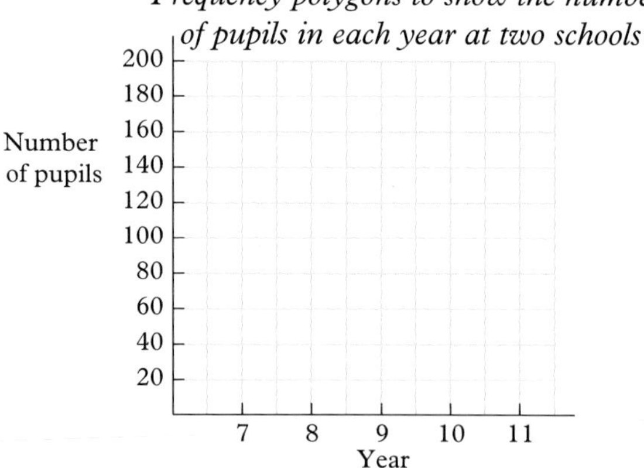

b Plot the points for The Burton School. Join them with straight lines.
c Plot the points for The Bravo School. Join them with straight lines.
Use a different colour.

- **Mean** To find the **mean** of a set of data:
  (1) Find the total of all the data values.
  (2) Divide by the number of data values.

  Mode The **mode** is the most common or the most popular data value.

  Median The **median** is the middle value when the data is in order from smallest to largest.

- **Range** The **range** is the biggest value take away the smallest value.

- **Grouping data** It is sensible to put data in groups before you make a tally-table.

  Example

Length of sentence (words)	Tally	Total
1–5		
6–10		
11–15		

Sentences with 1, 2, 3, 4 or 5 words go into the 1–5 group.
Sentences with 6, 7, 8, 9 or 10 words go into the 6–10 group and so on.
Then you can draw a bar-chart from the grouped data.

- **Frequency polygons** are often used to compare two sets of data.

  Trend
  The points are joined together to show the **trend**.
  The trend shows how the data is changing.
  You do not read information from the lines in between the points.

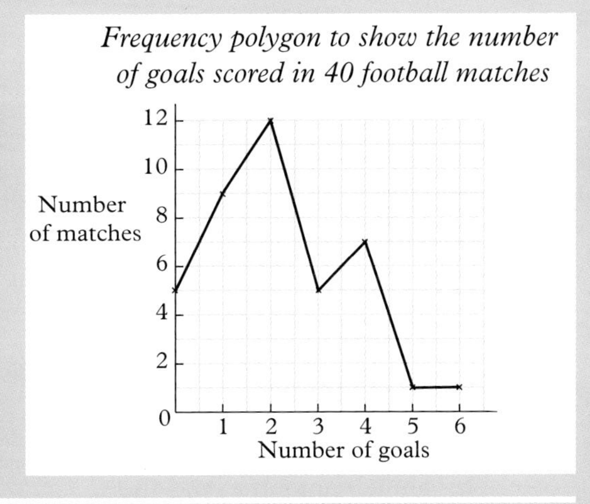

1 Look at these numbers:

7 6 9 0 3 4 7 6 4 7

a Work out the mean.
b Write down the mode.
c Find the median.
d Work out the range.

2 8J recorded the numbers of people in 50 cars passing the school.
Here are their results:
a Write down the mode.
b Copy the table.
Fill it in.
c Work out the mean number of people per car.

Number of people	Number of cars	Total number of people
1	23	$1 \times 23 =$
2	17	$2 \times 17 =$
3	7	$3 \times 7 =$
4	3	$4 \times 3 =$
Total		

3 Here are the results of 8M's Maths test:

86 78 45 65 71 49 63 80 91 37
67 64 87 75 69 81 79 68 48 26
37 62 90 71 61 78 65 19 85 44

a Copy this tally-table.
Fill it in.
b Write down the modal group.
c Draw a bar-chart from your tally-table.

Mark	Tally	Total
1–20		
21–40		
41–60		
61–80		
81–100		
	Total	

4 The frequency polygon shows the number of goals a team scored in some football matches.
a What was the modal number of goals scored?
b How many times did the team fail to score?
c How many times did the team score three goals?
d How many matches did the team play altogether?

Frequency polygon to show the number of goals scored in some football matches

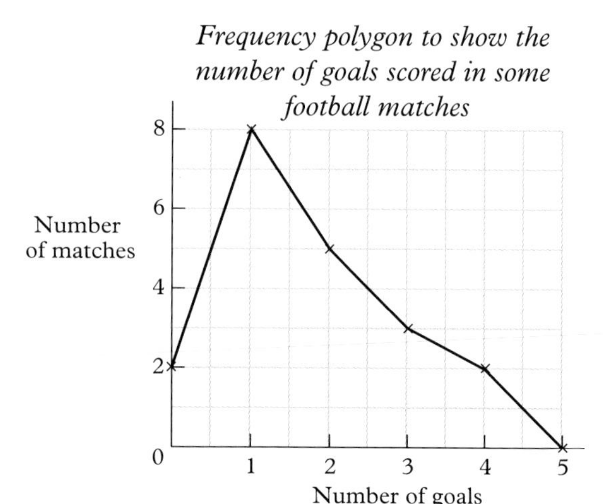

14 Volume: filling the space

CORE

QUESTIONS

EXTENSION

SUMMARY

TEST YOURSELF

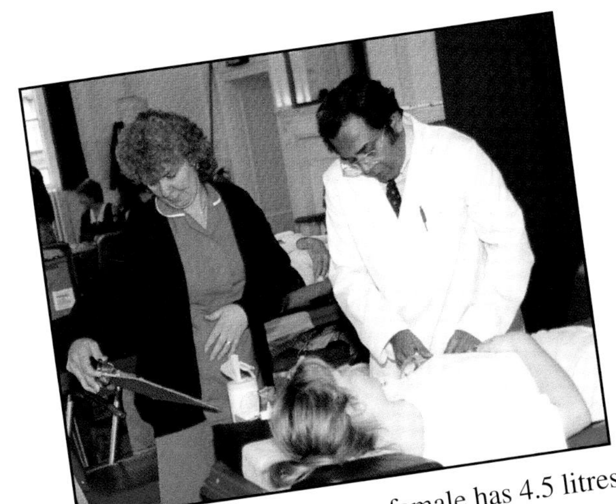

The average adult human female has 4.5 litres of blood in her body.

A male has slightly more.

If you give blood to the National Blood Service they take less than half a litre.

Altogether they collect 1.5 million litres each year.

This is the same as about 300 000 full bodies worth!

1 Pack it in!

The world record for the number of people in a phone box is 23.
This is a lot of people in a very small space!

Volume The amount of space that an object takes up is called its **volume**.

Exercise 14:1

1 Look at these objects.

(1)

(2)

(3)

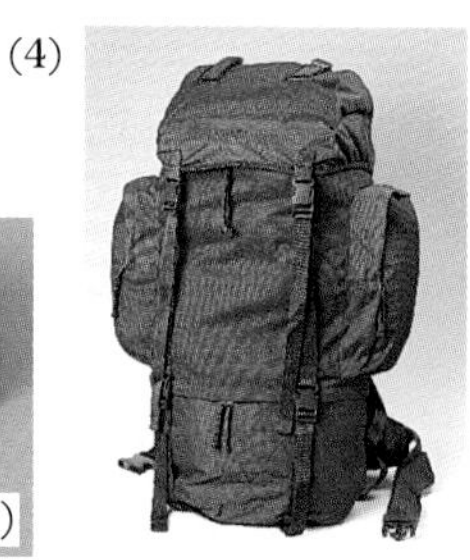
(4)

a Which has the biggest volume?
b Which has the smallest volume?
c List the objects in order of volume. Start with the *biggest.*

2 Look at these objects.

(1)

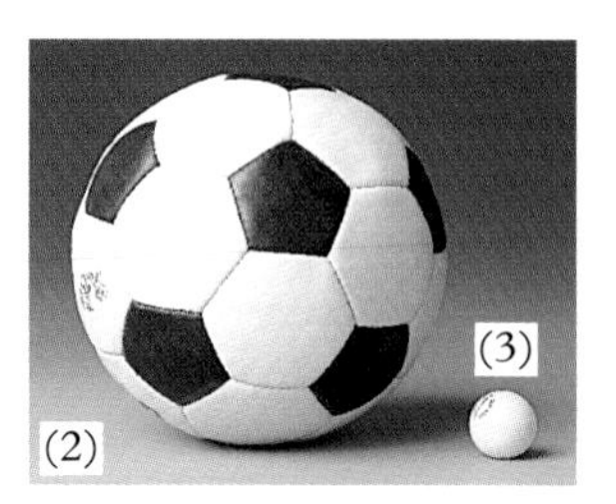
(2) (3)

(4)

List the objects in order of volume. Start with the *biggest.*

Capacity	The **capacity** of a hollow object is the volume of space inside it.

3 Look at these containers.

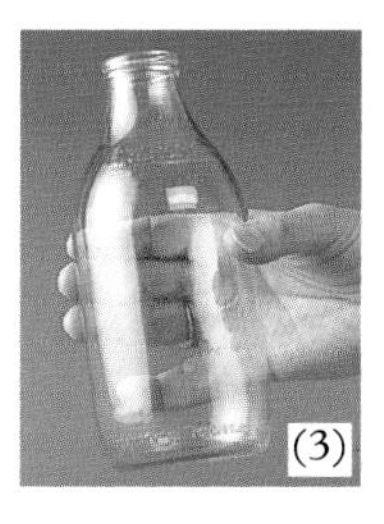

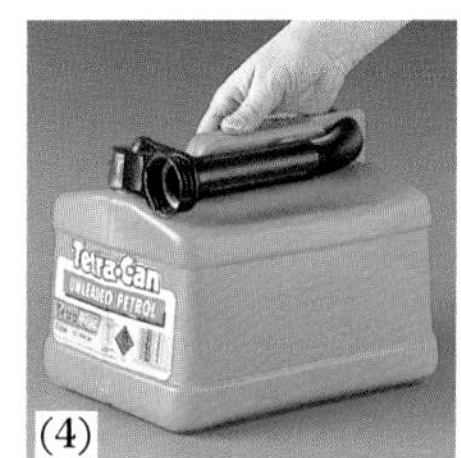

a Which has the biggest capacity?
b Which has the smallest capacity?
c List the objects in order of capacity. Start with the *biggest*.

Units of volume

Volume is measured in cubic units.
These can be mm^3, cm^3 or m^3

1 cm³	**1 cm³** is the space taken up by a cube with all its edges 1 cm long.

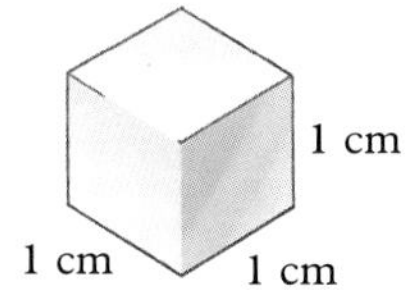

Units of capacity

1 m*l*	This cube is filled with water. The volume of water inside is **1 millilitre**. This is written **1 m*l*** **1 m*l*** is the same as **1 cm³**

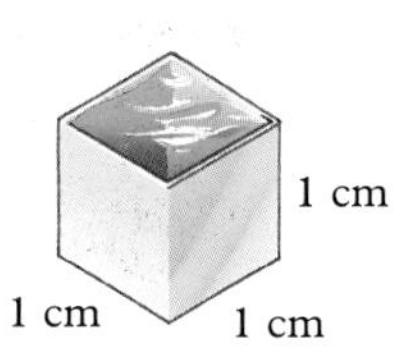

4 Look at these containers.

a List the containers in order of volume. Start with the *smallest*.

● **b** How much more space is there inside the can of Coke than in the sauce bottle?

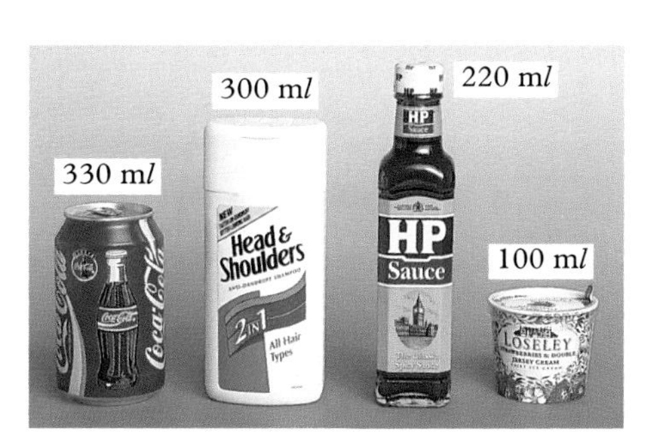

We measure large volumes in **litres**.
1 litre = 1000 m*l*

This lemonade bottle holds 2 litres.
This petrol can holds 5 litres.
A petrol tanker holds 34 000 litres.

Exercise 14:2

1 Estimate the volume of these containers.
Write your answers in litres.

a 

c 

e 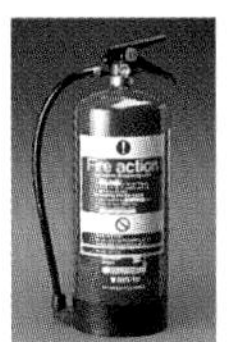

b 

d 

2 Estimate the volume of these containers.
Write your answers in millilitres.

f 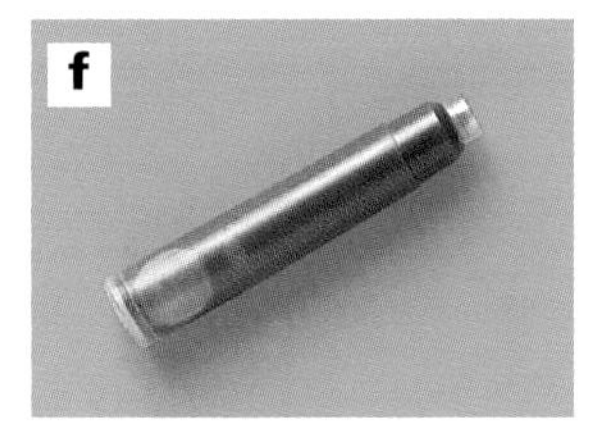

3 Estimate the volume of these containers.
You need to choose millilitres or litres.

a  

b 

c 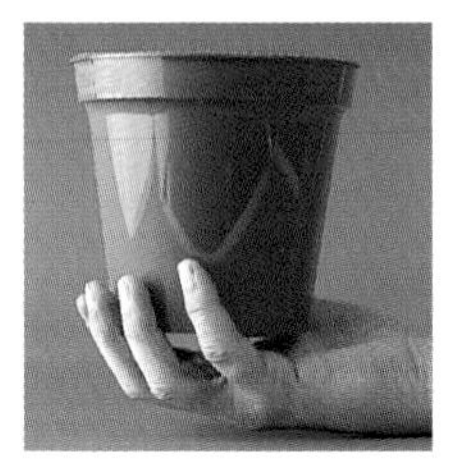

2 Stacking

Supermarkets stack their shelves so that you can see what they are selling.
They want to fit in as much as they can.
The shelf stackers need to work out how much they can fit in.

Example

Rachel is stacking cornflakes boxes.
First she sees how many boxes fit along the shelf.
5 boxes fit on this shelf.

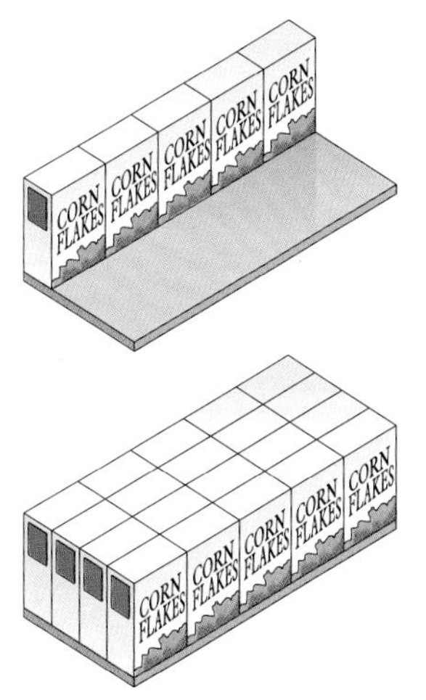

Then she sees how many rows of boxes she can fit in.
She can fit 4 rows on this shelf.

She multiplies the number of boxes in each row by the number of rows.
This tells her how many boxes will fit in.

$5 \times 4 = 20$ boxes
20 boxes will fit on the shelf.

Exercise 14:3

For each question:
a Write down the number of boxes in one row.
b Write down the number of rows that will fit on the shelf.
c Work out how many boxes will fit altogether.

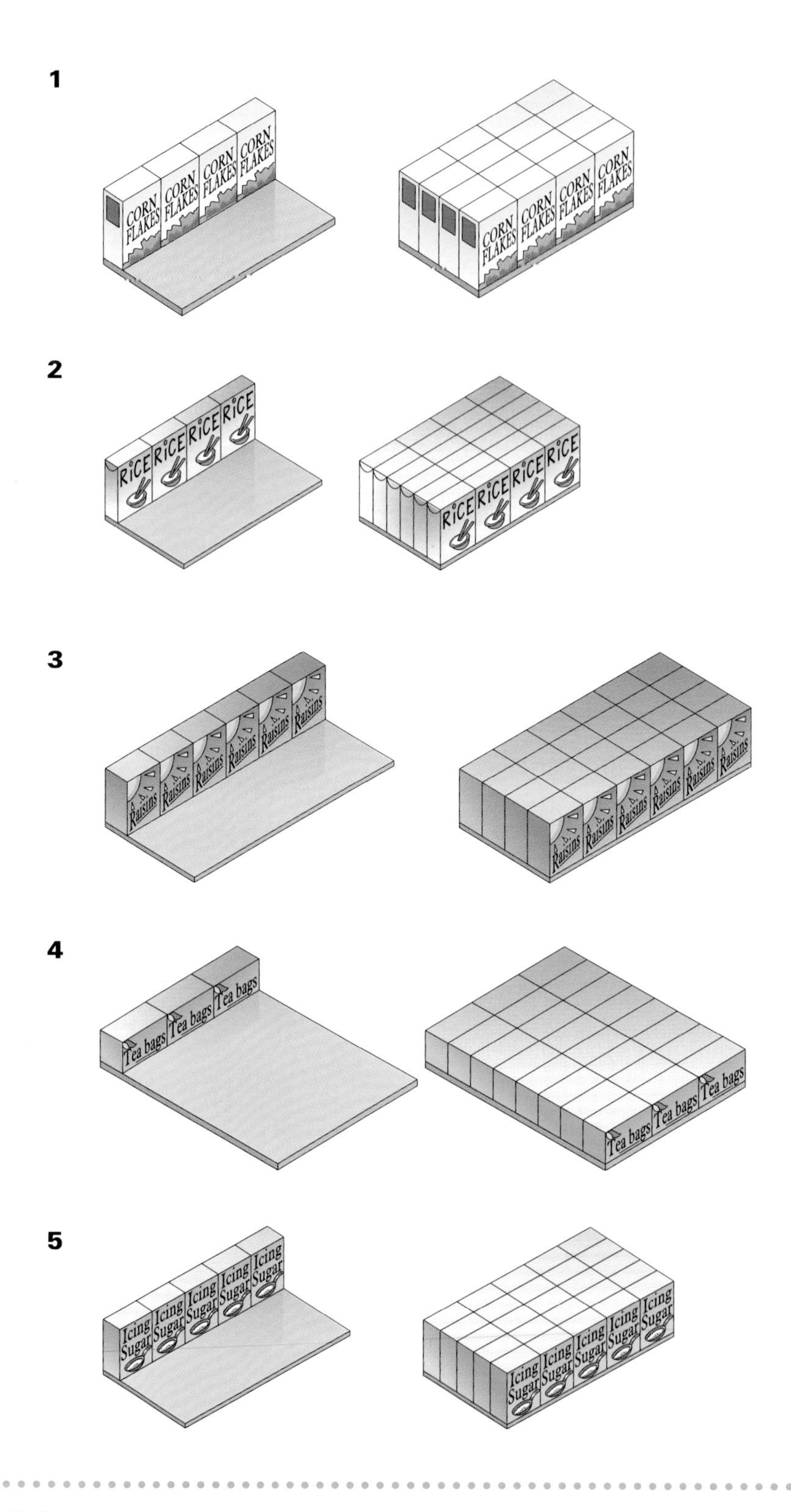
1
CORN FLAKES
CORN FLAKES
CORN FLAKES
CORN FLAKES
2
RiCE
RiCE
RiCE
RiCE
3
Raisins
Raisins
Raisins
Raisins
Raisins
Raisins
4
Tea bags
Tea bags
Tea bags
5
Icing Sugar
Icing Sugar
Icing Sugar
Icing Sugar
Icing Sugar

James is playing with his building bricks.
He likes to lay them out in rectangles.

Exercise 14:4

For each question work out:

a How many bricks James has in each row.
b How many rows of bricks James has.
c How many bricks James has altogether.

1

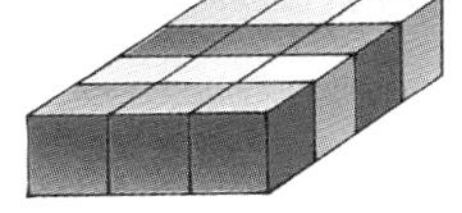

4

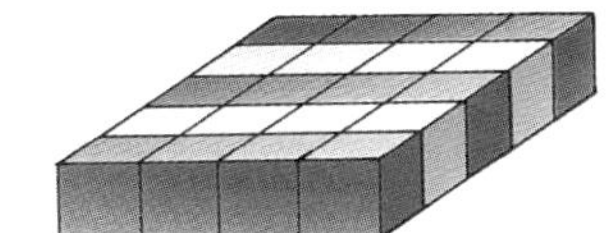

2

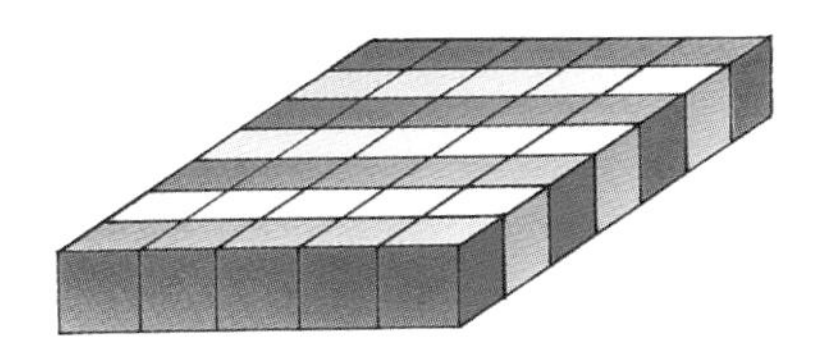

5

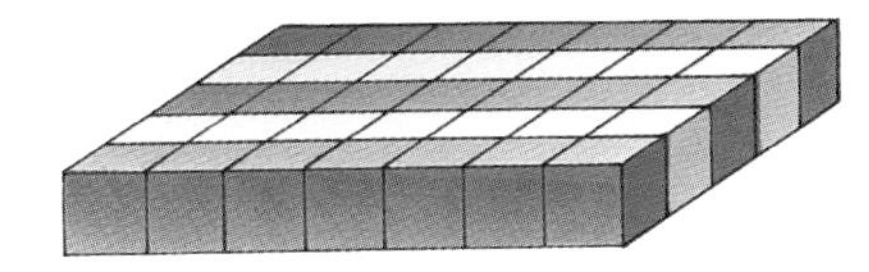

3

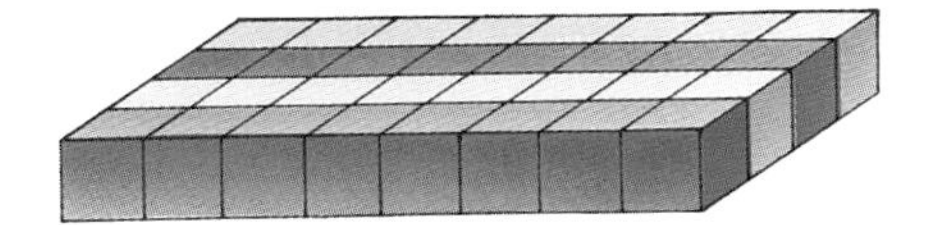

6

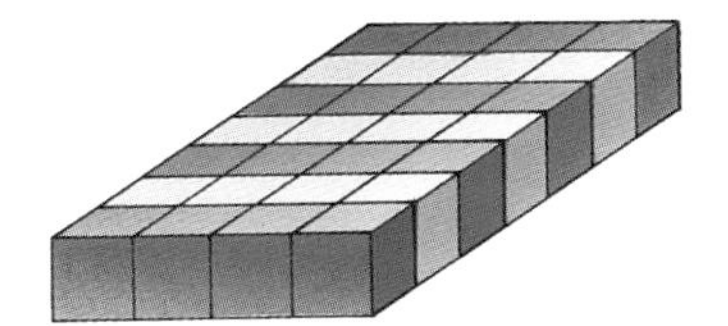

Exercise 14:5

Look at these pictures.
Work out how many boxes there are in each picture.

1

2

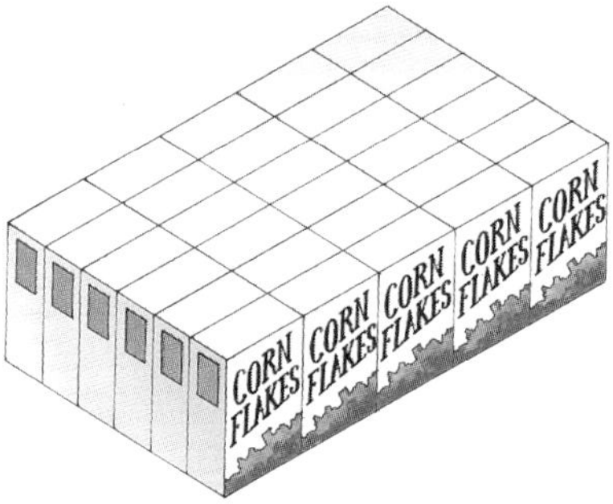

3

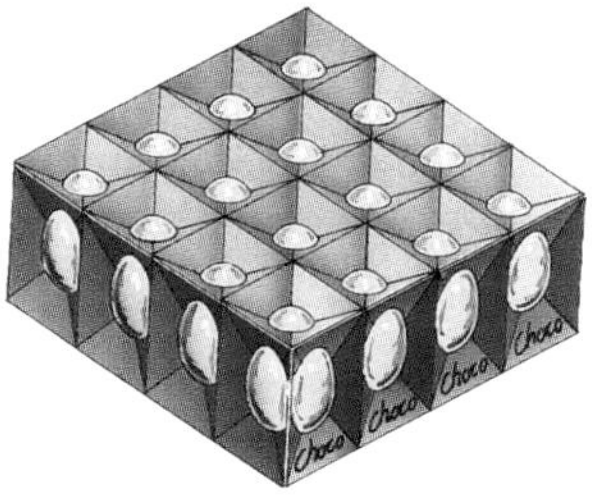

4

5

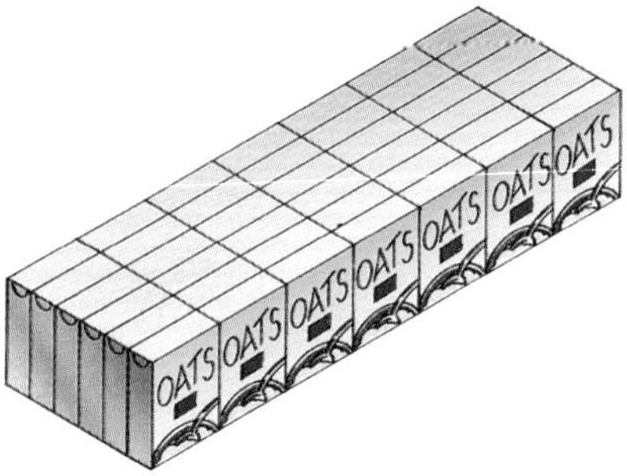

6

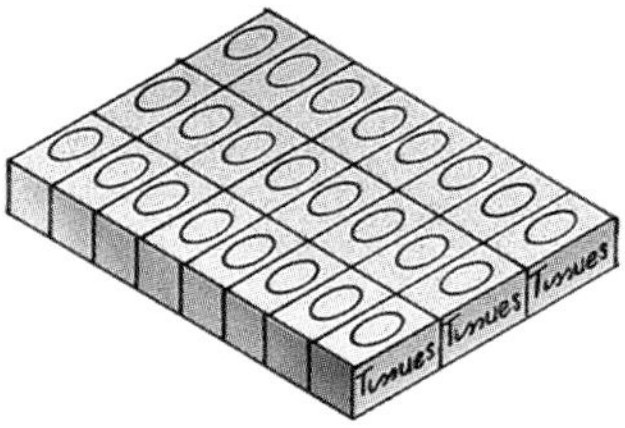

7

8

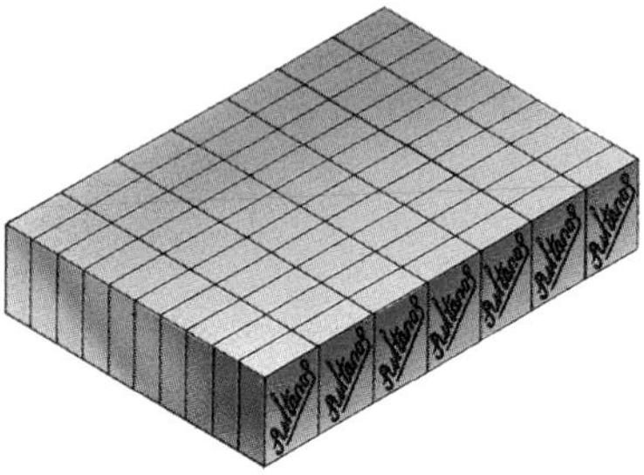

1 cm³

A cube that has sides of 1 cm is called a 1 cm cube.
We say that it has a volume of 1 cm cubed.
We write this as $\mathbf{1\ cm^3}$

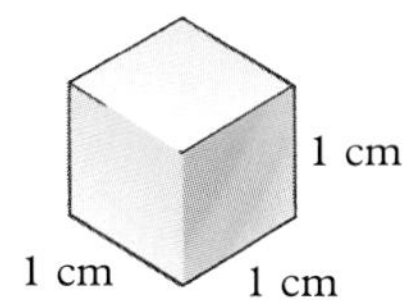

Example

This rectangle of 1 cm cubes has a volume of $12\ cm^3$

Work out the volume of these rectangles of 1 cm cubes.
Write your answers in cm^3

9

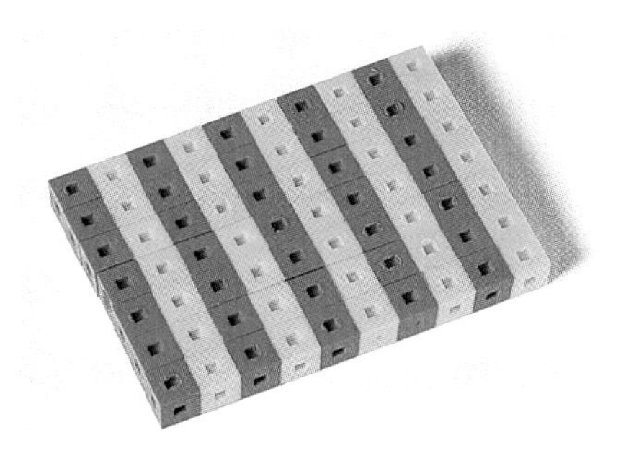

11

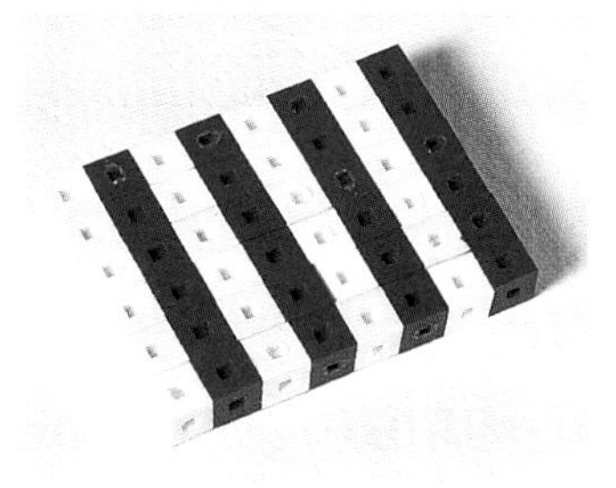

10

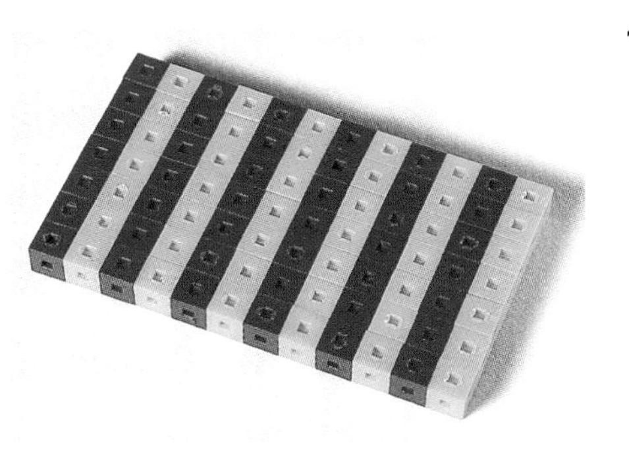

12

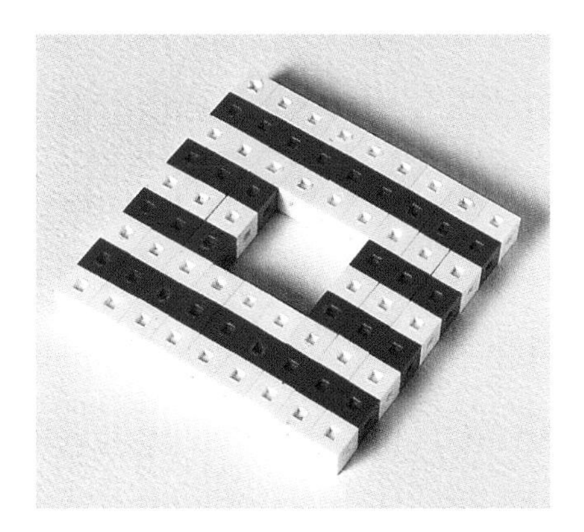

3 Stacking it higher

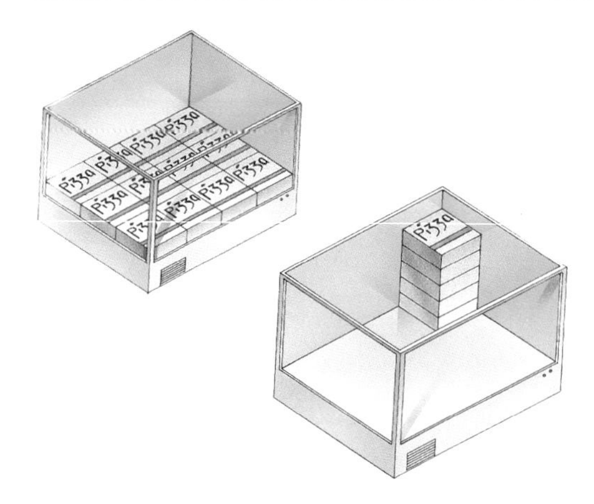

Rachel has to stack boxes of pizza in the freezer.
She works out how many will fit in one layer.

Then she works out how many layers she can fit in.
She multiplies the number in one layer by the number of layers.
This tells her the total number of pizzas she can fit in.

In this freezer she can fit 12 boxes in each layer and 5 layers.
She can fit $12 \times 5 = 60$ pizzas in altogether.

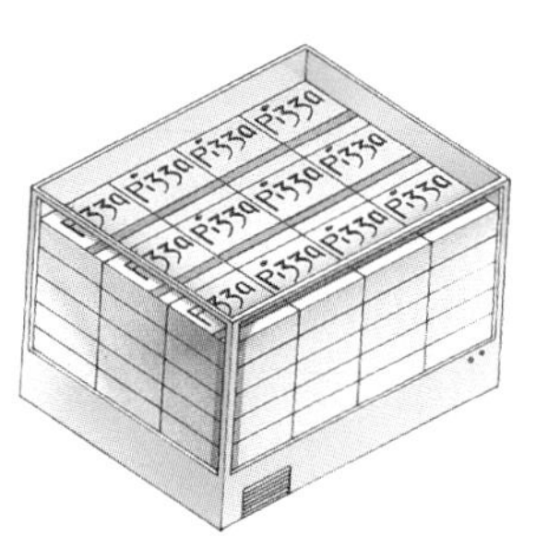

Exercise 14:6

For each question work out:

a The number of boxes in one layer.
b The number of layers.
c The total number of boxes in the stack.

1

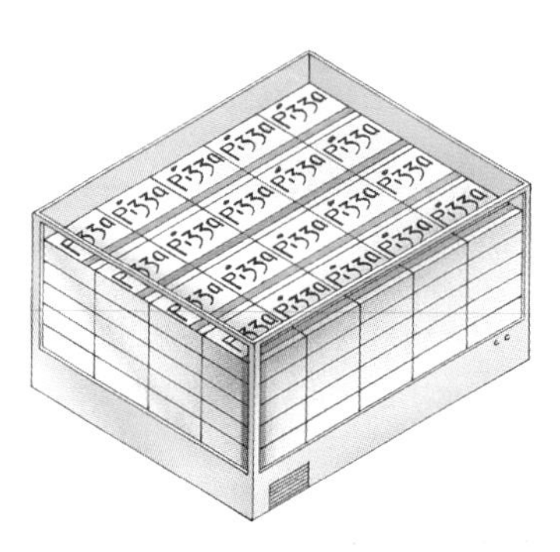

2

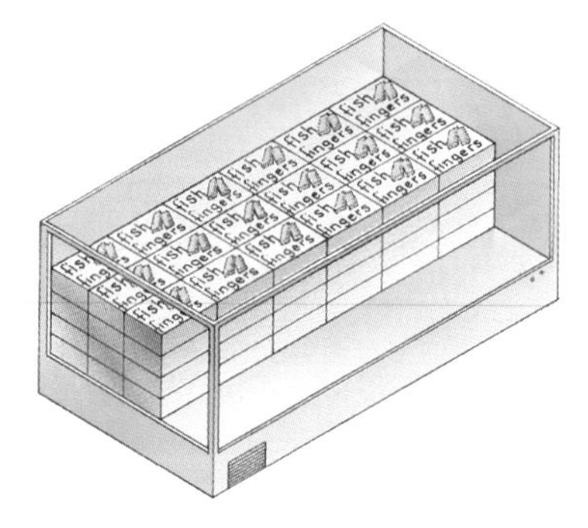

3

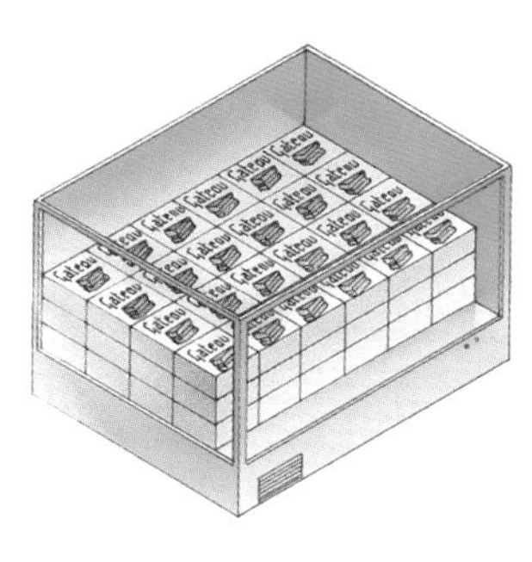

5

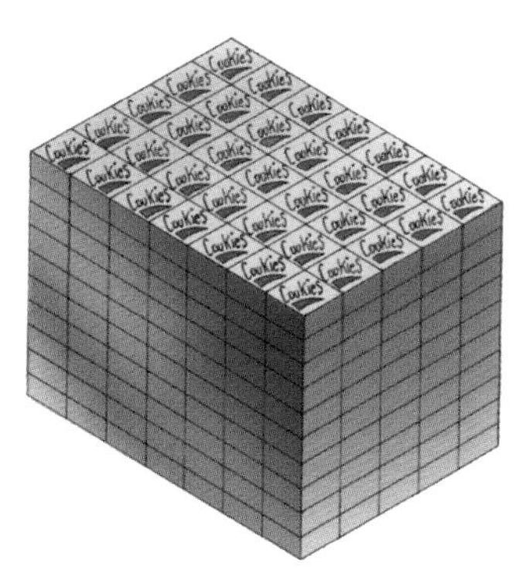

4

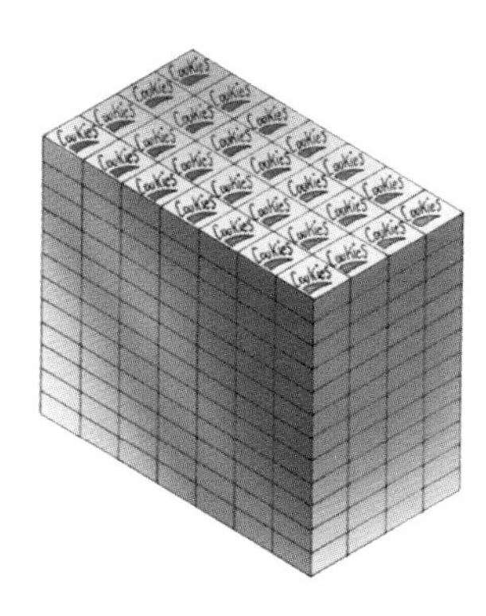

6

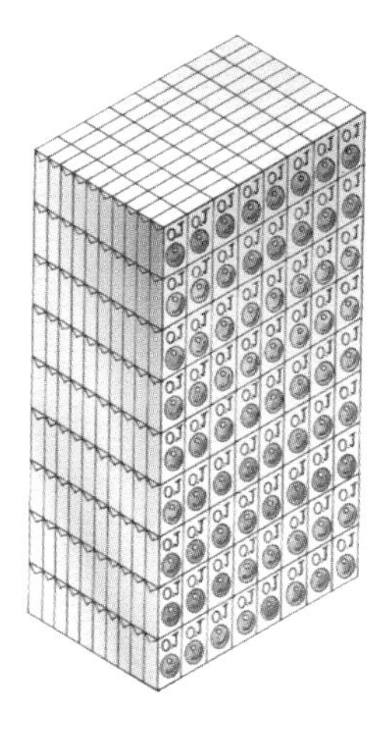

James has learned to build towers with wooden cubes.

Exercise 14:7

For each question work out:

a How many cubes James has in each layer.

b How many layers of cubes James has.

c How many cubes James has altogether.

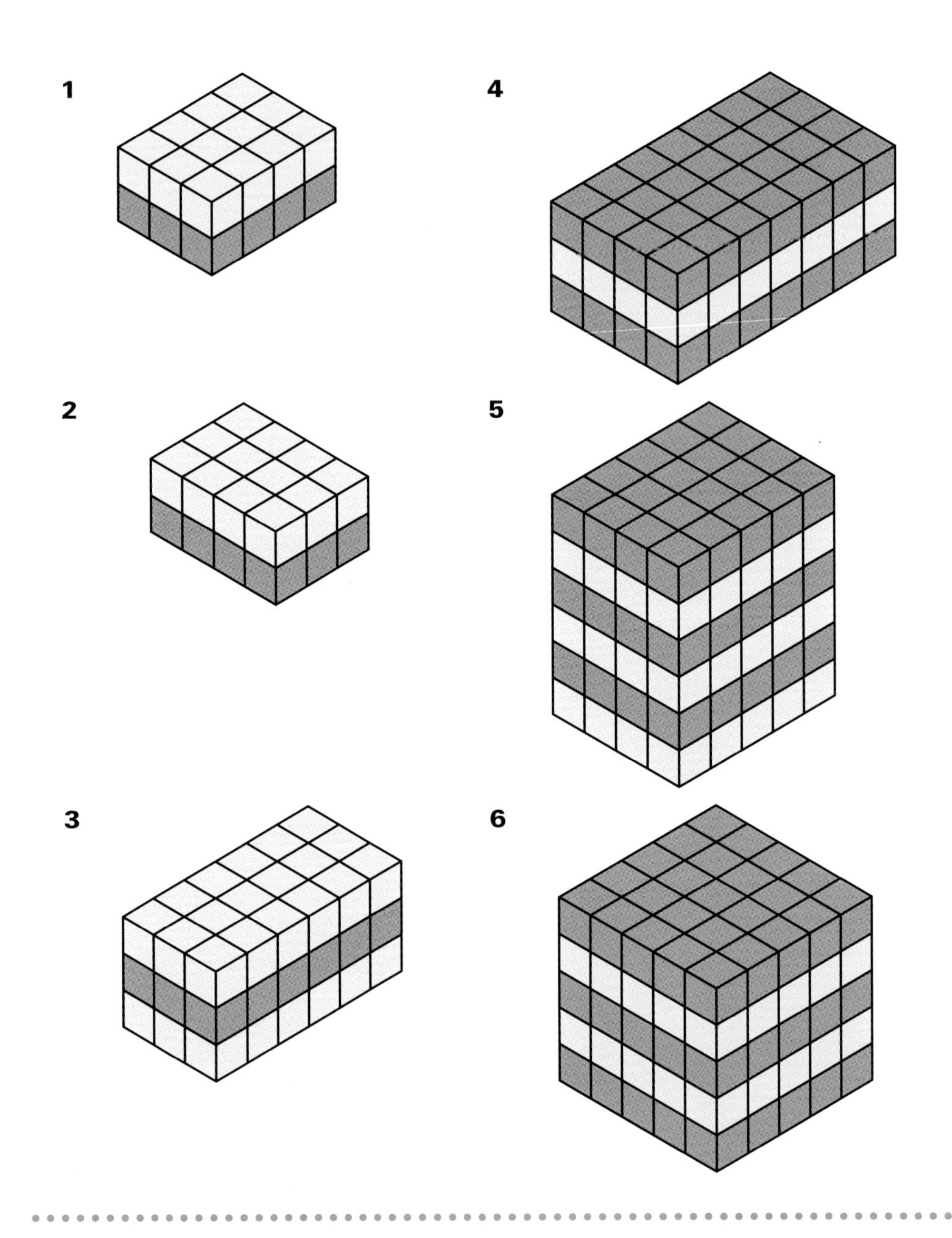

There is a faster way to find the volume of a block of 1 cm cubes.

(1) **Multiply the length by the width**.
This tells you how many cubes there are in one layer.

(2) **Multiply your answer by the height**.
This tells you how many cubes there are all together.

You can do this all at once: **Volume = length × width × height**

Example Work out the volume of this block of 1 cm cubes.

Volume = length × width × height
$= 6 \times 3 \times 4$
$= 72\ \text{cm}^3$

Exercise 14:8

Find the volume of these blocks of 1 cm cubes.
Write your answers in cm^3

1

2

3

4

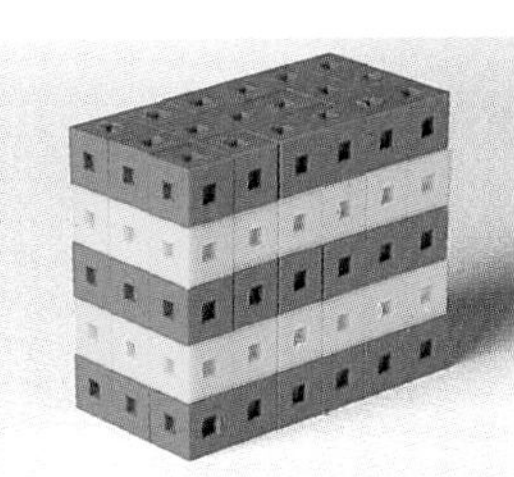

5

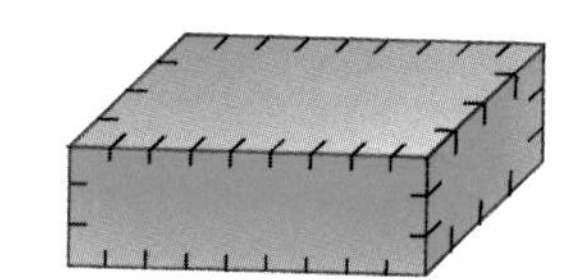

6

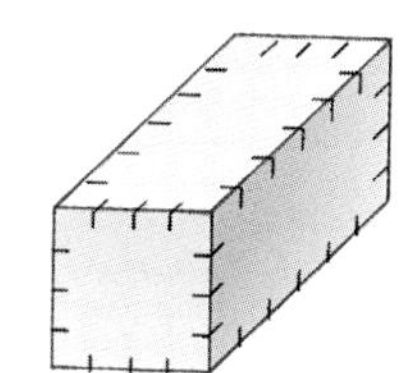

• **7**

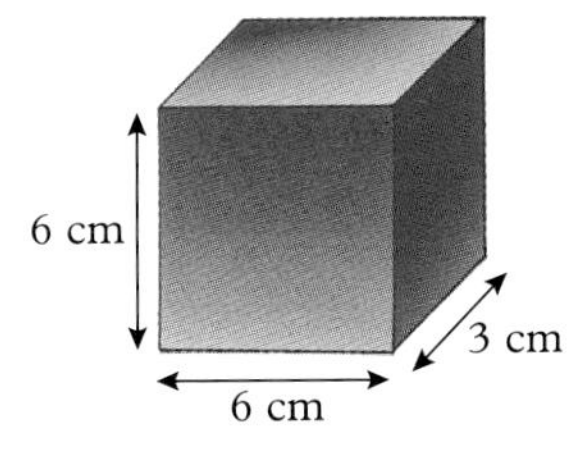

• **8**

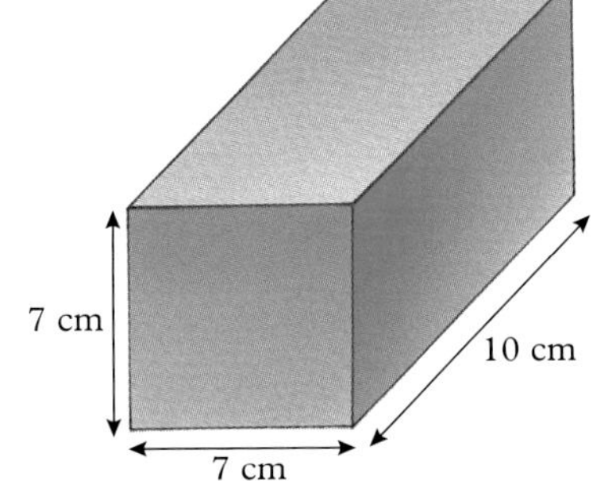

Exercise 14:9 Building a box

Get a piece of squared paper exactly 18 cm by 24 cm.

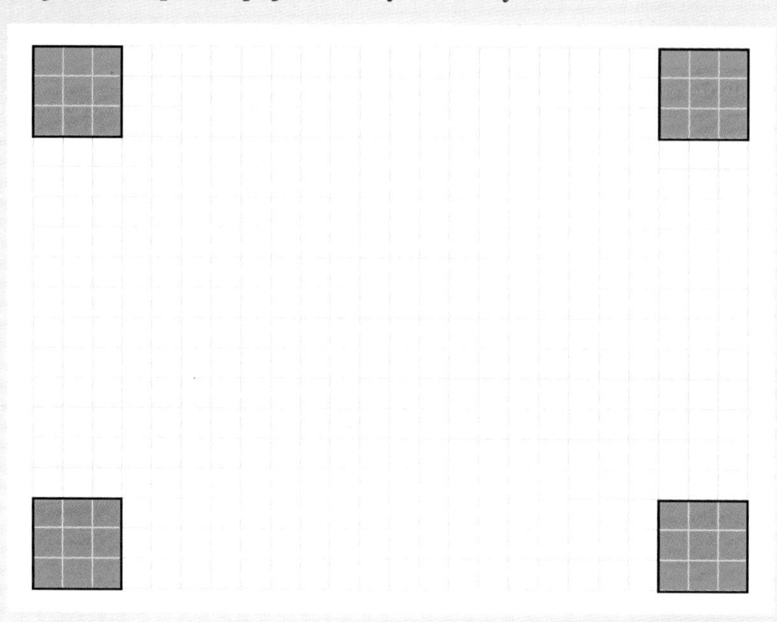

Cut squares out of each corner. This makes your paper into the net of a box.
Fold the paper to make the box.
Stick the corners with sticky tape.
The box will not have a lid.

Find the volume of the box.

Use more pieces of squared paper 18 cm by 24 cm to make more boxes. Try changing the size of the squares at the corners.

Find the volume of each box you make.
You will need to organise your results.

What is the biggest volume you can get?

Other things to try:

- The sides of the corner squares do not need to be a whole number of centimetres.
- You could make a box with a lid.
  How would this affect the volume?
- You could start with a piece of A4 paper.

Write a report on what you have found out.

1 Estimate the volume of these containers.
You need to choose millilitres or litres.

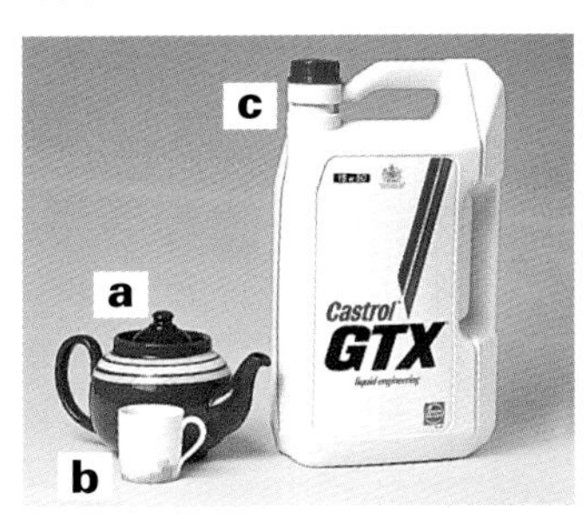

2 Work out the volume of these rectangles of 1 cm cubes.
Write your answers in cm^3

a

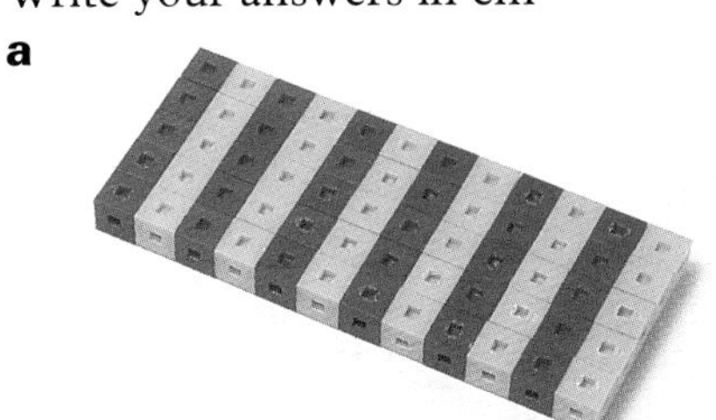

b

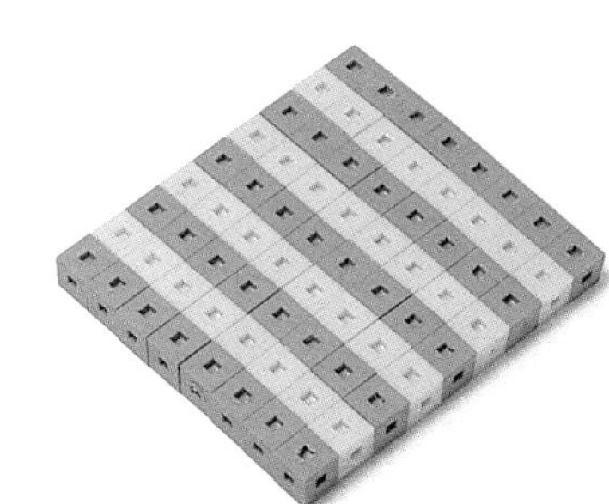

3 For each picture work out:
(1) The number of boxes in one layer.
(2) The number of boxes in the stack.
(3) The total number of boxes that would fill the fridge level with the stack.

a

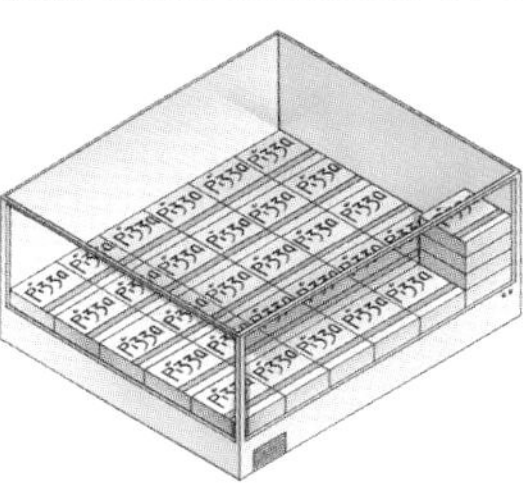

b

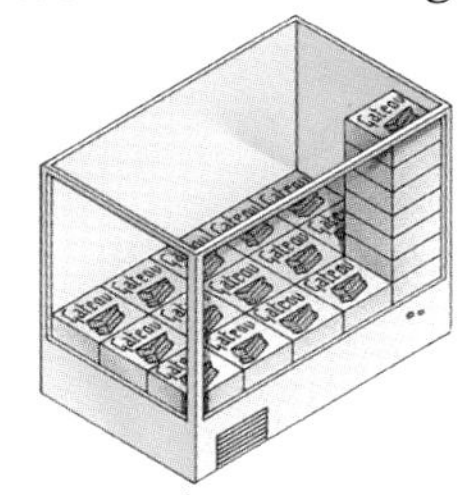

4 Find the volume of these blocks of 1 cm cubes.
Write your answers in cm^3

a

b

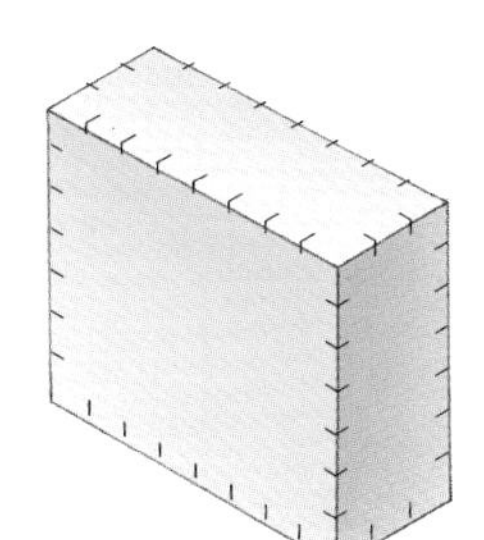

1 For each question:
(1) Write down the number of bricks in each layer.
(2) Write down the number of layers.
(3) Work out the total number of bricks.

a

b

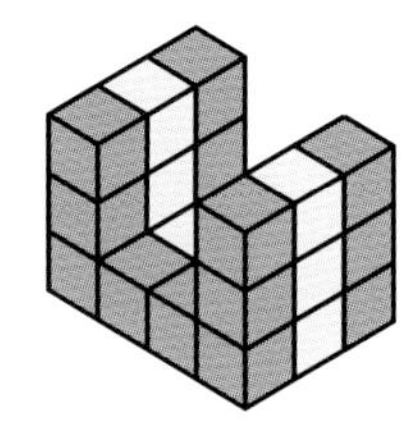

c

d

2 Work out the volume of these shapes.
(1) Split them up into blocks if you need to.
(2) Work out the volume of each block.
(3) Add up the volumes of the blocks to give the total volume.

a

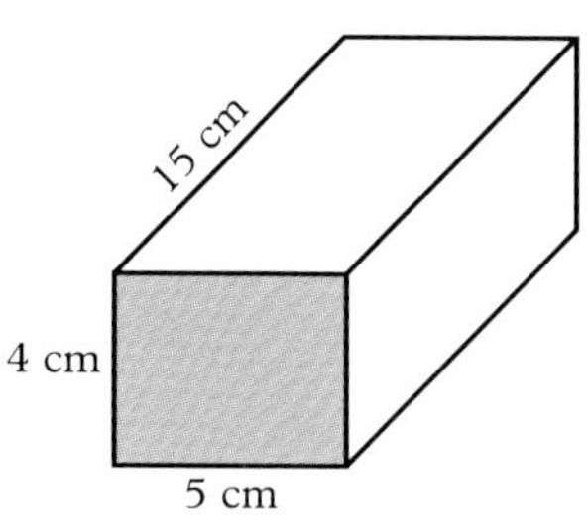

b

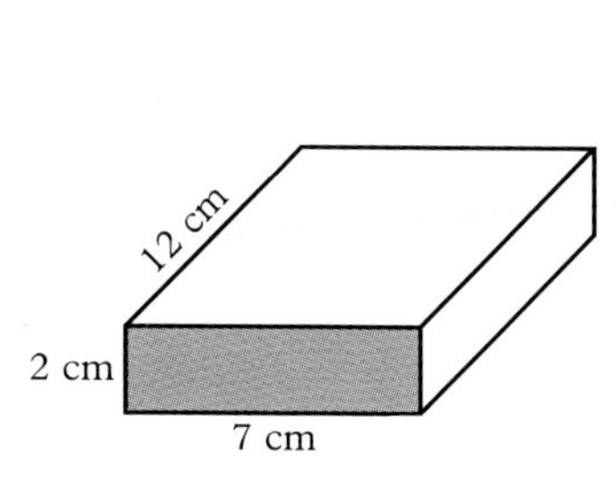

c

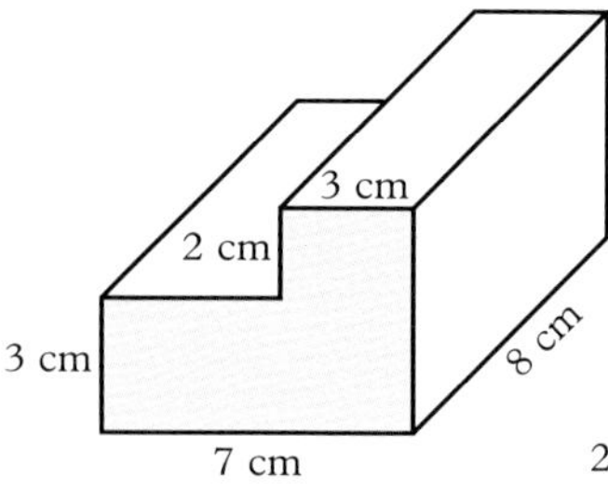

d

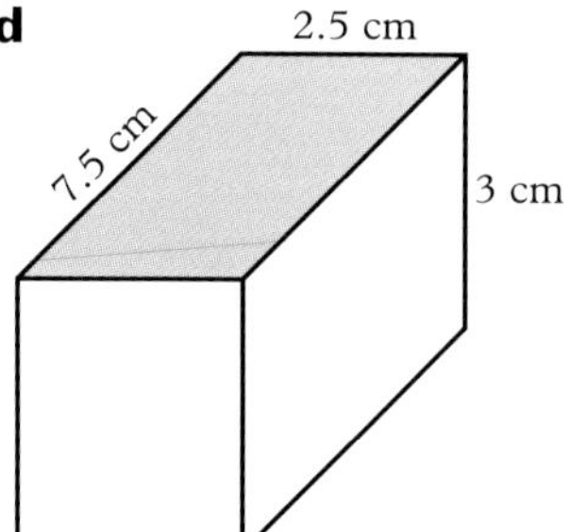

e

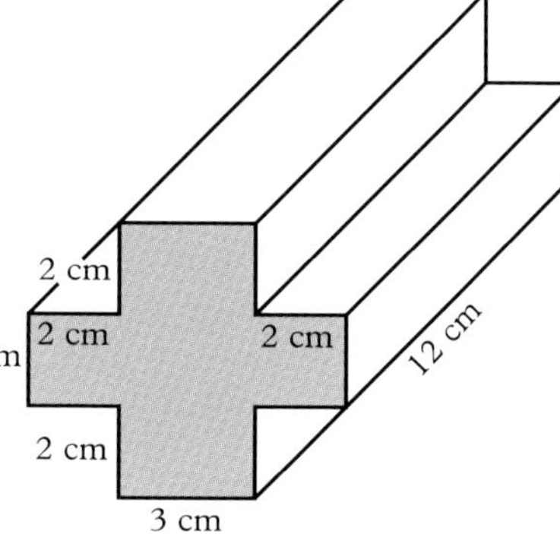

f

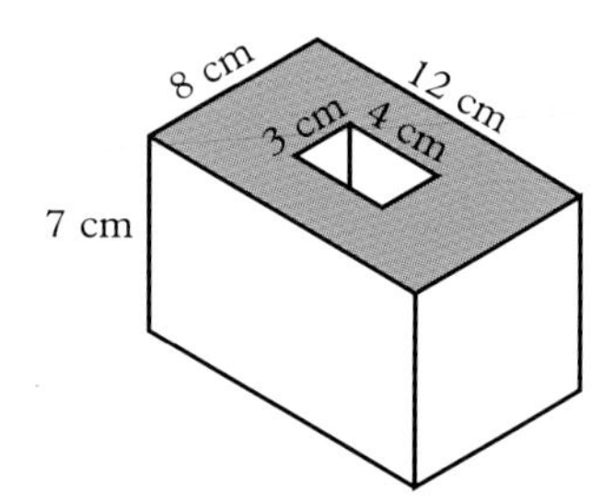

- **Volume** — The amount of space that an object takes up is called its **volume**.

- **Capacity** — The **capacity** of a hollow object is the volume of space inside it.

- **Units of volume** — Volume is measured in cubic units. These can be mm^3, cm^3 or m^3

  1 cm³ — **1 cm³** is the space taken up by a cube with all its edges 1 cm long.

  Units of capacity — This cube is filled with water. The volume of water inside is **1 millilitre**. This is written **1 m*l***

  1 m*l* — **1 m*l* is the same as 1 cm³**

  We measure large volumes in litres.
  1 litre = 1000 m*l*

- There is a quick way to find the volume of a block of 1 cm cubes.

  Volume = length × width × height

  Example — Work out the volume of this block of 1 cm cubes.

$$\text{Volume} = \text{length} \times \text{width} \times \text{height}$$
$$= 6 \times 3 \times 4$$
$$= 72\ \text{cm}^3$$

1 Look at these objects.

a Which has the biggest volume?

b Which has the smallest volume?

c List the objects in order of volume. Start with the *biggest*.

2 Estimate the volume of these containers.
You need to choose millilitres or litres.

3 Find the volume of these blocks of 1 cm cubes.
Write your answers in cm^3

a

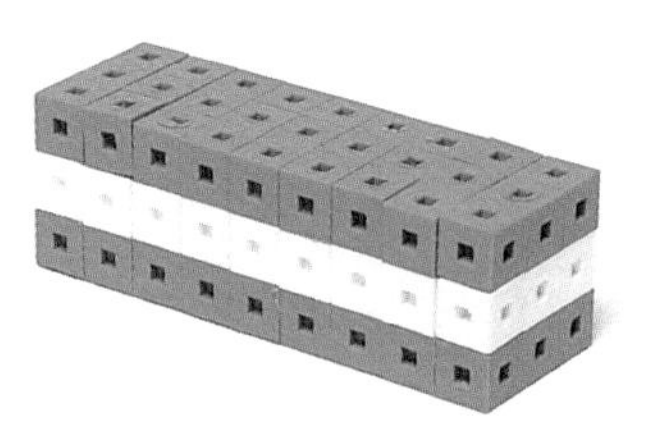

c

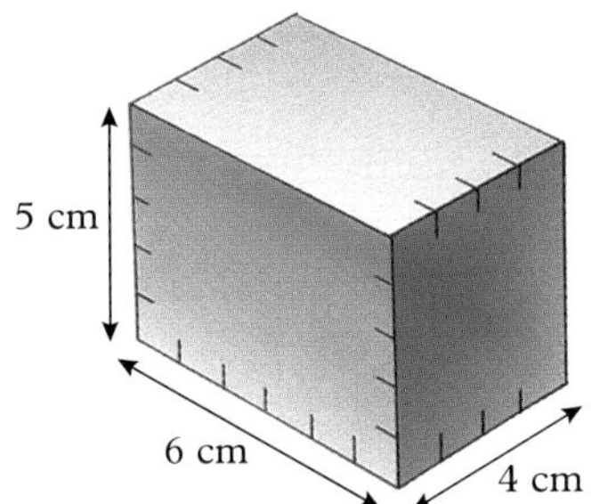

b

d

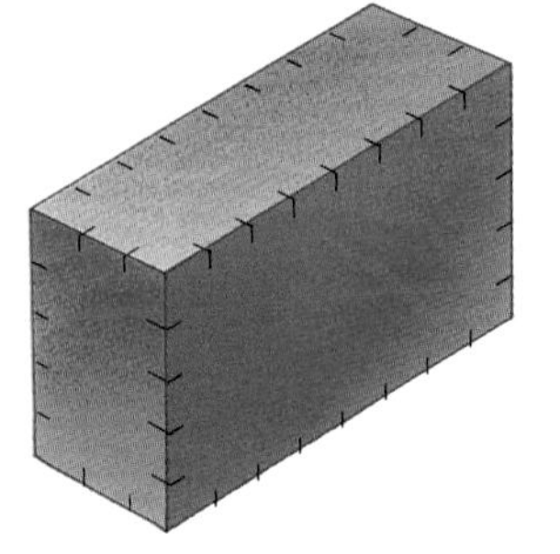

15 More or less?

CORE

1 **Trial and improvement**

2 **Simple equations**

3 **Order in number**

QUESTIONS

EXTENSION

SUMMARY

TEST YOURSELF

A supertanker holds 300 000 tonnes of crude oil.
This makes about 267 million litres of petrol.

A Mini covers about 13 km on 1 litre of petrol.
The distance of the Sun from the Earth is about 150 million km.

So Bill could drive his car to the Sun and back more than 11 times!

1 Trial and improvement

◀◀ REPLAY ▶

Josie is practising her passing and shooting in hockey.
She sets up a target and tries to hit it.
If her ball goes to the right of the target she aims to the left next time.
If the ball goes to the left of the target she aims to the right next time.
She is getting closer to the target.

This happens in Maths.
You can solve equations by guessing different values. You then try to get closer to the right answer.

This method is called **trial and improvement**.

Example

To solve $3x + 3 = 45$ by trial and improvement:
(1) try different values of x
(2) write your results in a table like this.

Value of x	Value of $3x + 3$	
10	$3 \times 10 + 3 = 33$	too small
15	$3 \times 15 + 3 = 48$	too big
14	$3 \times 14 + 3 = 45$	correct

Answer: $x = 14$

Exercise 15:1

Solve these equations by trial and improvement.
For each question:
copy the table
fill it in
add more rows until you find the answer.

1 $x + 27 = 43$

Value of x	Value of $x + 27$	
10	$10 + 27 = 37$	too small
20		

2 $x - 33 = 68$

Value of x	Value of $x - 33$	
90		

3 $3x = 144$

Value of x	Value of $3x$	
40		

4 $3x + 6 = 78$

Value of x	Value of $3x + 6$	
10		
20		

5 $5x - 4 = 36$

Value of x	Value of $5x - 4$	
5		
10		

Example Solve $12x - 35 = 163$

Value of x	Value of $12x - 35$	
10	85	too small
20	205	too big
16	157	too small
17	169	too big
16.5	163	correct

Answer: $x = 16.5$

Exercise 15:2

Solve these equations by trial and improvement.

1 $4x - 23 = 27$

Value of x	Value of $4x - 23$	
10	17	too small
15		too big
12		

2 $6x - 21 = 90$

Value of x	Value of $6x - 21$	
10		
20		

3 $8x + 25 = 221$

Value of x	Value of $8x + 25$	
20		
30		

4 $16c + 36 = 492$

Value of c	Value of $16c + 36$	

2 Simple equations

You have already learned about inverses.

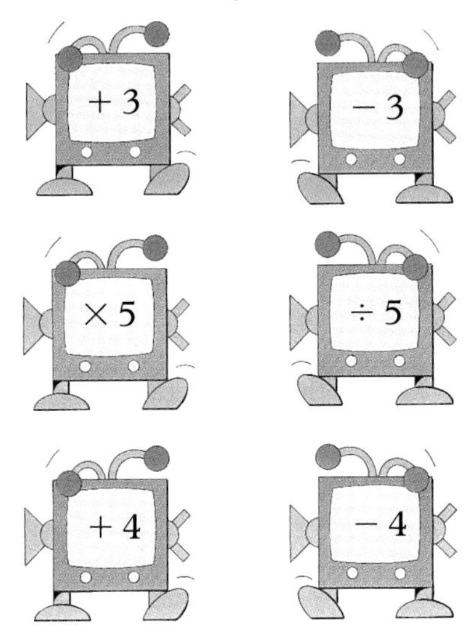

We can solve equations using inverses.
In the picture each robot is paired with its inverse.

Inverse An **inverse** returns you to where you started.

Example Write down the inverse of: **a** $+5$ **b** $\times 7$

a The inverse of $+5$ is -5
b The inverse of $\times 7$ is $\div 7$

Exercise 15:3

Write down the inverse of:

1 $+3$

2 -8

3 $\times 2$

4 $\div 6$

5 $+10$

6 $\div 4$

7 $+5$

8 $\times 9$

9 -7

The inverse of this function machine:

is this function machine:

We only draw the screens. The inverse of 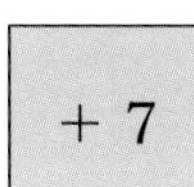

is − 7

Exercise 15:4

Draw the inverses of these function machines.

1 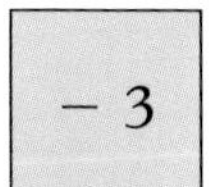

2 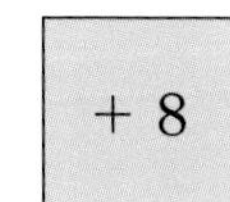

3 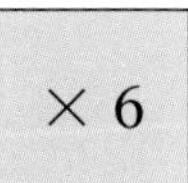

4 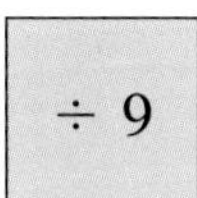

5 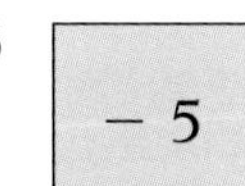

6 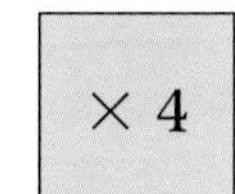

7 ÷ 7

8 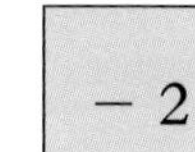

A function machine can have 2 steps.

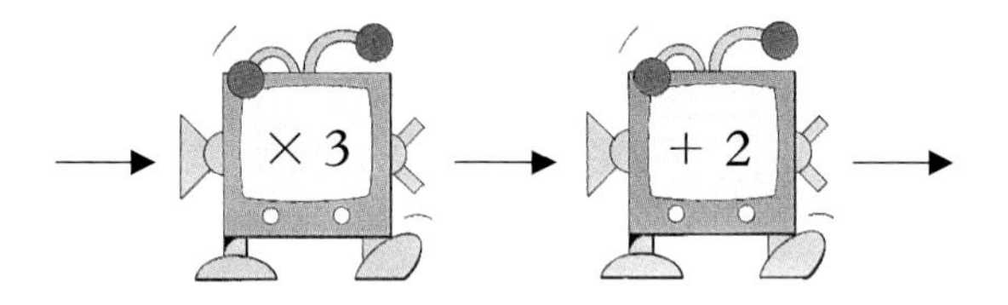

The inverse function machine is:

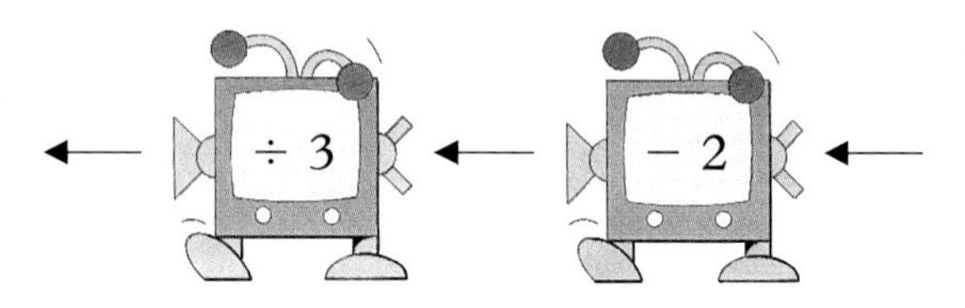

Draw the inverse function machines.

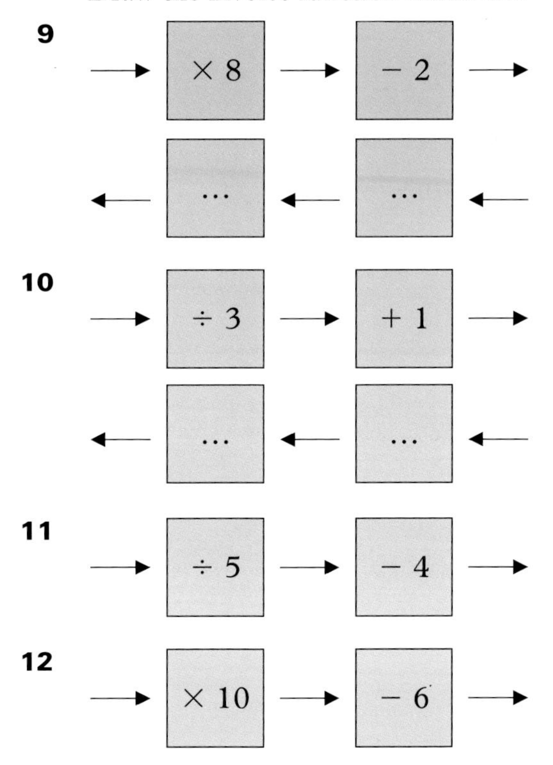

We can use function machines to solve equations.

Example Solve the equation $x + 9 = 28$

The function machine is:

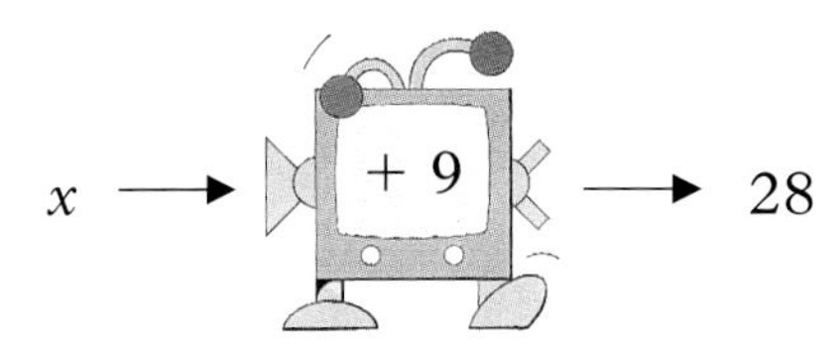

The inverse machine is:

Answer: $x = 19$

Exercise 15:5

Solve these equations by drawing inverse machines.

1 $x + 12 = 23$

2 $a + 8 = 21$

3 $x - 7 = 34$

4 $x - 9 = 33$

5 $x + 6 = 41$

6 $a - 16 = 44$

Example

Solve the equation $4a = 64$

Remember: $4a$ means $4 \times a$

The function machine is:

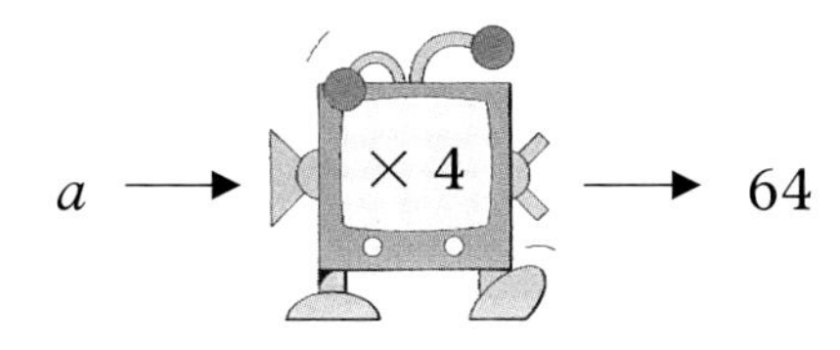

The inverse machine is:

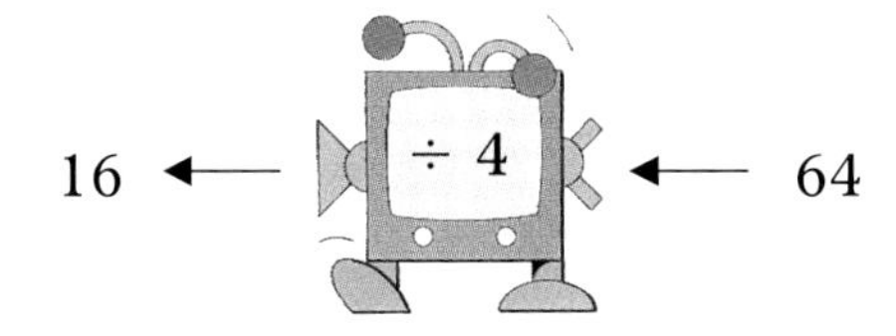

Answer: $a = 16$

Exercise 15:6

Solve these equations by drawing inverse machines.

1 $6a = 90$

2 $7x = 98$

3 $4y = 144$

4 $5x = 85$

5 $3m = 75$

6 $10a = 160$

Example Solve the equation $\frac{x}{5} = 12$

Remember: $\frac{x}{5}$ means $x \div 5$

The function machine is:

The inverse machine is:

Answer: $x = 60$

Exercise 15:7

Solve these equations by drawing inverse machines.

1 $\frac{x}{3} = 28$

2 $\frac{a}{6} = 14$

3 $\frac{d}{4} = 23$

4 $\frac{x}{7} = 25$

5 $\frac{m}{8} = 10$

6 $\frac{d}{5} = 20$

A function machine can have 2 steps.

Example Solve the equation $3a - 5 = 16$

The function machine is:

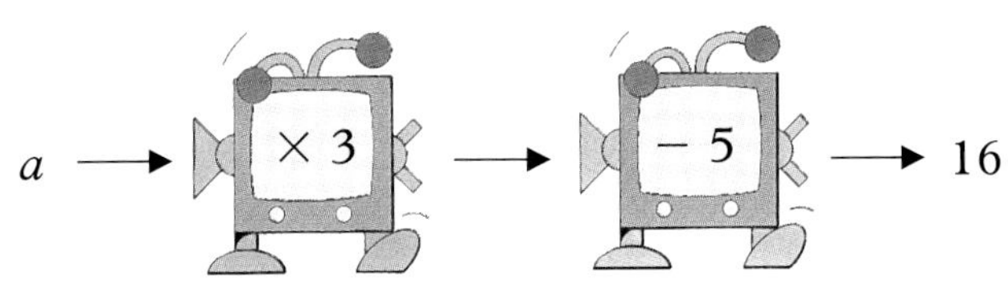

The inverse machine is:

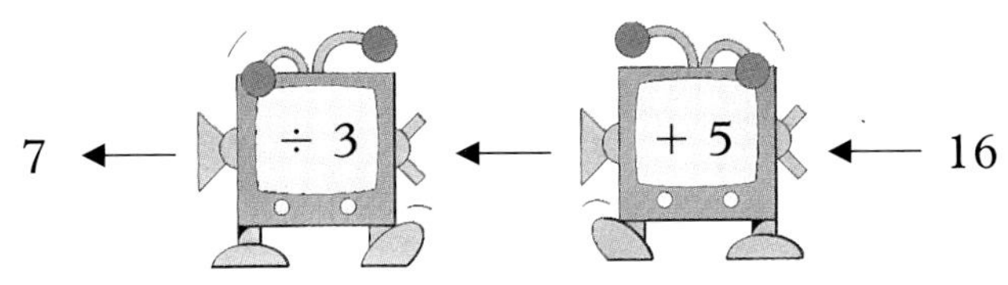

Answer: $a = 7$

Exercise 15:8

Solve these equations by drawing inverse machines.

1 $3x - 7 = 23$

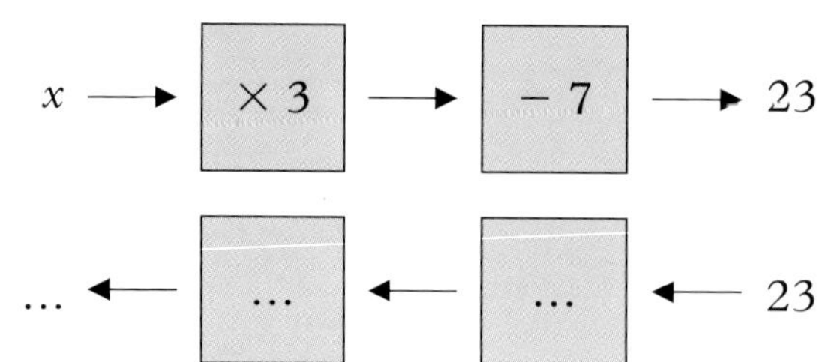

2 $6a + 13 = 61$

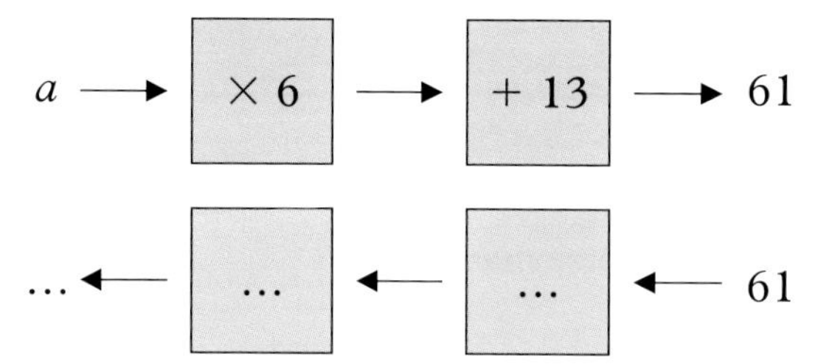

3 $4e + 8 = 44$

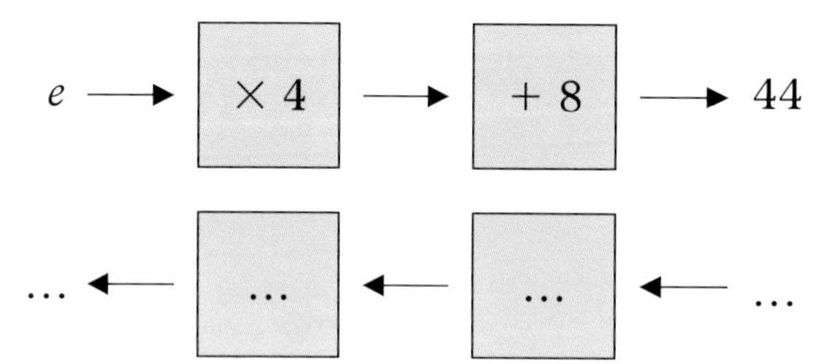

4 $7c - 6 = 29$

$c \rightarrow$ [× 7] $\rightarrow$ [− 6] $\rightarrow$ …

… $\leftarrow$ […] $\leftarrow$ […] $\leftarrow$ …

● **5** $5y + 13 = 43$

● **6** $8f - 26 = 70$

3 Order in number

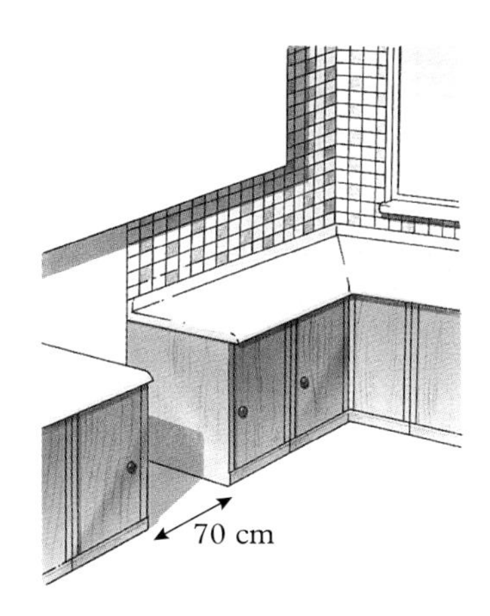

Mrs Jones is buying a new cooker.

She wants to know which of these cookers will fit the space in her kitchen.

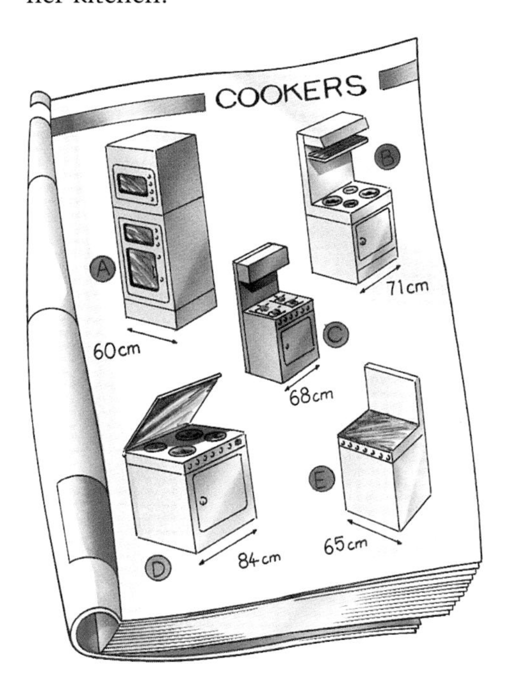

A will fit because 60 cm is less than 70 cm.
B will not fit because 71 cm is more than 70 cm.
C and E will also fit.
D is too big. It won't fit.

Exercise 15:9

1 Mr Khan is buying a new fridge. It must fit in a space 150 cm high.
Which of these fridges will fit?

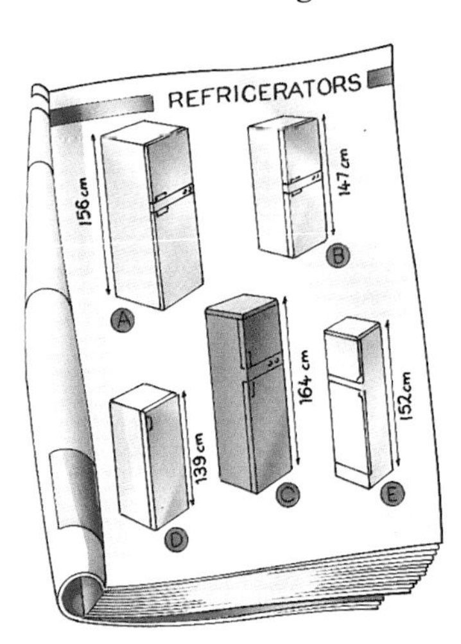

2 Janina's bedroom window is 6.6 m from the ground.
She wants a safety ladder that she can use in case of fire.
These are the ladders in a catalogue.

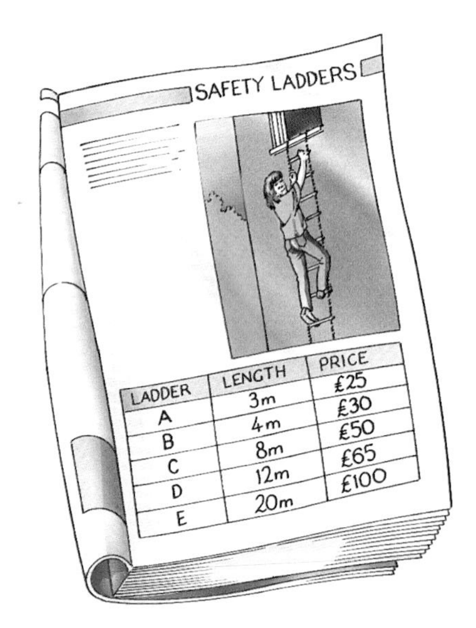

LADDER	LENGTH	PRICE
A	3m	£25
B	4m	£30
C	8m	£50
D	12m	£65
E	20m	£100

a Which ladders would not reach the ground?
b Which ladder should she buy?

3 Write true or false for each of these.

a 80 cm is more than 79.9 cm.

b 14 months is less than 1 year.

c 140 seconds is more than 3 minutes.

d 79 p is less than £0.08

e 0.5 m is more than 45 cm.

f 1 kg of lead is heavier than 1 kg of feathers.

4 **a** Which is larger 127 or 153?

b Which is smaller 1005 or 1050?

c Which is larger 8.93 or 8.79?

d Which is smaller 0.03 or 0.304?

e Which is hotter -4 °C or -8 °C?

f Which is smaller 1 mm^2 or 1 cm^2?

5 Write down the number that is:

a 5 more than 100

b 5 less than 300

c 1 less than 1000

d 10 more than 1000

e 20 less than 2000

f twice as big as 205

6 Mr Brown buys this packet of chicken pieces.

a What is the least number of chicken pieces that he will get?

b Could the packet contain 10 pieces? Explain your answer.

● **7** These are the times taken by three girls to run 100 metres. Who ran the fastest?

	Time (s)
Pardeep	12.3
Tina	13.1
Ursula	11.9

Example

The price of a Christmas tree depends on its height.
What is the cost of a tree of height:

a 5 feet
b $2\frac{1}{2}$ feet

a Cost = £7 because 5 feet is between 4 and 6 feet.
b Cost = £5 because $2\frac{1}{2}$ feet is less than 4 feet.

Exercise 15:10

1 What is the cost of a tree of height:
a 3 feet **b** 8 feet **c** $5\frac{1}{2}$ feet

2 Barry is selling pumpkins for Halloween.

What is the cost of a pumpkin that weighs:
a 3 kg **c** 1.5 kg
b 5 kg **d** $2\frac{1}{2}$ kg

3 On sports day points are given for the high jump.

Less than 80 cm	1 point
Between 80 cm and 100 cm	2 points
Between 100 cm and 120 cm	4 points
Over 120 cm	8 points

Work out the points for these pupils.
a David 115 cm
b Peter 79 cm
c Charlene 122 cm
d Kerri 81 cm

1 Solve these equations by trial and improvement.
Copy the table. Fill it in.
Add more rows until you find the answer.

a $2x + 39 = 69$

Value of x	Value of $2x + 39$	
10		
20		

b $5x - 12 = 28$

Value of x	Value of $5x - 12$	
5		
10		

2 Draw the inverses of these function machines.

a -12 **c** $\div 16$ **e** $\div 20$

b $+5$ **d** $\times 14$ **f** -7

3 Draw the inverses of these function machines.

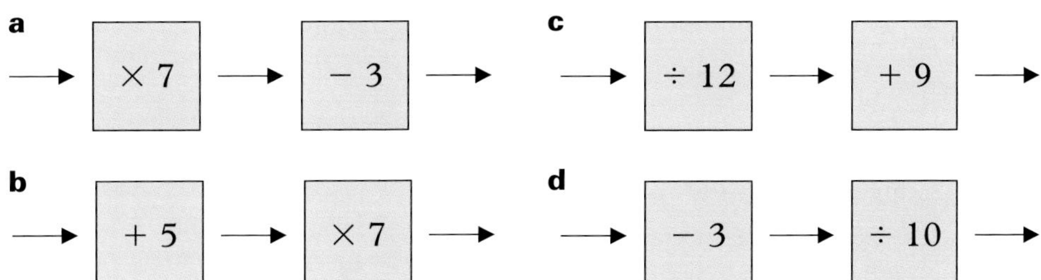

a → $\times 7$ → -3 →

b → $+5$ → $\times 7$ →

c → $\div 12$ → $+9$ →

d → -3 → $\div 10$ →

4 Solve these equations by drawing inverse machines.

a $x - 8 = 20$

b $x + 5 = 13$

c $10a = 120$

d $\frac{d}{4} = 12$

e $\frac{x}{5} = 24$

f $6p = 84$

1 Solve these equations by trial and improvement.
Copy the table. Fill it in.
Add more rows until you find the answer.

a $x^2 = 289$ *Remember:* x^2 means $x \times x$

Value of x	Value of x^2	
10		
20		

b $x^2 = 2025$

Value of x	Value of x^2	
40		
50		

Solve these equations by drawing inverse machines.

2 $4x + 15 = 39$

3 $5c - 14 = 36$

4 $9f + 14 = 77$

5 $10g - 23 = 57$

6 Solve these equations by drawing inverse machines.

a $\frac{x}{8} + 13 = 20$ **b** $\frac{a}{6} - 8 = 3$ **c** $\frac{m}{2} - 13 = 0$

7 **a** This is the function machine for the equation $\frac{3x}{5} = 6$

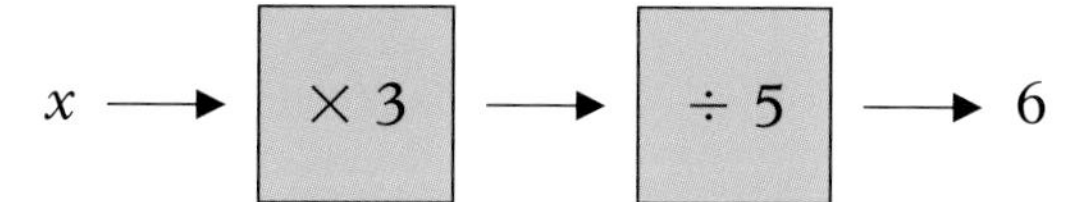

Copy and fill in the inverse machine.

… ← … ← … ← 6

Answer: $x = \ldots$

Solve these equations in the same way.

b $\frac{2x}{3} = 8$ **d** $\frac{3x}{8} = 6$ **f** $\frac{2a}{7} = 4$

c $\frac{5m}{6} = 10$ **e** $\frac{4x}{9} = 12$ **g** $\frac{3t}{10} = 9$

- ***Trial and improvement***

Example To solve $3x + 3 = 45$ by trial and improvement:
(1) try different values of x
(2) write your results in a table like this:
Remember: $3x$ means $3 \times x$

Value of x	Value of $3x + 3$	
10	$3 \times 10 + 3 = 33$	too small
15	$3 \times 15 + 3 = 48$	too big
14	$3 \times 14 + 3 = 45$	correct

Answer: $x = 14$

- **Inverse** An **inverse** returns you to where you started.

The inverse of 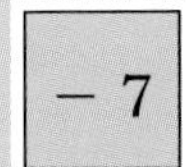

is + 7

- *Example* Solve the equation $x + 9 = 28$

The function machine is:

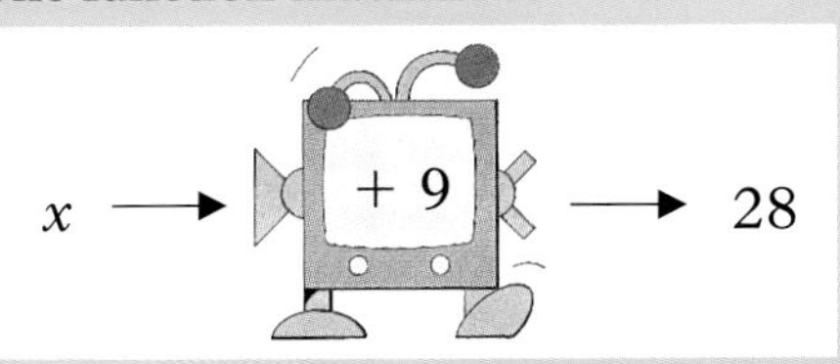

The inverse machine is:

Answer: $x = 19$

- *Example* Solve the equation $3a - 5 = 16$

The function machine is:

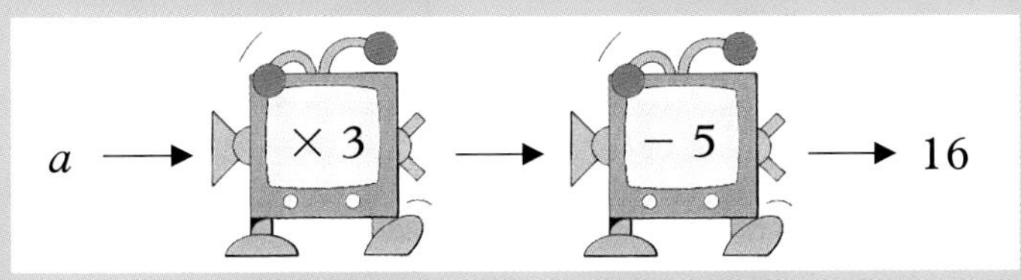

The inverse machine is:

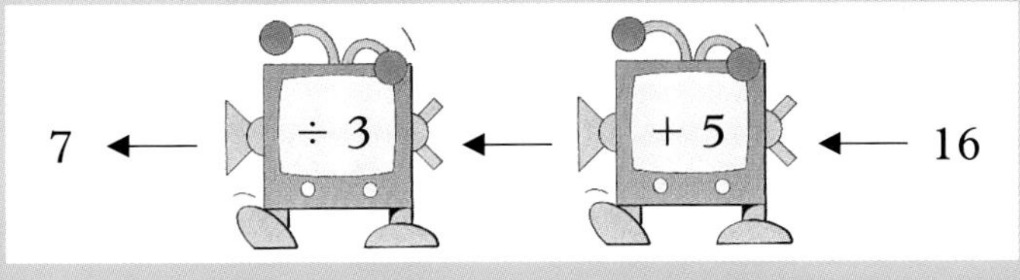

Answer: $a = 7$

1 Solve this equation by trial and improvement: $5x - 3 = 62$
Copy the table. Fill it in.
Add more rows until you find the answer.

Value of x	Value of $5x - 3$	
10		
20		

2 Write down the inverse of:
a $+4$ **b** -10 **c** $\times 6$ **d** $\div 11$

3 Draw the inverse of these function machines.

a → $\times 5$ → -8 →

b → $\div 7$ → $+4$ →

4 Solve these equations by drawing inverse machines.
a $x - 11 = 25$ **b** $6a = 102$ **c** $\frac{x}{12} = 108$

5 Solve these equations by copying and filling in the inverse machines.
a $2x - 13 = 15$

x → $\times 2$ → -13 → 15

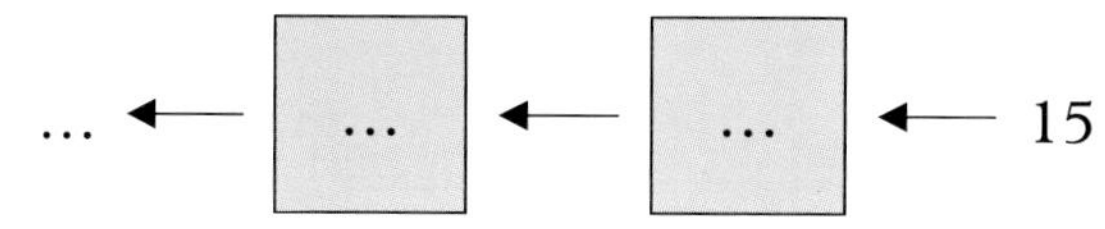

b $4c - 16 = 52$

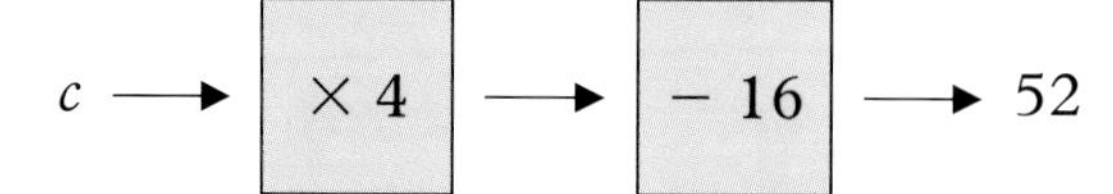

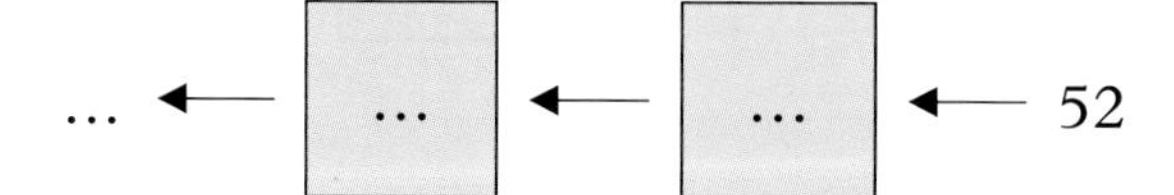

16 The crossing point

CORE

1 Intersecting lines

2 Graphs of patterns

3 Solving puzzles

QUESTIONS

EXTENSION

SUMMARY

TEST YOURSELF

Each symbol in the diagram has a value. The total values are placed alongside some rows and columns. What number should replace the question mark to give the value of the bottom row?

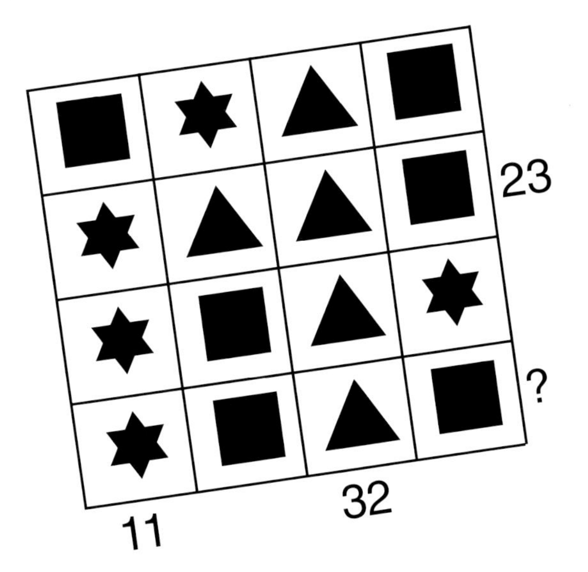

1 Intersecting lines

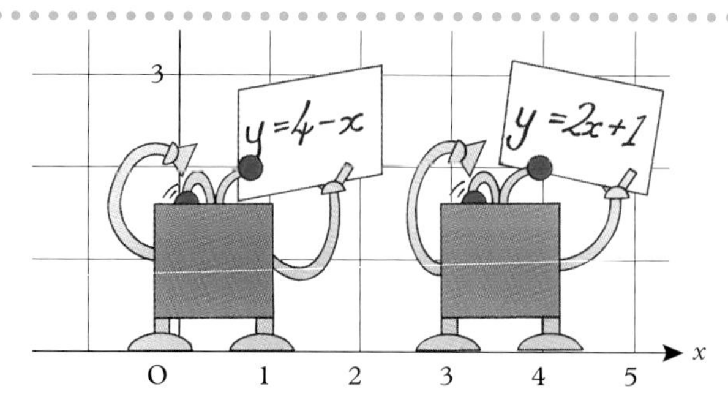

You can use robots to draw lines.

Example Draw the line $y = x + 3$ using robot screens.

x				y	
1	→		→	4	(1, 4)
2	→	$+\,3$	→	5	(2, 5)
3	→		→	6	(3, 6)

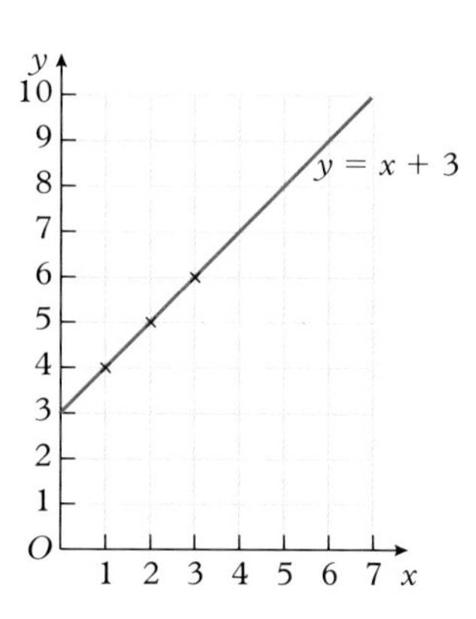

You only need two points to draw a straight line.
The third point acts as a check.

Exercise 16:1

1 **a** Use this robot screen to find three points on the line $y = 3x$

x				y	
1	→		→	3	(1, 3)
2	→	$\times\,3$	→	…	(2, …)
3	→		→	…	(3, …)

b Copy the axes from the example on to squared paper.

c Plot your three points.
Draw a line through them with a ruler.

d Label the line with its equation $y = 3x$

2 **a** Use this robot screen to find three points on the line $y = x + 6$

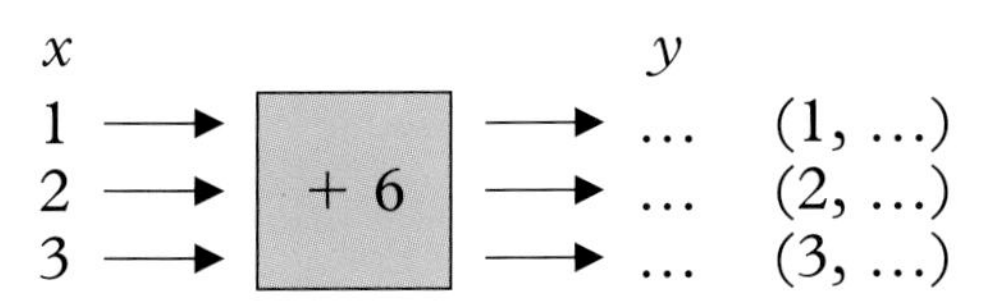

b Plot your three points on your diagram for question **1**.
Draw a line through them with a ruler.

c Label the line with its equation $y = x + 6$

3 Write down the co-ordinates of the point where your two lines cross.
Remember: This point is called a **point of intersection**.

Exercise 16:2

1 **a** Use this robot screen to find three points on the line $y = 2x$

x			y	
1 →		→	...	(1, ...)
2 →	$\times 2$	→	...	(2, ...)
3 →		→	...	(3, ...)

b Copy the axes from the example on to squared paper.

c Plot your three points.
Draw a line through them with a ruler.

d Label the line with its equation $y = 2x$

2 **a** Use this robot screen to find three points on the line $y = x + 4$

x			y	
1 →		→	...	(1, ...)
2 →	$+ 4$	→	...	(2, ...)
3 →		→	...	(3, ...)

b Plot your three points on your diagram for question **1**.
Draw a line through them with a ruler.

c Label the line with its equation $y = x + 4$

3 Write down the co-ordinates of the point where your two lines from questions **1** and **2** cross.

Exercise 16:3

1 **a** Copy the axes on to squared paper.
b Plot the points (1,1) (3,3) (5,5)
Draw a line through the points with a ruler.
c For each of these points
$\boldsymbol{y}$ co-ordinate = $\boldsymbol{x}$ co-ordinate
The equation is $y = x$
Label your line $y = x$

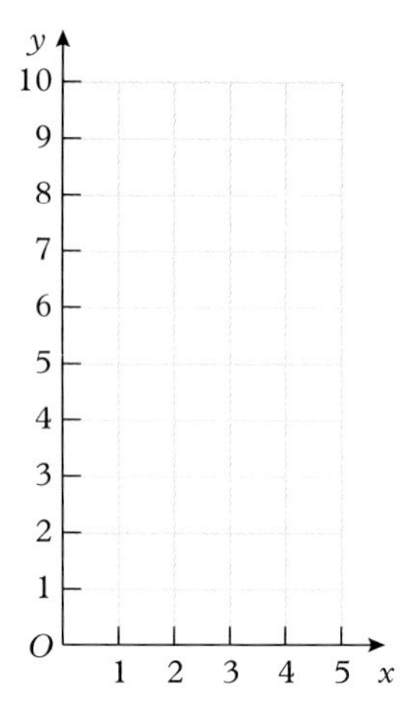

2 **a** Use these robot screens to find three points on the line $y = 3x - 2$

x						y	
1 →		3 →		→		1	(1, 1)
2 →	× 3	… →		− 2	→	…	(2, …)
3 →		… →		→		…	(3, …)

b Plot your three points on your diagram for question **1**.
Draw a line through them with a ruler.
c Label the line with its equation $y = 3x - 2$

3 Write down the co-ordinates of the point of intersection of your two lines from questions **1** and **2**.

● **4** **a** Use these robot screens to find three points on the line $y = 2x + 1$

x						y	
1 →		… →		→		…	(1, …)
2 →	× 2	… →		+ 1	→	…	(2, …)
3 →		… →		→		…	(3, …)

b Copy the axes from question **1** again.
Plot your three points.
Draw a line through them with a ruler.
c Label the line with its equation $y = 2x + 1$
d Use robot screens to find three points on the line $y = 2x + 4$
Plot your three points on your axes.
Draw a line through them with a ruler.
e What can you say about your two lines?

2 Graphs of patterns

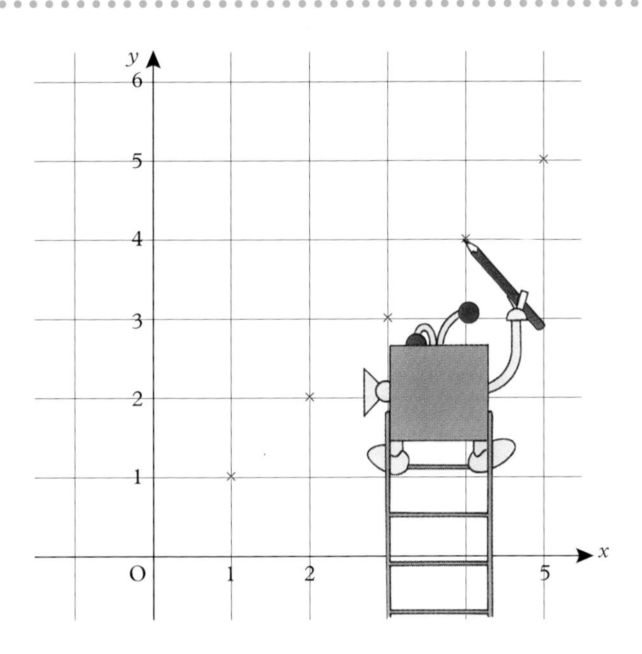

Exercise 16:4

1 Mr Green arranges tables and chairs like this.

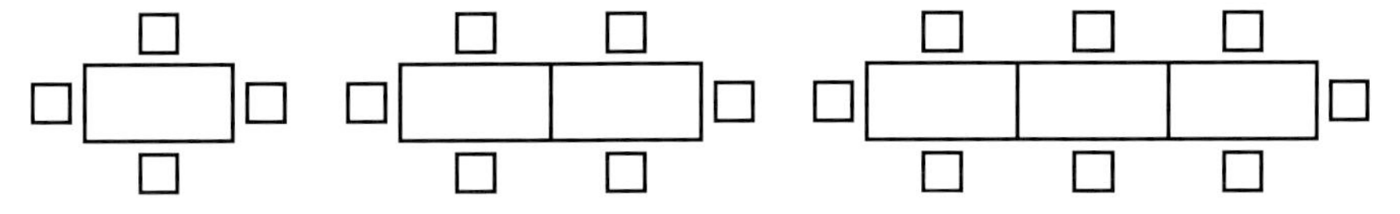

a Draw the pattern for four tables.

b Copy this table.

Number of tables	1	2	3	4	5	6	7
Number of chairs	4	6	8				

c The number of chairs goes up like this:

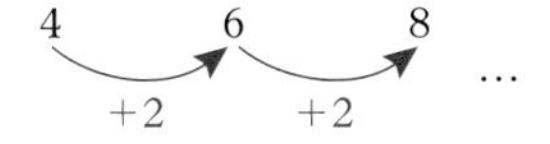

What is the rule for this pattern?

d Use the rule to fill in your table.

2 **a** Copy the axes on to squared paper.

b

Number of tables	1	2	3		
Number of chairs	4	6			

You can get co-ordinates of points from your table.
Copy these co-ordinates.
Fill them in.
(1, 4) (2, 6) (3, …) (4, …)
(5, …) (6, …) (7, …)

c Plot all seven points on your axes.
Do not join them up.
Your points should be in a straight line.

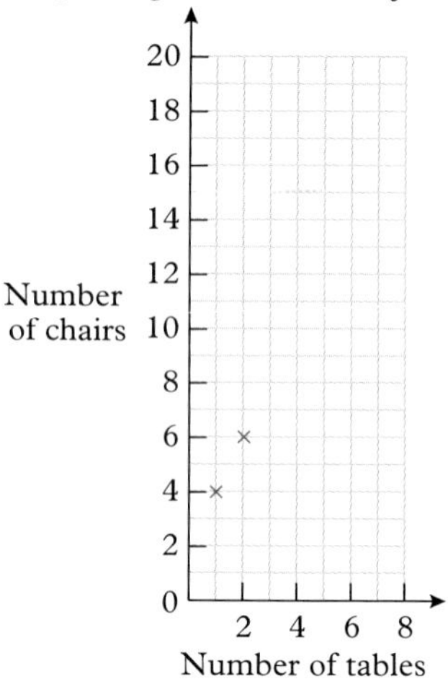

Exercise 16:5

1 Marcia is putting up photos of the school play using drawing pins.
Her display looks like this.

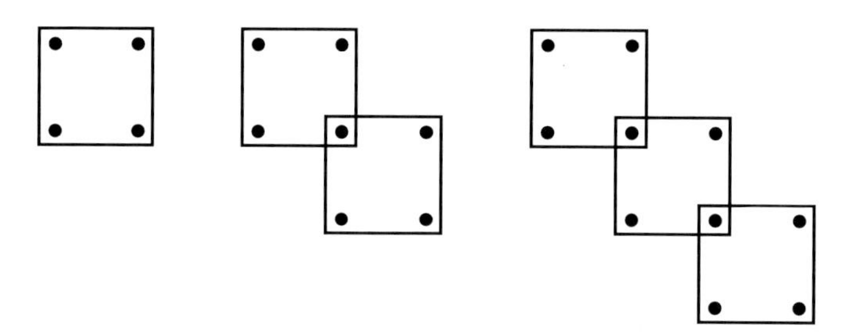

a Draw the pattern for four photos.

b Copy this table.

Number of photos	1	2	3	4	5	6	7
Number of pins	4	7	10				

c The number of pins goes up like this:
4 7 10 …
What is the rule for this pattern?

d Use the rule to fill in your table.

2 **a** Copy the axes on to squared paper.

b

Number of photos	1	2		
Number of pins	4			

You can get co-ordinates of points from your table.
The first point is (1, 4).
Write down the other six points.

c Plot all seven points on your axes.
Do not join them up.
Your points should be in a straight line.

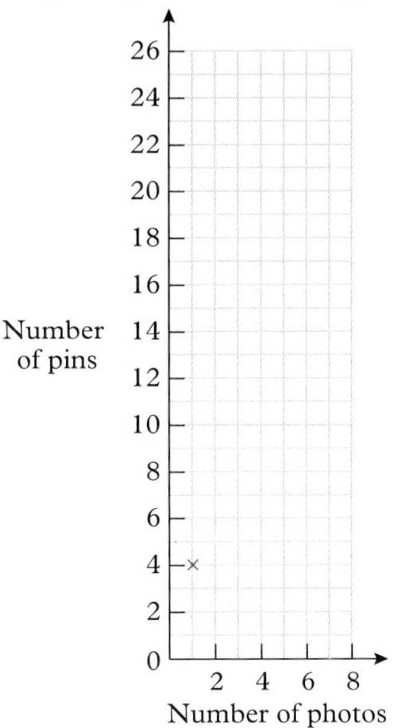

Exercise 16:6

1 Hitesh is making house patterns with matchsticks.

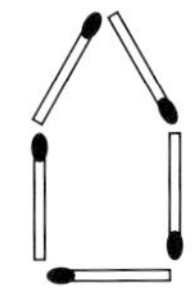

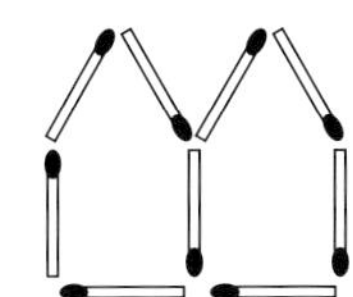

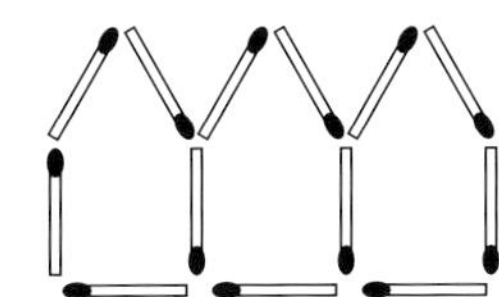

a Draw the pattern for four houses.

b Copy this table.

Number of houses	1	2	3	4	5	6
Number of matchsticks	5	9				

c Describe in words how the pattern goes up.

d Use the rule to fill in the missing numbers.

e Draw a set of axes like the ones at the top of this page.
Label the short axis 'Number of houses'.
Label the long axis 'Number of matchsticks'.

f Plot the points from your table.
Do not join them up.
Your points should be in a straight line.

g Give your graph a title.

3 Solving puzzles

John has found a puzzle in a newspaper.

Exercise 16:7

1 A number pattern starts like this:

2	3
4	5

5	6
7	8

8	9
10	11

Here are some more parts of the same pattern.
Copy the squares.
Fill in the missing numbers.

a

14	…
16	…

b

17	…
…	20

c

…	21
…	23

2 Here is another pattern.

2	4
6	8

8	♥
12	14

14	♠
♣	20

Write down the value of **a**  **b**  **c** 

Example

Here is John's newspaper problem.
The shapes add up to the number shown.
John has to find the value of each shape.

▲	▲	8
▲	●	10

He sees that two triangles add up to 8.
One triangle must be 4.

He sees that one triangle and one circle add up to 10.
One circle must be 6.
Because: $4 + 6 = 10$

Exercise 16:8

Solve these picture puzzles.

1

■	■	14
■	◆	9

2

	)	14
)	)	18

3

● ●)	18
● ● ●	15

4

▲ ▲ ▲	21
▲ ◆ ◆	15

5

A B B	24
A A A	12

● **6**

	48
● ●	26

7 Make up a puzzle of your own.
Give it to a friend to solve.

Exercise 16:9

1 The numbers in ◯ and ◯ add up to the number in ☐ like this:

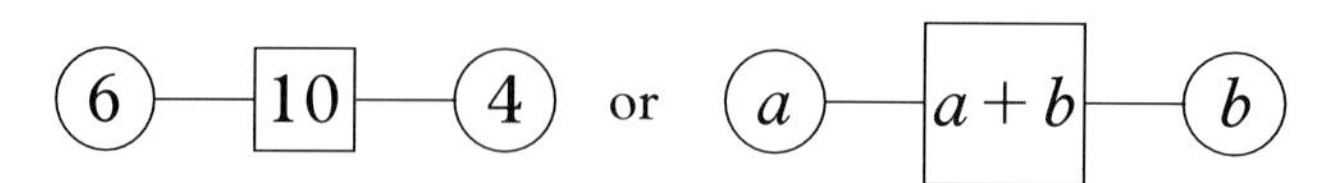

a Copy these.
Fill in the missing numbers.

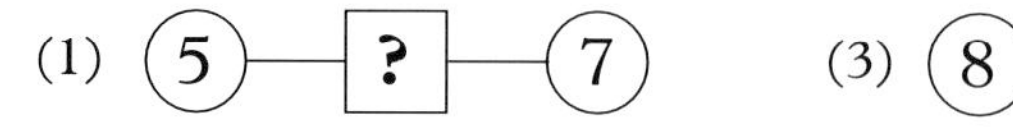

b Write down the value of each letter.

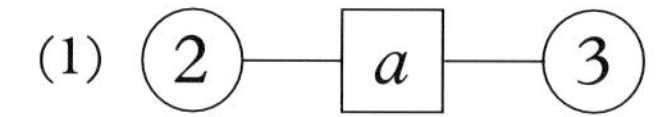

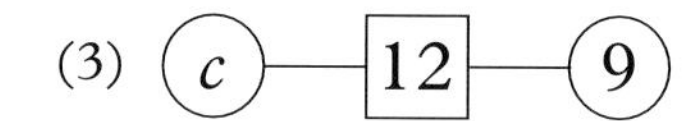

(2) 10 b 5

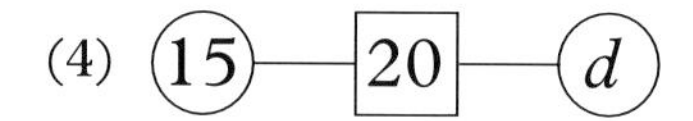

2 The numbers in △ and △ are multiplied to give the number in ☐ like this:

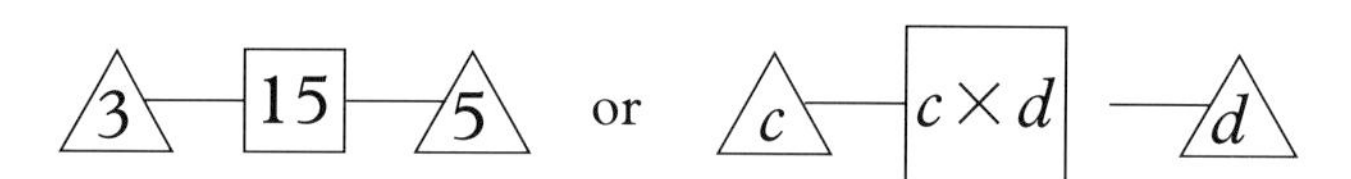

a Copy these.
Fill in the missing numbers.

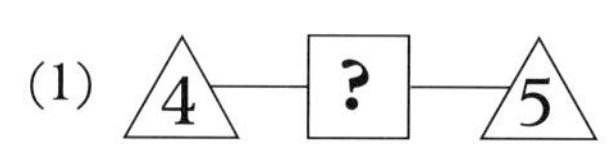

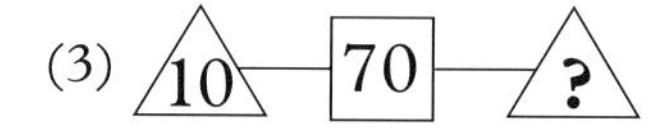

(2) ? 12 4

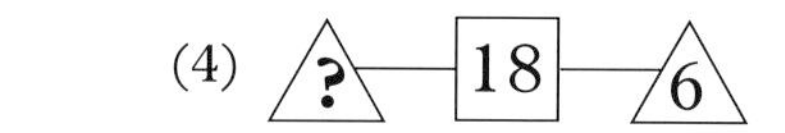

b Write down the value of each letter.

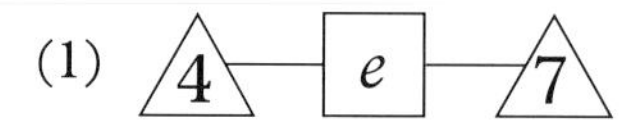

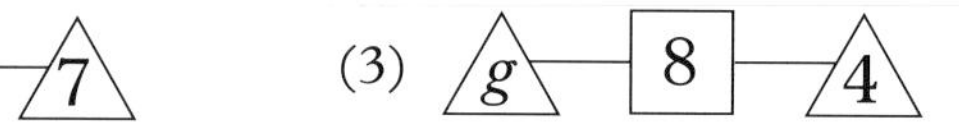

(2) 3 f 11

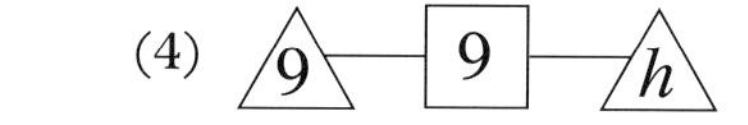

1 **a** Use this robot screen to find three points on the line $y = x + 3$

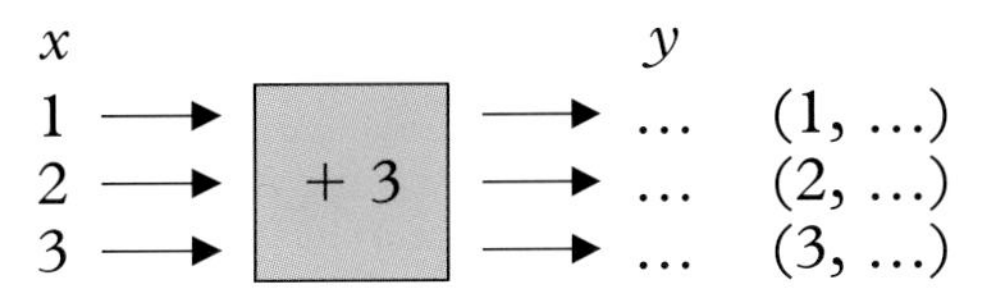

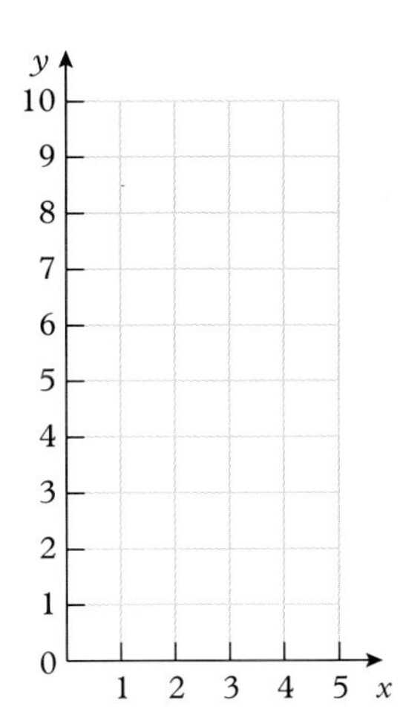

b Copy the axes on to squared paper.
Plot your three points.
Draw a line through them with a ruler.
Label the line with its equation $y = x + 3$

c (1) Use these robot screens to find three points on the line $y = 2x + 2$

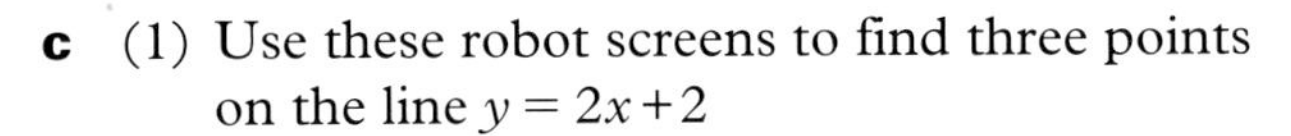

(2) Plot your three points on your diagram for part **b**.
Draw a line through them with a ruler.
(3) Label the line with its equation $y = 2x + 2$

d Write down the co-ordinates of the point of intersection.

2 **a** Copy this pattern.
Fill in the missing numbers.

1	2	3		7	8	9		…	14	…
		4	5	6		…	11	12		

b Here is another pattern.
Write down the value of each letter.

1	2	3		a	6	7		9	c	11		
		3	4	5		7	8	b		d	12	13

c Copy this pattern.
Continue the pattern up to 21.

1	2	3			6	7	8			11	…
		3	4	5	6		8	9	10	11	

3 The Art Room has a washing line.
Tom is hanging 8W's pictures up to dry.
For one picture he uses two pegs.
Two pictures need three pegs, etc.

a Draw the pattern for four pictures.

b Copy this table.

Number of pictures	1	2	3	4	5	6	7
Number of pegs	2	3	4				

Graph to show number of pegs for a given number of pictures

Number of pegs: 0 1 2 3 4 5 6 7 8 9 10

Number of pictures: 1 2 3 4 5 6 7 8

c Describe in words the rule for the pattern.

d Use the rule to fill in your table.

e Copy the axes on to squared paper.

f You can get the co-ordinates of points from the table.
The first point is (1, 2).
Write down the other six points.

g Plot all seven points on your axes.
Do not join them up.
Your points should be in a straight line.

4 The numbers 1 to 9 are drawn in a 3×3 square.

1	2	3
4	5	6
7	8	9

Here is a 2×2 square from inside the larger square.

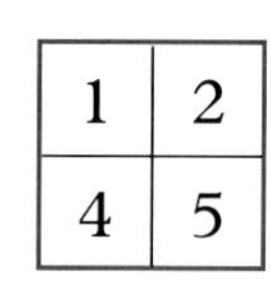

These 2×2 squares are from inside the large square.
Write down the value of each letter.

2	3
5	6

4	5
7	a

5	b
c	9

5 The numbers in ◯ and ◯ add up to the number in △ like this:

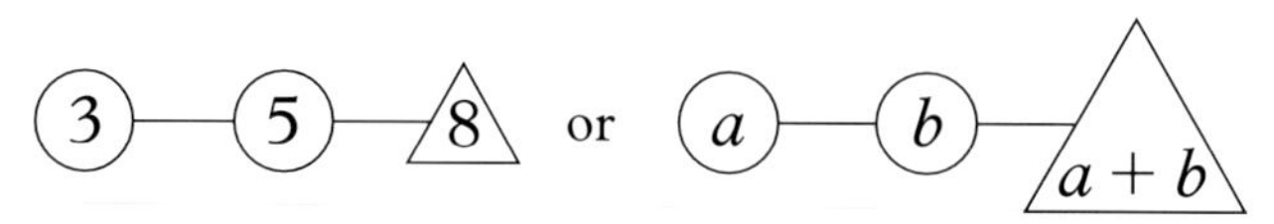

Write down the value of each letter.

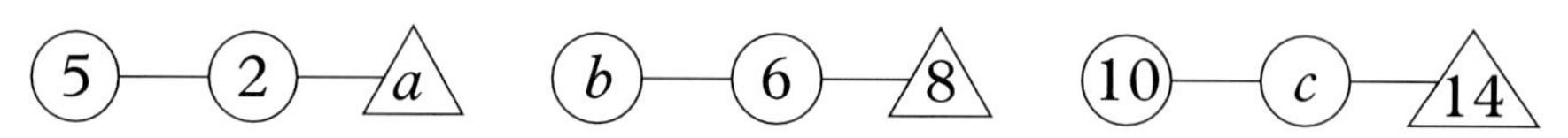

1 **a** Use these robot screens to find three points on the line $y = 3x - 1$

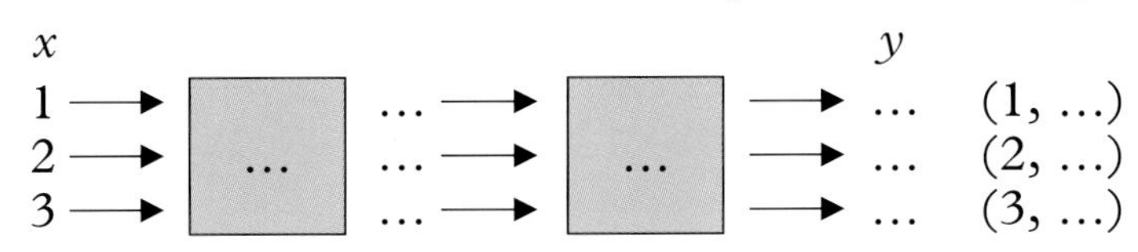

b Copy the axes on to squared paper.
Plot your three points on your axes.
Draw a line through them with a ruler.
Label the line with its equation.

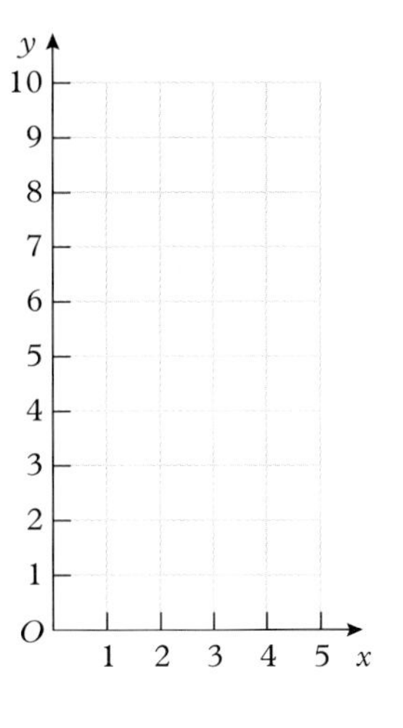

c (1) Use robot screens to find three points on the line $y = 3x - 3$
(2) Plot your three points on your diagram from **b**.
Draw a line through them with a ruler.
Label the line with its equation.

d What can you say about your two lines?

e Use robot screens to find three points on the line $y = 2x + 1$
Plot your three points on your diagram from **c**.
Draw a line through them with a ruler.
Label the line with its equation.

f Write down the co-ordinates of the two points of intersection.

2 **a** In this pattern the pairs of co-ordinates add up to 6.
(1) Copy and fill in:
(0, 6) (1, 5) (2, ...) (3, ...) (4, ...) (5, ...) (6, 0)
(2) Copy the axes from question **1** on to squared paper.
Plot the points.
Join them up with a ruler.
(3) Label your line with its equation $x + y = 6$

b In this pattern the pairs of co-ordinates add up to 5.
(1) Copy and fill in:
(0, 5) (1, 4) (2, ...) (3, ...) (4, ...) (5, ...)
(2) Plot the points on your diagram from **a**.
Join them up with a ruler.
(3) Label your line with its equation $x + y = 5$

c (1) Predict where the line $x + y = 4$ will go.
(2) Write down the pairs of co-ordinates that add up to 4.
(0, 4) (1, ...) ...
(3) Plot the points on your diagram from **a**.
Join them up with a ruler.
(4) Label your line with its equation $x + y = 4$
(5) Was your prediction correct?

3 The numbers in △ and △ and △ add up to the number in ○

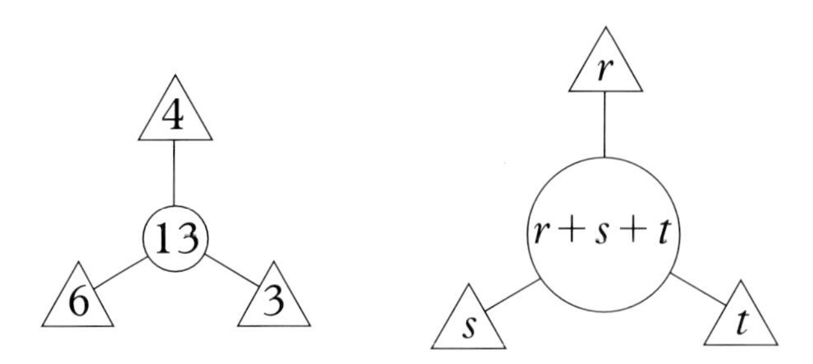

a Copy these.
Fill in the missing numbers.

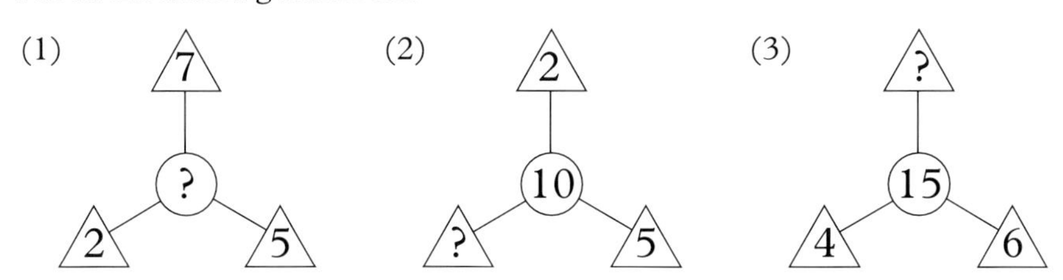

b Write down the value of each letter.

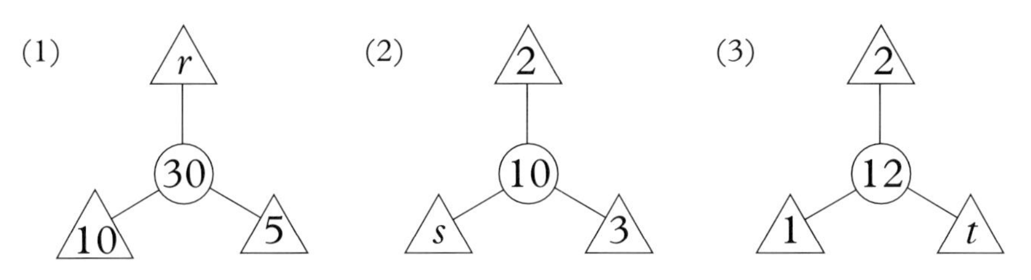

4 **a** Look at this pattern.

1	4
2	3

4	5
3	6

5	8
6	7

8	9
7	10

Draw the next two terms in the pattern.

b Write down the value of each letter.

13	a
14	15

16	17
b	18

c	20
18	19

20	21
d	22

- *Example* Draw the line $y = x + 3$ using robot screens.

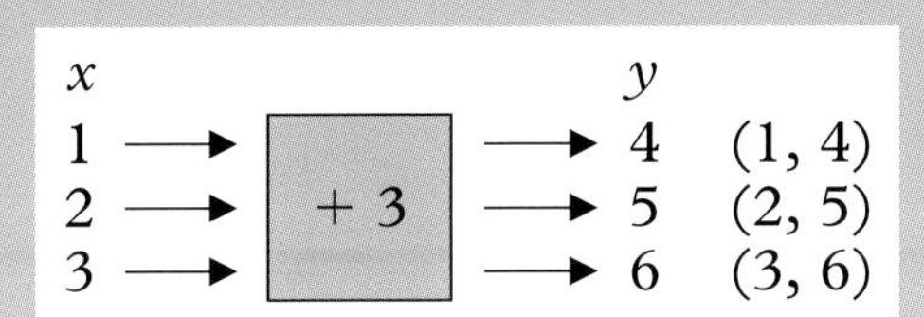

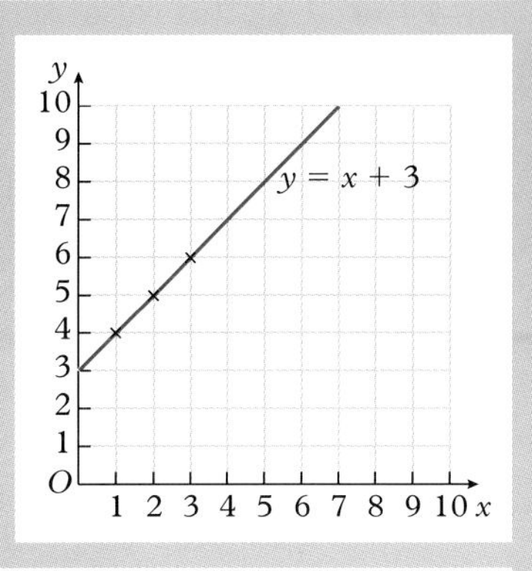

- *Example* You can put patterns of numbers in tables.

x	1	2	3	4	5
y	4	9	14		

The y numbers make a pattern.

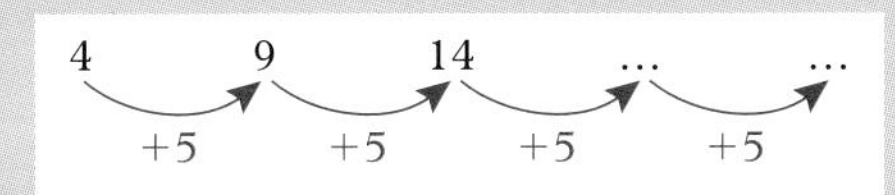

The rule is + 5.

You can use the rule to fill in the table.

x	1	2	3	4	5
y	4	9	14	19	24

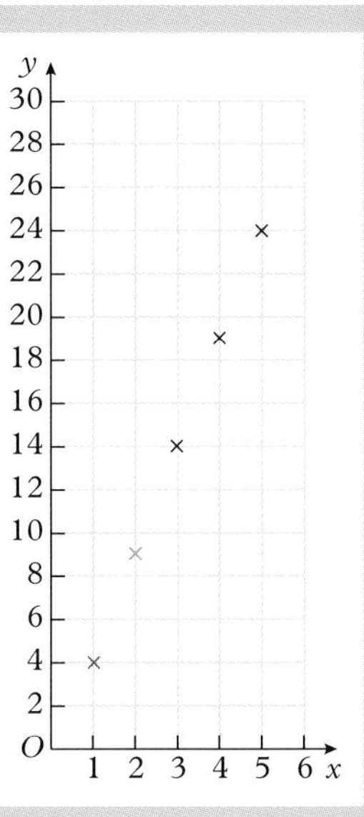

You can get pairs of co-ordinates from the table:
(1, 4) (2, 9) (3, 14) (4, 19) (5, 24)

- *Example* A number pattern starts like this:

2	3
4	5

5	6
7	8

8	9
10	11

…

Find the missing numbers.

a

14	15
16	…

b

…	18
…	20

c

20	♥
♣	23

Answers: **a** 17 **b** 17, 19 **c** ♥ = 21, ♣ = 22

1 **a** Use this robot screen to find three points on the line $y = x + 2$

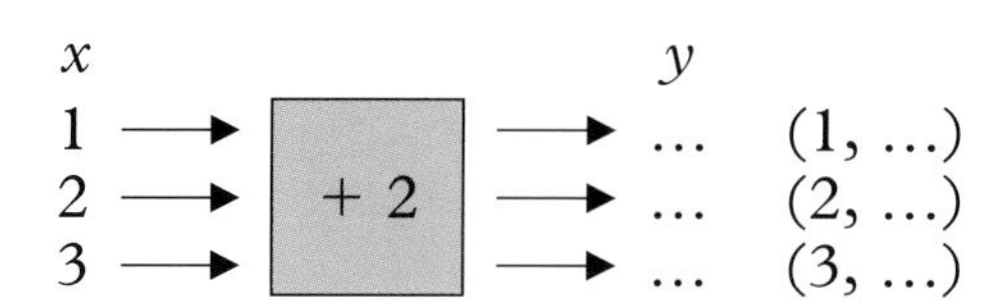

b Copy the axes on to squared paper.
Plot your three points.
Draw a line through them with a ruler.
Label the line with its equation $y = x + 2$

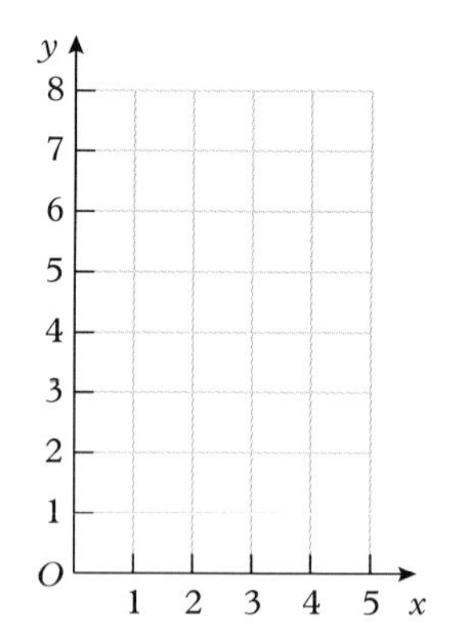

2 Jane is making triangle patterns with matchsticks.

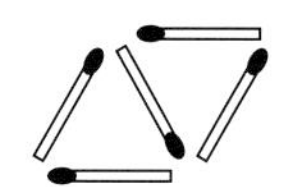
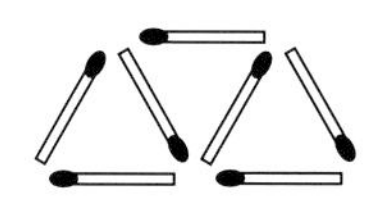

a Draw the pattern for four triangles.
b Copy this table.

Number of triangles	1	2	3	4	5	6
Number of matchsticks	3	5	7			

c Describe in words the rule for this pattern.
d Use the rule to fill in your table.
e Copy the axes on to squared paper.
f You can get the co-ordinates of points from the table.
The first point is (1, 3).
Write down the other five points.
g Plot all six points on your axes.
Do not join them up.
Your points should be in a straight line.

Graph to show number of triangles for a given number of matchsticks

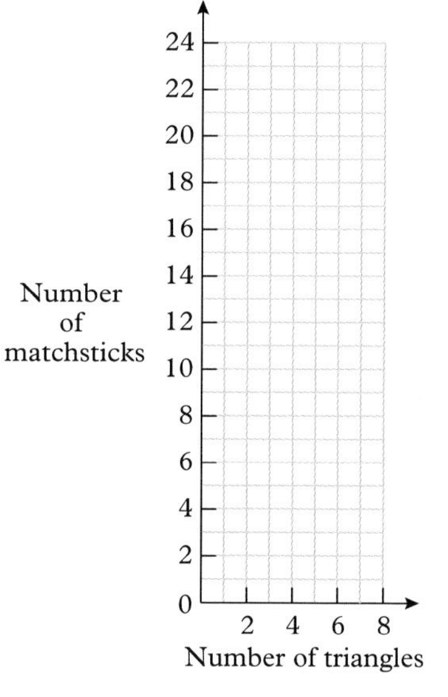

3 Look at this pattern.
Write down the value of each letter.

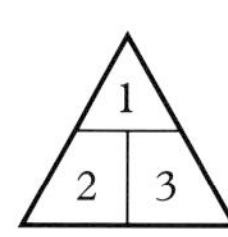

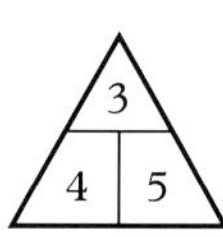

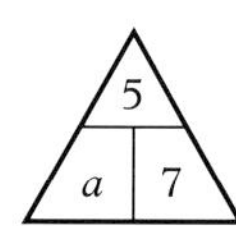

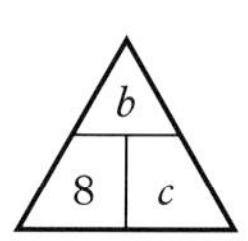

Help yourself

1 Adding
2 Subtracting
3 Multiplying
4 Multiplying by 10
5 Multiplying by 100, 1000, ...
6 Multiplying by 20, 30, ...
7 Long multiplication
8 Dividing
9 Dividing by 10
10 Dividing by 100, 1000, ...
11 Dividing by 20, 30, ...
12 Adding fractions
13 Subtracting fractions

1 Adding

You should set out additions in columns.

Example

13 + 2 should be set out like this:

$$\begin{array}{r} 13 \\ +\ \underline{2} \\ \underline{15} \end{array}$$

Here are some more examples.

27 + 21 431 + 26 542 + 136

$$\begin{array}{r} 27 \\ +\ \underline{21} \\ \underline{48} \end{array} \qquad \begin{array}{r} 431 \\ +\ \underline{26} \\ \underline{457} \end{array} \qquad \begin{array}{r} 542 \\ +\ \underline{136} \\ \underline{678} \end{array}$$

Sometimes we need to 'carry'. This happens when a column adds up to 10 or more.

Example

13 + 9

$$\begin{array}{r} 13 \\ +\ \underline{9} \\ \underline{22} \\ {\scriptstyle 1} \end{array}$$

Here are some more examples.

27 + 29 246 + 28 558 + 67

$$\begin{array}{r} 27 \\ +\ \underline{29} \\ \underline{56} \\ {\scriptstyle 1} \end{array} \qquad \begin{array}{r} 246 \\ +\ \underline{28} \\ \underline{274} \\ {\scriptstyle 1} \end{array} \qquad \begin{array}{r} 558 \\ +\ \underline{67} \\ \underline{625} \\ {\scriptstyle 1\,1} \end{array}$$

Exercise 1

Copy these into your book.
Work out the answers.

1 $\begin{array}{r} 25 \\ +\ \underline{3} \\ \underline{} \end{array}$

2 $\begin{array}{r} 36 \\ +\ \underline{32} \\ \underline{} \end{array}$

3 $\begin{array}{r} 43 \\ +\ \underline{12} \\ \underline{} \end{array}$

4 $\begin{array}{r} 235 \\ +\ \underline{134} \\ \underline{} \end{array}$

5 $\begin{array}{r} 730 \\ +\ \underline{48} \\ \underline{} \end{array}$

6 $\begin{array}{r} 35 \\ +\ \underline{432} \\ \underline{} \end{array}$

7 $\begin{array}{r} 4032 \\ +\ \underline{645} \\ \underline{} \end{array}$

8 $\begin{array}{r} 2509 \\ +\ \underline{7290} \\ \underline{} \end{array}$

9 21 + 8

10 43 + 35

11 524 + 31

12 814 + 130

Exercise 2

Copy these into your book.
Work out the answers.

1 $\begin{array}{r} 25 \\ +\ \underline{9} \\ \underline{} \end{array}$

2 $\begin{array}{r} 28 \\ +\ \underline{16} \\ \underline{} \end{array}$

3 $\begin{array}{r} 37 \\ +\ \underline{25} \\ \underline{} \end{array}$

4 $\begin{array}{r} 147 \\ +\ \underline{28} \\ \underline{} \end{array}$

5 $\begin{array}{r} 275 \\ +\ \underline{26} \\ \underline{} \end{array}$

6 $\begin{array}{r} 568 \\ +\ \underline{93} \\ \underline{} \end{array}$

7 $\begin{array}{r} 248 \\ +\ \underline{185} \\ \underline{} \end{array}$

8 $\begin{array}{r} 526 \\ +\ \underline{419} \\ \underline{} \end{array}$

9 38 + 57

10 95 + 46

11 114 + 97

12 57 + 253

Other words

All these words can also mean **add**.

plus **sum** **total**

Examples
Work out 24 **plus** 13
Find the **sum** of 24 and 13
Find the **total** of 24 and 13

all mean $$\begin{array}{r} 24 \\ +\ 13 \\ \hline 37 \\ \hline \end{array}$$

---

2 Subtracting

Subtractions should also be set out in columns.

Example

28 − 10 should be set out like this:

$$\begin{array}{r} 28 \\ -\ 10 \\ \hline 18 \\ \hline \end{array}$$

Here are some more examples.

29 − 16 $$\begin{array}{r} 29 \\ -\ 16 \\ \hline 13 \\ \hline \end{array}$$

436 − 25 $$\begin{array}{r} 436 \\ -\ 25 \\ \hline 411 \\ \hline \end{array}$$

587 − 226 $$\begin{array}{r} 587 \\ -\ 226 \\ \hline 361 \\ \hline \end{array}$$

Exercise 3

Copy these into your book.
Work out the answers.

1 $$\begin{array}{r} 68 \\ -\ 24 \\ \hline \\ \hline \end{array}$$

2 $$\begin{array}{r} 869 \\ -\ 245 \\ \hline \\ \hline \end{array}$$

3 $$\begin{array}{r} 468 \\ -\ 236 \\ \hline \\ \hline \end{array}$$

4 $$\begin{array}{r} 965 \\ -\ 51 \\ \hline \\ \hline \end{array}$$

5 $$\begin{array}{r} 648 \\ -\ 302 \\ \hline \\ \hline \end{array}$$

6 $$\begin{array}{r} 1928 \\ -\ 705 \\ \hline \\ \hline \end{array}$$

7 $$\begin{array}{r} 4861 \\ -\ 520 \\ \hline \\ \hline \end{array}$$

8 $$\begin{array}{r} 7243 \\ -\ 102 \\ \hline \\ \hline \end{array}$$

9 659 − 38

10 784 − 352

11 292 − 140

12 3579 − 1468

Sometimes we need to 'borrow'. This happens when the number on the bottom of a column is bigger than the one on the top.

Example

42 − 19

The 4 is worth 4 lots of 10.
We can 'borrow' → one of these 10s.
We change it into ten ones.

$$\begin{array}{r} 42 \\ -\ 19 \\ \hline \\ \hline \end{array}$$

← The 9 is bigger than the 2.

Our working now looks like this:

$$\begin{array}{r} {}^{3}\not{4}\,{}^{1}2 \\ -\ 19 \\ \hline 23 \end{array}$$

← We can now take the 9 away from the 12.

Here is another example:

64 − 28

$$\begin{array}{r} 64 \\ -\ 28 \\ \hline \end{array} \rightarrow \begin{array}{r} {}^{5}\not{6}\,{}^{1}4 \\ -\ 28 \\ \hline \end{array} \rightarrow \begin{array}{r} {}^{5}\not{6}\,{}^{1}4 \\ -\ 28 \\ \hline 36 \end{array}$$

Here are some more difficult examples:

82 − 67 231 − 119 623 − 487

$$\begin{array}{r} {}^{7}\not{8}\,{}^{1}2 \\ -\ 67 \\ \hline 15 \end{array} \qquad \begin{array}{r} 2\,{}^{2}\not{3}\,{}^{1}1 \\ -\ 119 \\ \hline 112 \end{array} \qquad \begin{array}{r} {}^{5}\not{6}\,{}^{11}\not{2}\,{}^{1}3 \\ -\ 487 \\ \hline 136 \end{array}$$

Exercise 4

Copy these into your book.
Work out the answers.

1 $\begin{array}{r} 37 \\ -\ 18 \\ \hline \end{array}$

2 $\begin{array}{r} 86 \\ -\ 49 \\ \hline \end{array}$

3 $\begin{array}{r} 54 \\ -\ 27 \\ \hline \end{array}$

4 $\begin{array}{r} 253 \\ -\ 35 \\ \hline \end{array}$

5 $\begin{array}{r} 423 \\ -\ 319 \\ \hline \end{array}$

6 $\begin{array}{r} 634 \\ -\ 166 \\ \hline \end{array}$

7 $\begin{array}{r} 193 \\ -\ 58 \\ \hline \end{array}$

8 $\begin{array}{r} 275 \\ -\ 167 \\ \hline \end{array}$

9 513 − 374

10 621 − 438

11 417 − 309

12 526 − 438

You cannot borrow from the next column if there is a zero in it.
You may need to borrow across more than one column.

Example

$$\begin{array}{r} 300 \\ -\ 196 \\ \hline \end{array} \rightarrow \begin{array}{r} {}^{2}\not{3}\,{}^{1}00 \\ -\ 196 \\ \hline \end{array} \rightarrow \begin{array}{r} {}^{2}\not{3}\,{}^{9}\not{1}\not{0}\,{}^{1}0 \\ -\ 196 \\ \hline 104 \end{array}$$

Exercise 5

Copy these into your book.
Work out the answers.

1 $\begin{array}{r} 400 \\ -\ 173 \\ \hline \end{array}$

2 $\begin{array}{r} 800 \\ -\ 236 \\ \hline \end{array}$

3 $\begin{array}{r} 8000 \\ -\ 364 \\ \hline \end{array}$

4 $\begin{array}{r} 7000 \\ -\ 4328 \\ \hline \end{array}$

Other words

All these words can also mean **subtract**.

take away **take**
minus **difference**

Examples
Find 73 **take away** 24
Work out 73 **take** 24
Find 73 **minus** 24
Find the **difference** between 73 and 24

Checking

You can always check a subtraction by adding.

Example

256 − 183

$$\begin{array}{r} \overset{1}{\not 2}\overset{1}{5}6 \\ -\ 183 \\ \hline 73 \end{array} \qquad \text{check} \qquad \begin{array}{r} 183 \\ +\ 73 \\ \hline 256 \end{array}$$

Go back to your answers for Exercise **5**. Check each of them by adding.

3 Multiplying

When we are adding lots of the same number it is quicker to multiply.

Example

$$\begin{array}{r} 31 \\ 31 \\ 31 \\ 31 \\ +\ 31 \\ \hline 155 \end{array} \quad \text{is the same as} \quad \begin{array}{r} 31 \\ \times\ 5 \\ \hline 155 \end{array}$$

To do $\begin{array}{r} 31 \\ \times\ 5 \\ \hline \end{array}$ first do 5×1 $\begin{array}{r} 31 \\ \times\ 5 \\ \hline 5 \end{array}$

then do 5×3 $\begin{array}{r} 31 \\ \times\ 5 \\ \hline 155 \end{array}$

Remember to keep your numbers in columns.

Here are some more examples:

$$\begin{array}{r} 62 \\ \times\ 4 \\ \hline 248 \end{array} \qquad \begin{array}{r} 51 \\ \times\ 9 \\ \hline 459 \end{array}$$

Exercise 6

1 $\begin{array}{r} 23 \\ \times\ 2 \\ \hline \end{array}$

2 $\begin{array}{r} 213 \\ \times\ 3 \\ \hline \end{array}$

3 $\begin{array}{r} 52 \\ \times\ 4 \\ \hline \end{array}$

4 $\begin{array}{r} 331 \\ \times\ 3 \\ \hline \end{array}$

Sometimes we need to carry.

Example

$$\begin{array}{r} 26 \\ \times\ 3 \\ \hline 8 \\ {\scriptstyle 1} \end{array} \quad \rightarrow \quad \begin{array}{r} 26 \\ \times\ 3 \\ \hline 78 \\ {\scriptstyle 1} \end{array}$$

$3 \times 2 = 6$
Then add the 1 to give 7

Exercise 7

1 $\begin{array}{r} 37 \\ \times\ 2 \\ \hline \end{array}$

2 $\begin{array}{r} 45 \\ \times\ 2 \\ \hline \end{array}$

3 $\begin{array}{r} 46 \\ \times\ 4 \\ \hline \end{array}$

4 $\begin{array}{r} 124 \\ \times\ 3 \\ \hline \end{array}$

5 $\begin{array}{r} 259 \\ \times\ 2 \\ \hline \end{array}$

6 $\begin{array}{r} 637 \\ \times\ 5 \\ \hline \end{array}$

7 $\begin{array}{r} 146 \\ \times\ 9 \\ \hline \end{array}$

8 $\begin{array}{r} 178 \\ \times\ 9 \\ \hline \end{array}$

9 $\begin{array}{r} 357 \\ \times\ 5 \\ \hline \end{array}$

10 $\begin{array}{r} 803 \\ \times\ 4 \\ \hline \end{array}$

Other words

These words can also mean **multiply**.

times **product** **of**

Examples

Find 24 **times** 16
Find the **product** of 24 and 16
Find one half **of** 24

4 Multiplying by 10

When we multiply by 10, all the digits move across **one** column to the **left**.
This makes the number 10 times bigger.
We can use the headings **Th H T U** to help.
They mean **Th**ousands, **H**undreds, **T**ens and **U**nits. Units is another way of saying 'ones'.

Example

$23 \times 10 = 230$

H	T	U
	2	3
2	3	0

Here are some more examples:

Th	H	T	U	
		4	6	$46 \times 10 = 460$
	4	6	0	
	2	5	3	$253 \times 10 = 2530$
2	5	3	0	
	6	0	1	$601 \times 10 = 6010$
6	0	1	0	

Exercise 8

Multiply these numbers by 10.

1 39 **4** 756 **7** 5000

2 45 **5** 684 **8** 8007

3 128 **6** 1562

5 Multiplying by 100, 1000, ...

When we multiply by 100, all the digits move across **two** columns to the **left**.
This makes the number 100 times bigger.
This is because $100 = 10 \times 10$.
So multiplying by 100 is like multiplying by 10 twice.

Example

$74 \times 100 = 7400$

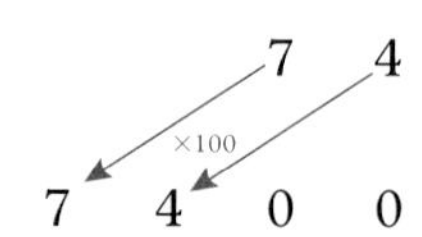

When we multiply by 1000 all the numbers move across three columns to the left.

This is because $1000 = 10 \times 10 \times 10$.
This means that multiplying by 1000 is like multiplying by 10 three times.

Example

$74 \times 1000 = 74\,000$

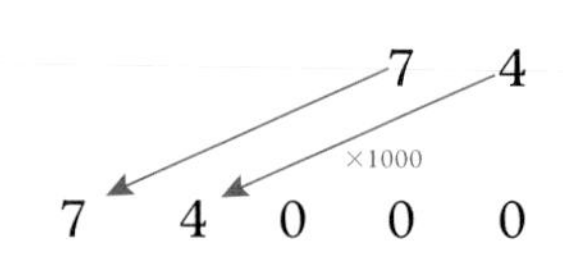

Exercise 9

Write down the answers to these.

1 75×100

2 82×100

3 36×1000

4 178×100

5 3190×100

6 420×1000

7 5243×100

8 800×1000

9 5004×1000

10 $815 \times 10\,000$

11 $302 \times 10\,000$

12 $835 \times 100\,000$

Exercise 10

Work these out.

1 28×20

2 36×20

3 27×30

4 34×30

5 58×30

6 26×40

7 83×40

8 45×50

9 62×50

10 213×20

11 371×30

12 425×70

6 Multiplying by 20, 30, ...

When we multiply by 20 it is like multiplying by 2 then by 10. This is because $20 = 2 \times 10$.

Example

To do 18×20
first do

$$\begin{array}{r} 18 \\ \times \quad 2 \\ \hline 36 \\ \hline {}_{1} \end{array}$$

Then do $36 \times 10 = 360$

So $18 \times 20 = 360$

In the same way multiplying by 30 is the same as multiplying by 3 and then multiplying by 10.

Example

To do 26×30:
first do

$$\begin{array}{r} 26 \\ \times \quad 3 \\ \hline 78 \\ \hline {}_{1} \end{array}$$

Then do $78 \times 10 = 780$

So $26 \times 30 = 780$

7 Long multiplication

When we want to multiply two quite large numbers we have to do it in stages. Here are two methods. You only have to know one of them.

Method 1

Example 146 × 24

First do 146 × 4

$$\begin{array}{r} 146 \\ \times \quad 4 \\ \hline 584 \\ \hline \end{array}$$

1 2

Then do 146 × 20

$$\begin{array}{r} 146 \\ \times \quad 2 \\ \hline 292 \\ \hline \end{array}$$

1

292 × 10 = 2920

Now add the two answers together.

$$\begin{array}{r} 584 \\ +\ 2920 \\ \hline 3504 \\ \hline \end{array}$$

Usually the working out looks like this:

$$\begin{array}{r} 146 \\ \times \quad 24 \\ \hline 584 \\ 2920 \\ \hline 3504 \\ \hline \end{array}$$

Here is another example.

$$\begin{array}{rl} 223 & \\ \times \quad 36 & \\ \hline 1338 & \leftarrow (223 \times 6) \\ 6690 & \leftarrow (223 \times 30) \\ \hline 8028 & \\ \hline \end{array}$$

1 1

Method 2

Example 125 × 23

First set out the numbers with boxes, like this:

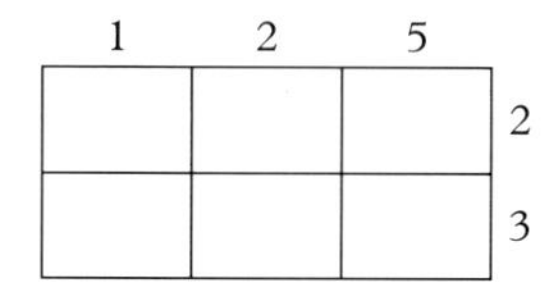

Now draw in the diagonals like this:

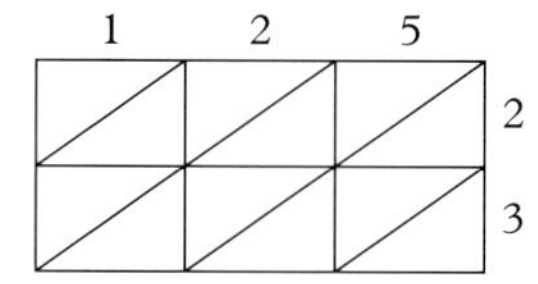

Fill in like a table square then add along the diagonals like this:

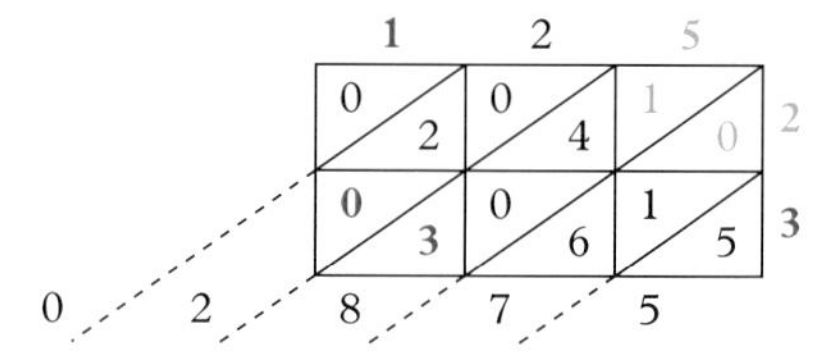

1 × 3 = 3

Notice the 0 in the top box when the answer is a single digit.

So 125 × 23 = **2875**

Here is another example.
When the diagonal adds up to more than 10, we carry into the next one.

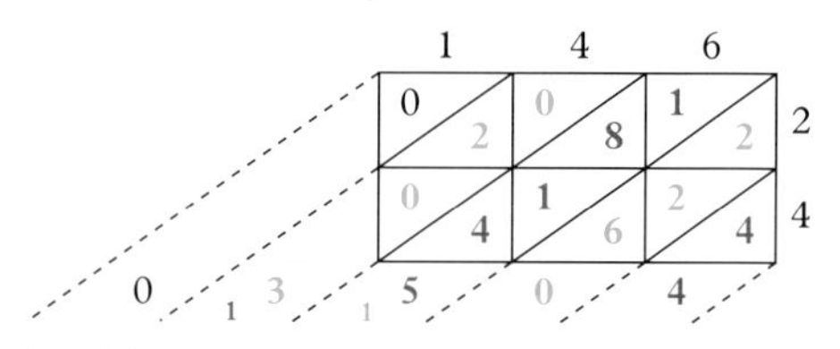

So 146 × 24 = **3504**

Exercise 11

Use the method you prefer to work these out.

1 34×25

2 63×34

3 123×42

4 314×26

5 271×35

6 257×53

7 391×43

8 172×84

9 545×33

10 612×65

11 754×61

12 989×98

8 Dividing

Multiplying is like doing lots of additions. In the same way dividing is like doing lots of subtractions.

To find out how many 4s make 12 we can see how many times we can take 4 away from 12.

$12 - 4 = 8$ (once)
$8 - 4 = 4$ (twice)
$4 - 4 = 0$ (three times)

So there are 3 lots of 4 in 12.

We can say 12 divided by 4 is 3

or $12 \div 4 = 3$

Example

$15 \div 3 = ?$
$15 - 3 = 12$ (once)
$12 - 3 = 9$ (twice)
$9 - 3 = 6$ (three times)
$6 - 3 = 3$ (four times)
$3 - 3 = 0$ (five times)

So $15 \div 3 = 5$

Exercise 12

Work these out.

1 $12 \div 3$

2 $45 \div 5$

3 $30 \div 6$

4 $20 \div 4$

5 $32 \div 4$

6 $21 \div 7$

7 $45 \div 9$

8 $80 \div 10$

9 $14 \div 2$

10 $42 \div 6$

11 $40 \div 8$

12 $54 \div 9$

When the numbers get bigger, this method takes too long. We need a new way to work it out.

Example

$68 \div 2$

$2\overline{)68}$

First work out $6 \div 2 = 3$. Put the 3 above the 6:

$$\begin{array}{r} 3 \\ 2\overline{)68} \end{array}$$

Now work out $8 \div 2 = 4$. Put the 4 above the 8:

$$\begin{array}{r} 34 \\ 2\overline{)68} \end{array}$$

So $68 \div 2 = 34$

Here is another example: $84 \div 4$

$$\begin{array}{r} 21 \\ 4\overline{)84} \end{array}$$

So $84 \div 4 = 21$

Exercise 13

Work these out.

1 $2\overline{)84}$

2 $3\overline{)93}$

3 $5\overline{)55}$

4 $96 \div 3$

5 $64 \div 2$

6 $884 \div 4$

Sometimes we need to 'carry'. This happens when a number does not divide exactly.

Example

$72 \div 4$

$4\overline{)72}$

First do $7 \div 4$. This is 1 with 3 left over.
Put the 1 above the 7 and carry the 3 like this.

$$\begin{array}{r} 1 \\ 4\overline{)7^{3}2} \end{array}$$

Now do $32 \div 4$. This is 8. Put the 8 above the $^{3}2$ like this

$$\begin{array}{r} 18 \\ 4\overline{)7^{3}2} \end{array}$$

So $72 \div 4 = 18$

Here is another example: $85 \div 5$

$$\begin{array}{r} 17 \\ 5\overline{)8^{3}5} \end{array}$$

So $85 \div 5 = 17$

Exercise 14

Work these out.

1 $2\overline{)58}$

2 $3\overline{)54}$

3 $72 \div 4$

4 $64 \div 4$

5 $84 \div 7$

6 $76 \div 4$

7 $96 \div 6$

8 $128 \div 8$

9 $424 \div 4$

10 $276 \div 2$

11 $621 \div 3$

12 $364 \div 7$

9 Dividing by 10

When we divide by 10, all the digits move across **one** column to the **right**. This makes the number smaller.

Example

$230 \div 10 = 23$

H	T	U
2	3	0
	2	3

Here are some more examples.

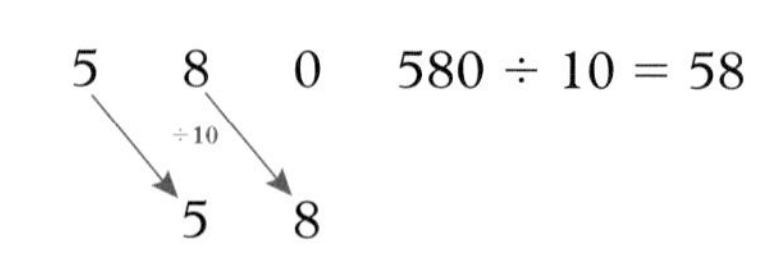

$580 \div 10 = 58$

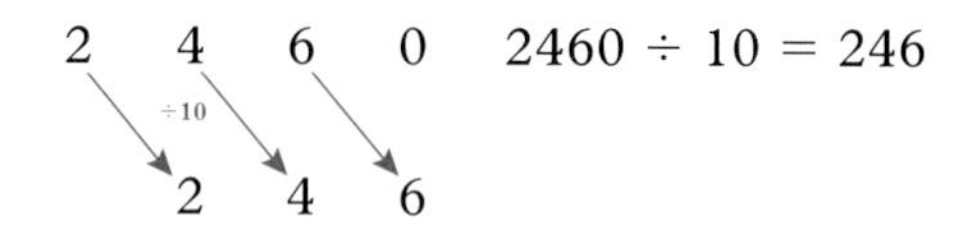

$2460 \div 10 = 246$

Exercise 15

Divide these numbers by 10.

1 740

2 80

3 5960

4 830

5 9040

6 7200

7 5000

8 700 000

10 Dividing by 100, 1000, ...

When we divide by 100, all the digits move across **two** columns to the **right**. This is because $100 = 10 \times 10$. So dividing by 100 is like dividing by 10 twice.

Example

$7400 \div 100 = 74$

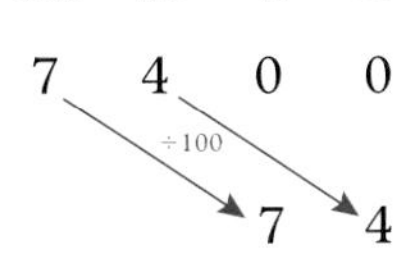

When we divide by 1000, all the numbers move across **three** columns to the **right**.

Example

$74\,000 \div 1000 = 74$

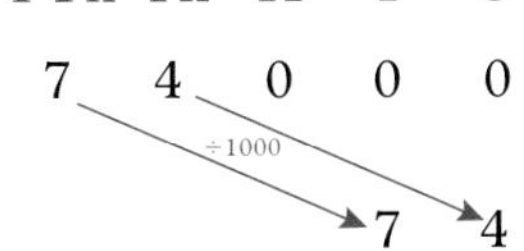

11 Dividing by 20, 30, ...

When we divide by 20, it is like dividing by 2 then by 10. This is because $20 = 2 \times 10$.

Example

To do $360 \div 20$

first do $2\overline{)3^{1}60}$ = 180

Then do $180 \div 10 = 18$

So $360 \div 20 = 18$

In the same way dividing by 30 is the same as dividing by 3 then by 10.

Example

To do $780 \div 30$

first do $3\overline{)7^{1}80}$ = 260

Then do $260 \div 10 = 26$

So $780 \div 30 = 26$

Exercise 16

Work these out.

1 $7800 \div 100$

2 $5300 \div 100$

3 $6400 \div 100$

4 $42\,000 \div 1000$

5 $78\,000 \div 100$

6 $78\,000 \div 1000$

7 $200\,000 \div 1000$

8 $200\,000 \div 10\,000$

Exercise 17

Work these out.

1 $640 \div 20$

2 $240 \div 30$

3 $5680 \div 40$

4 $2350 \div 50$

5 $7540 \div 20$

6 $2820 \div 30$

7 $1890 \div 90$

8 $24\,240 \div 80$

Other words

These words can also mean **divide**.

share **quotient**

Examples

Share 240 by 12
Find the **quotient** of 240 and 12

} both mean 240 ÷ 12

12 Adding fractions

To add fractions, the bottom numbers (denominators) **must** be the same.

Examples

$\frac{1}{3} + \frac{1}{3} = \frac{2}{3}$

one third + one third = two thirds

$\frac{2}{7} + \frac{3}{7} = \frac{5}{7}$

two sevenths + three sevenths = five sevenths

$\frac{3}{5} + \frac{3}{5} = \frac{6}{5} = 1\frac{1}{5}$

three fifths + three fifths = six fifths = one and one fifth

Exercise 18

Work these out.

1 $\frac{3}{5} + \frac{1}{5}$

2 $\frac{1}{6} + \frac{3}{6}$

3 $\frac{7}{9} + \frac{1}{9}$

4 $\frac{4}{11} + \frac{3}{11}$

5 $\frac{5}{13} + \frac{7}{13}$

6 $\frac{3}{8} + \frac{2}{8}$

7 $\frac{2}{9} + \frac{5}{9}$

8 $\frac{5}{12} + \frac{4}{12}$

9 $\frac{8}{12} + \frac{5}{12}$

10 $\frac{4}{5} + \frac{3}{5}$

11 $\frac{6}{8} + \frac{5}{8}$

12 $\frac{9}{11} + \frac{5}{11}$

Sometimes the two bottom numbers are different. Before we can add the fractions we **must** make them the same.

Example

$\frac{1}{3} + \frac{1}{6}$

We need to find a number that 3 and 6 both divide into exactly.

Numbers that 3 goes into:
3 (6) 9 12 …
Numbers that 6 goes into:
(6) 12 18 …

The first number that is in both lists is 6. The 6 is called the common denominator.

Now write the fractions with 6 as the bottom number:

$\frac{2}{3} = \frac{?}{6}$ (×2) so $\frac{2}{3} = \frac{4}{6}$ (×2, ×2) so $\frac{2}{3} = \frac{4}{6}$

We can see this in a diagram.

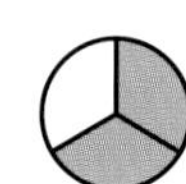
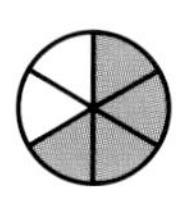

The $\frac{1}{6}$ does not need changing.

So $\frac{2}{3} + \frac{1}{6} = \frac{4}{6} + \frac{1}{6} = \frac{5}{6}$

Here is another example:

$\frac{2}{3} + \frac{1}{4}$

Numbers that 3 goes into:
3 6 9 (12) 15 ...

Numbers that 4 goes into:
4 8 (12) 16 ...

We need to change both fractions to twelfths. 12 is the common denominator.

$\frac{2}{3} = \frac{?}{12}$ (×4) $\quad \frac{2}{3} = \frac{8}{12}$ (×4)

$\frac{1}{4} = \frac{?}{12}$ (×3) $\quad \frac{1}{4} = \frac{3}{12}$ (×3)

So $\frac{2}{3} + \frac{1}{4} = \frac{8}{12} + \frac{3}{12} = \frac{11}{12}$

13 Subtracting fractions

This works just like adding fractions.

Example

$\frac{3}{5} - \frac{2}{5} = \frac{1}{5}$

The two bottom numbers must still be the same.

Example

$\frac{3}{8} - \frac{1}{4}$

Numbers that 8 goes into:
(8) 16 24 ...
Numbers that 4 goes into:
4 (8) 12 16 ...

$\frac{1}{4} = \frac{?}{8}$ (×2) $\quad \frac{1}{4} = \frac{2}{8}$ (×2)

The $\frac{3}{8}$ does not need changing.

So $\frac{3}{8} - \frac{1}{4} = \frac{3}{8} - \frac{2}{8} = \frac{1}{8}$

Exercise 19

Work these out.

1 $\frac{1}{4} + \frac{1}{2}$

2 $\frac{1}{5} + \frac{1}{10}$

3 $\frac{2}{5} + \frac{3}{10}$

4 $\frac{5}{8} + \frac{1}{4}$

5 $\frac{5}{12} + \frac{1}{6}$

6 $\frac{5}{9} + \frac{1}{3}$

7 $\frac{1}{3} + \frac{1}{5}$

8 $\frac{2}{7} + \frac{1}{2}$

9 $\frac{2}{5} + \frac{1}{3}$

10 $\frac{1}{7} + \frac{4}{5}$

11 $\frac{1}{8} + \frac{3}{7}$

12 $\frac{1}{2} + \frac{1}{3} + \frac{1}{4}$

Exercise 20

Work these out.

1 $\frac{7}{8} - \frac{2}{8}$

2 $\frac{2}{5} - \frac{1}{5}$

3 $\frac{7}{13} - \frac{3}{13}$

4 $\frac{3}{5} - \frac{1}{10}$

5 $\frac{5}{8} - \frac{1}{4}$

6 $\frac{11}{12} - \frac{2}{3}$

7 $\frac{1}{4} - \frac{1}{5}$

8 $\frac{3}{6} - \frac{1}{3}$

9 $\frac{6}{7} - \frac{2}{3}$

10 $\frac{3}{4} - \frac{2}{3}$

11 $\frac{5}{8} - \frac{2}{5}$

12 $\frac{10}{11} - \frac{5}{8}$

CHAPTER 1

1 **a** DM10 = £5 **b** DM12 = £6 **c** DM6 = £3

2 **a**

Number of hours	1	2	3	4	5
Wages £	5	10	15	20	25

b

Graph to show Alison's wages

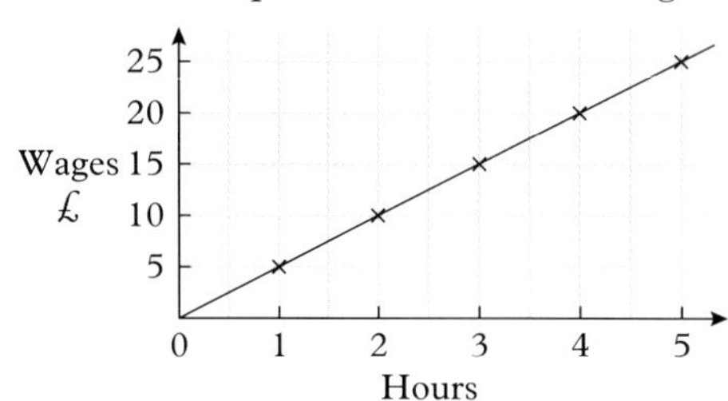

3 **a** (1) 6.30 am (2) 11.40 am (3) 3.02 pm (4) 10.57 pm
b (1) 07 15 (2) 12 30 (3) 17 27 (4) 21 25

4 **a** May has 31 days **b** November has 30 days
c 2010 is not a leap year so February has 28 days.
d 2007 is not a leap year so it has 365 days.

5 **a** 11.25 + 15 minutes = 11.40 am **b** 3.40 + 45 minutes = 4.25 pm

6 **a** 18 minutes
b From 08 56 to 09 00 is 4 minutes.
From 09 00 to 11 00 is 2 hours.
From 11 00 to 11 23 is 23 minutes.
Journey takes 2 hours + 4 minutes + 23 minutes = 2 hours 27 minutes

CHAPTER 2

1 **a** 289 **b** 12.96 **c** 6400

2 **a** 25 **b** 40 **c** 0.2 **d** 14

3 **a** $\sqrt{6} = 2.44948\ldots$
$= 2.4$ to 1 dp
b $\sqrt{7.9} = 2.81069\ldots$
$= 2.8$ to 1 dp
c $\sqrt{600} = 24.49489$
$= 24.5$ to 1 dp
d $\sqrt{45} = 6.70820$
$= 6.7$ to 1 dp

4 Area of square $= 7.3 \times 7.3$
$= 7.3^2$
$= 53.29\ \text{cm}^2$

5 Length of side $= \sqrt{250}$
$= 15.81138$
$= 15.8$ to 1 dp

6 **a** 23 **c** 12 **e** 35 **g** 6
b 23 **d** 9 **f** 36 **h** 3

7 **a** 6 **b** 70 **c** 600 **d** 1700

8 **a** (1) estimate $30 + 90 = 120$ (3) estimate $6 \times 3 = 18$
(2) estimate $70 - 40 = 30$ (4) estimate $50 \div 2 = 25$
b (1) 116 (2) 29.3 (3) 17.92 (4) 30
The estimates are all quite close to the correct answers.
Parts (2) and (3) are very close.

CHAPTER 3

1 **a**

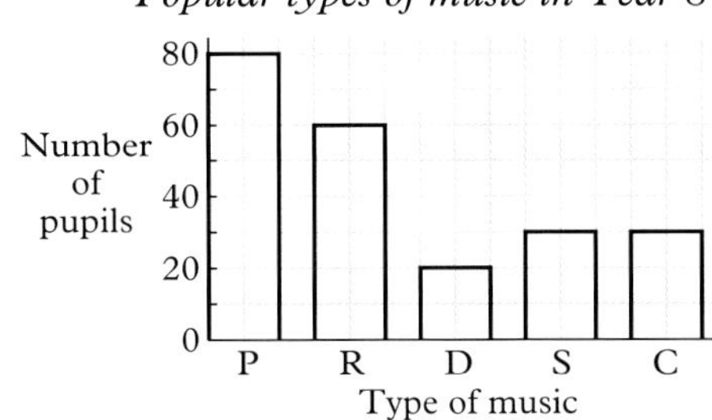

b pop **c** dance

2 **a, b, c**

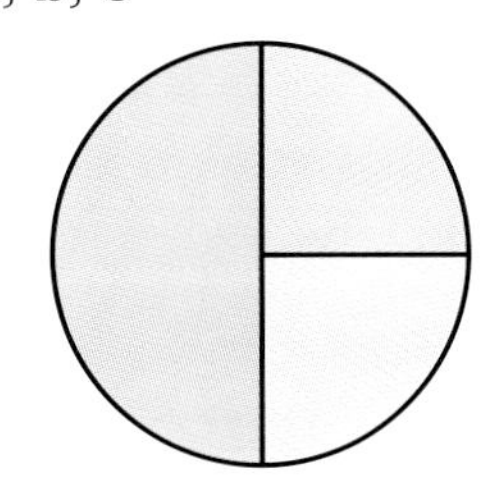

Year 8's favourite radio station

Key: Radio 1
Atlantic 252
Radio 5 Live

3 **a** $360° \div 30 = 12°$ for each pupil

b

	Number of pupils	Working	Angle
Radio 1	12	12×12	144°
Radio 5 Live	10	10×12	120°
Atlantic 252	8	8×12	96°

c

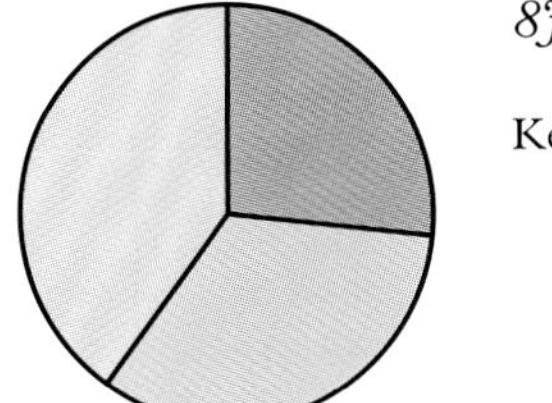

8J's favourite radio station

Key: Radio 1
Atlantic 252
Radio 5 Live

CHAPTER 4

1 **a** ← -3 ← **c** ← $\div 5$ ←

b ← $\times 7$ ←

2 ← $\times 3$ ← $+8$ ←

3 **a** the next two are:

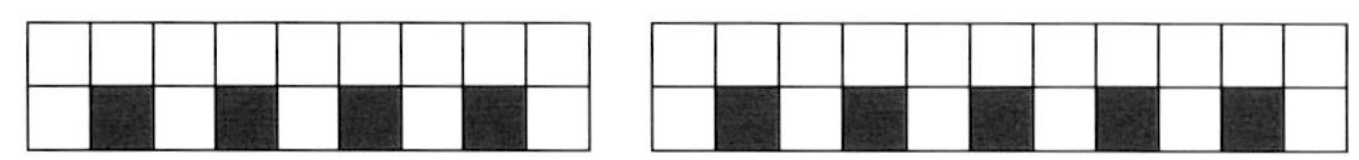

b

Number of red slabs	1	2	3	4	5
Number of white slabs	5	8	11	14	17

c Add 3 white slabs each time.

d The first part of the formula is:
number of white slabs = 3 × number of red slabs

e

Number of red slabs	1	2	3	4	5
	3 +?	6 +?	9 +?	12 +?	15 +?
Number of white slabs	5	8			

f Add 2

g **number of *white* slabs = 3 × number of *red* slabs + 2**

h $3 \times 20 + 2 = 60 + 2 = 62$

i → $\times 3$ → $+2$ →

j ← $\div 3$ ← -2 ←

k 20 ← $\div 3$ ← 60 ← -2 ← 62 = 20 red slabs

CHAPTER 5

1 **a**

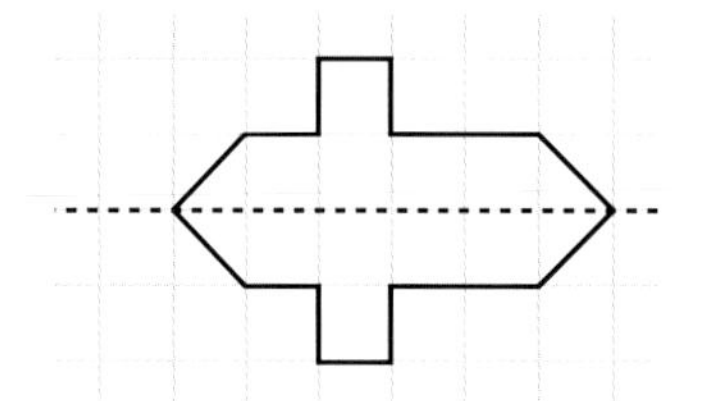

b

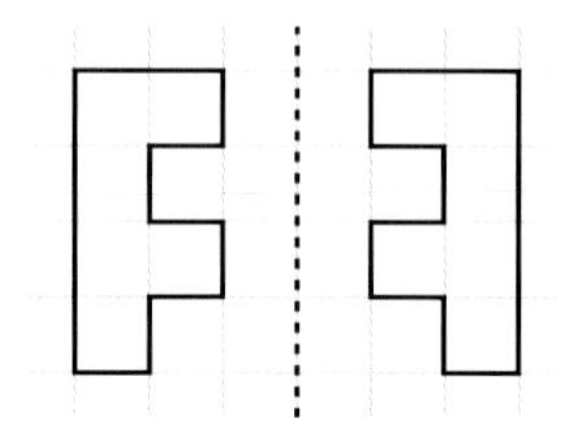

2 a 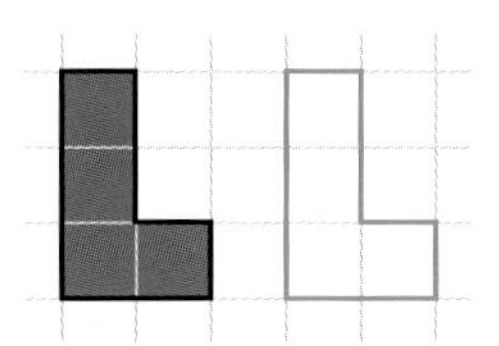

b 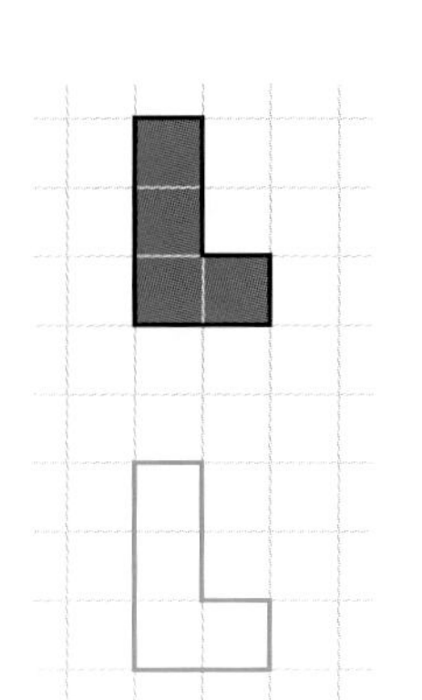

c 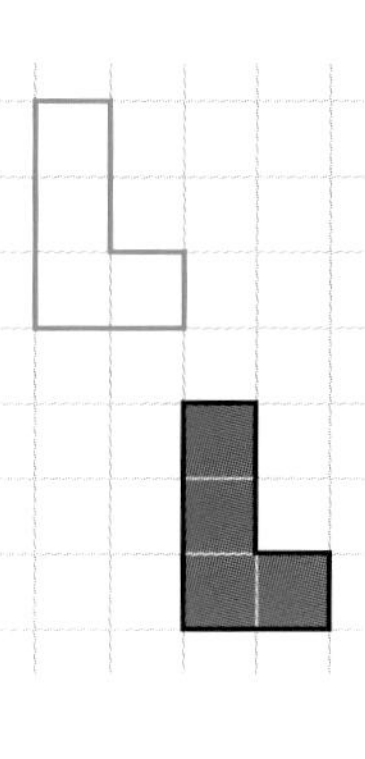

3 a 

b 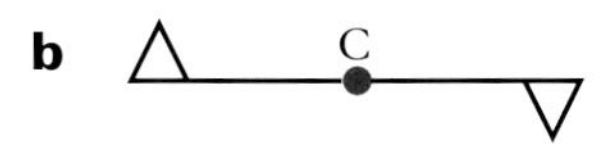

4

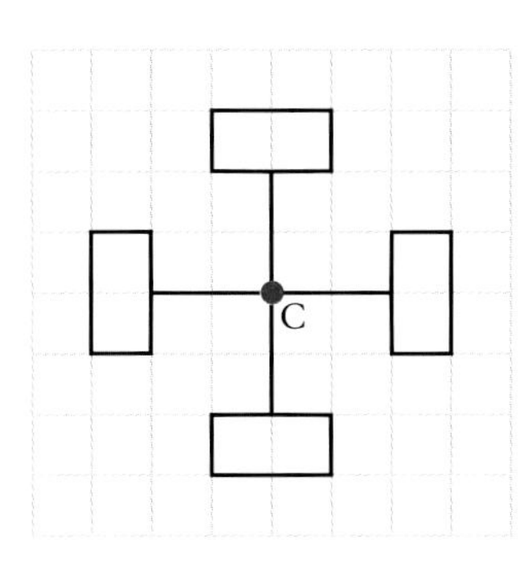

5 a 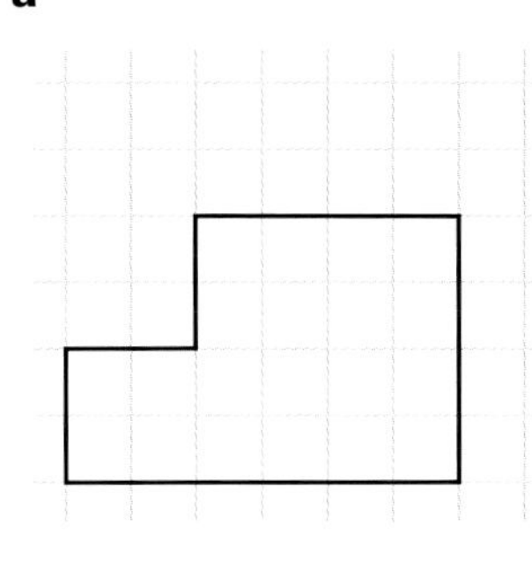

b 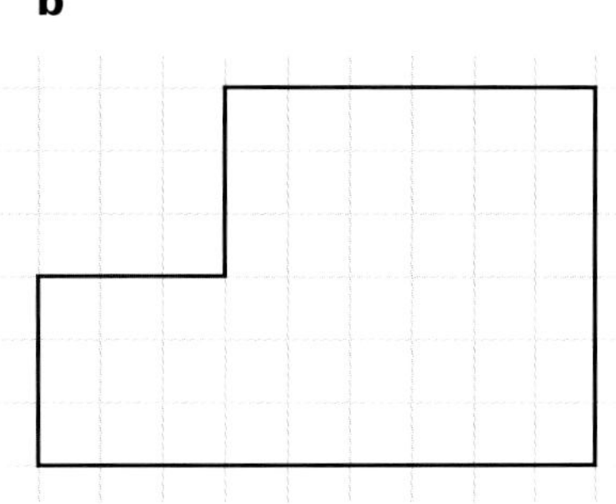

CHAPTER 6

1 $-5\,°C$, $-3\,°C$, $-1\,°C$, $0\,°C$, $1\,°C$, $2\,°C$, $6\,°C$

2 a $5\,°C > 3\,°C$ **b** $-6\,°C > -8\,°C$ **c** $-4\,°C < 0\,°C$

3 $9 + 43 = 52\,°C$

4 50 p + 20 p + 20 p + 10 p + 10 p + 10 p + 5 p; total £1.25

5 **a** £1 − 40 p = 60 p **b** £1 − 87 p = 13 p **c** £1 − 24 p = 76 p

6 **a** £5.72 + £0.69 = £6.41
b £0.85 + £4 + £0.78 = £5.63
c £6.80 − £2.07 = £4.73
d £5 − £0.69 = £4.31

7 £7.48 + £4.55 = £12.03

8 £12 − £5.75 = £6.25

9 **a** £4.86 **b** £6.39 **c** £0.31

10 £452 ÷ 12 = £37.67

11

Item	Number bought	Cost
pencils	5 at 38 p each	£1.90
ruler	1 at 55 p	£0.55
files	3 at £1.45 each	£4.35
	TOTAL COST	£6.80

CHAPTER 7

1 **a** D is acute
b C is obtuse
c A is a right angle
d B is reflex

2 **a** $a = 180° - 42° = 138°$
b $b = 360° - 265° = 95°$
c $c = 180° - 95° - 25° = 60°$
d $d = 132°$ (opposite angles), $e = 48°$ (opposite angles)

3 **a** $p = 61°$ $q = 119°$
$r = 61°$ $s = 119°$
b $w = 99°$ $x = 81°$
$y = 99°$ $z = 81°$

4

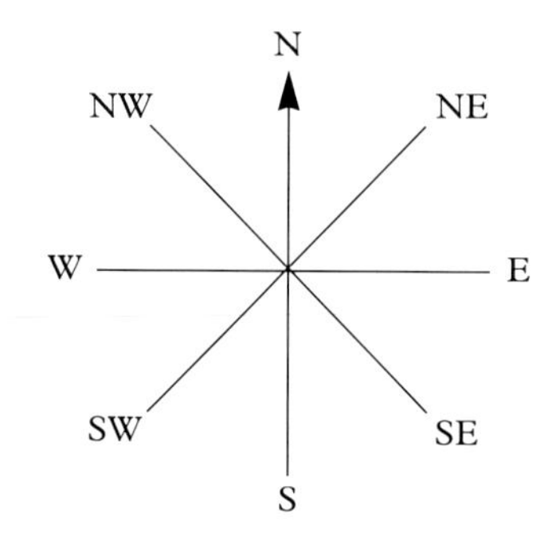

CHAPTER 8

1 There are 6 letters in SCHOOL.

a $\frac{1}{6}$ **b** $\frac{2}{6} = \frac{1}{3}$ **c** 0, there is no letter A in SCHOOL

2 There are 14 sweets in the bag.

a $\frac{4}{14} = \frac{2}{7}$ **b** $\frac{10}{14} = \frac{5}{7}$

3 There are 5 pencils in the case.

a (1) $1 \times 2 = 2$ (2) $1 \times 2 = 2$ (3) $3 \times 2 = 6$

b (1) $1 \times 6 = 6$ (2) $1 \times 6 = 6$ (3) $3 \times 6 = 18$

4 **a** $\frac{1}{6}$ **b** $\frac{1}{3}$ **c** $\frac{9}{10}$

5 green and red, green and blue, red and blue

CHAPTER 9

1 23 toffees out of 100 is 23%

2 12 out of 50 is the same as 24 out of 100, which is 24%

3 **a** 10% of £8 = 80 p
b 10% of £20 = £2
c 10% of £9.50 = 95 p
d 10% of £12.50 = £1.25
e 10% of £14.80 = £1.48

4 **a** 10% of £400 = £40
b 40% of £400 = $4 \times$ £40 = £160
c 50% of £340 = £170, so 25% is £170 $\div$ 2 = £85

5 **a** 46% of 1100 = $0.46 \times 1100 = 506$
b 67% of 1700 = $0.67 \times 1700 = 1139$
c 73% of 8600 = $0.73 \times 8600 = 6278$

6 **a** 48% of 6700 = $0.48 \times 6700 = 3216$ people
b 38% of 1200 = $0.38 \times 1200 = 456$ m
c 96% of 750 = $0.96 \times 750 = 720$ g
d 7% of 1327 = 0.07×1327 = £92.89

7 $\frac{1}{3}$ of $60 = 60 \div 3 = 20$ g

8 **a** $\frac{1}{7}$ of $28 = 28 \div 7 = 4$, so $\frac{2}{7}$ of $28 = 4 \times 2 = 8$ pupils

b $1 - \frac{2}{7}$ are not blonde, so $\frac{5}{7}$ of pupils are not blonde

9 **a** $\frac{1}{4}$ of 28 = 7 fillings

b $1 - \frac{1}{4}$ are not filled, so $\frac{3}{4}$ of Paul's teeth are not filled

CHAPTER 10

1 **a** $x = 1$ **b** $x = 4$ **c** $y = 5$ **d** $y = 2$

2

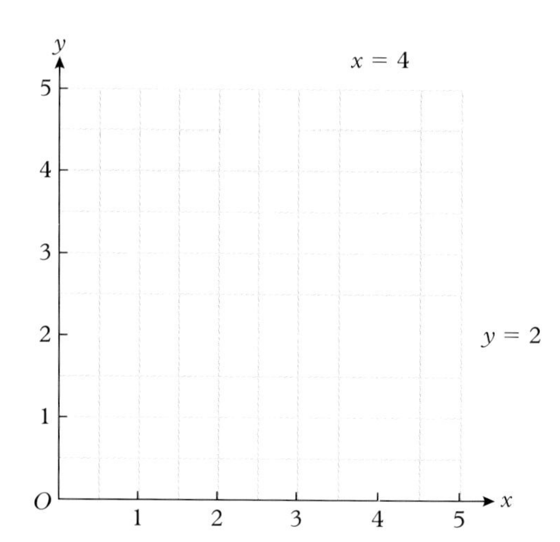

d The lines cross at (4, 2)

3 $x = 5,\ y = 3$

4 (1, 6)

5 **a** $y = 5x$ is the steepest **b** $y = x$ is the least steep

6 **a** $y = x + 3$ crosses the y axis at 3
b $y = x + 5$ crosses the y axis at 5
c $y = x$ crosses the y axis at 0

7 **a** the lines are parallel
b $y = x + 7$ is highest up the grid
c $y = x$ is lowest on the grid
d $y = x + 2$ would be between $y = x$ and $y = x + 4$ on the grid

CHAPTER 11

1 **a** 300 cm = 300 ÷ 100 m = 3 m
b 25 mm = 25 ÷ 10 cm = 2.5 cm
c 7 km = 7 × 1000 m = 7000 m
d 8.6 m = 8.6 × 100 cm = 860 cm
e 4500 g = 4500 ÷ 1000 kg = 4.5 kg
f 7.2 kg = 7.2 × 1000 g = 7200 g
g 0.4 t = 0.4 × 1000 kg = 400 kg
h 3000 ml = 3000 ÷ 1000 l = 3 l
i 4.8 l = 4.8 × 1000 ml = 4800 ml

2 **a** 3 in = 3×2.5 cm = 7.5 cm
b 177 yd = 177×0.9 m = 159.3 m
c 30 miles an hour = 30×1.6 km an hour = 48 km an hour
d 4 ounces = 4×28 g = 112 g
e 165 pounds = 165×0.45 kg = 74.25 kg
f 3 gallons = $3 \times 4.5\,l = 13.5\,l$
g 1 pint = $0.57\,l$

3 **a** The rectangle is 3.5 cm long and 1.5 cm wide.
b The new rectangle is 7 cm long and 3 cm wide

4 $18 \div 6 = 3$, so Keith is 3 times older than Melanie.

5 **a** You add $3 \times 250\,ml = 750\,ml$ of water
b $250 + 750 = 1000\,ml = 1\,l$ of orange drink is made

6 **a** (1) A to B measures 3 cm (2) $3 \times 2 = 6$ km
b (1) B to C measures 6 cm (2) $6 \times 2 = 12$ km
c (1) C to A measures 5 cm (2) $5 \times 2 = 10$ km

CHAPTER 12

1 **a** Perimeter = $2 + 2 + 1 + 2 + 1 + 4 = 12$ cm
b Area = 6 cm^2

2 **a** Area = length × width = $10 \times 8 = 80$ cm^2
b Perimeter = $8 + 10 + 8 + 10 = 36$ cm

3 **a**

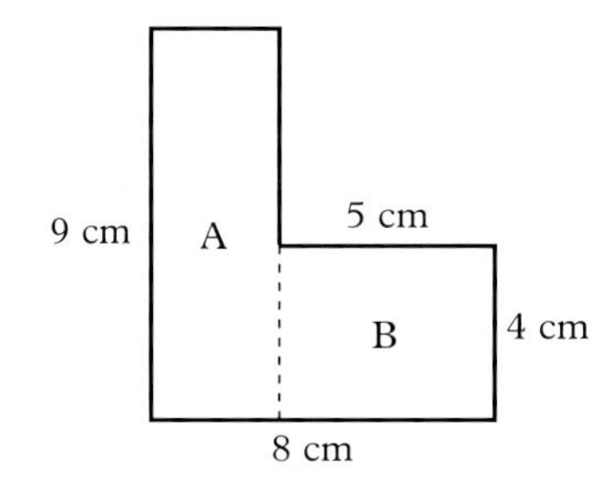

Blue line + 5 = 8
Blue line = 3 cm
Area A = $9 \times 3 = 27$ cm^2
Area B = $5 \times 4 = 20$ cm^2
Total area = $27 + 20 = 47$ cm^2

b Area of whole = $10 \times 6 = 60$ cm^2
Area of piece cut out = $6 \times 2 = 12$ cm^2
Area of green shape = $60 - 12 = 48$ cm^2

4 **a** Area = $\frac{\text{base} \times \text{height}}{2} = \frac{9 \times 5}{2} = 22.5$ cm^2

b Area = $\frac{12 \times 7}{2} = 42$ cm^2

CHAPTER 13

1 **a** Mean $= \dfrac{7+6+9+0+3+4+7+6+4+7}{10}$

$= 53 \div 10 = 5.3$

b Mode is the most common number = 7

c Writing the numbers in order:

0 3 4 4 6 6 7 7 7 9

Median is the middle number = 6

d Range = biggest number − smallest number

$= 9 - 0 = 9$

2 **a** Mode is the most common number of people in cars = 1

b

Number of people	Number of cars	Total number of people
1	23	$1 \times 23 = 23$
2	17	$2 \times 17 = 34$
3	7	$3 \times 7 = 21$
4	3	$4 \times 3 = 12$
Total	50	90

Mean number of people per car $= 90 \div 50 = 1.8$

3 **a**

Mark	Tally	Total
1–20	|	1
21–40	|||	3
41–60	||||	4
61–80	~~||||~~ ~~||||~~ ~~||||~~ |	16
81–100	~~||||~~ |	6
	Total	30

b Modal group is the most common group, = 61–80

c *Bar chart of 8M's Maths test marks*

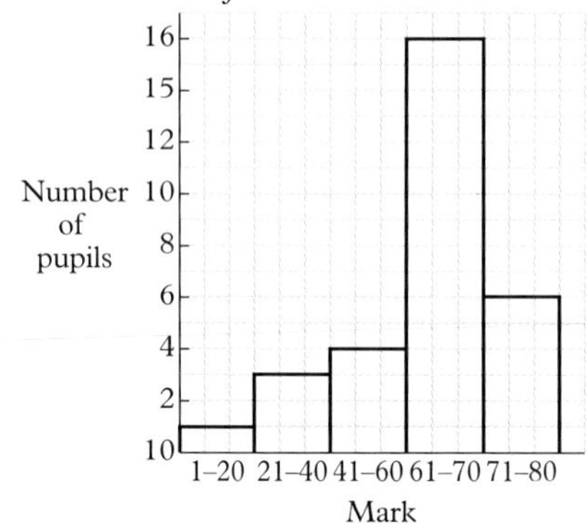

4 **a** Modal score is the most common score, = 1 goal
b Team failed to score in 2 matches
c Team scored 3 goals in 3 matches
d Team played $2 + 8 + 5 + 3 + 2 = 20$ matches

CHAPTER 14

1 **a** (3) Ariel Automatic
b (4) Butter
c (3) Ariel, (1) Corn Flakes, (2) Dairy Milk, (4) Butter

2 **a** 1 litre **b** 60 ml
As both these answers are estimates allow yourself any answer that is close to them.

3 **a** $9 \times 3 \times 3 = 81\ \text{cm}^3$
b $7 \times 3 \times 3 = 63\ \text{cm}^3$
c $4 \times 6 \times 5 = 120\ \text{cm}^3$
d $3 \times 8 \times 5 = 120\ \text{cm}^3$

CHAPTER 15

1 $5x - 3 = 62$

Value of x	Value of $5x - 3$	
10	$5 \times 10 - 3 = 47$	too small
20	$5 \times 20 - 3 = 97$	too big
12	$5 \times 12 - 3 = 57$	too small
13	$5 \times 13 - 3 = 62$	correct

Answer: $x = 13$

2 **a** -4 **b** $+10$ **c** $\div 6$ **d** $\times 11$

3 **a** ← $\div 5$ ← $+ 8$ ←

b ← $\times 7$ ← $- 4$ ←

4 **a** $x \longrightarrow$ $-\ 11$ $\longrightarrow 25$

$36 \longleftarrow$ $+\ 11$ $\longleftarrow 25$

so $x = 36$

b $x \longrightarrow$ $\times\ 6$ $\longrightarrow 102$

$17 \longleftarrow$ $\div\ 6$ $\longleftarrow 102$

so $x = 17$

c $x \longrightarrow$ $\div\ 12$ $\longrightarrow 108$

$1296 \longleftarrow$ $\times\ 12$ $\longleftarrow 108$

so $x = 1296$

5 **a** $x \longrightarrow$ $\times\ 2$ $\longrightarrow$ $-\ 13$ $\longrightarrow 15$

$14 \longleftarrow$ $\div\ 2$ $\longleftarrow$ $+\ 13$ $\longleftarrow 15$

so $x = 14$

b $c \longrightarrow$ $\times\ 4$ $\longrightarrow$ $-\ 16$ $\longrightarrow 52$

$17 \longleftarrow$ $\div\ 4$ $\longleftarrow$ $+\ 16$ $\longleftarrow 52$

so $c = 17$

CHAPTER 16

1 **a**

x			y	
1	$\longrightarrow$	$+\ 2$	$\longrightarrow$ 3	(1, 3)
2	$\longrightarrow$	$+\ 2$	$\longrightarrow$ 4	(2, 4)
3	$\longrightarrow$	$+\ 2$	$\longrightarrow$ 5	(3, 5)

b

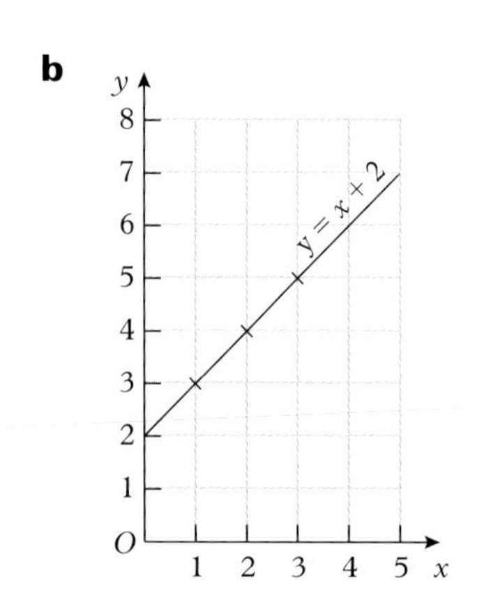

2 a

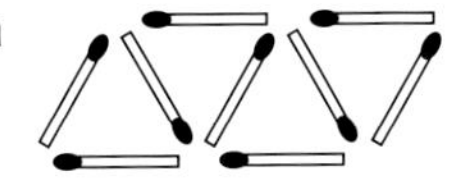

b, d

Number of triangles	1	2	3	4	5	6	7
Number of matchsticks	3	5	7	9	11	13	15

c Add 2

f (1, 3), (2, 5), (3, 7), (4, 9), (5, 11), (6,13)

g

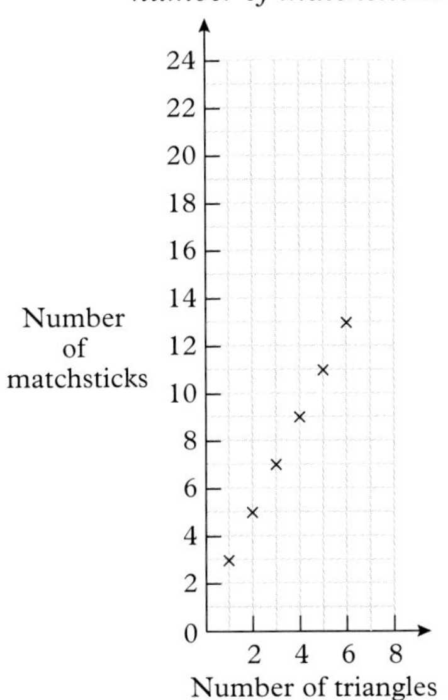

3 $a = 6, b = 7, c = 9$

Exercise 1

1	28	**5**	778	**9**	29
2	68	**6**	467	**10**	78
3	55	**7**	4677	**11**	555
4	369	**8**	9799	**12**	944

Exercise 2

1	34	**5**	301	**9**	95
2	44	**6**	661	**10**	141
3	62	**7**	433	**11**	211
4	175	**8**	945	**12**	310

Exercise 3

1	44	**5**	346	**9**	621
2	624	**6**	1223	**10**	432
3	232	**7**	4341	**11**	152
4	914	**8**	7141	**12**	2111

Exercise 4

1	19	**5**	104	**9**	139
2	37	**6**	468	**10**	183
3	27	**7**	135	**11**	108
4	218	**8**	108	**12**	88

Exercise 5

1	227	**3**	7636
2	564	**4**	2672

Exercise 6

1	46	**3**	208
2	639	**4**	993

Exercise 7

1	74	**6**	3185
2	90	**7**	1314
3	184	**8**	1602
4	372	**9**	1785
5	518	**10**	3212

Exercise 8

1	390	**5**	6840
2	450	**6**	15 620
3	1280	**7**	50 000
4	7560	**8**	80 070

Exercise 9

1	7500	**7**	524 300
2	8200	**8**	800 000
3	36 000	**9**	5 004 000
4	17 800	**10**	8 150 000
5	319 000	**11**	3 020 000
6	420 000	**12**	83 500 000

Exercise 10

1	560	**5**	1740	**9**	3100
2	720	**6**	1040	**10**	4260
3	810	**7**	3320	**11**	11 130
4	1020	**8**	2250	**12**	29 750

Exercise 11

1	850	**5**	9485	**9**	17 985
2	2142	**6**	13 621	**10**	39 780
3	5166	**7**	16 813	**11**	45 994
4	8164	**8**	14 448	**12**	96 922

Exercise 12

1 4 **2** 9 **3** 5 **4** 5 **5** 8 **6** 3 **7** 5 **8** 8 **9** 7 **10** 7 **11** 5 **12** 6

Exercise 13

1 42 **2** 31 **3** 11 **4** 32 **5** 32 **6** 221

Exercise 14

1 29 **2** 18 **3** 18 **4** 16 **5** 12 **6** 19 **7** 16 **8** 16 **9** 106 **10** 138 **11** 207 **12** 52

Exercise 15

1 74 **2** 8 **3** 596 **4** 83 **5** 904 **6** 720 **7** 500 **8** 70 000

Exercise 16

1 78 **2** 53 **3** 64 **4** 42 **5** 780 **6** 78 **7** 200 **8** 20

Exercise 17

1 32 **2** 8 **3** 142 **4** 47 **5** 377 **6** 94 **7** 21 **8** 303

Exercise 18

1 $\frac{4}{5}$ **2** $\frac{4}{6}$ **3** $\frac{8}{9}$ **4** $\frac{7}{11}$ **5** $\frac{12}{13}$ **6** $\frac{5}{8}$ **7** $\frac{7}{9}$ **8** $\frac{9}{12}$ **9** $\frac{13}{12} = \frac{1}{12}$ **10** $\frac{7}{5} = 1\frac{2}{5}$ **11** $\frac{11}{8} = 1\frac{3}{8}$ **12** $\frac{14}{11} = 1\frac{3}{11}$

Exercise 19

1 $\frac{3}{4}$ **2** $\frac{3}{10}$ **3** $\frac{7}{10}$ **4** $\frac{7}{8}$ **5** $\frac{7}{12}$ **6** $\frac{8}{9}$ **7** $\frac{8}{15}$ **8** $\frac{11}{14}$ **9** $\frac{11}{15}$ **10** $\frac{33}{35}$ **11** $\frac{31}{56}$ **12** $\frac{13}{12} = 1\frac{1}{12}$

Exercise 20

1 $\frac{5}{8}$ **2** $\frac{1}{5}$ **3** $\frac{4}{11}$ **4** $\frac{5}{10} = \frac{1}{2}$ **5** $\frac{3}{8}$ **6** $\frac{3}{12} = \frac{1}{4}$ **7** $\frac{1}{20}$ **8** $\frac{1}{6}$ **9** $\frac{4}{21}$ **10** $\frac{1}{12}$ **11** $\frac{9}{40}$ **12** $\frac{25}{88} = \frac{1}{2}$